The Strange Adventures of H.P. Lovecraft

The Strange Adventures of H.P. Lovecraft

MAC CARTER
Story

TONY SALMONS
Pencils and Inks

ADAM BYRNE
Producer, Cover Art and Colors

KEATON KOHL
Flats

IMAGE COMICS, INC.

Robert Kirkman - chief operating officer
Erik Larsen - chief financial officer
Todd McFarlane - president
Marc Silvestri - chief executive officer
Jim Valentino - vice-president

Eric Stephenson - publisher
Todd Martinez - sales & licensing coordinator
Betsy Gomez - pr & marketing coordinator
Branwyn Bigglestone - accounts manager
Sarah deLaine - administrative assistant
Tyler Shainline - production manager
Drew Gill - art director
Jonathan Chan - production artist
Monica Howard - production artist
Vincent Kukua - production artist

www.imagecomics.com

CHAPTER ONE:
ABOUT A WRITER AND HIS BOOK

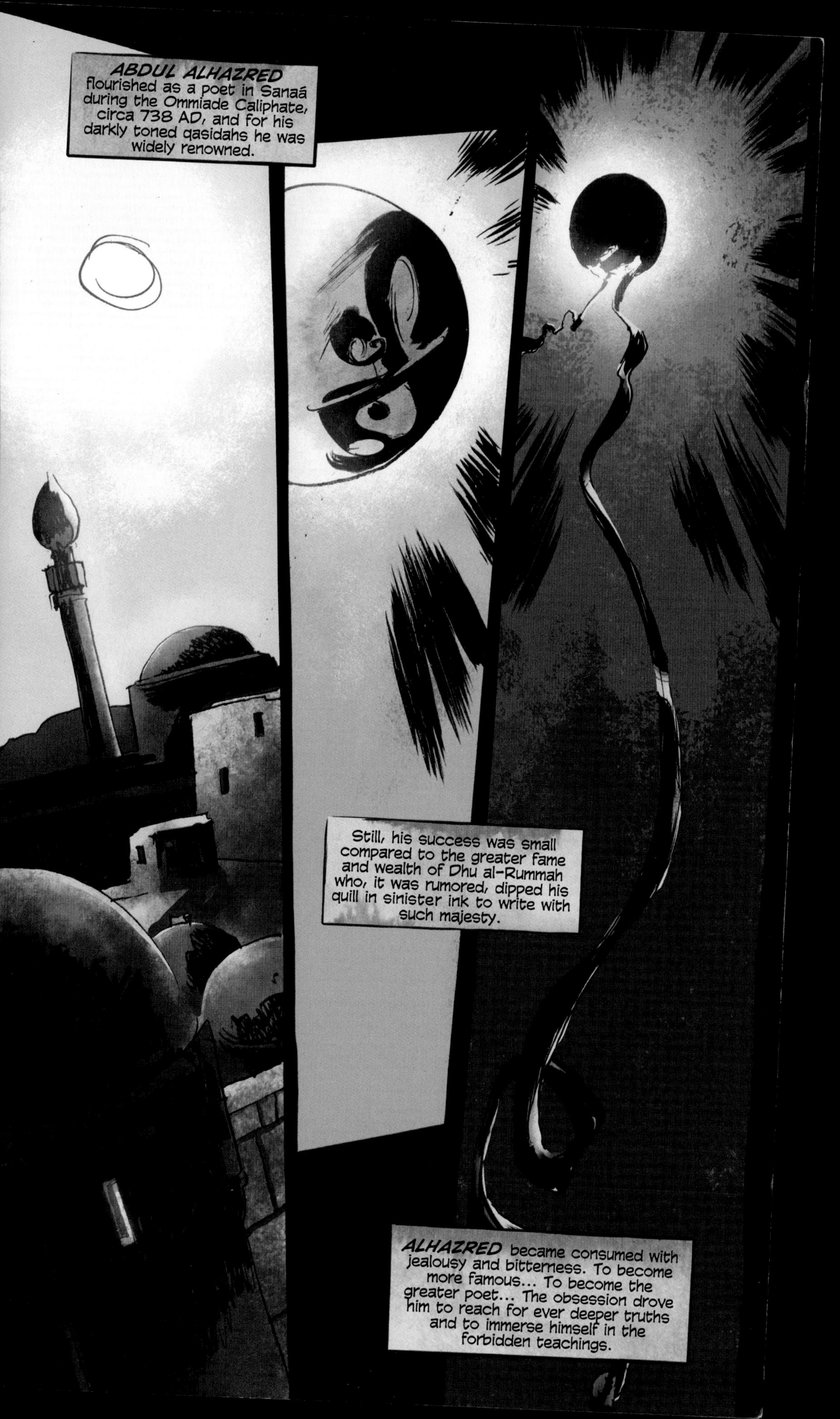
ABDUL ALHAZRED flourished as a poet in Sanaá during the Ommiade Caliphate, circa 738 AD, and for his darkly toned qasidahs he was widely renowned.
Still, his success was small compared to the greater fame and wealth of Dhu al-Rummah who, it was rumored, dipped his quill in sinister ink to write with such majesty.
ALHAZRED became consumed with jealousy and bitterness. To become more famous... To become the greater poet... The obsession drove him to reach for ever deeper truths and to immerse himself in the forbidden teachings.

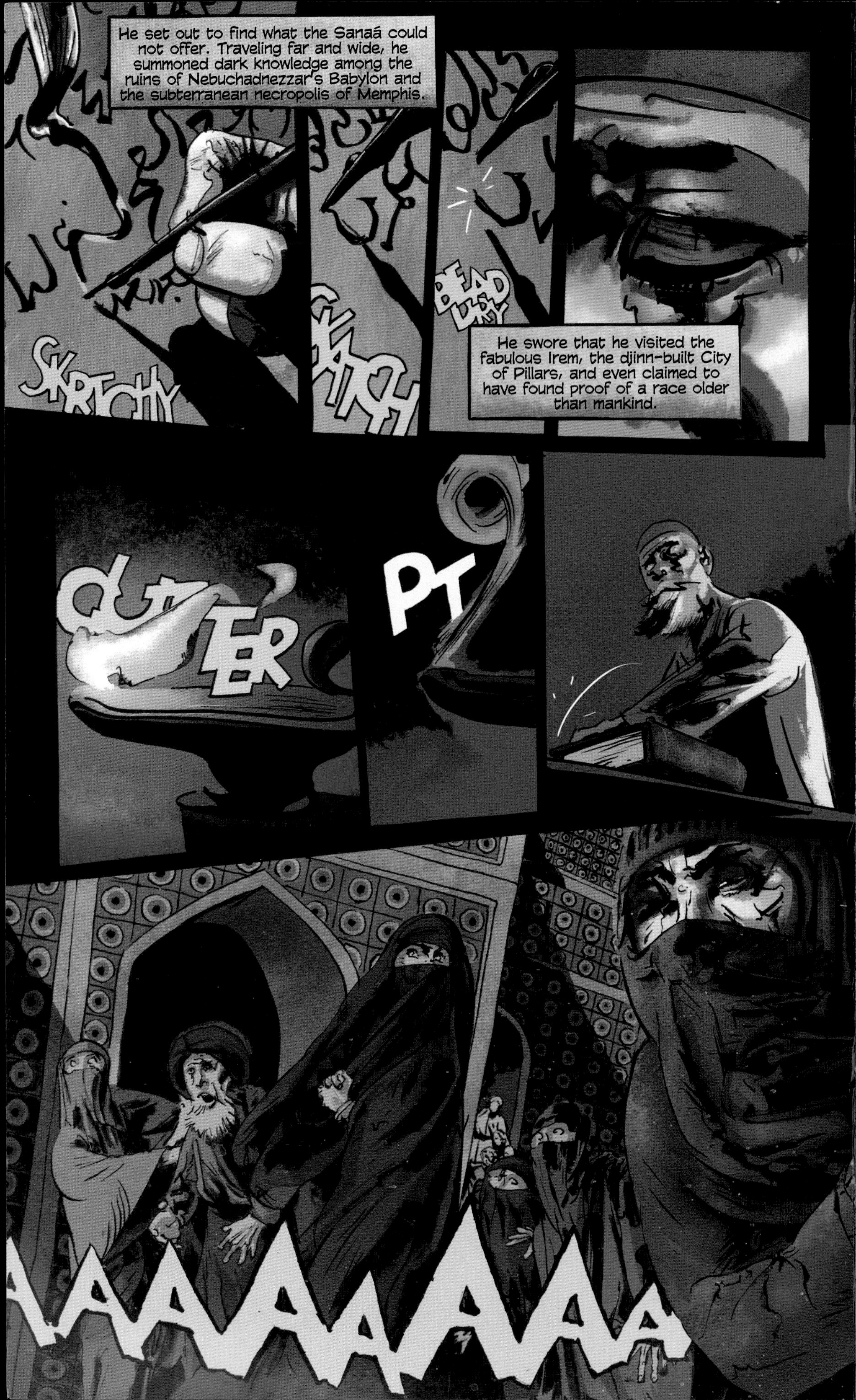
He set out to find what the Sanaá could not offer. Traveling far and wide, he summoned dark knowledge among the ruins of Nebuchadnezzar's Babylon and the subterranean necropolis of Memphis.
SKRTCHY
DEAD DRY
He swore that he visited the fabulous Irem, the djinn-built City of Pillars, and even claimed to have found proof of a race older than mankind.
PT
AAAAAAAAA

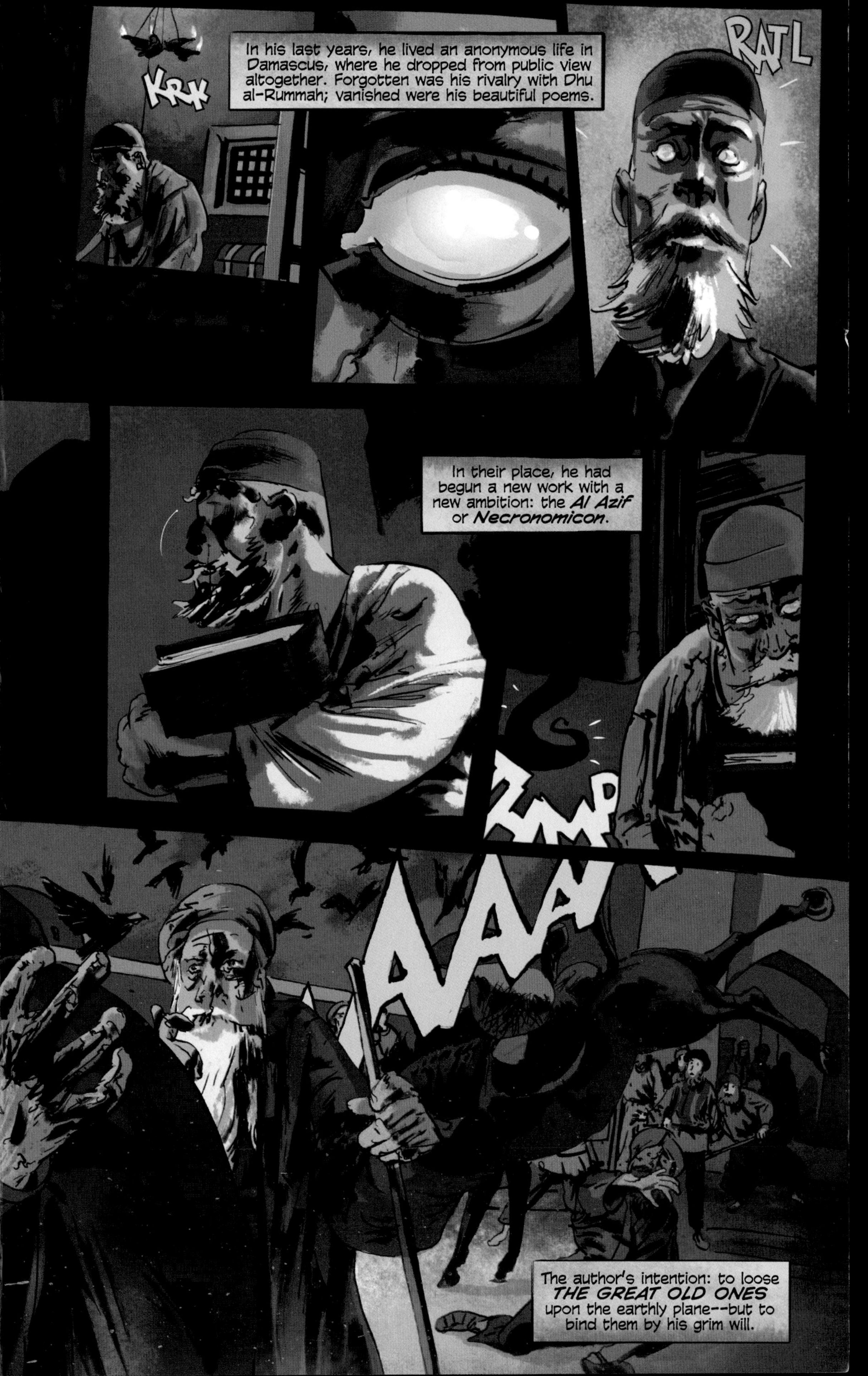

In his last years, he lived an anonymous life in Damascus, where he dropped from public view altogether. Forgotten was his rivalry with Dhu al-Rummah; vanished were his beautiful poems.
KRK
RATL
In their place, he had begun a new work with a new ambition: the *Al Azif* or *Necronomicon*.
AAA
The author's intention: to loose **THE GREAT OLD ONES** upon the earthly plane--but to bind them by his grim will.

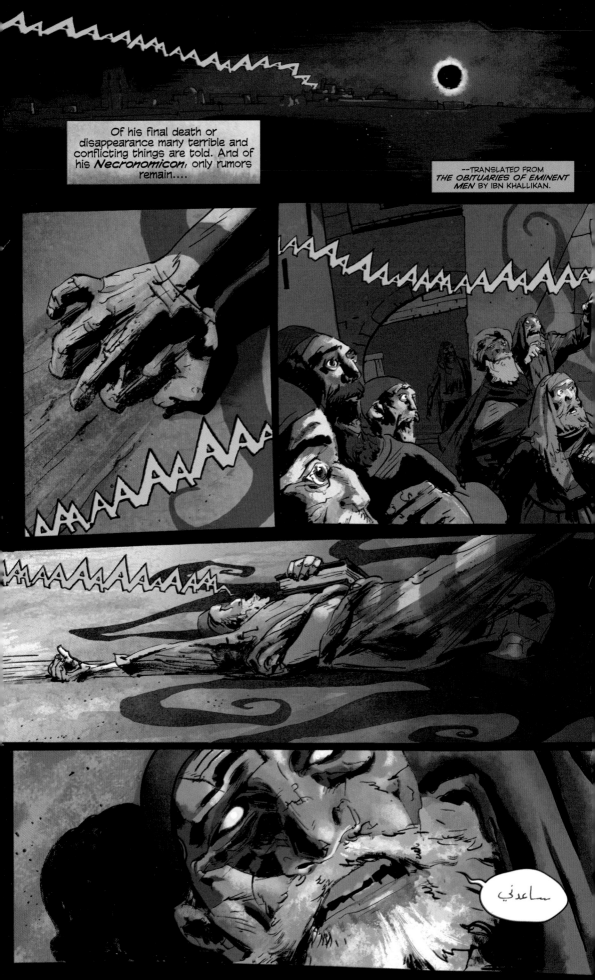

Of his final death or disappearance many terrible and conflicting things are told. And of his *Necronomicon*, only rumors remain....

--TRANSLATED FROM *THE OBITUARIES OF EMINENT MEN* BY IBN KHALLIKAN.

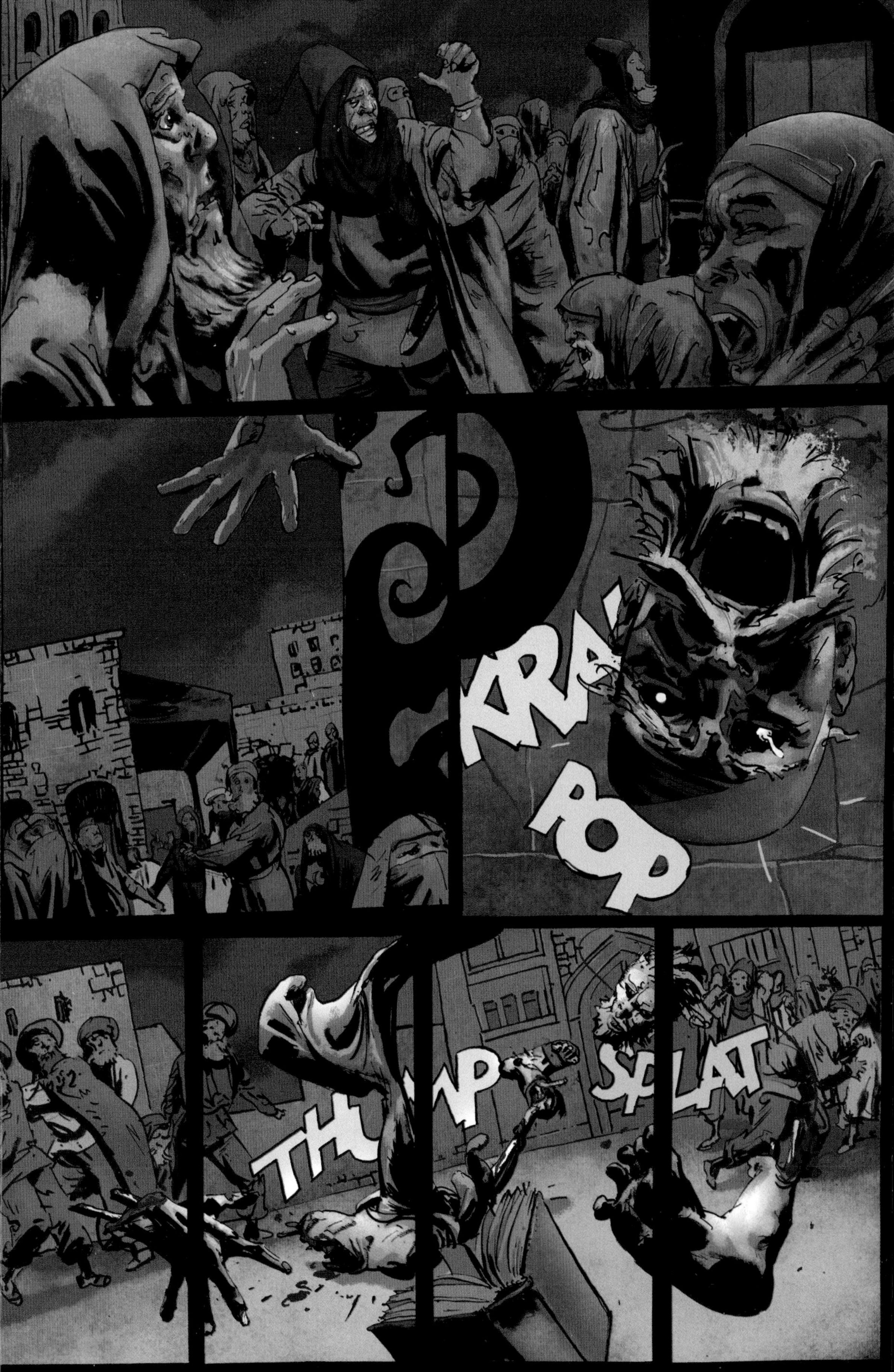
POP
SPLAT

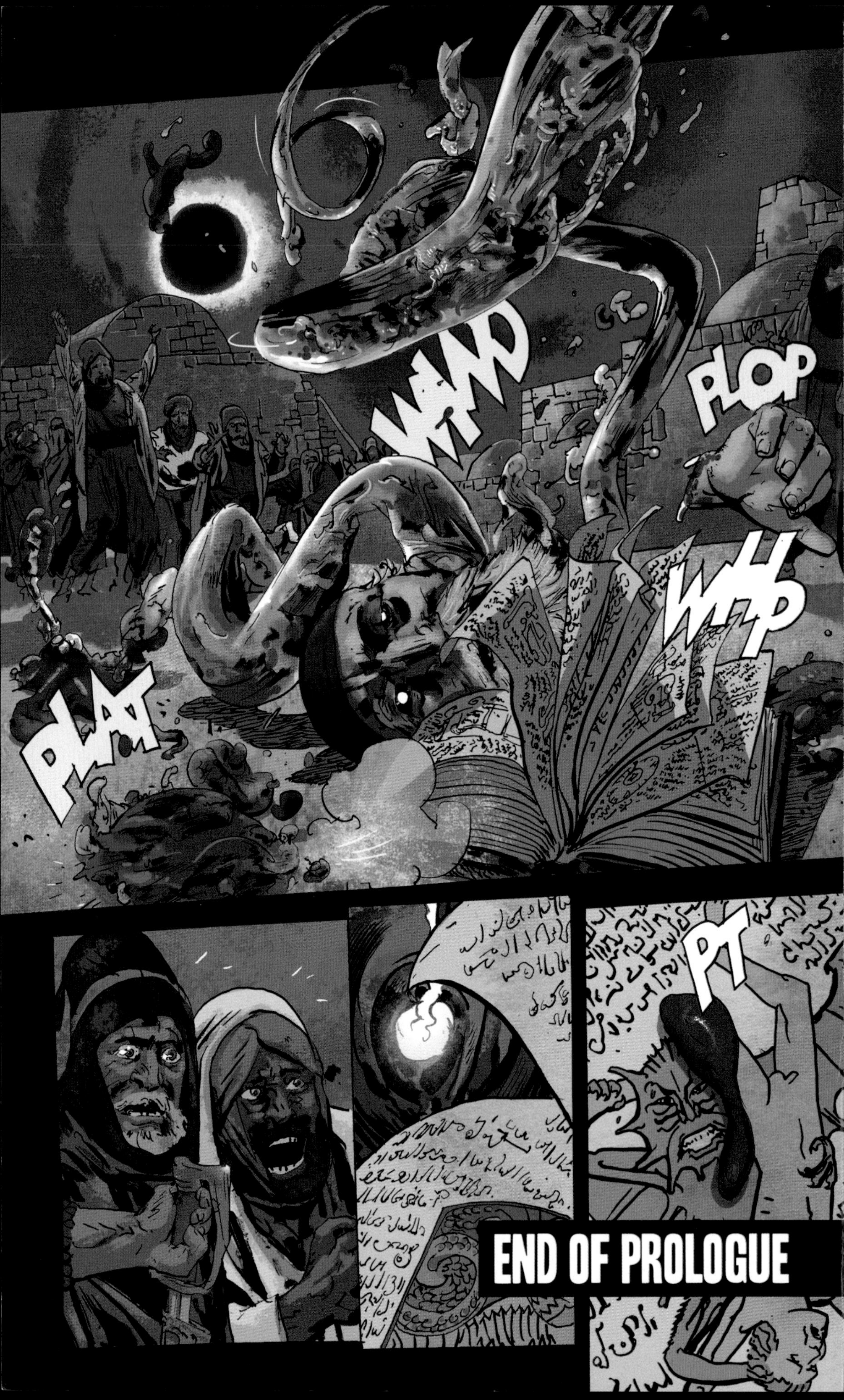
WHAP
PLOP
WHP
PLAT
PT
END OF PROLOGUE

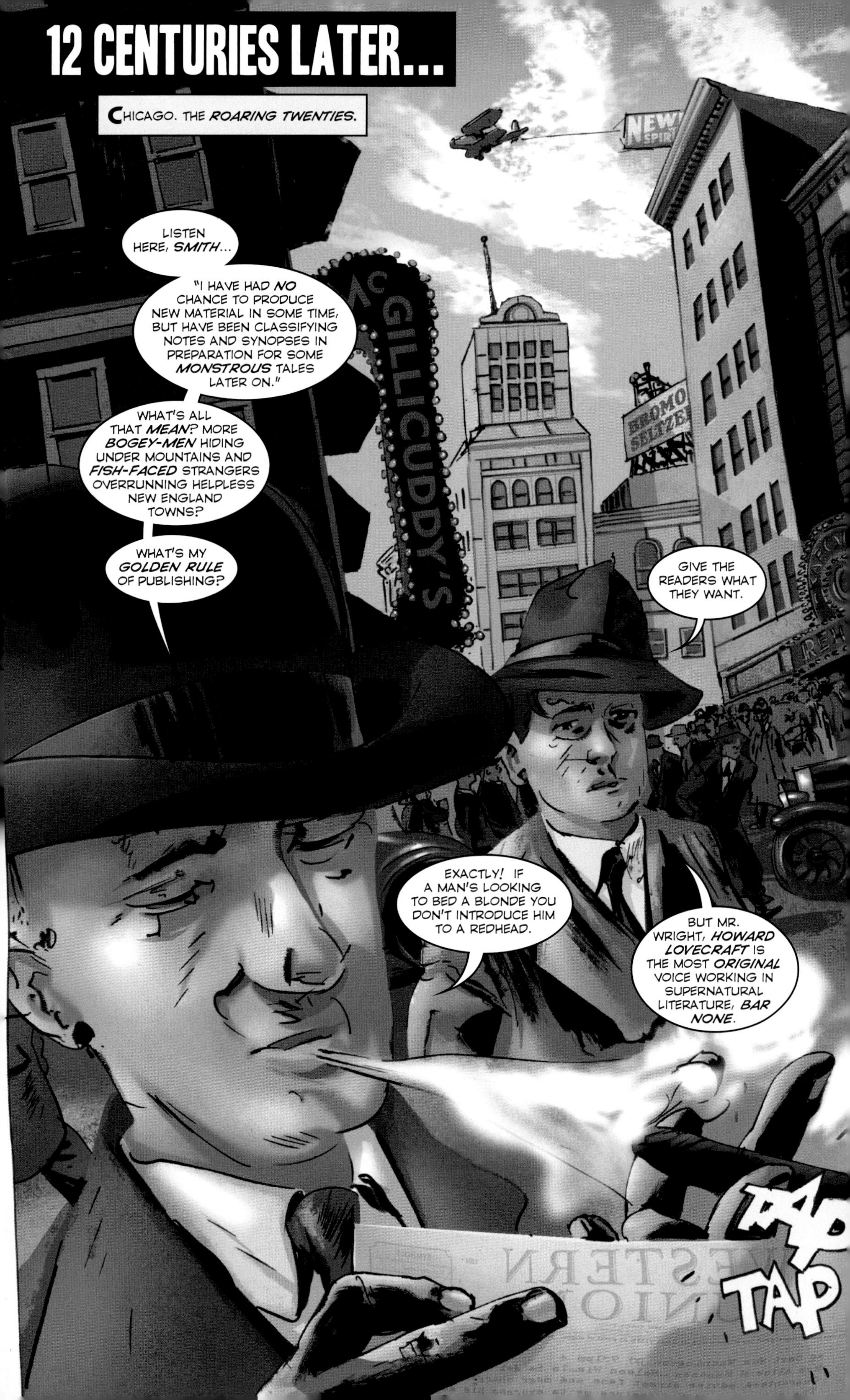
12 CENTURIES LATER...
CHICAGO. THE ROARING TWENTIES.
McGILLICUDDY'S
LISTEN HERE, SMITH...
"I HAVE HAD NO CHANCE TO PRODUCE NEW MATERIAL IN SOME TIME, BUT HAVE BEEN CLASSIFYING NOTES AND SYNOPSES IN PREPARATION FOR SOME MONSTROUS TALES LATER ON."
WHAT'S ALL THAT MEAN? MORE BOGEY-MEN HIDING UNDER MOUNTAINS AND FISH-FACED STRANGERS OVERRUNNING HELPLESS NEW ENGLAND TOWNS?
WHAT'S MY GOLDEN RULE OF PUBLISHING?
GIVE THE READERS WHAT THEY WANT.
EXACTLY! IF A MAN'S LOOKING TO BED A BLONDE YOU DON'T INTRODUCE HIM TO A REDHEAD.
BUT MR. WRIGHT, HOWARD LOVECRAFT IS THE MOST ORIGINAL VOICE WORKING IN SUPERNATURAL LITERATURE, BAR NONE.
TAP
TAP

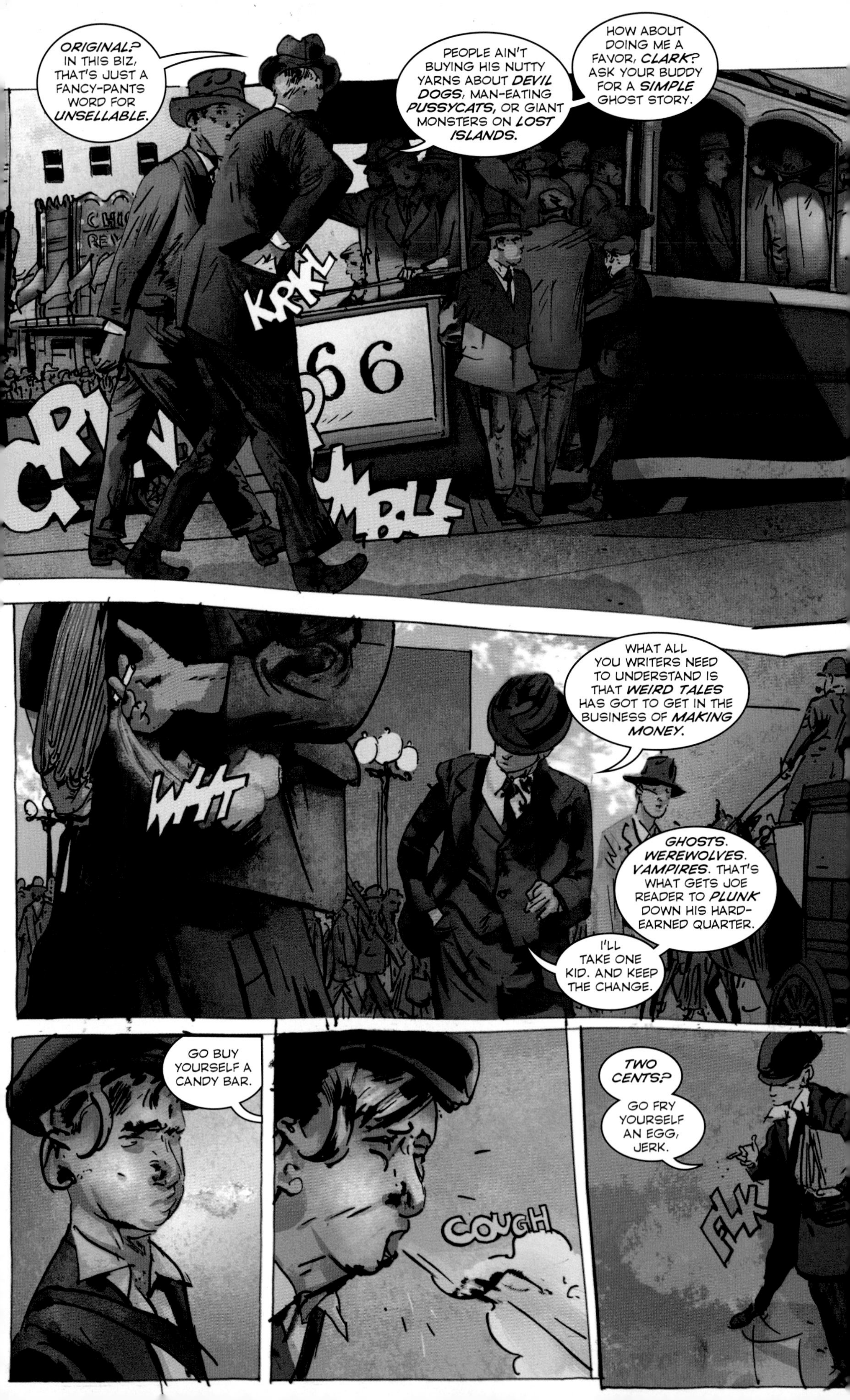
ORIGINAL? IN THIS BIZ, THAT'S JUST A FANCY-PANTS WORD FOR UNSELLABLE.
PEOPLE AIN'T BUYING HIS NUTTY YARNS ABOUT DEVIL DOGS, MAN-EATING PUSSYCATS, OR GIANT MONSTERS ON LOST ISLANDS.
HOW ABOUT DOING ME A FAVOR, CLARK? ASK YOUR BUDDY FOR A SIMPLE GHOST STORY.
KRKL
66
CRUMBLL
WHAT ALL YOU WRITERS NEED TO UNDERSTAND IS THAT WEIRD TALES HAS GOT TO GET IN THE BUSINESS OF MAKING MONEY.
WHT
GHOSTS. WEREWOLVES. VAMPIRES. THAT'S WHAT GETS JOE READER TO PLUNK DOWN HIS HARD-EARNED QUARTER.
I'LL TAKE ONE KID. AND KEEP THE CHANGE.
GO BUY YOURSELF A CANDY BAR.
COUGH
TWO CENTS?
GO FRY YOURSELF AN EGG, JERK.
FLK

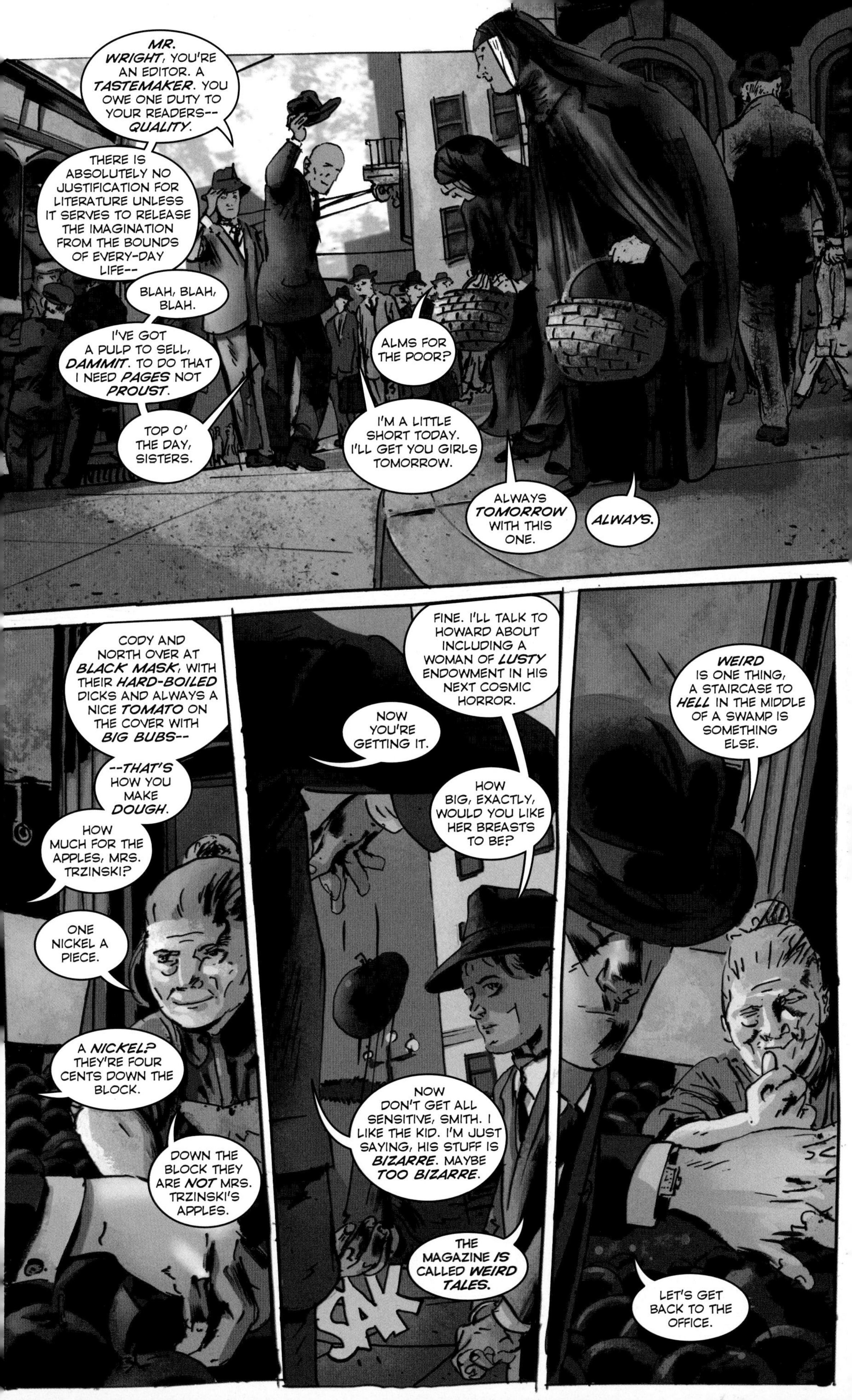
MR. WRIGHT, YOU'RE AN EDITOR. A TASTEMAKER. YOU OWE ONE DUTY TO YOUR READERS-- QUALITY.
THERE IS ABSOLUTELY NO JUSTIFICATION FOR LITERATURE UNLESS IT SERVES TO RELEASE THE IMAGINATION FROM THE BOUNDS OF EVERY-DAY LIFE--
BLAH, BLAH, BLAH.
I'VE GOT A PULP TO SELL, DAMMIT. TO DO THAT I NEED PAGES NOT PROUST.
TOP O' THE DAY, SISTERS.
ALMS FOR THE POOR?
I'M A LITTLE SHORT TODAY. I'LL GET YOU GIRLS TOMORROW.
ALWAYS TOMORROW WITH THIS ONE.
ALWAYS.
CODY AND NORTH OVER AT BLACK MASK, WITH THEIR HARD-BOILED DICKS AND ALWAYS A NICE TOMATO ON THE COVER WITH BIG BUBS--
--THAT'S HOW YOU MAKE DOUGH.
HOW MUCH FOR THE APPLES, MRS. TRZINSKI?
ONE NICKEL A PIECE.
A NICKEL? THEY'RE FOUR CENTS DOWN THE BLOCK.
DOWN THE BLOCK THEY ARE NOT MRS. TRZINSKI'S APPLES.
FINE. I'LL TALK TO HOWARD ABOUT INCLUDING A WOMAN OF LUSTY ENDOWMENT IN HIS NEXT COSMIC HORROR.
NOW YOU'RE GETTING IT.
HOW BIG, EXACTLY, WOULD YOU LIKE HER BREASTS TO BE?
NOW DON'T GET ALL SENSITIVE, SMITH. I LIKE THE KID. I'M JUST SAYING, HIS STUFF IS BIZARRE. MAYBE TOO BIZARRE.
THE MAGAZINE IS CALLED WEIRD TALES.
SAK
WEIRD IS ONE THING, A STAIRCASE TO HELL IN THE MIDDLE OF A SWAMP IS SOMETHING ELSE.
LET'S GET BACK TO THE OFFICE.

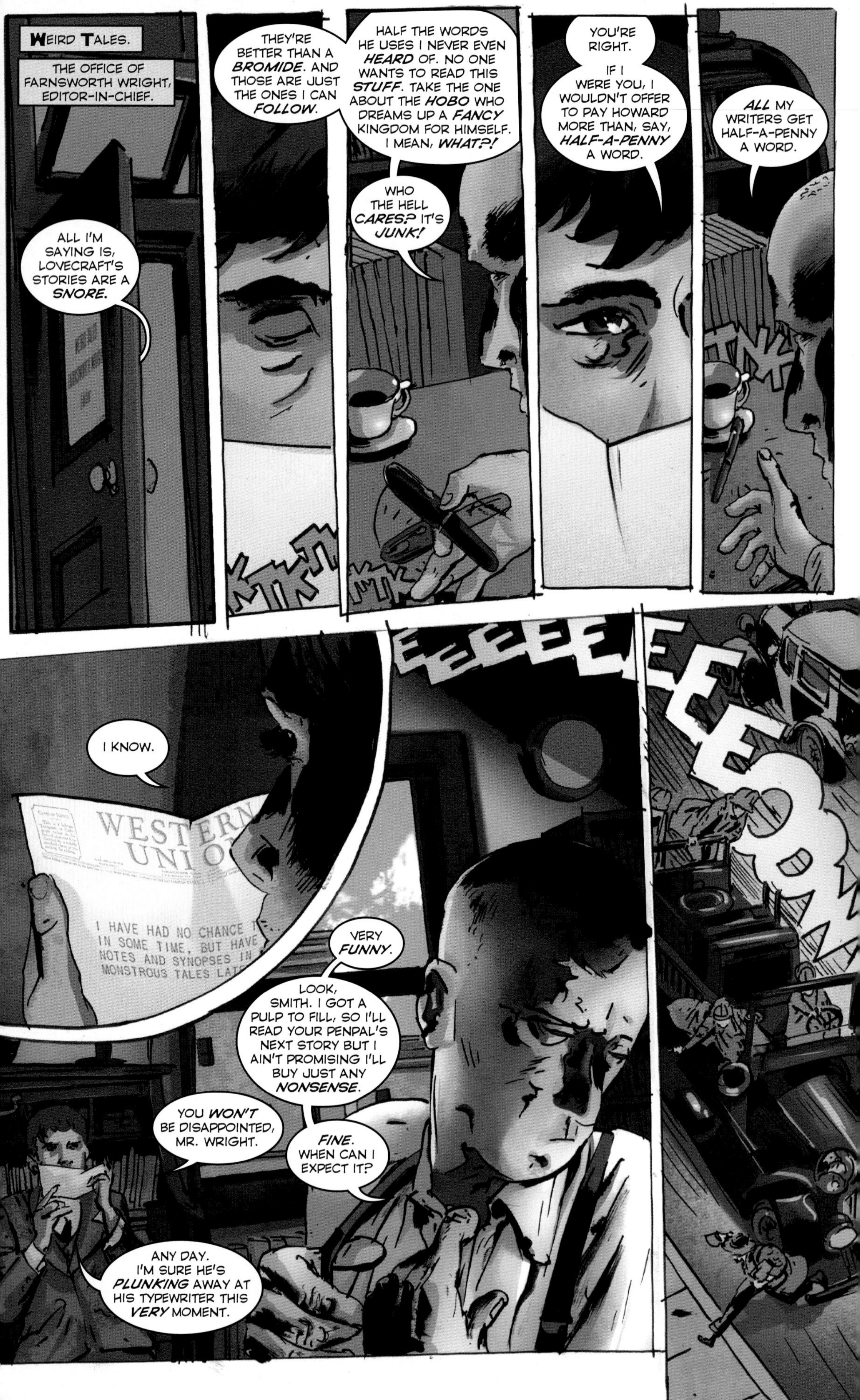
WEIRD TALES.
THE OFFICE OF FARNSWORTH WRIGHT, EDITOR-IN-CHIEF.
ALL I'M SAYING IS, LOVECRAFT'S STORIES ARE A SNORE.
THEY'RE BETTER THAN A BROMIDE. AND THOSE ARE JUST THE ONES I CAN FOLLOW.
HALF THE WORDS HE USES I NEVER EVEN HEARD OF. NO ONE WANTS TO READ THIS STUFF. TAKE THE ONE ABOUT THE HOBO WHO DREAMS UP A FANCY KINGDOM FOR HIMSELF. I MEAN, WHAT?!
WHO THE HELL CARES? IT'S JUNK!
YOU'RE RIGHT.
IF I WERE YOU, I WOULDN'T OFFER TO PAY HOWARD MORE THAN, SAY, HALF-A-PENNY A WORD.
ALL MY WRITERS GET HALF-A-PENNY A WORD.
I KNOW.
VERY FUNNY.
LOOK, SMITH. I GOT A PULP TO FILL, SO I'LL READ YOUR PENPAL'S NEXT STORY BUT I AIN'T PROMISING I'LL BUY JUST ANY NONSENSE.
YOU WON'T BE DISAPPOINTED, MR. WRIGHT.
FINE. WHEN CAN I EXPECT IT?
ANY DAY. I'M SURE HE'S PLUNKING AWAY AT HIS TYPEWRITER THIS VERY MOMENT.

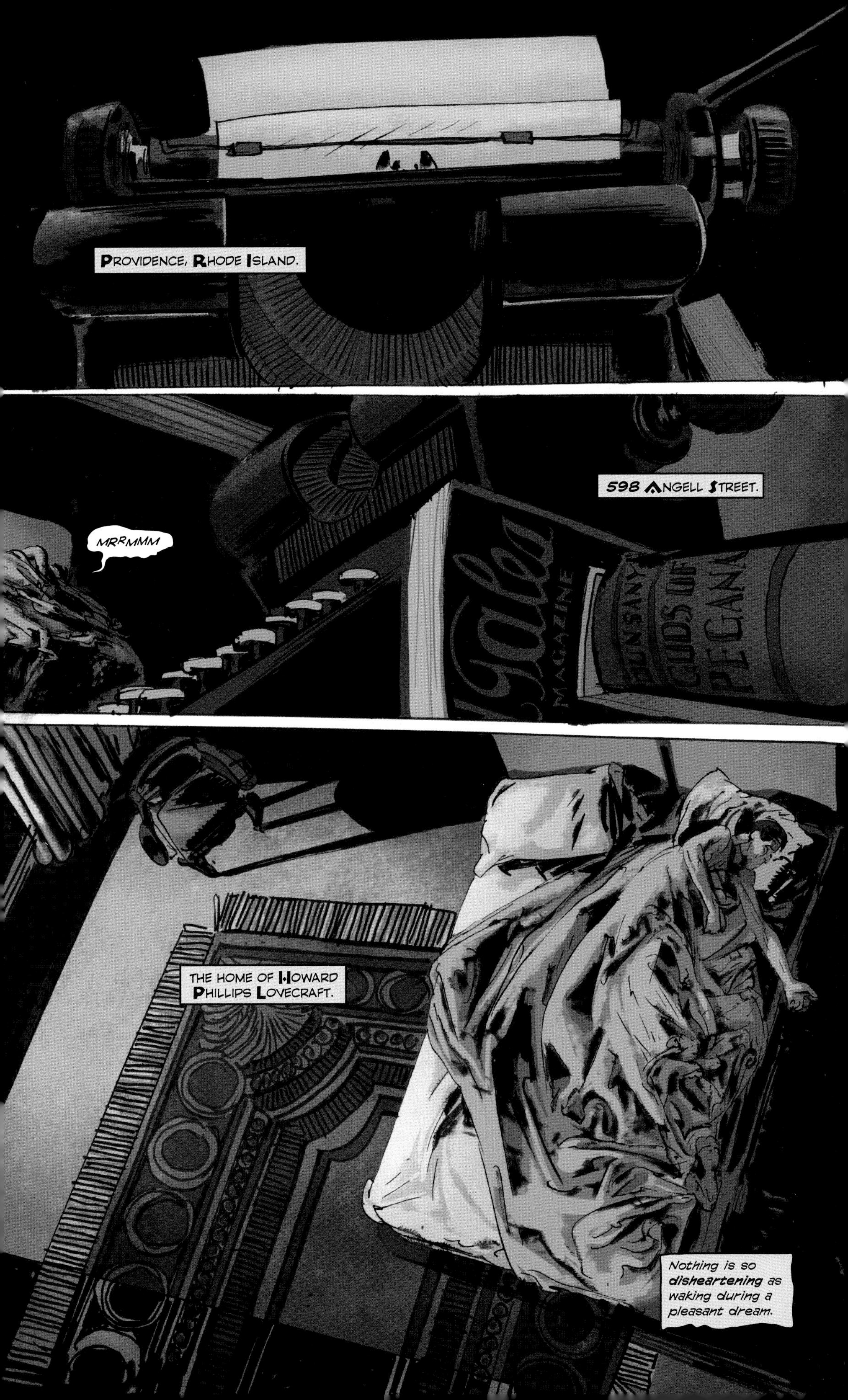
PROVIDENCE, RHODE ISLAND.
598 ANGELL STREET.
MRRMMM
MAGAZINE
THE HOME OF HOWARD PHILLIPS LOVECRAFT.
Nothing is so ***disheartening*** as waking during a pleasant dream.

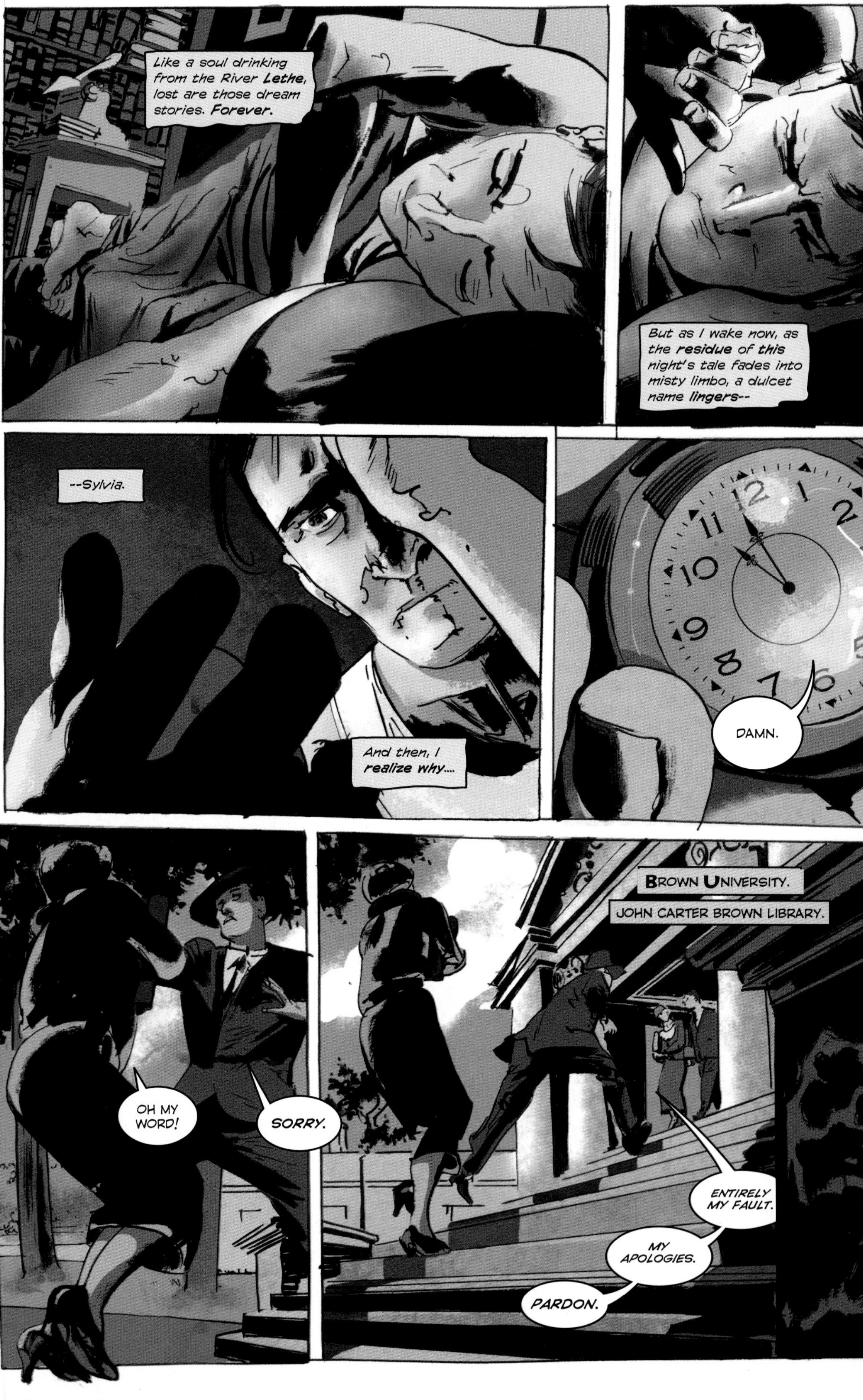
Like a soul drinking from the River Lethe, lost are those dream stories. Forever.
But as I wake now, as the residue of this night's tale fades into misty limbo, a dulcet name lingers--
--Sylvia.
And then, I realize why....
DAMN.
OH MY WORD!
SORRY.
BROWN UNIVERSITY.
JOHN CARTER BROWN LIBRARY.
ENTIRELY MY FAULT.
MY APOLOGIES.
PARDON.

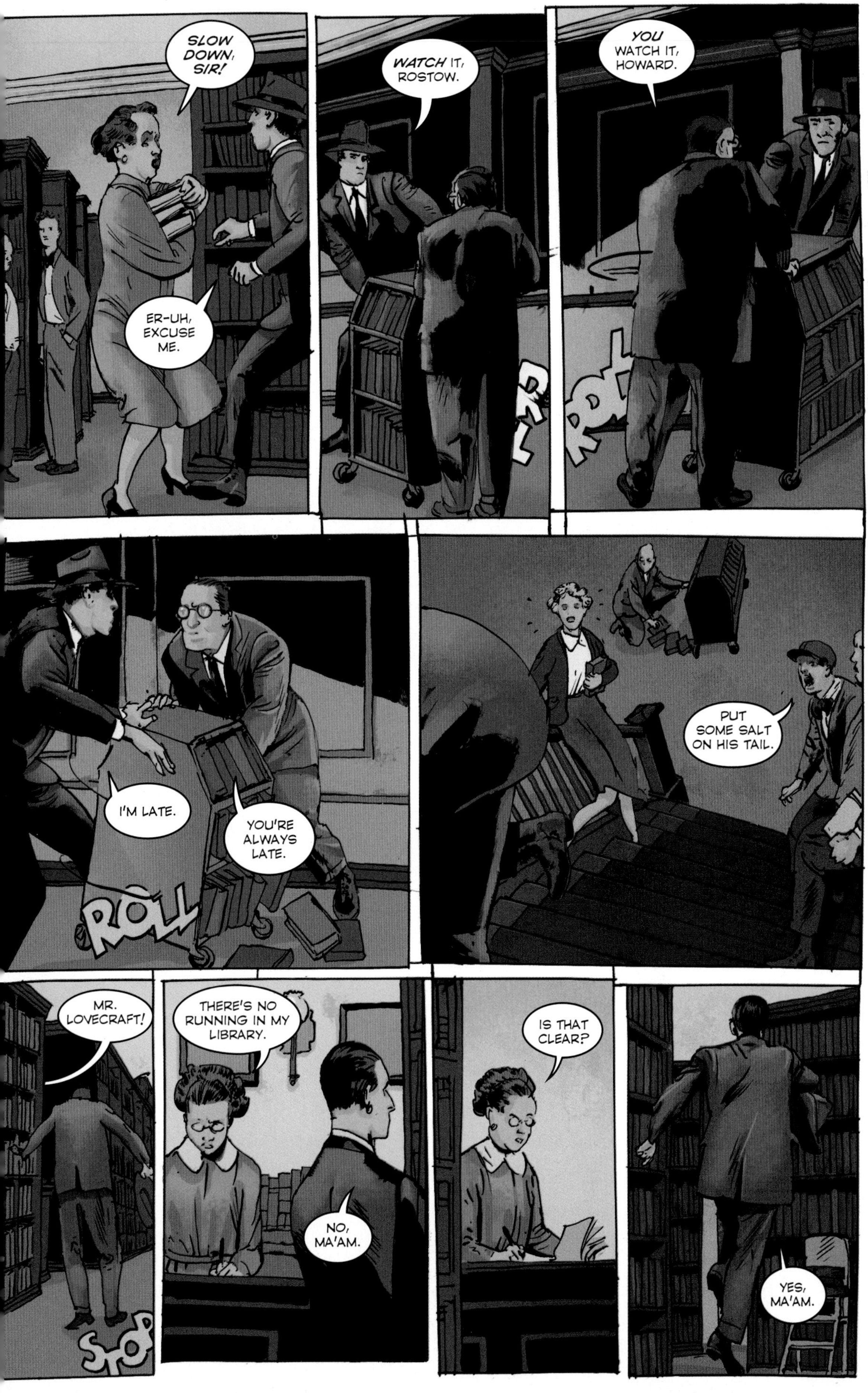
SLOW DOWN, SIR!
ER-UH, EXCUSE ME.
WATCH IT, ROSTOW.
ROLL
YOU WATCH IT, HOWARD.
ROLL
I'M LATE.
YOU'RE ALWAYS LATE.
ROLL
PUT SOME SALT ON HIS TAIL.
MR. LOVECRAFT!
STOP
THERE'S NO RUNNING IN MY LIBRARY.
NO, MA'AM.
IS THAT CLEAR?
YES, MA'AM.

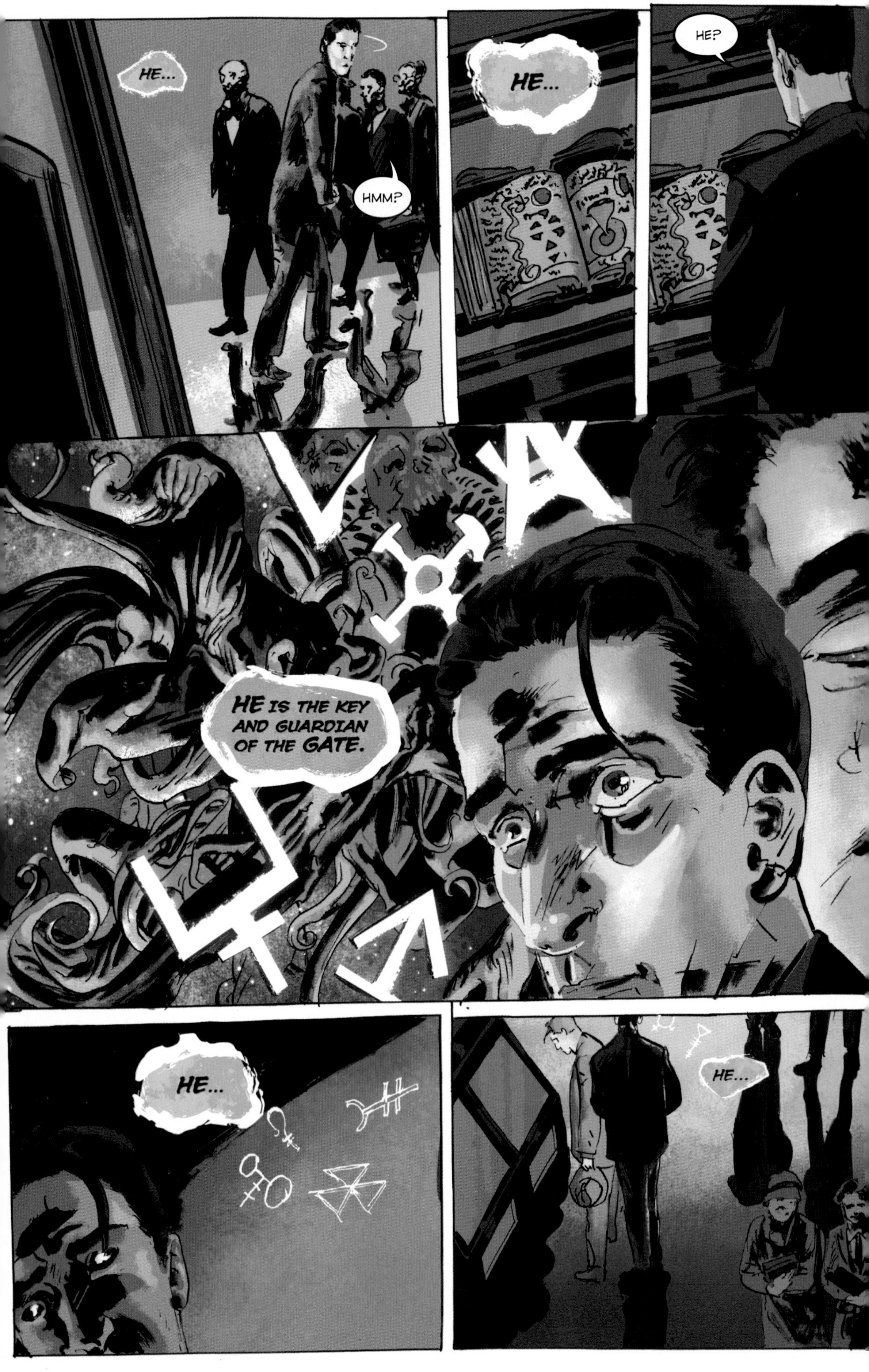
HE...
HMM?
HE...
HE?
HE IS THE KEY AND GUARDIAN OF THE GATE.
HE...
HE...

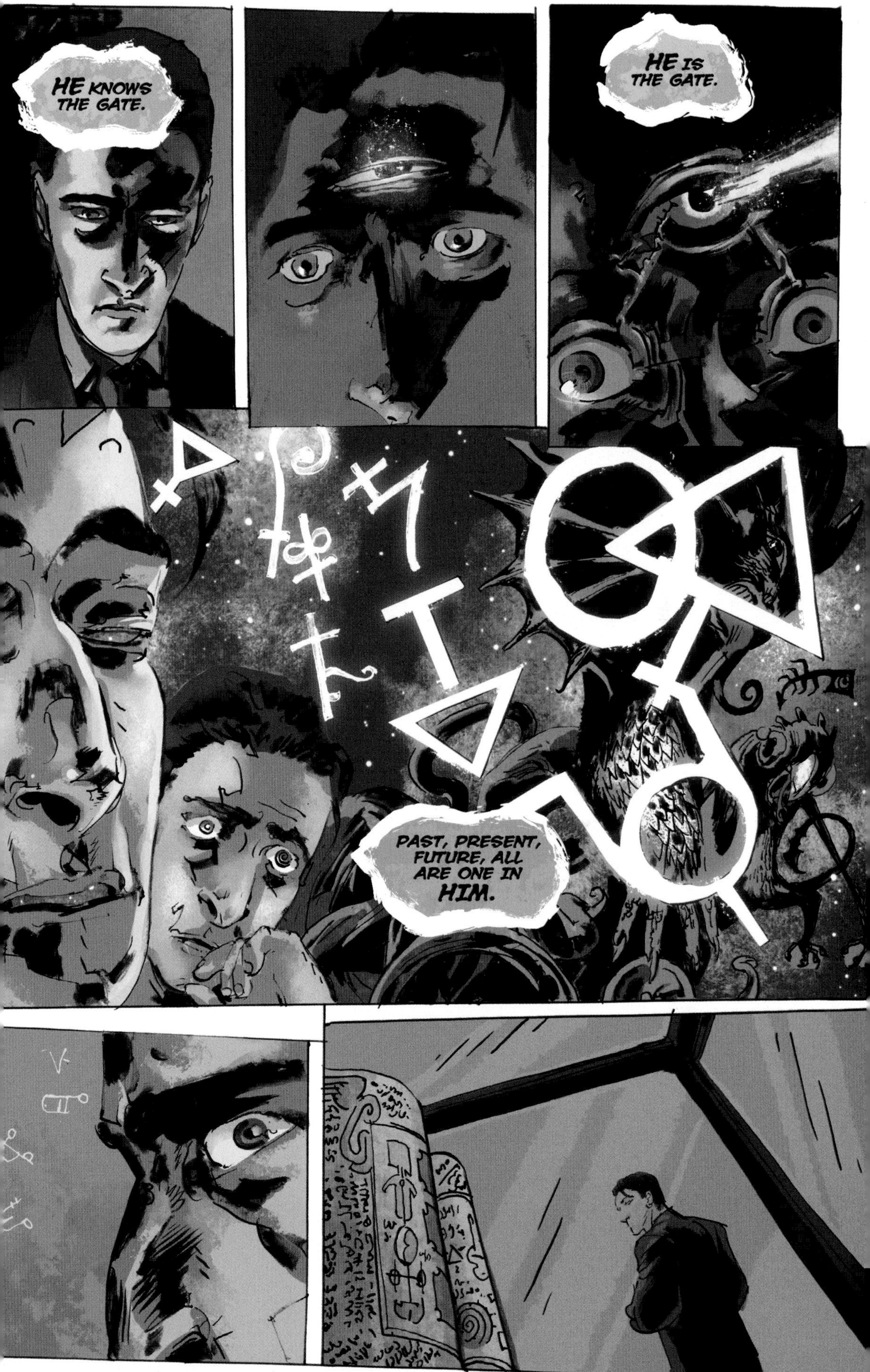
HE KNOWS THE GATE.
HE IS THE GATE.
PAST, PRESENT, FUTURE, ALL ARE ONE IN HIM.

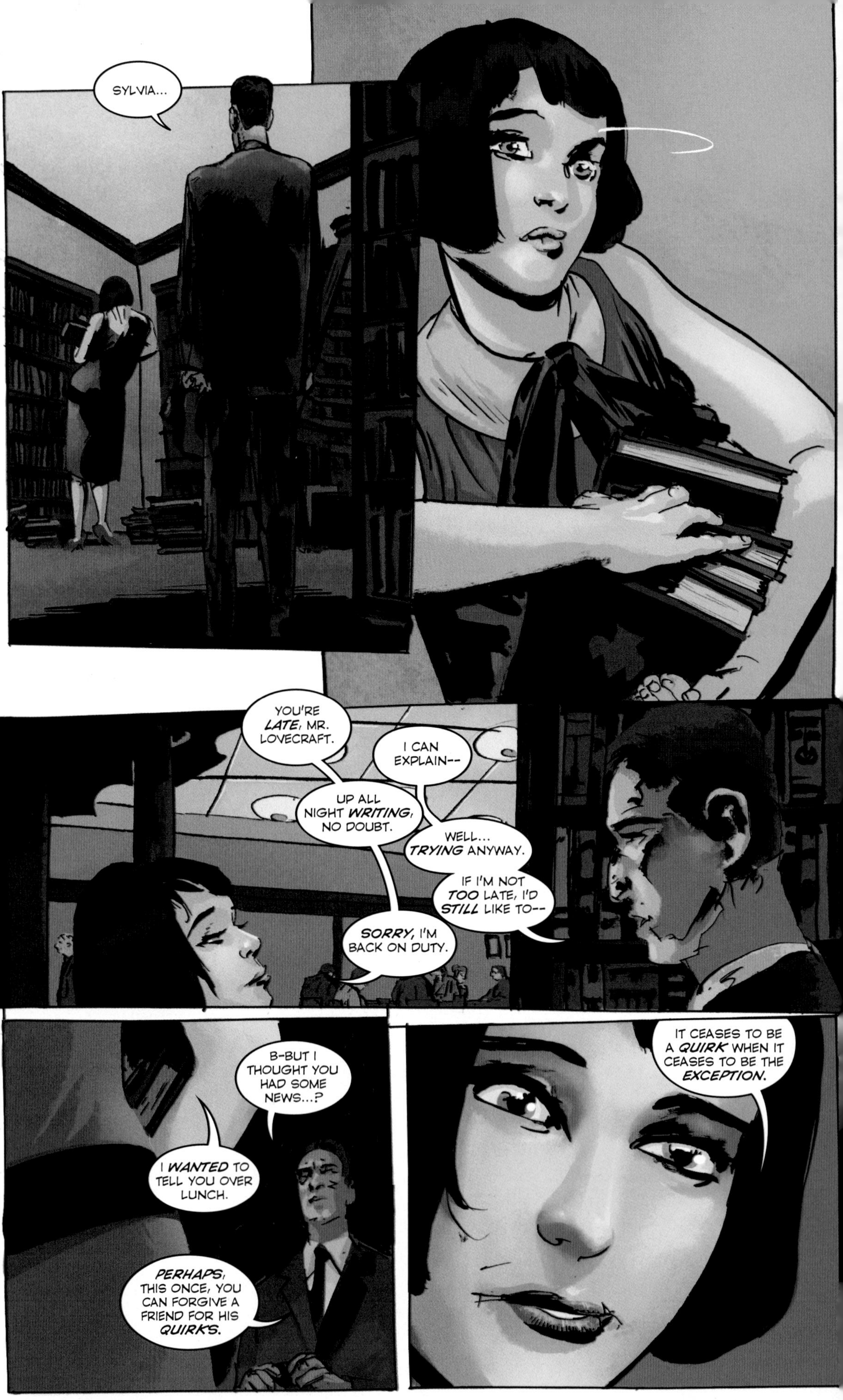
SYLVIA...
YOU'RE LATE, MR. LOVECRAFT.
I CAN EXPLAIN--
UP ALL NIGHT WRITING, NO DOUBT.
WELL... TRYING ANYWAY.
IF I'M NOT TOO LATE, I'D STILL LIKE TO--
SORRY, I'M BACK ON DUTY.
B-BUT I THOUGHT YOU HAD SOME NEWS...?
I WANTED TO TELL YOU OVER LUNCH.
PERHAPS, THIS ONCE, YOU CAN FORGIVE A FRIEND FOR HIS QUIRKS.
IT CEASES TO BE A QUIRK WHEN IT CEASES TO BE THE EXCEPTION.

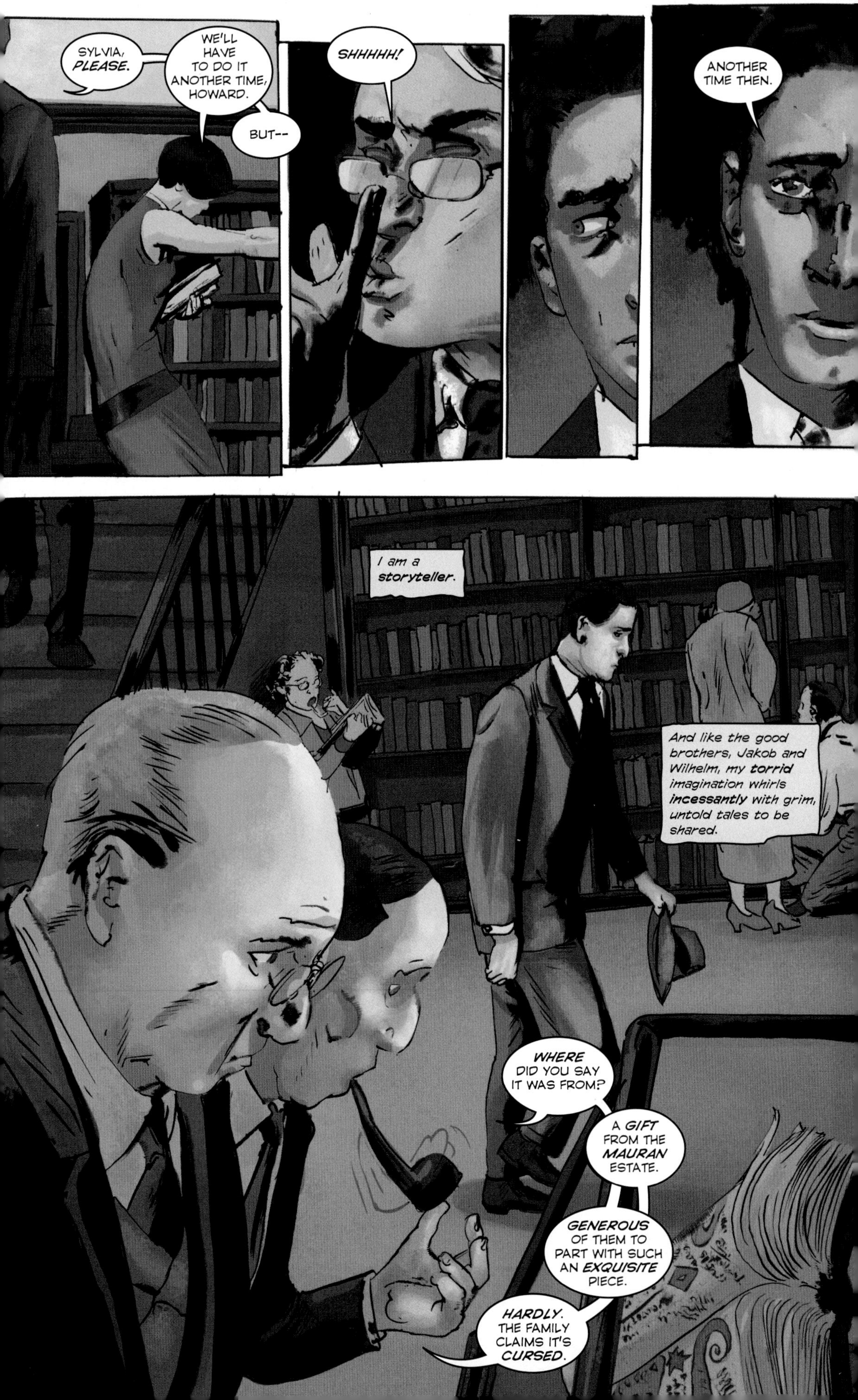
SYLVIA, PLEASE.
WE'LL HAVE TO DO IT ANOTHER TIME, HOWARD.
BUT--
SHHHHH!
ANOTHER TIME THEN.
I am a storyteller.
And like the good brothers, Jakob and Wilhelm, my torrid imagination whirls incessantly with grim, untold tales to be shared.
WHERE DID YOU SAY IT WAS FROM?
A GIFT FROM THE MAURAN ESTATE.
GENEROUS OF THEM TO PART WITH SUCH AN EXQUISITE PIECE.
HARDLY. THE FAMILY CLAIMS IT'S CURSED.

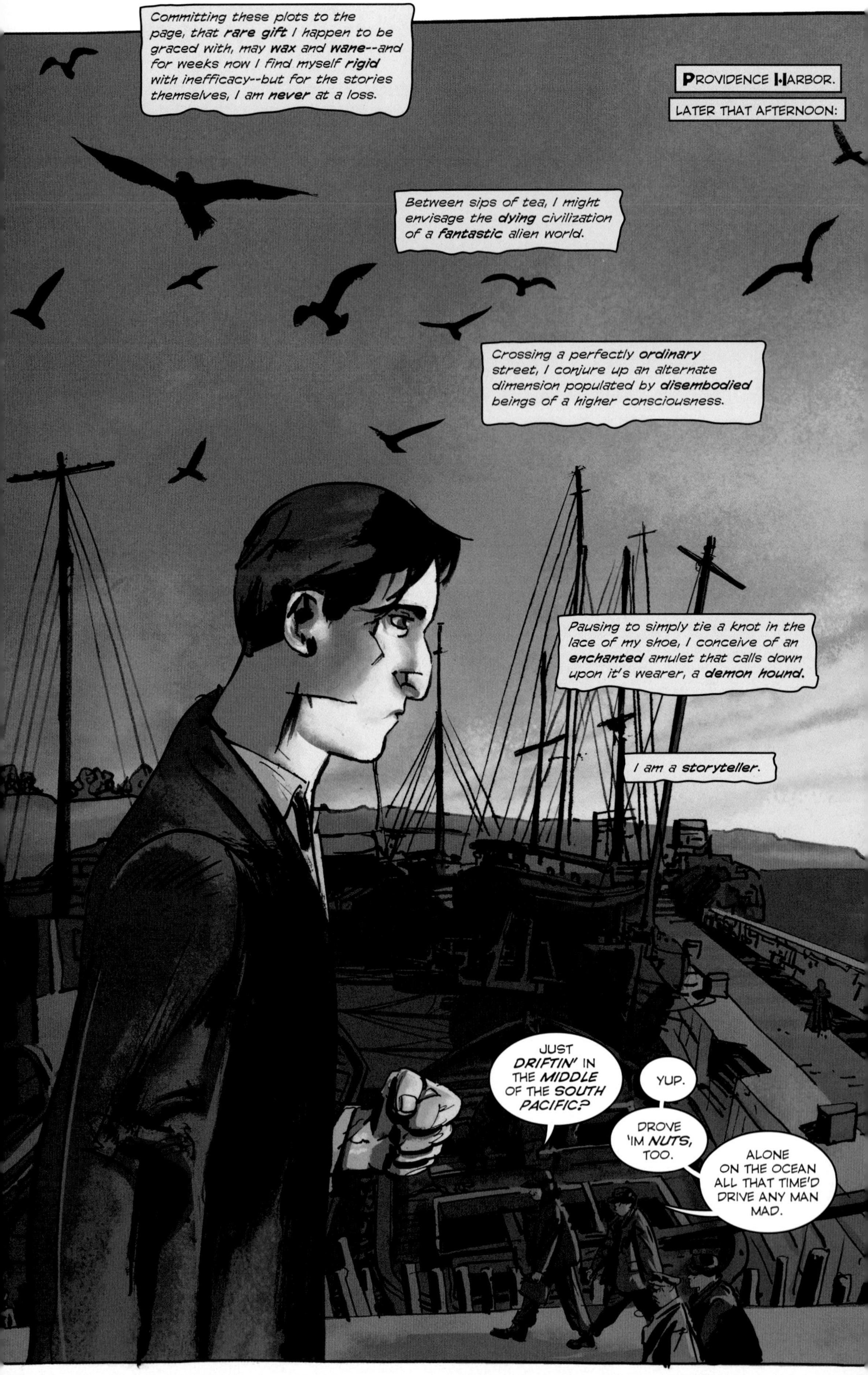
Committing these plots to the page, that rare gift I happen to be graced with, may wax and wane--and for weeks now I find myself rigid with inefficacy--but for the stories themselves, I am never at a loss.
PROVIDENCE HARBOR.
LATER THAT AFTERNOON:
Between sips of tea, I might envisage the dying civilization of a fantastic alien world.
Crossing a perfectly ordinary street, I conjure up an alternate dimension populated by disembodied beings of a higher consciousness.
Pausing to simply tie a knot in the lace of my shoe, I conceive of an enchanted amulet that calls down upon it's wearer, a demon hound.
I am a storyteller.
JUST DRIFTIN' IN THE MIDDLE OF THE SOUTH PACIFIC?
YUP.
DROVE 'IM NUTS, TOO.
ALONE ON THE OCEAN ALL THAT TIME'D DRIVE ANY MAN MAD.

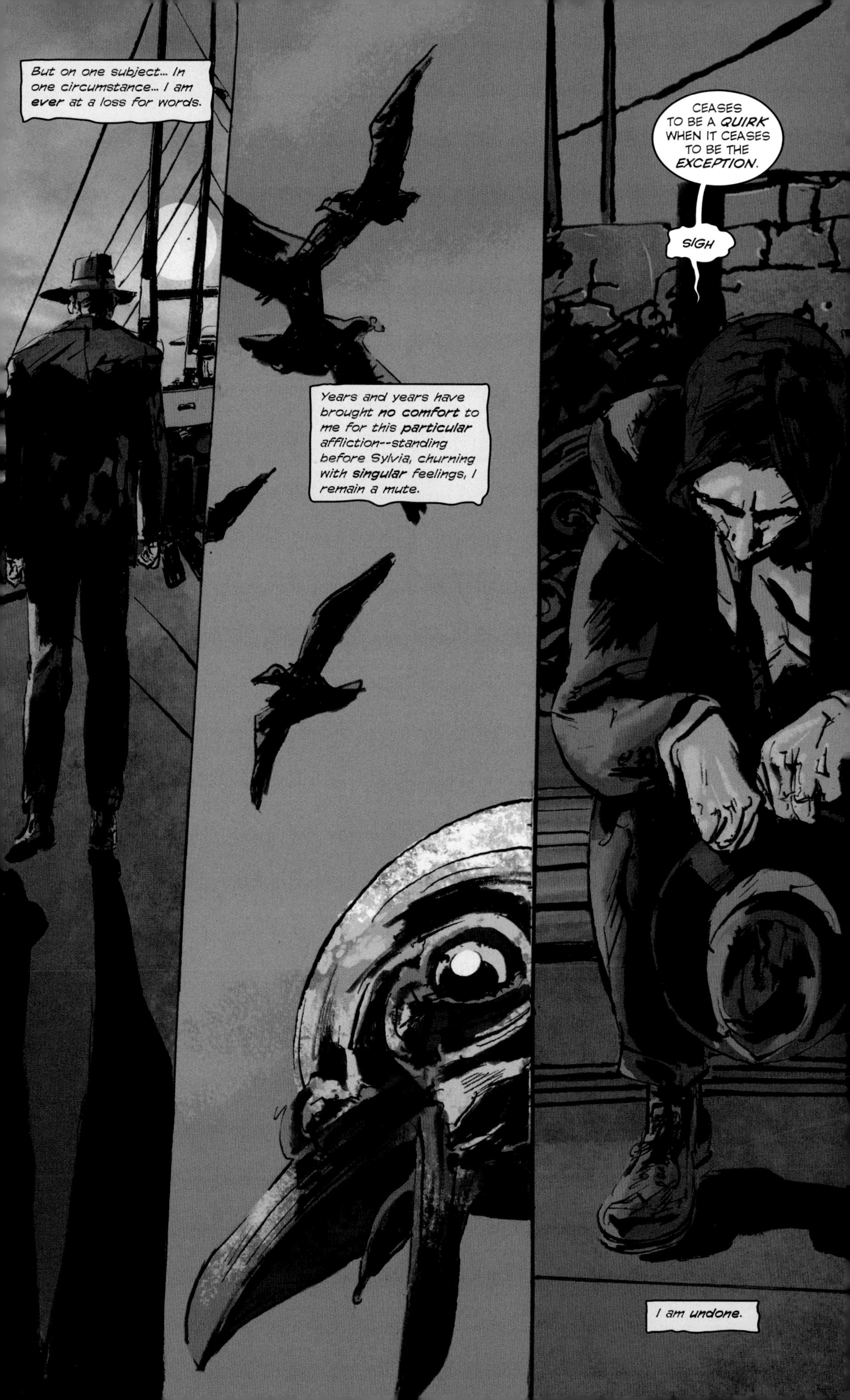
But on one subject... In one circumstance... I am ever at a loss for words.
Years and years have brought no comfort to me for this particular affliction--standing before Sylvia, churning with singular feelings, I remain a mute.
CEASES TO BE A QUIRK WHEN IT CEASES TO BE THE EXCEPTION.
SIGH
I am undone.

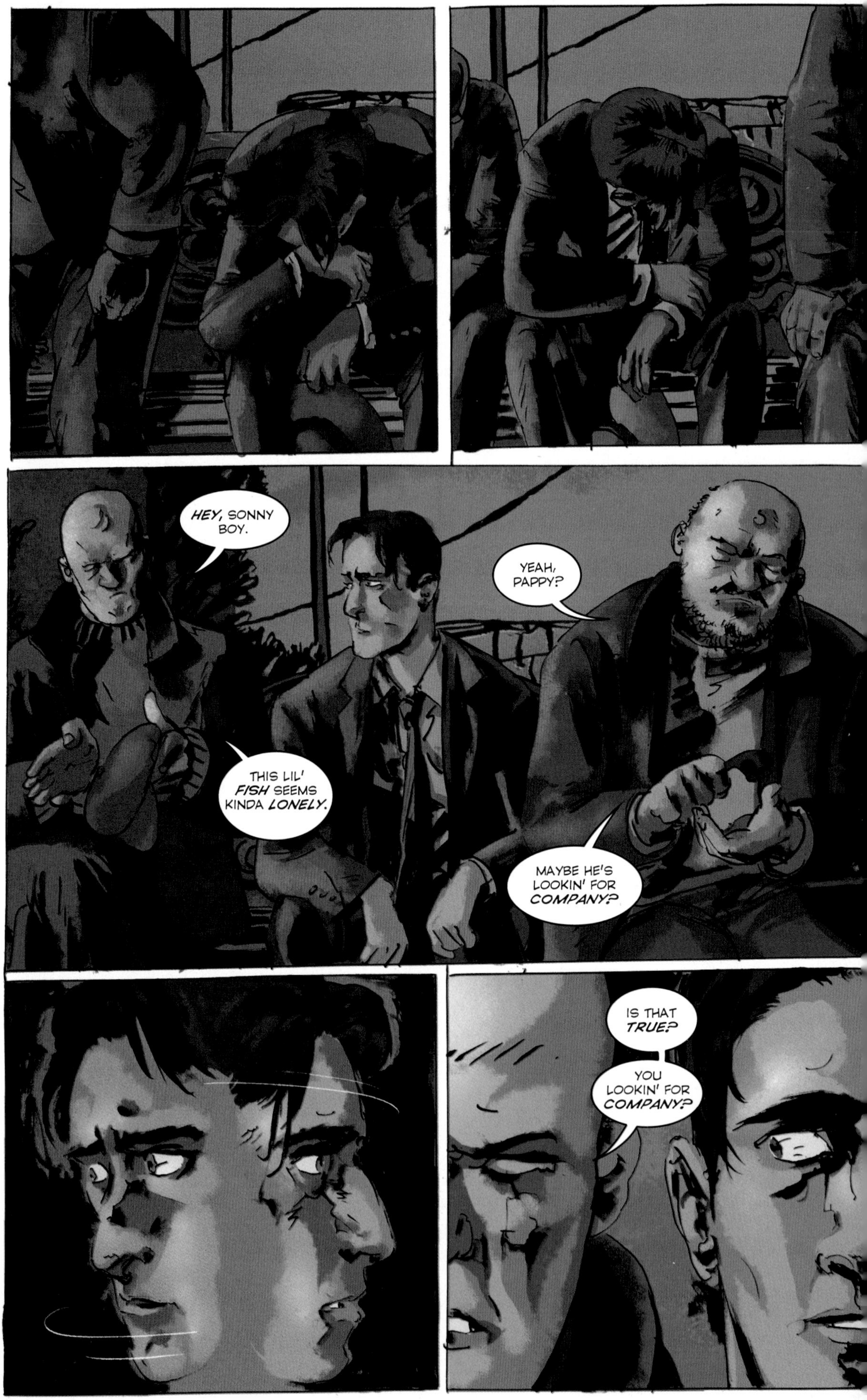
HEY, SONNY BOY.
YEAH, PAPPY?
THIS LIL' FISH SEEMS KINDA LONELY.
MAYBE HE'S LOOKIN' FOR COMPANY?
IS THAT TRUE?
YOU LOOKIN' FOR COMPANY?

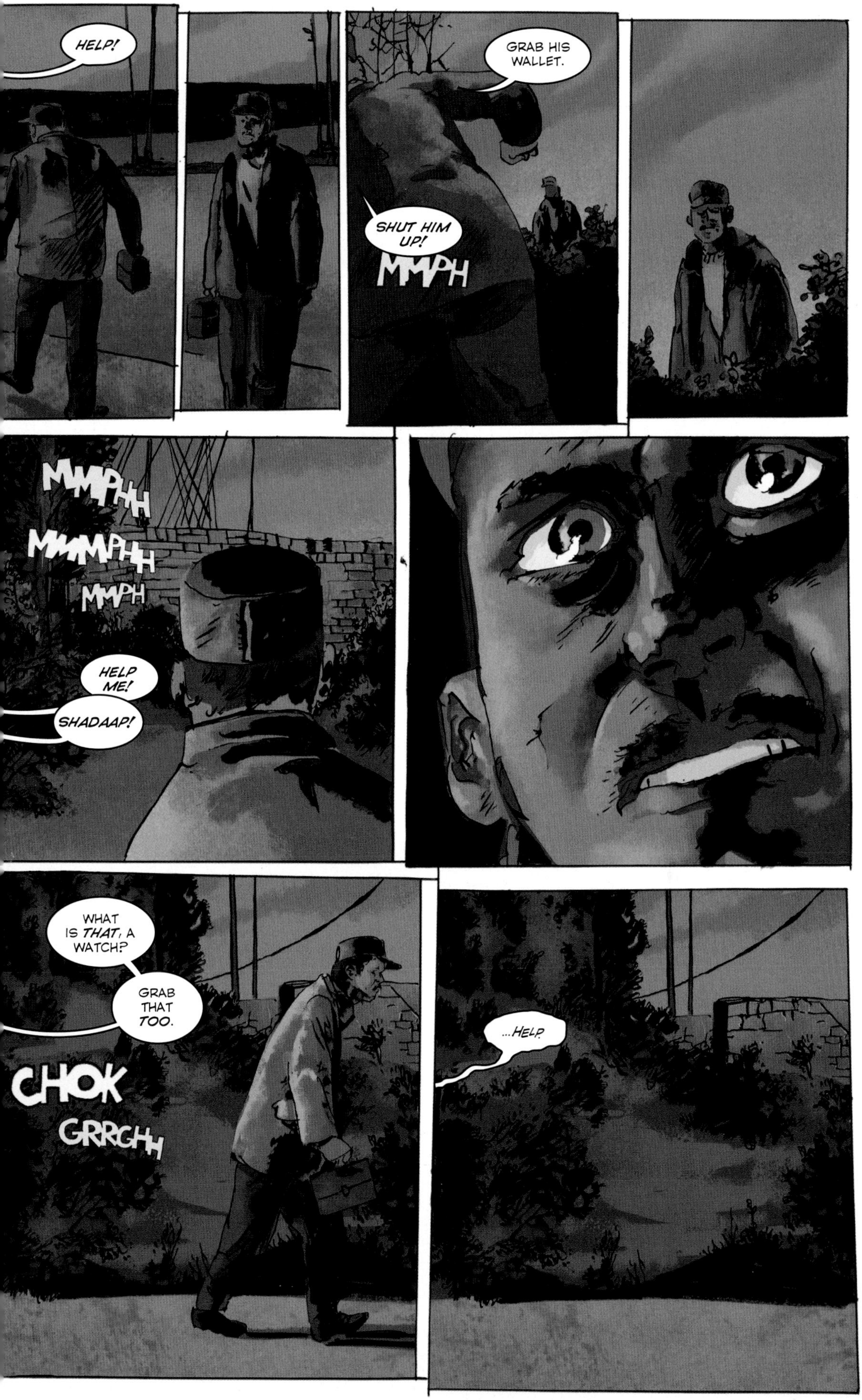
HELP!
GRAB HIS WALLET.
SHUT HIM UP!
MMPH
MMPHH
MMMPHH
MMPH
HELP ME!
SHADAAP!
WHAT IS THAT, A WATCH?
GRAB THAT TOO.
CHOK
GRRGHH
...HELP.

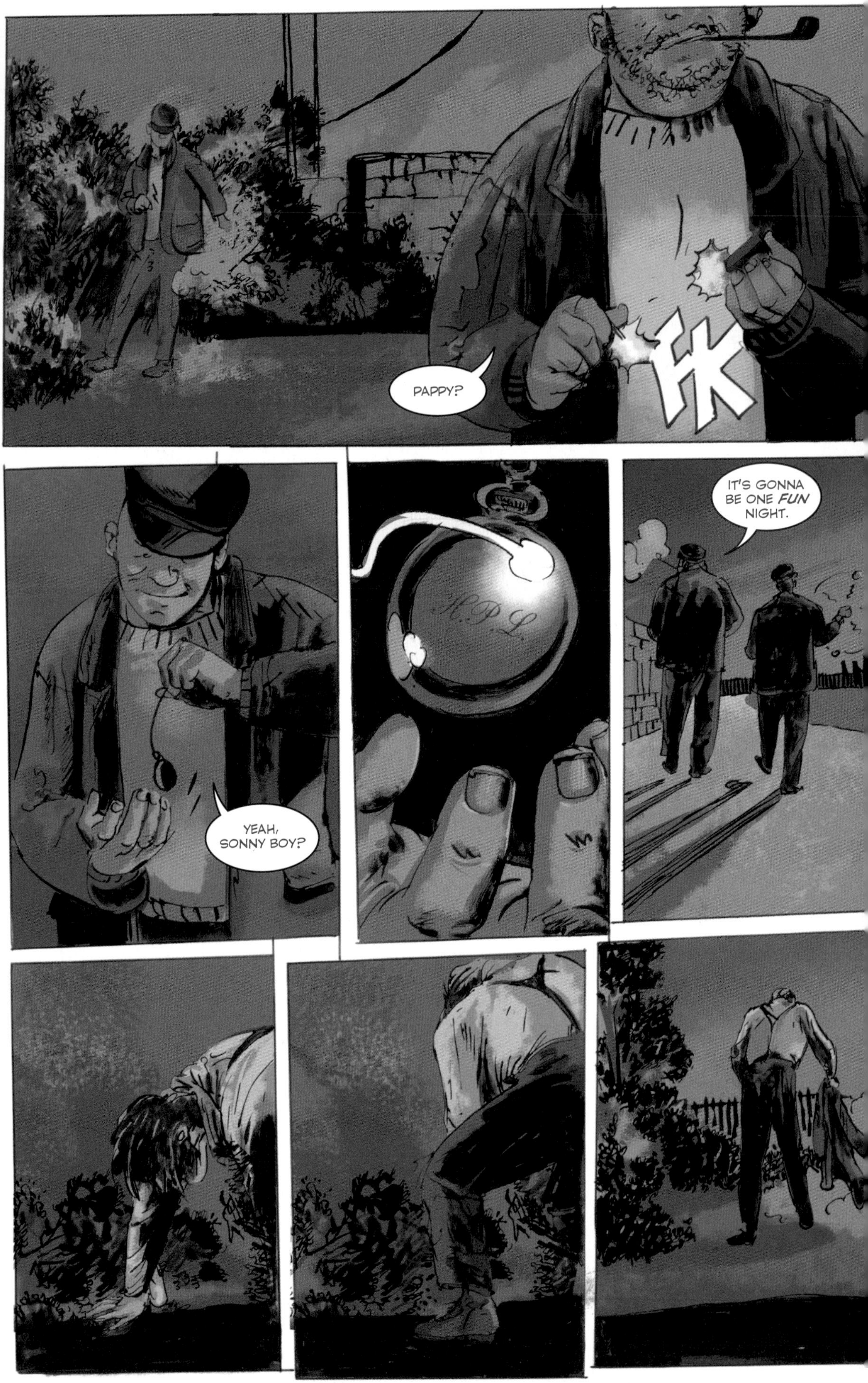
PAPPY?
FK
YEAH, SONNY BOY?
IT'S GONNA BE ONE *FUN* NIGHT.

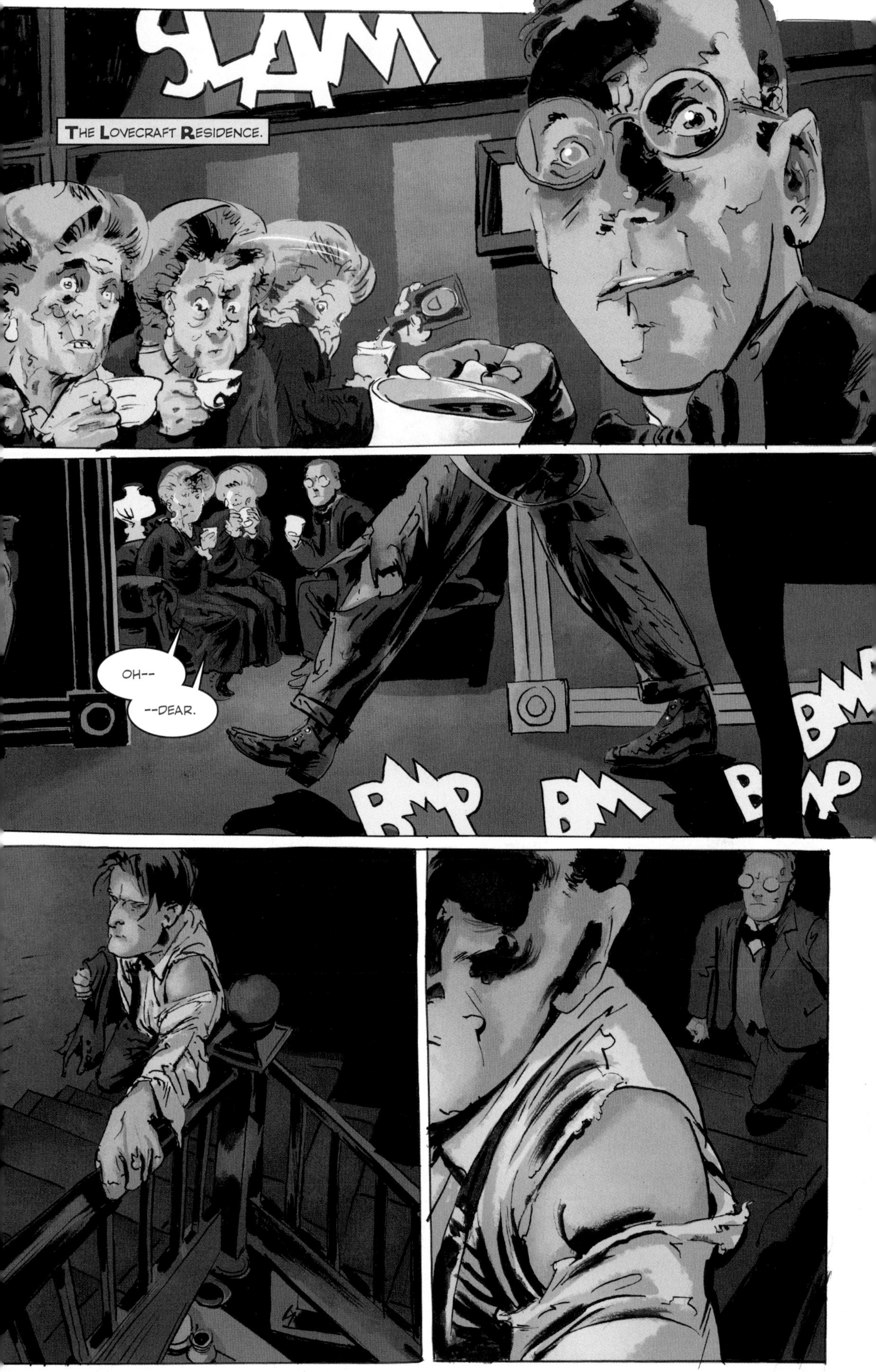
SLAM
THE LOVECRAFT RESIDENCE.
OH--
--DEAR.
BMP
BM
BMP
BMP

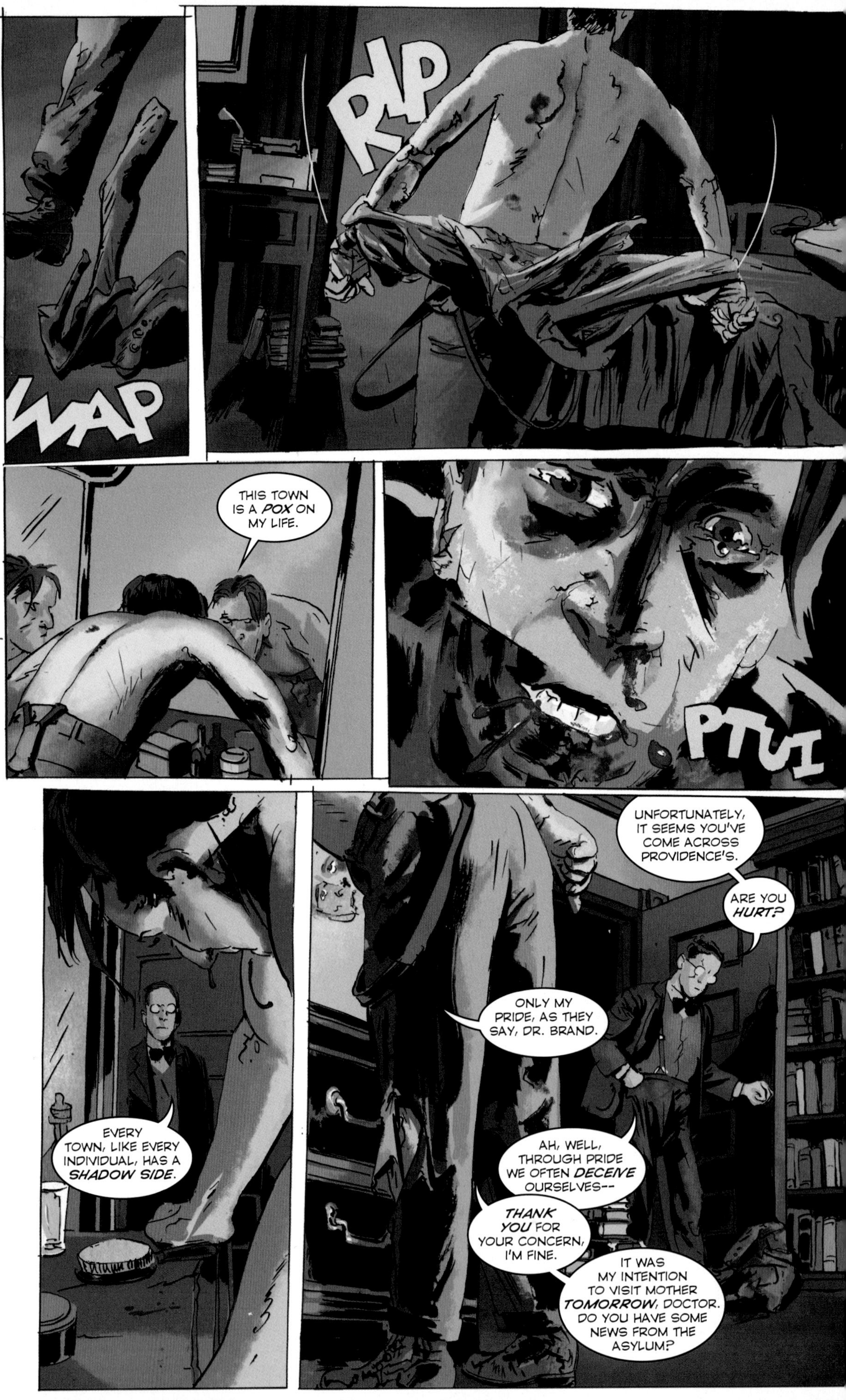
WAP
RIP
THIS TOWN IS A *POX* ON MY LIFE.
PTUI
EVERY TOWN, LIKE EVERY INDIVIDUAL, HAS A *SHADOW SIDE*.
UNFORTUNATELY, IT SEEMS YOU'VE COME ACROSS PROVIDENCE'S.
ARE YOU *HURT?*
ONLY MY PRIDE, AS THEY SAY, DR. BRAND.
AH, WELL, THROUGH PRIDE WE OFTEN *DECEIVE* OURSELVES--
THANK YOU FOR YOUR CONCERN, I'M FINE.
IT WAS MY INTENTION TO VISIT MOTHER *TOMORROW*, DOCTOR. DO YOU HAVE SOME NEWS FROM THE ASYLUM?

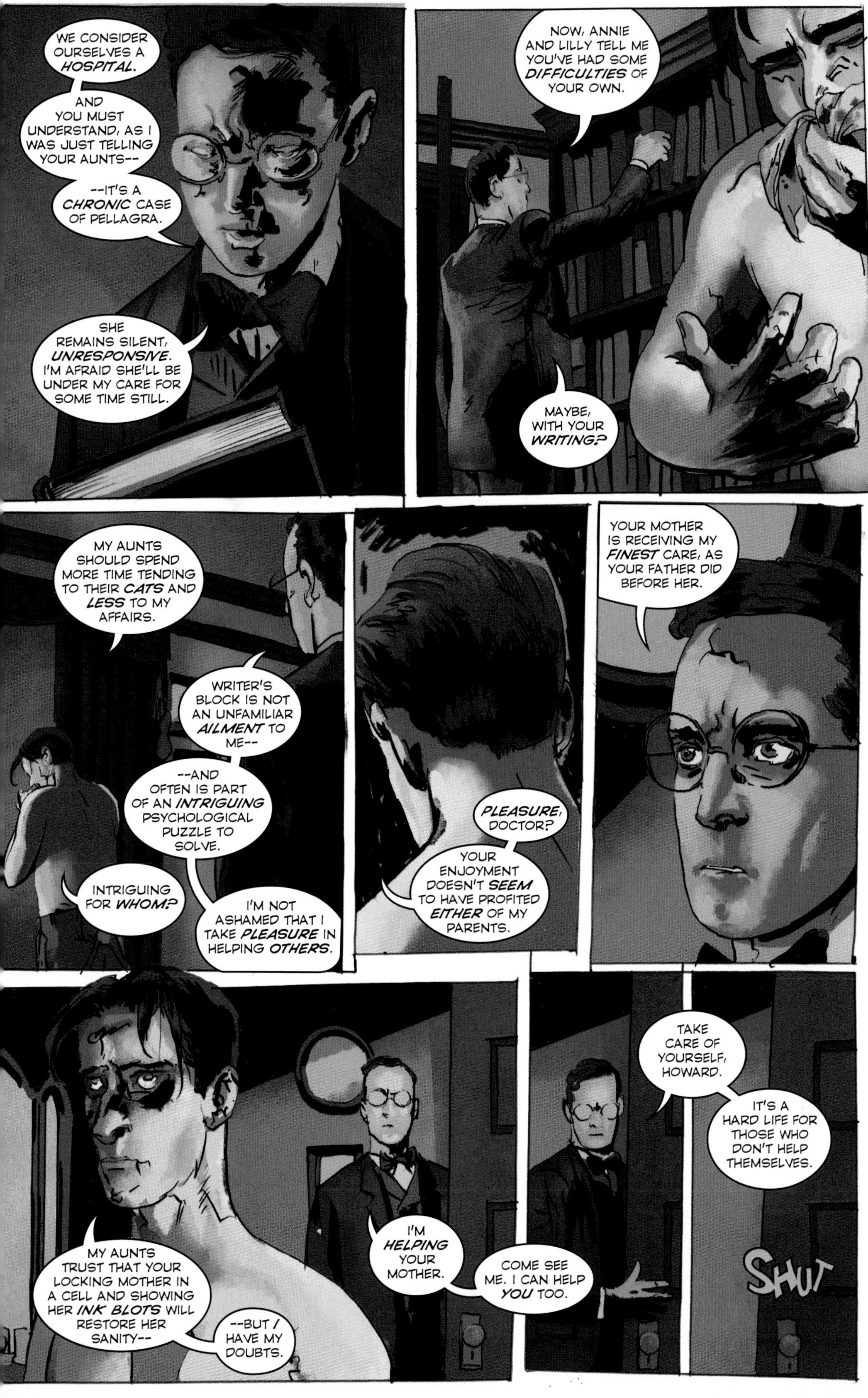
WE CONSIDER OURSELVES A *HOSPITAL.*
AND YOU MUST UNDERSTAND, AS I WAS JUST TELLING YOUR AUNTS--
--IT'S A *CHRONIC* CASE OF PELLAGRA.
SHE REMAINS SILENT, *UNRESPONSIVE*. I'M AFRAID SHE'LL BE UNDER MY CARE FOR SOME TIME STILL.
NOW, ANNIE AND LILLY TELL ME YOU'VE HAD SOME *DIFFICULTIES* OF YOUR OWN.
MAYBE, WITH YOUR *WRITING?*
MY AUNTS SHOULD SPEND MORE TIME TENDING TO THEIR *CATS* AND *LESS* TO MY AFFAIRS.
WRITER'S BLOCK IS NOT AN UNFAMILIAR *AILMENT* TO ME--
--AND OFTEN IS PART OF AN *INTRIGUING* PSYCHOLOGICAL PUZZLE TO SOLVE.
INTRIGUING FOR *WHOM?*
I'M NOT ASHAMED THAT I TAKE *PLEASURE* IN HELPING *OTHERS*.
PLEASURE, DOCTOR?
YOUR ENJOYMENT DOESN'T *SEEM* TO HAVE PROFITED *EITHER* OF MY PARENTS.
YOUR MOTHER IS RECEIVING MY *FINEST* CARE, AS YOUR FATHER DID BEFORE HER.
MY AUNTS TRUST THAT YOUR LOCKING MOTHER IN A CELL AND SHOWING HER *INK BLOTS* WILL RESTORE HER SANITY--
--BUT *I* HAVE MY DOUBTS.
I'M *HELPING* YOUR MOTHER.
COME SEE ME. I CAN HELP *YOU* TOO.
TAKE CARE OF YOURSELF, HOWARD.
IT'S A HARD LIFE FOR THOSE WHO DON'T HELP THEMSELVES.
SHUT

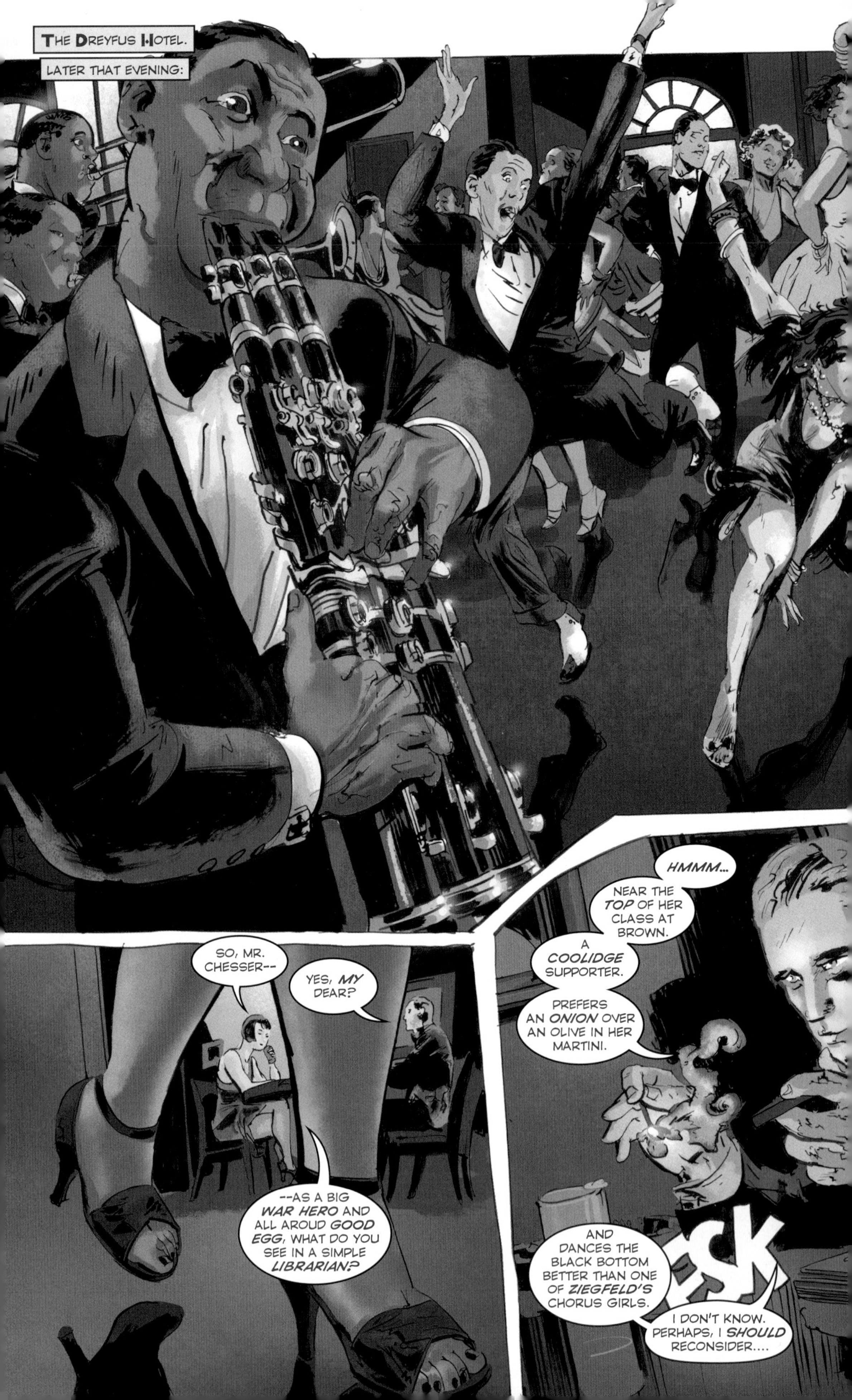
THE DREYFUS HOTEL.
LATER THAT EVENING:
HMMM...
NEAR THE TOP OF HER CLASS AT BROWN.
A COOLIDGE SUPPORTER.
PREFERS AN ONION OVER AN OLIVE IN HER MARTINI.
SO, MR. CHESSER--
YES, MY DEAR?
--AS A BIG WAR HERO AND ALL AROUD GOOD EGG, WHAT DO YOU SEE IN A SIMPLE LIBRARIAN?
AND DANCES THE BLACK BOTTOM BETTER THAN ONE OF ZIEGFELD'S CHORUS GIRLS.
FSK
I DON'T KNOW. PERHAPS, I SHOULD RECONSIDER....

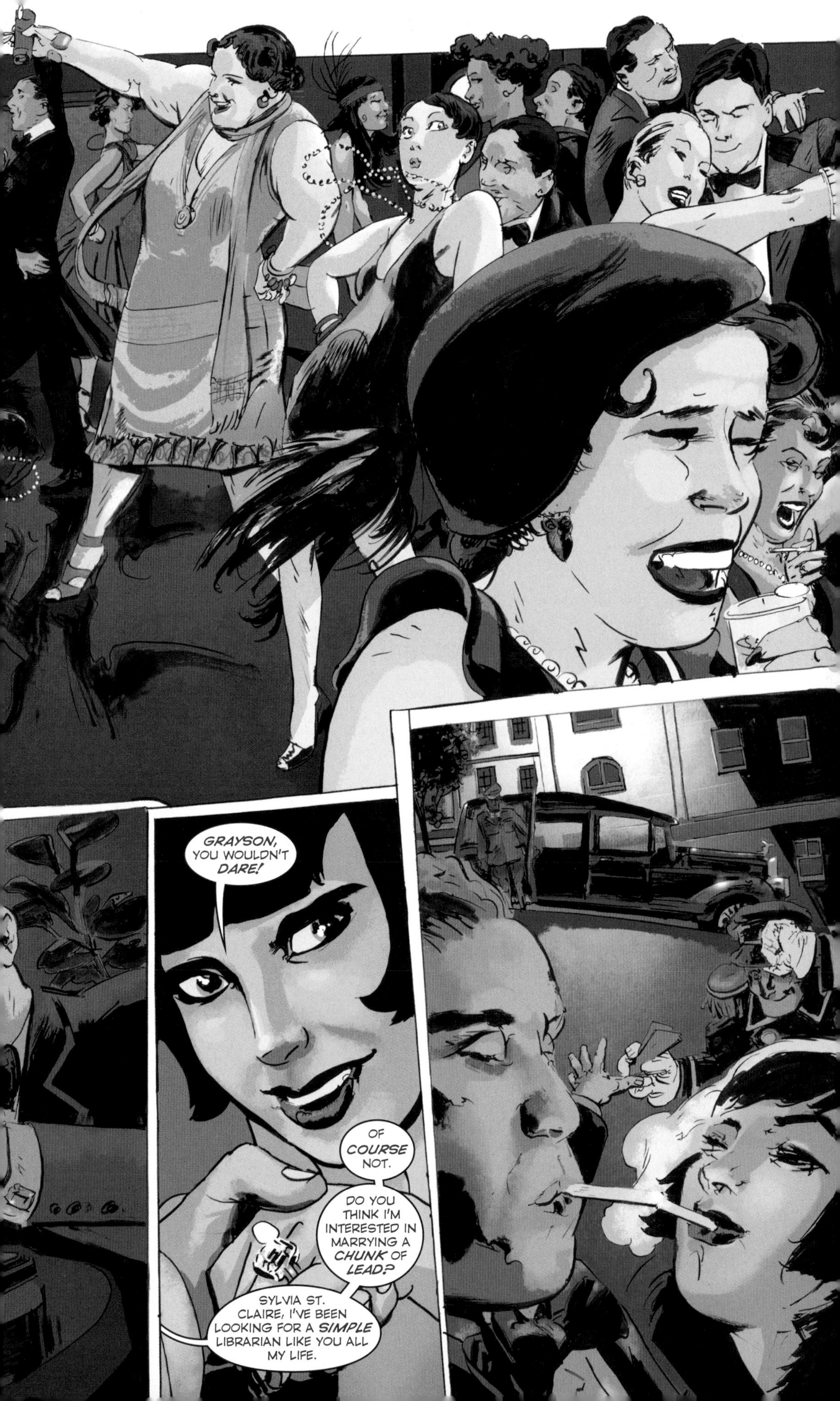
GRAYSON, YOU WOULDN'T DARE!
OF COURSE NOT.
DO YOU THINK I'M INTERESTED IN MARRYING A CHUNK OF LEAD?
SYLVIA ST. CLAIRE, I'VE BEEN LOOKING FOR A SIMPLE LIBRARIAN LIKE YOU ALL MY LIFE.

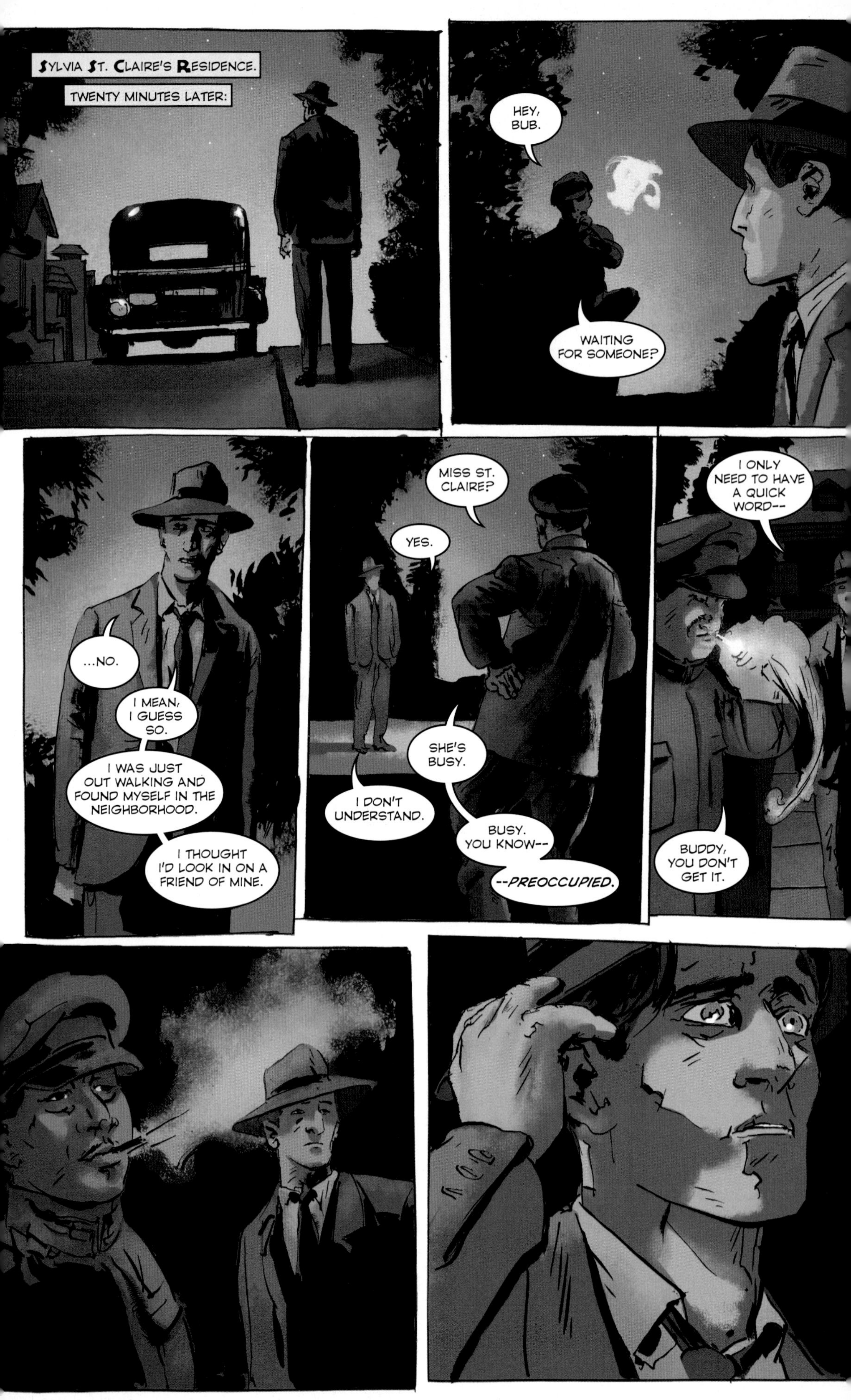
SYLVIA ST. CLAIRE'S RESIDENCE.
TWENTY MINUTES LATER:
HEY, BUB.
WAITING FOR SOMEONE?
...NO.
I MEAN, I GUESS SO.
I WAS JUST OUT WALKING AND FOUND MYSELF IN THE NEIGHBORHOOD.
I THOUGHT I'D LOOK IN ON A FRIEND OF MINE.
MISS ST. CLAIRE?
YES.
SHE'S BUSY.
I DON'T UNDERSTAND.
BUSY. YOU KNOW--
--PREOCCUPIED.
I ONLY NEED TO HAVE A QUICK WORD--
BUDDY, YOU DON'T GET IT.

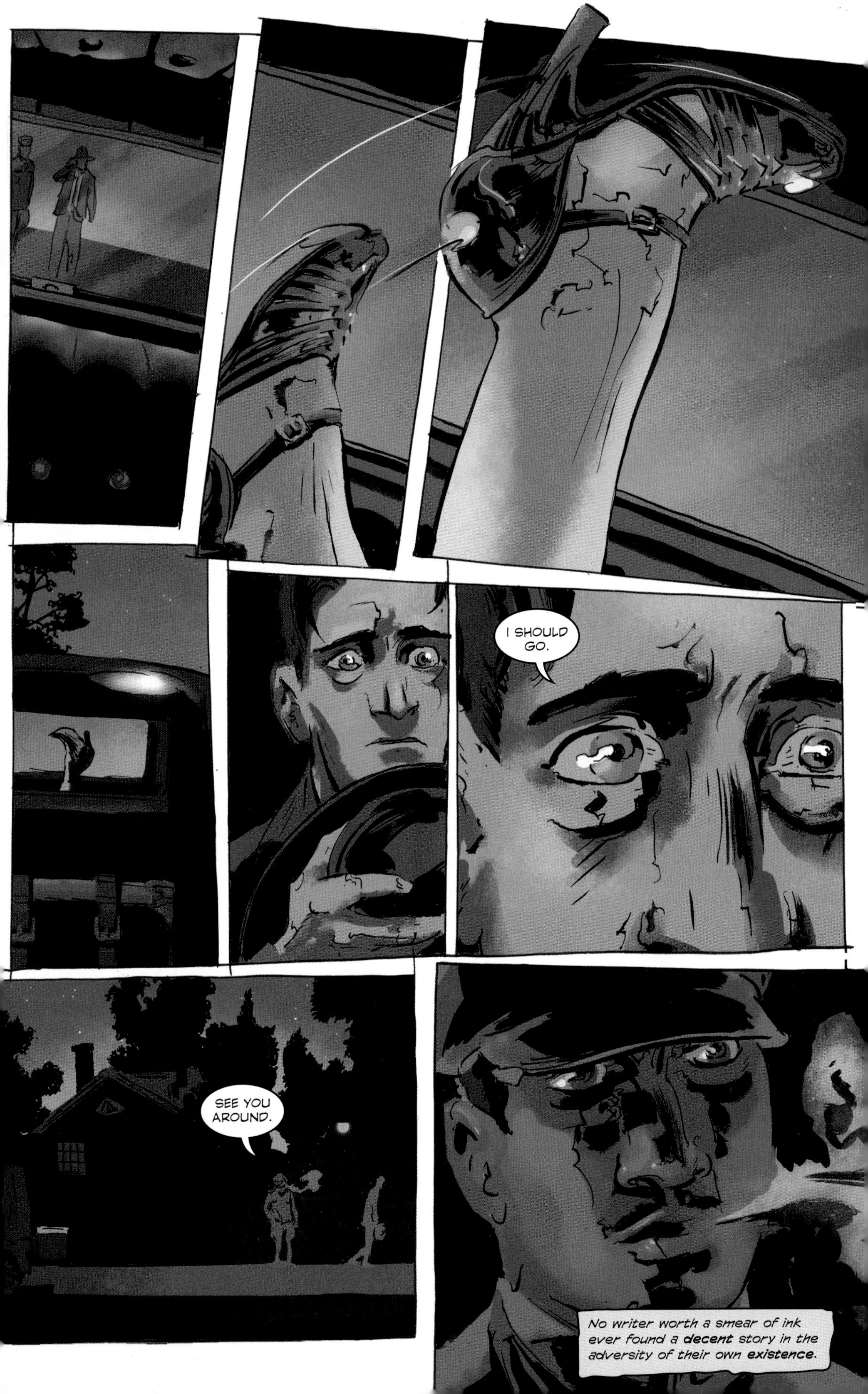
I SHOULD GO.
SEE YOU AROUND.
No writer worth a smear of ink ever found a **decent** story in the adversity of their own **existence**.

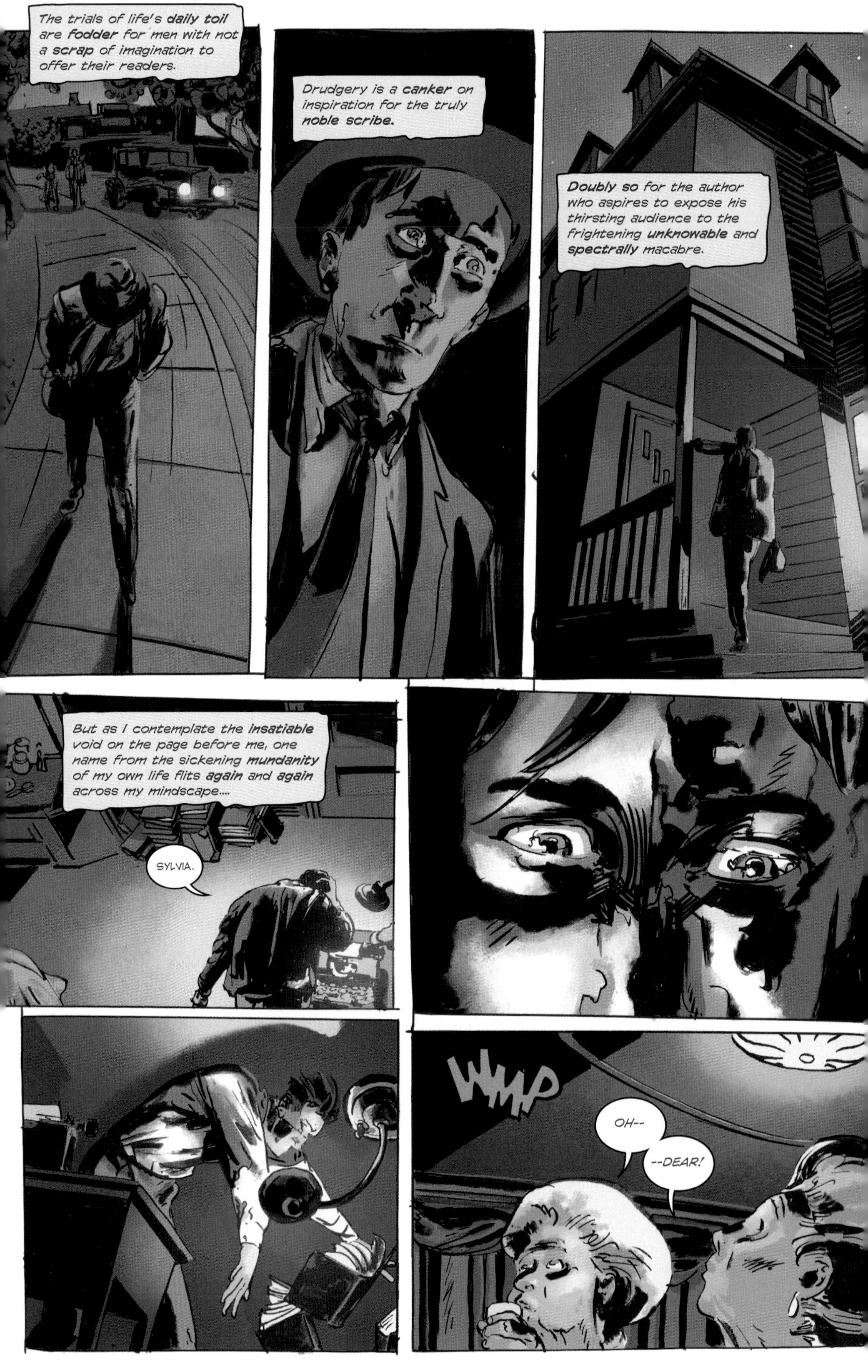
The trials of life's **daily toil** are **fodder** for men with not a **scrap** of imagination to offer their readers.
Drudgery is a **canker** on inspiration for the truly **noble scribe.**
Doubly so for the author who aspires to expose his thirsting audience to the frightening **unknowable** and **spectrally** macabre.
But as I contemplate the **insatiable** void on the page before me, one name from the sickening **mundanity** of my own life flits **again** and **again** across my mindscape....
SYLVIA.
WHAP
OH--
--DEAR!

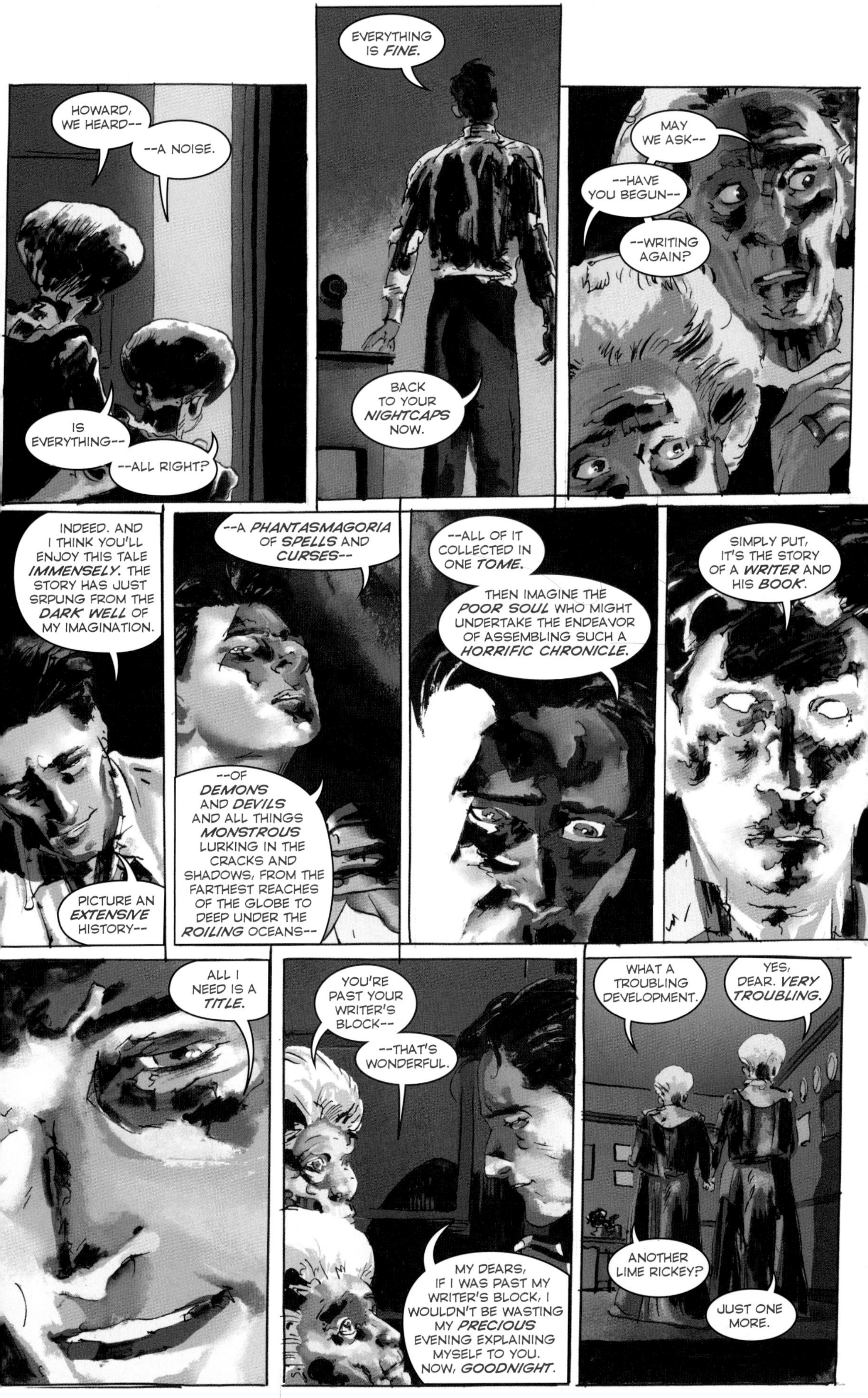
HOWARD, WE HEARD--
--A NOISE.
IS EVERYTHING--
--ALL RIGHT?
EVERYTHING IS *FINE.*
BACK TO YOUR *NIGHTCAPS* NOW.
MAY WE ASK--
--HAVE YOU BEGUN--
--WRITING AGAIN?
INDEED. AND I THINK YOU'LL ENJOY THIS TALE *IMMENSELY.* THE STORY HAS JUST SRPUNG FROM THE *DARK WELL* OF MY IMAGINATION.
PICTURE AN *EXTENSIVE* HISTORY--
--A *PHANTASMAGORIA* OF *SPELLS* AND *CURSES*--
--OF *DEMONS* AND *DEVILS* AND ALL THINGS *MONSTROUS* LURKING IN THE CRACKS AND SHADOWS, FROM THE FARTHEST REACHES OF THE GLOBE TO DEEP UNDER THE *ROILING* OCEANS--
--ALL OF IT COLLECTED IN ONE *TOME.*
THEN IMAGINE THE *POOR SOUL* WHO MIGHT UNDERTAKE THE ENDEAVOR OF ASSEMBLING SUCH A *HORRIFIC CHRONICLE.*
SIMPLY PUT, IT'S THE STORY OF A *WRITER* AND HIS *BOOK*.
ALL I NEED IS A *TITLE.*
YOU'RE PAST YOUR WRITER'S BLOCK--
--THAT'S WONDERFUL.
MY DEARS, IF I WAS PAST MY WRITER'S BLOCK, I WOULDN'T BE WASTING MY *PRECIOUS* EVENING EXPLAINING MYSELF TO YOU. NOW, *GOODNIGHT*.
WHAT A TROUBLING DEVELOPMENT.
YES, DEAR. *VERY TROUBLING.*
ANOTHER LIME RICKEY?
JUST ONE MORE.

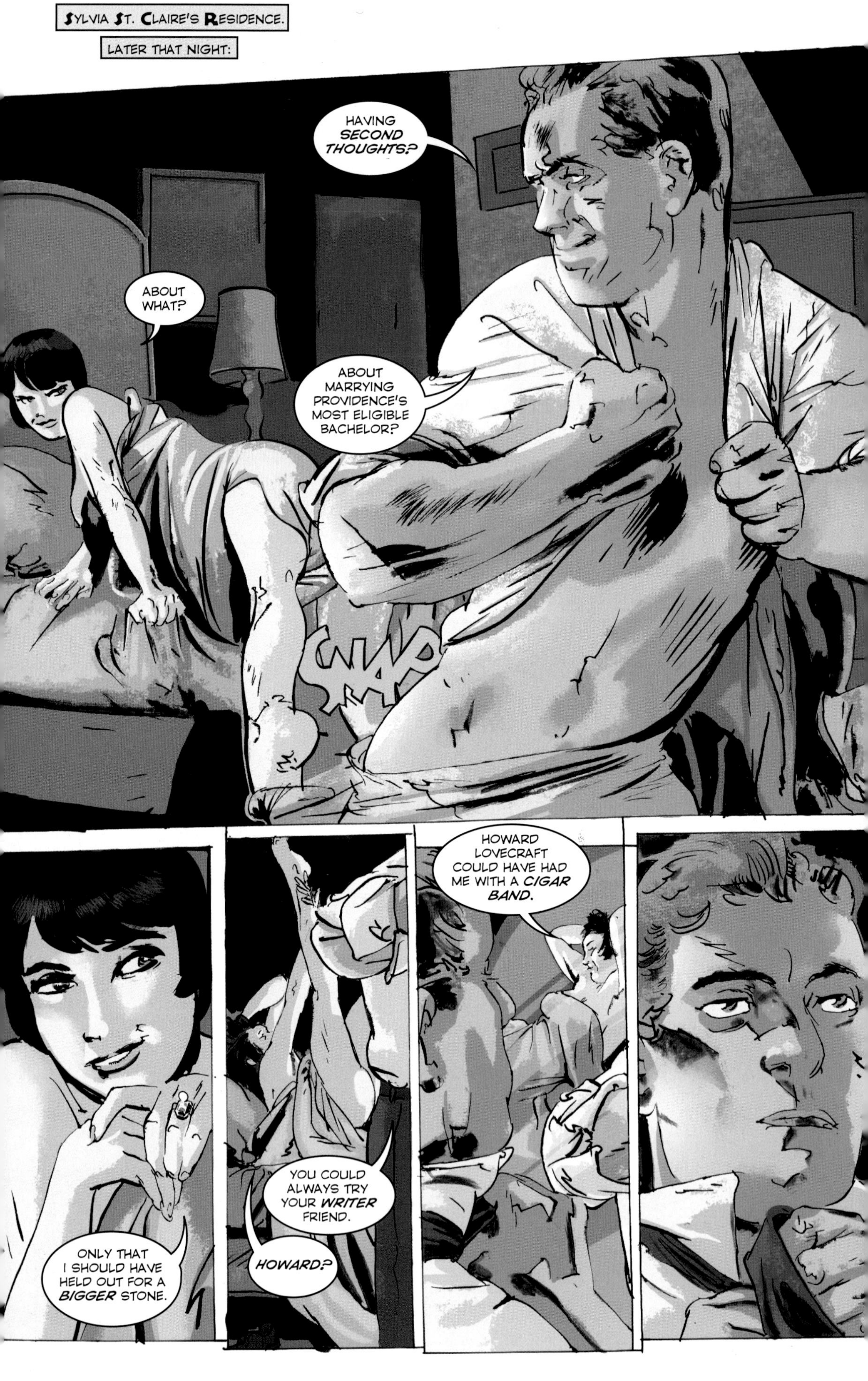

SYLVIA ST. CLAIRE'S RESIDENCE.
LATER THAT NIGHT:
HAVING *SECOND THOUGHTS?*
ABOUT WHAT?
ABOUT MARRYING PROVIDENCE'S MOST ELIGIBLE BACHELOR?
ONLY THAT I SHOULD HAVE HELD OUT FOR A *BIGGER* STONE.
YOU COULD ALWAYS TRY YOUR *WRITER* FRIEND.
HOWARD?
HOWARD LOVECRAFT COULD HAVE HAD ME WITH A *CIGAR BAND.*

The blank page.

Target of the many ghastly narratives that once poured forth from my imagination, like unabated rain falling from a **storm-darkened** sky.

Now, the flow of stories has been reduced to nothing more than a **slow trickle** from a leaking, rusted pipe.

And I wonder, will the swirling, vaporous haze **clear** from my mind's eye?

Perhaps not tonight.

But what of the weirdly horrible tale of a cosmically **maleficent** book?

A congeries of everything **vile** and **depraved**--

An **odious** tome that serves as a space-time portal between our **naive** world and some nether dimension--a realm of malign **suggestiveness**.

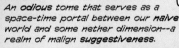

There's something **darkly promising** in the **baleful** idea. It festers with genuine possibility.

No. It's **gibberish**. There's nothing to it.

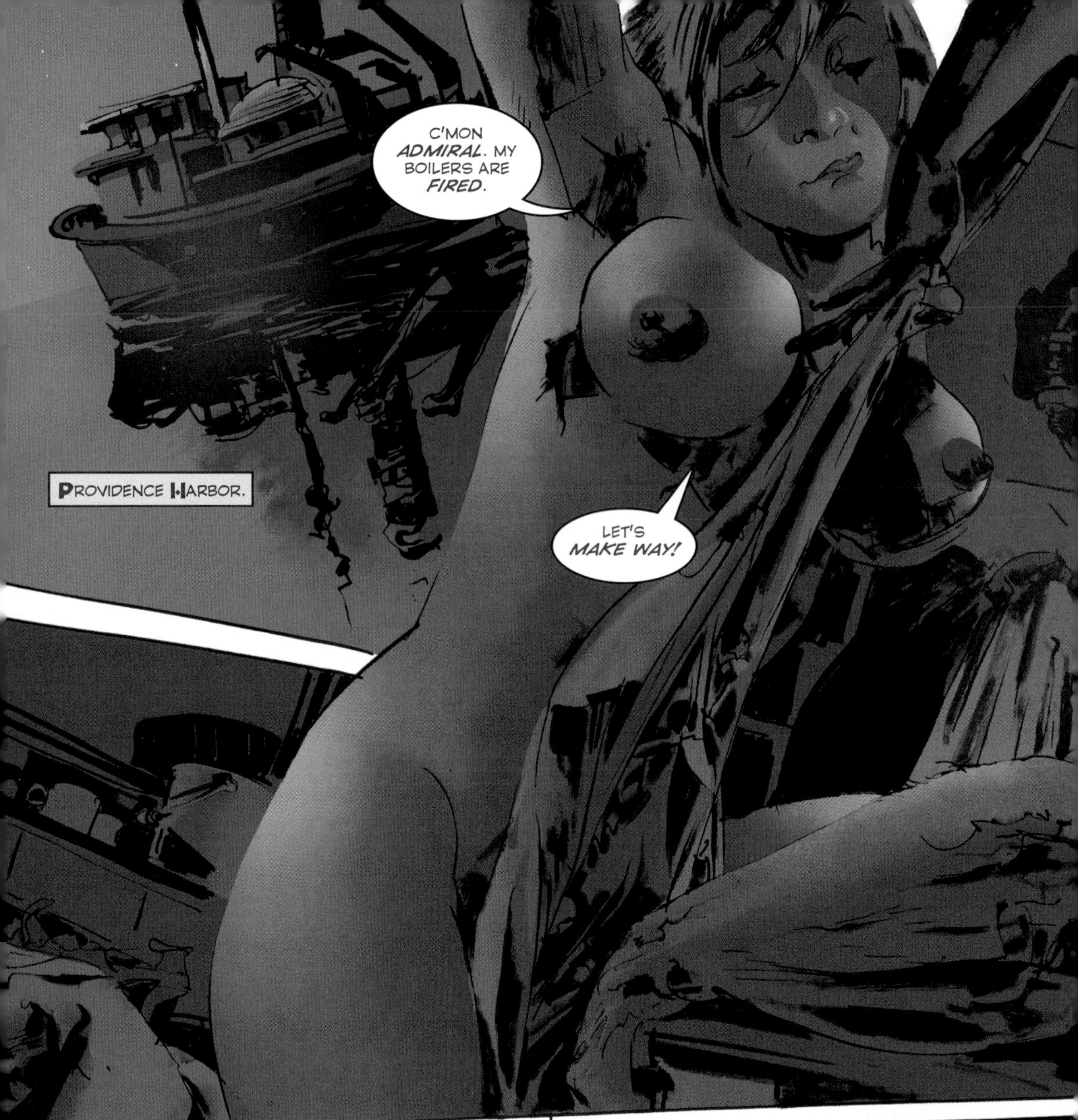
C'MON ADMIRAL. MY BOILERS ARE FIRED.
PROVIDENCE HARBOR.
LET'S MAKE WAY!

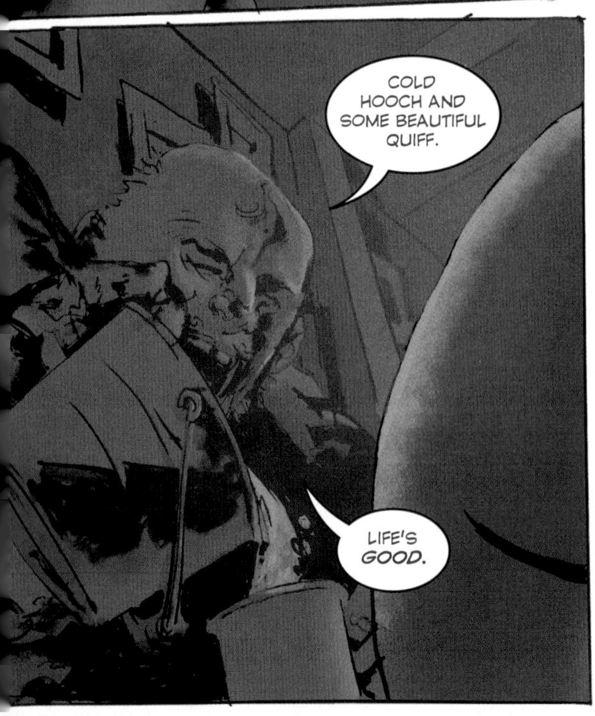
COLD HOOCH AND SOME BEAUTIFUL QUIFF.
LIFE'S GOOD.

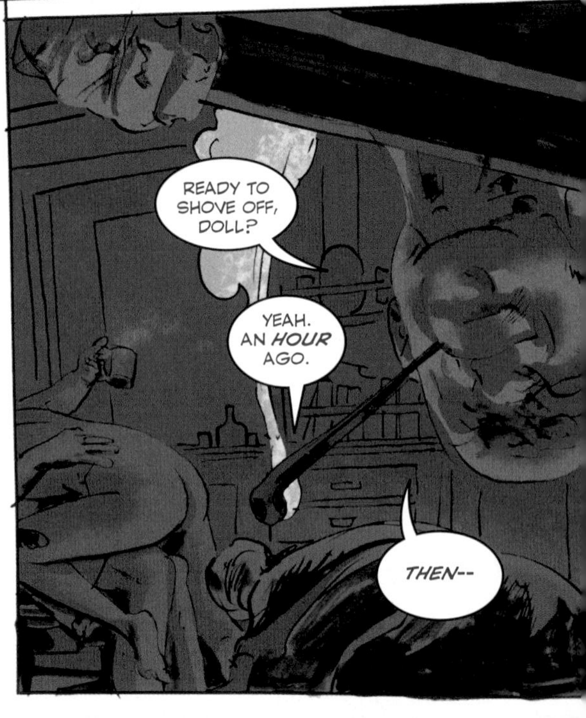
READY TO SHOVE OFF, DOLL?
YEAH. AN HOUR AGO.
THEN--

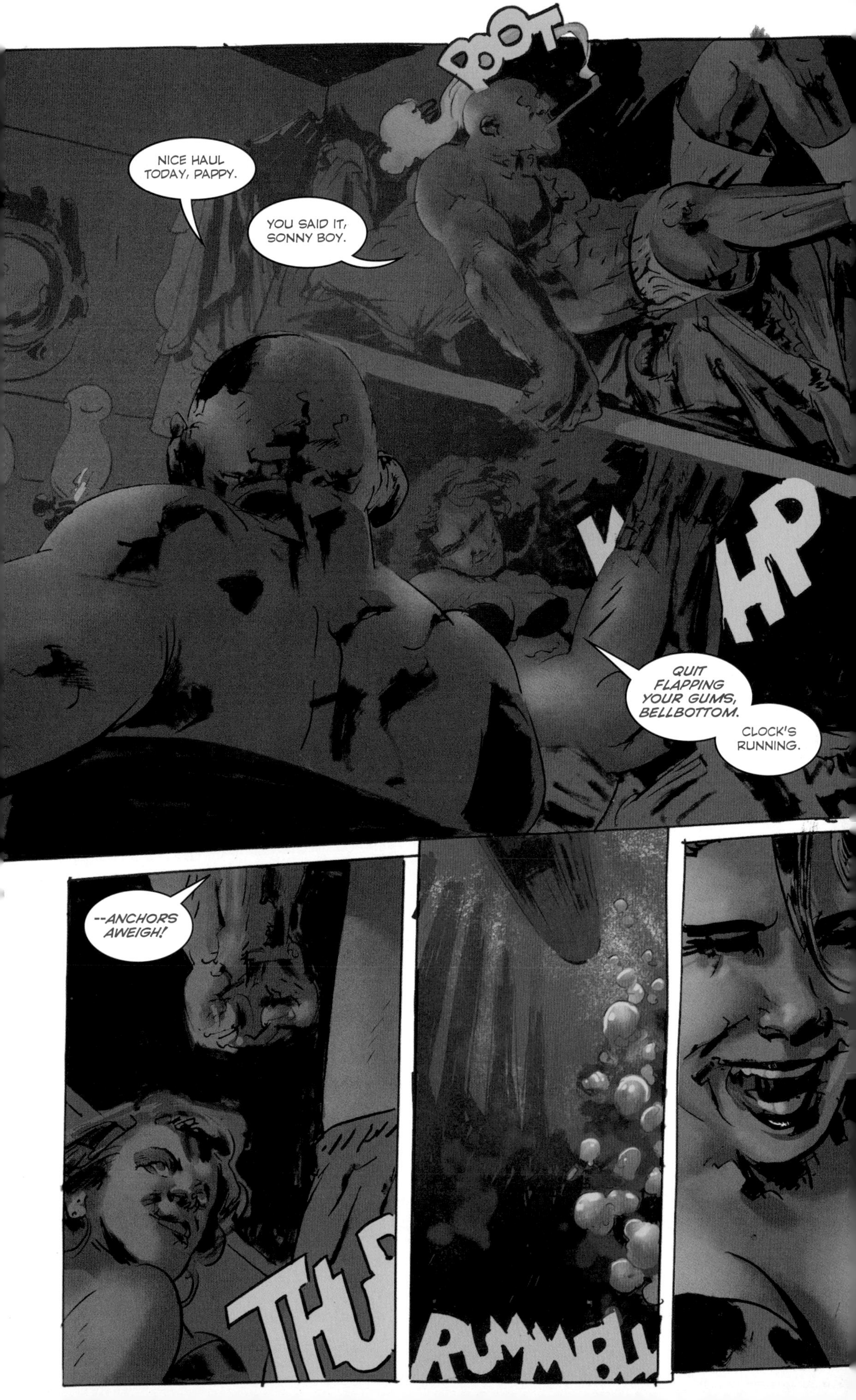
BOOT
NICE HAUL TODAY, PAPPY.
YOU SAID IT, SONNY BOY.
QUIT FLAPPING YOUR GUMS, BELLBOTTOM.
CLOCK'S RUNNING.
--ANCHORS AWEIGH!

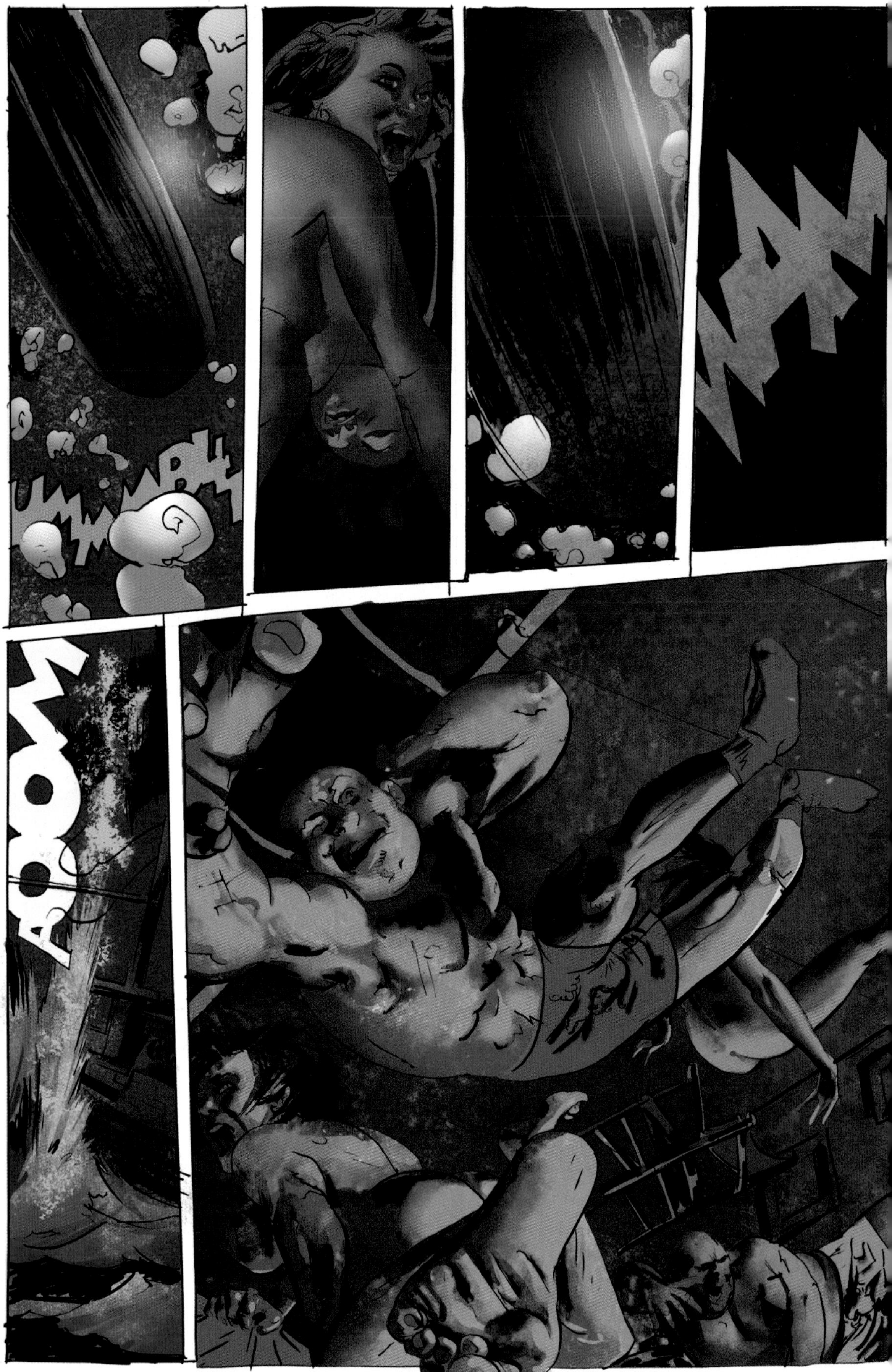

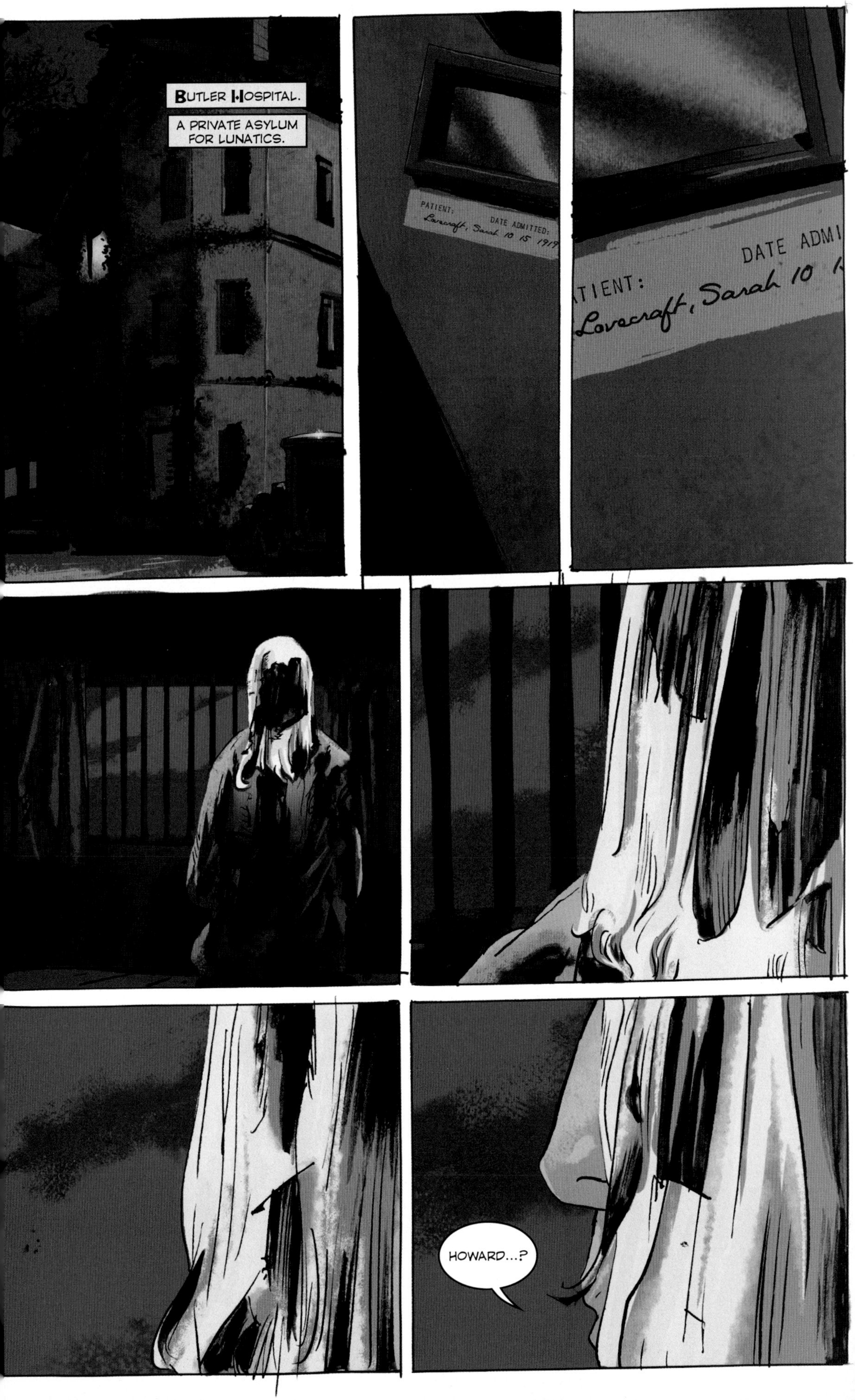
BUTLER HOSPITAL.
A PRIVATE ASYLUM FOR LUNATICS.
PATIENT: DATE ADMITTED:
Lovecraft, Sarah 10 15 1919
PATIENT: DATE ADMI
Lovecraft, Sarah 10
HOWARD...?

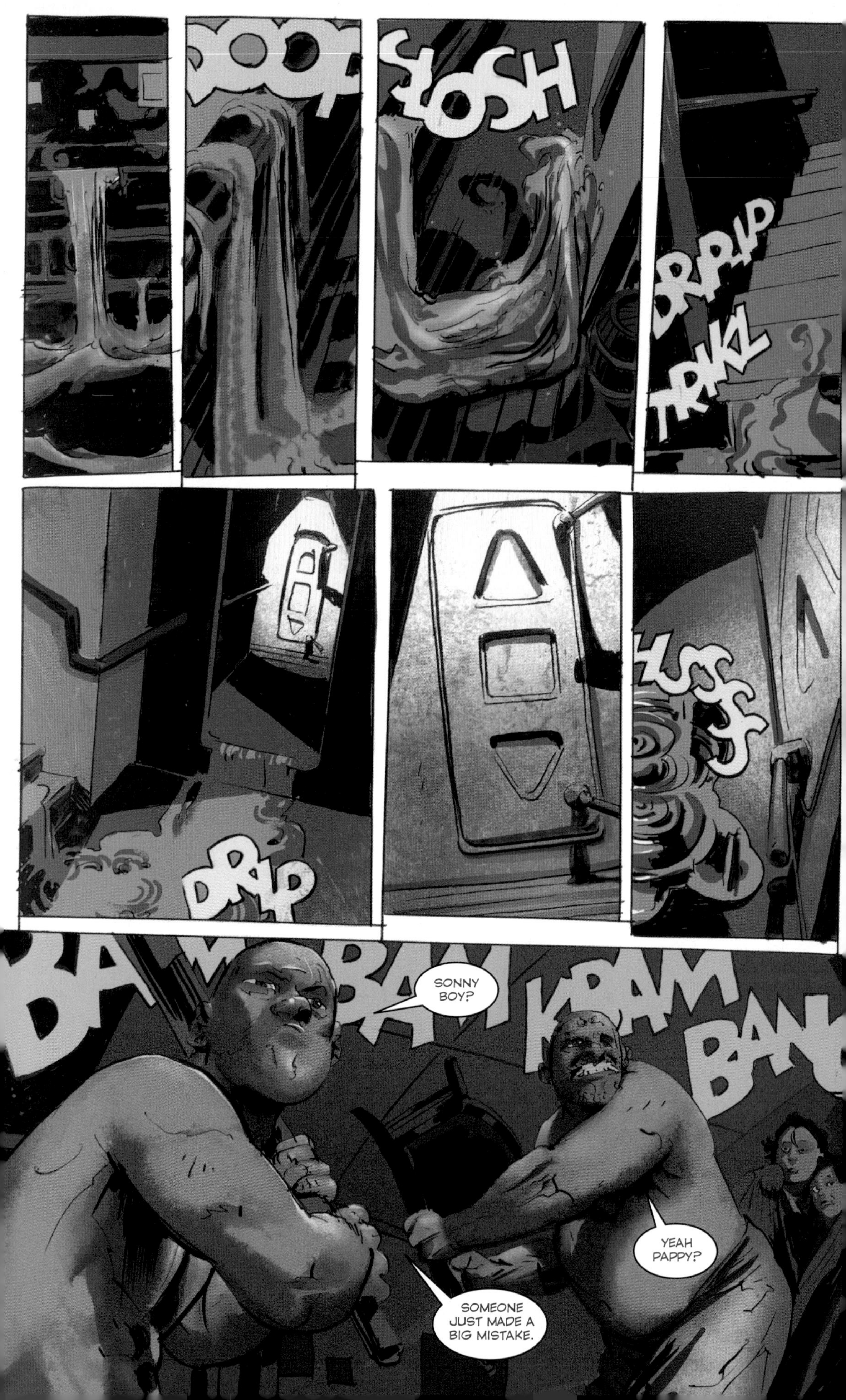
BLOOP
SLOSH
DRIP
TRKL
DRIP
HUSS
BAM
BAM
SONNY BOY?
KRAM
BANG
YEAH PAPPY?
SOMEONE JUST MADE A BIG MISTAKE.

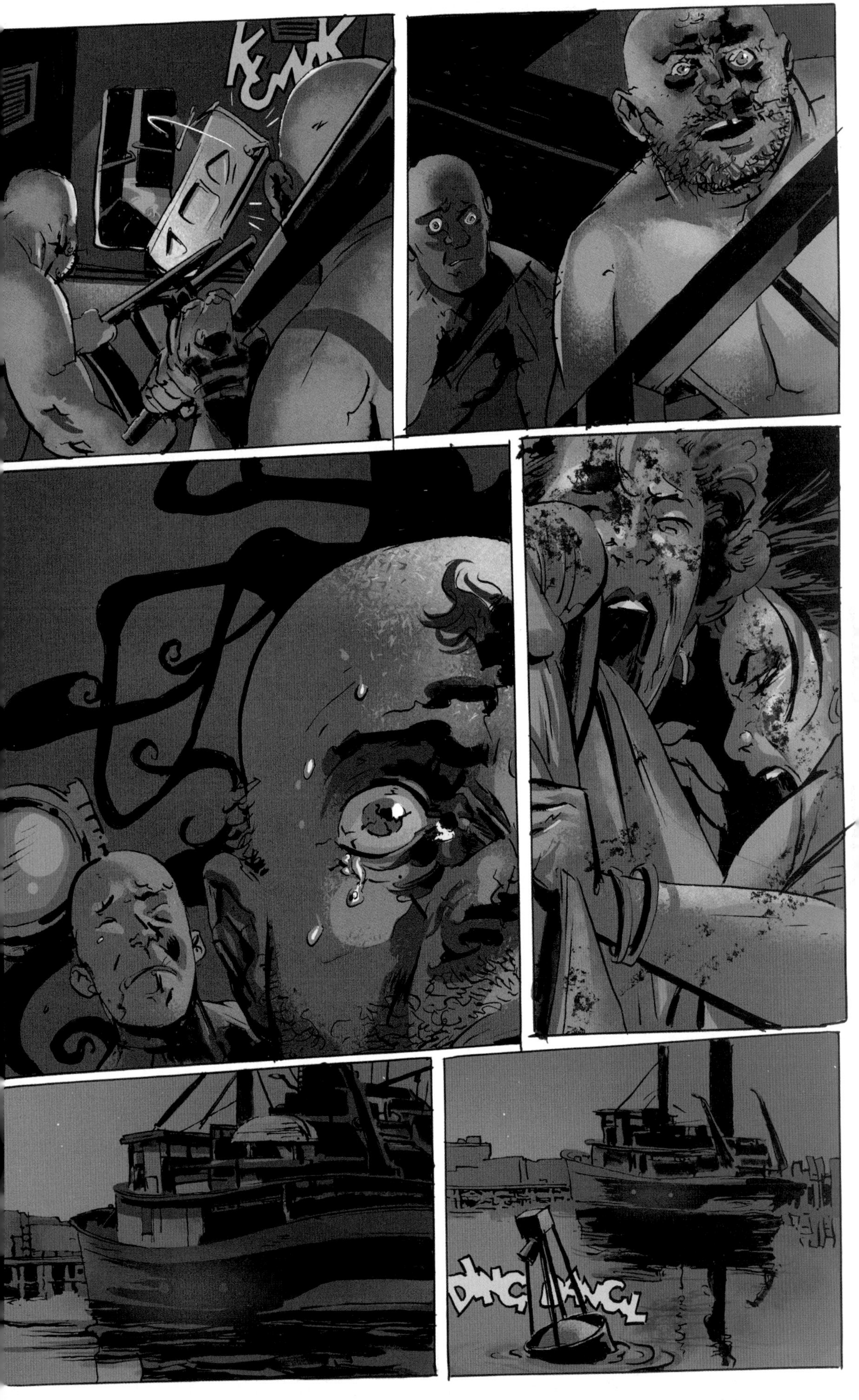
KLUNK
DNG CLANGL

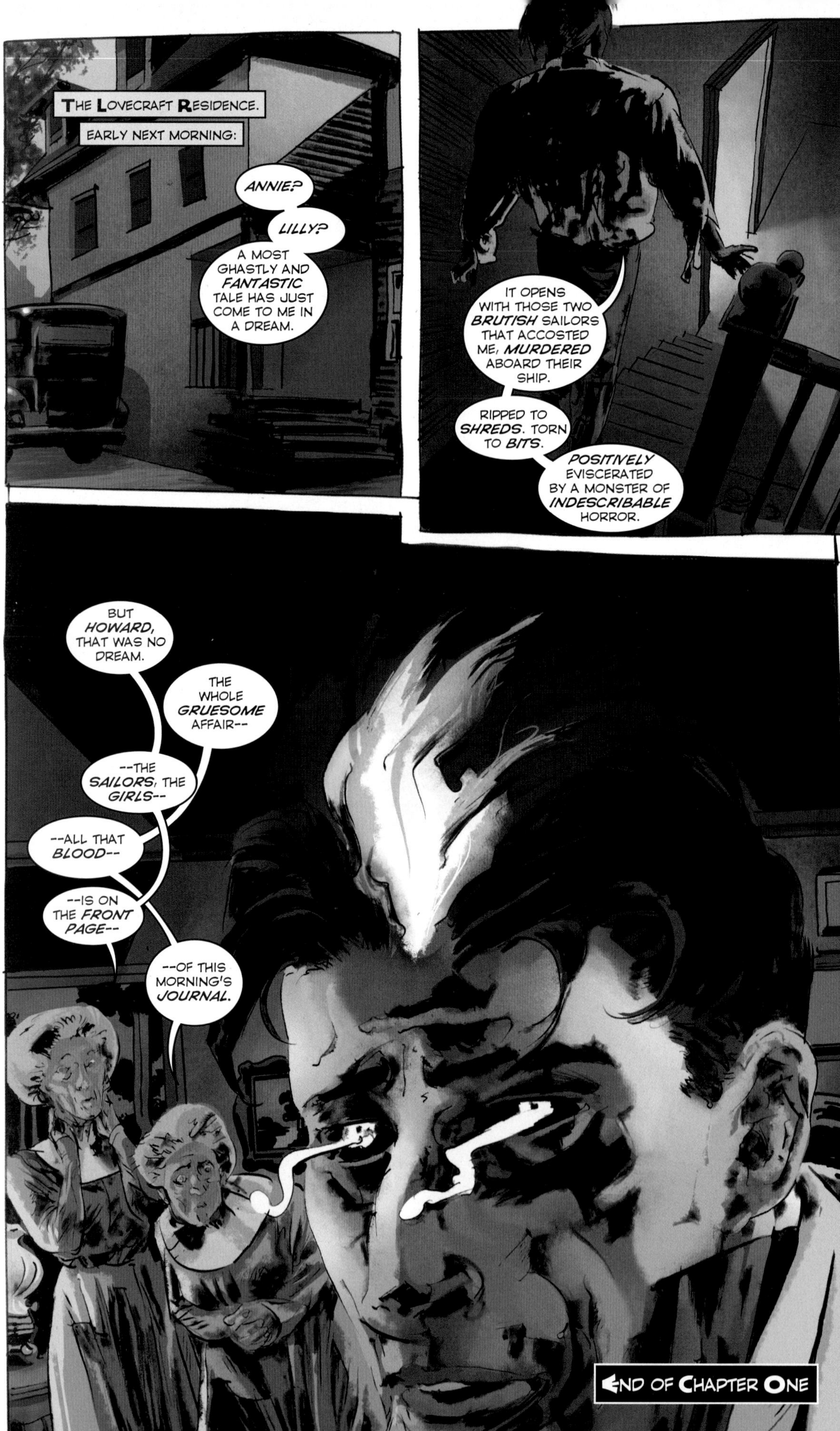
THE LOVECRAFT RESIDENCE.
EARLY NEXT MORNING:
ANNIE?
LILLY?
A MOST GHASTLY AND FANTASTIC TALE HAS JUST COME TO ME IN A DREAM.
IT OPENS WITH THOSE TWO BRUTISH SAILORS THAT ACCOSTED ME, MURDERED ABOARD THEIR SHIP.
RIPPED TO SHREDS. TORN TO BITS.
POSITIVELY EVISCERATED BY A MONSTER OF INDESCRIBABLE HORROR.
BUT HOWARD, THAT WAS NO DREAM.
THE WHOLE GRUESOME AFFAIR--
--THE SAILORS, THE GIRLS--
--ALL THAT BLOOD--
--IS ON THE FRONT PAGE--
--OF THIS MORNING'S JOURNAL.
END OF CHAPTER ONE

It is a frightening thought that man also has a shadow side to him, consisting not just of little weaknesses and foibles, but of a positively demonic dynamism. The individual seldom knows anything of this; to him, as an individual, it is incredible that he should ever in any circumstances go beyond himself. But let these harmless creatures form a mass, and there emerges a raging monster; and each individual is only one tiny cell in the monster's body, so that for better or worse he must accompany it on its bloody rampages and even assist it to the utmost.

-CARL JUNG

CHAPTER TWO:
PERCHANCE TO DREAM

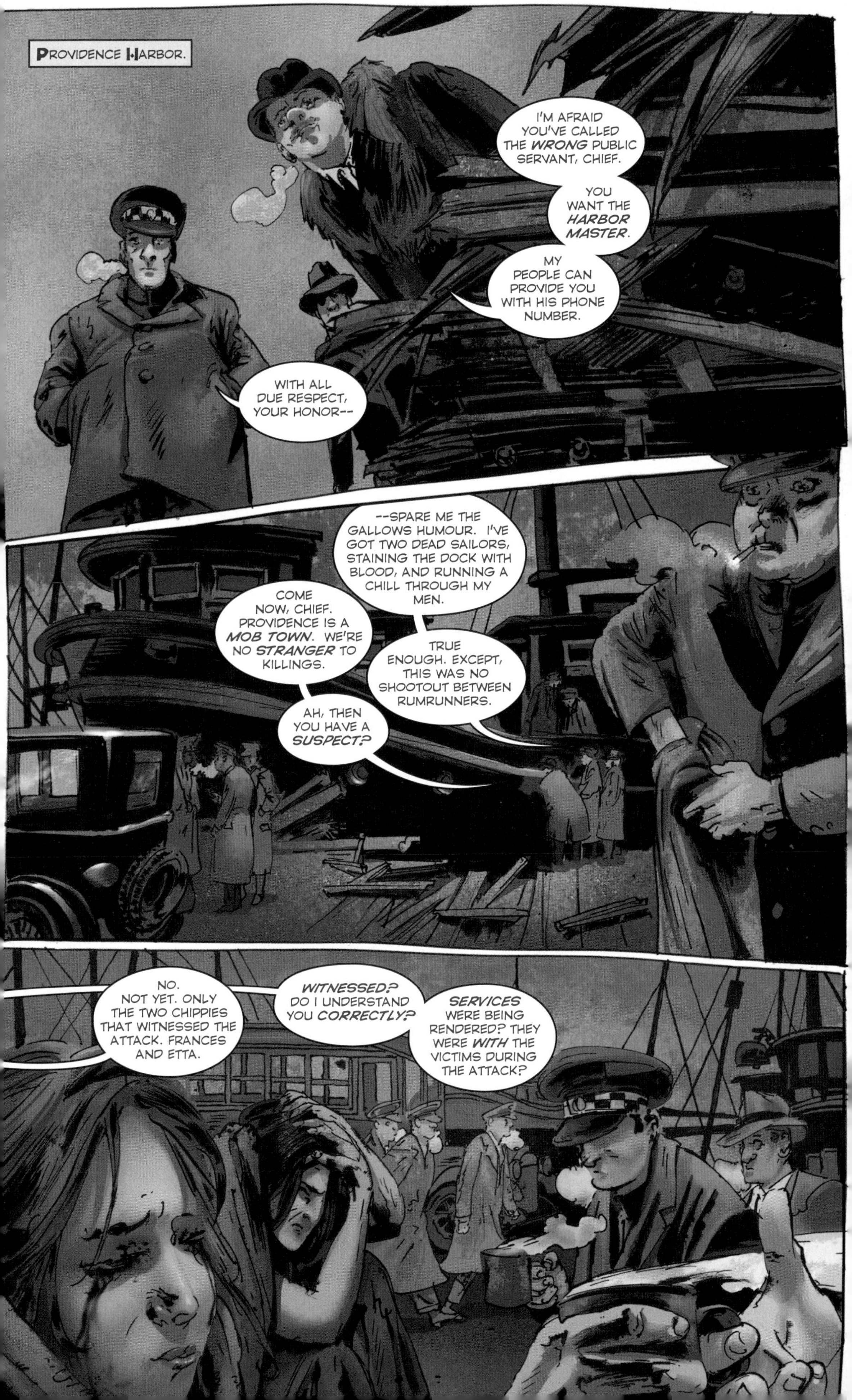
PROVIDENCE HARBOR.
I'M AFRAID YOU'VE CALLED THE *WRONG* PUBLIC SERVANT, CHIEF.
YOU WANT THE *HARBOR MASTER*.
MY PEOPLE CAN PROVIDE YOU WITH HIS PHONE NUMBER.
WITH ALL DUE RESPECT, YOUR HONOR--
--SPARE ME THE GALLOWS HUMOUR. I'VE GOT TWO DEAD SAILORS, STAINING THE DOCK WITH BLOOD, AND RUNNING A CHILL THROUGH MY MEN.
COME NOW, CHIEF. PROVIDENCE IS A *MOB TOWN*. WE'RE NO *STRANGER* TO KILLINGS.
TRUE ENOUGH. EXCEPT, THIS WAS NO SHOOTOUT BETWEEN RUMRUNNERS.
AH, THEN YOU HAVE A *SUSPECT?*
NO. NOT YET. ONLY THE TWO CHIPPIES THAT WITNESSED THE ATTACK. FRANCES AND ETTA.
WITNESSED? DO I UNDERSTAND YOU *CORRECTLY?*
SERVICES WERE BEING RENDERED? THEY WERE *WITH* THE VICTIMS DURING THE ATTACK?

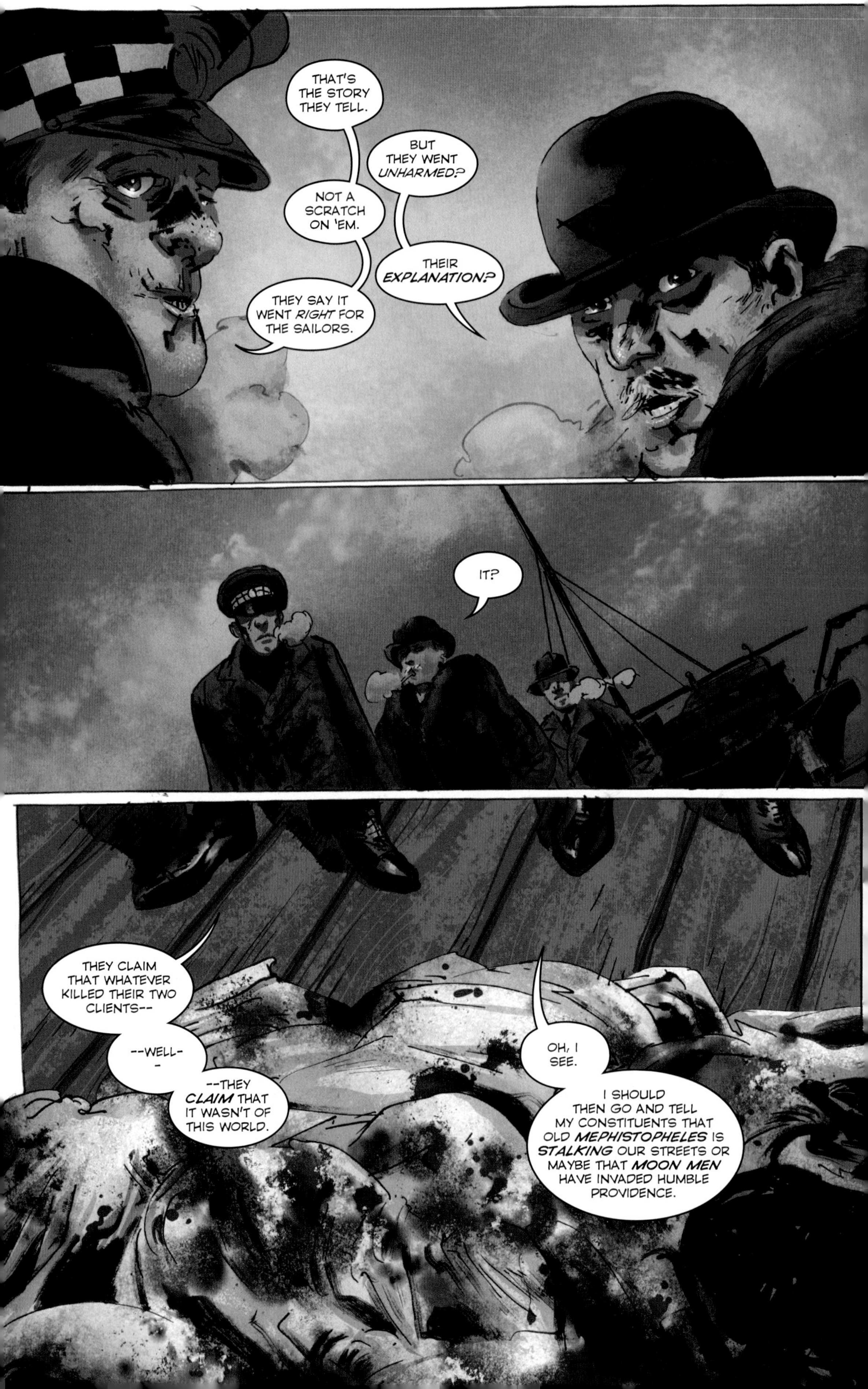
THAT'S THE STORY THEY TELL.
BUT THEY WENT UNHARMED?
NOT A SCRATCH ON 'EM.
THEIR EXPLANATION?
THEY SAY IT WENT RIGHT FOR THE SAILORS.
IT?
THEY CLAIM THAT WHATEVER KILLED THEIR TWO CLIENTS--
--WELL--
--THEY CLAIM THAT IT WASN'T OF THIS WORLD.
OH, I SEE.
I SHOULD THEN GO AND TELL MY CONSTITUENTS THAT OLD MEPHISTOPHELES IS STALKING OUR STREETS OR MAYBE THAT MOON MEN HAVE INVADED HUMBLE PROVIDENCE.

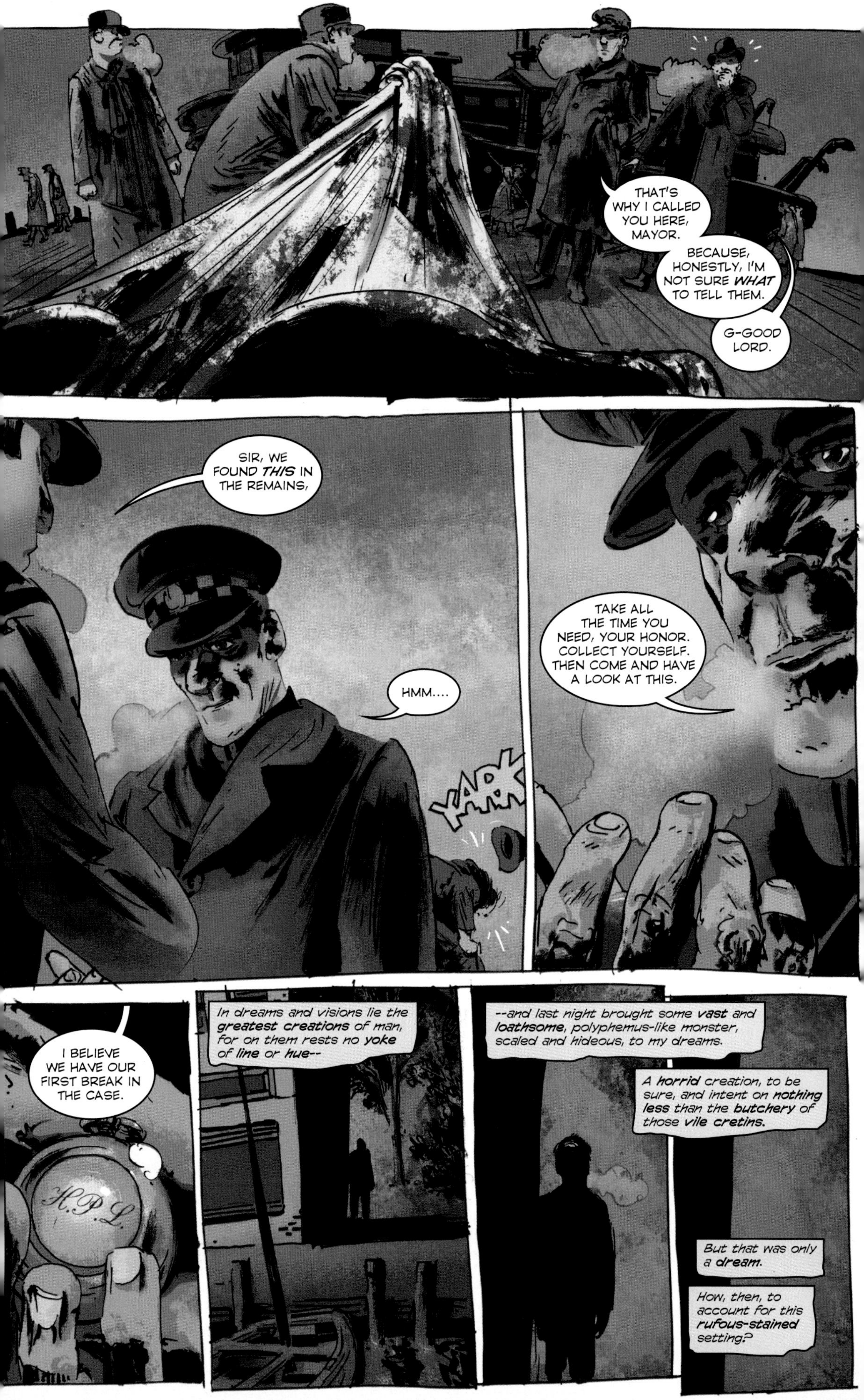
THAT'S WHY I CALLED YOU HERE, MAYOR.
BECAUSE, HONESTLY, I'M NOT SURE *WHAT* TO TELL THEM.
G-GOOD LORD.
SIR, WE FOUND *THIS* IN THE REMAINS,
HMM....
YARK
TAKE ALL THE TIME YOU NEED, YOUR HONOR. COLLECT YOURSELF. THEN COME AND HAVE A LOOK AT THIS.
I BELIEVE WE HAVE OUR FIRST BREAK IN THE CASE.
H.P.L.
*In dreams and visions lie the **greatest creations** of man, for on them rests no **yoke** of **line** or **hue**--*
*--and last night brought some **vast** and **loathsome**, polyphemus-like monster, scaled and hideous, to my dreams.*
*A **horrid** creation, to be sure, and intent on **nothing less** than the **butchery** of those **vile cretins**.*
*But that was only a **dream**.*
*How, then, to account for this **rufous-stained** setting?*

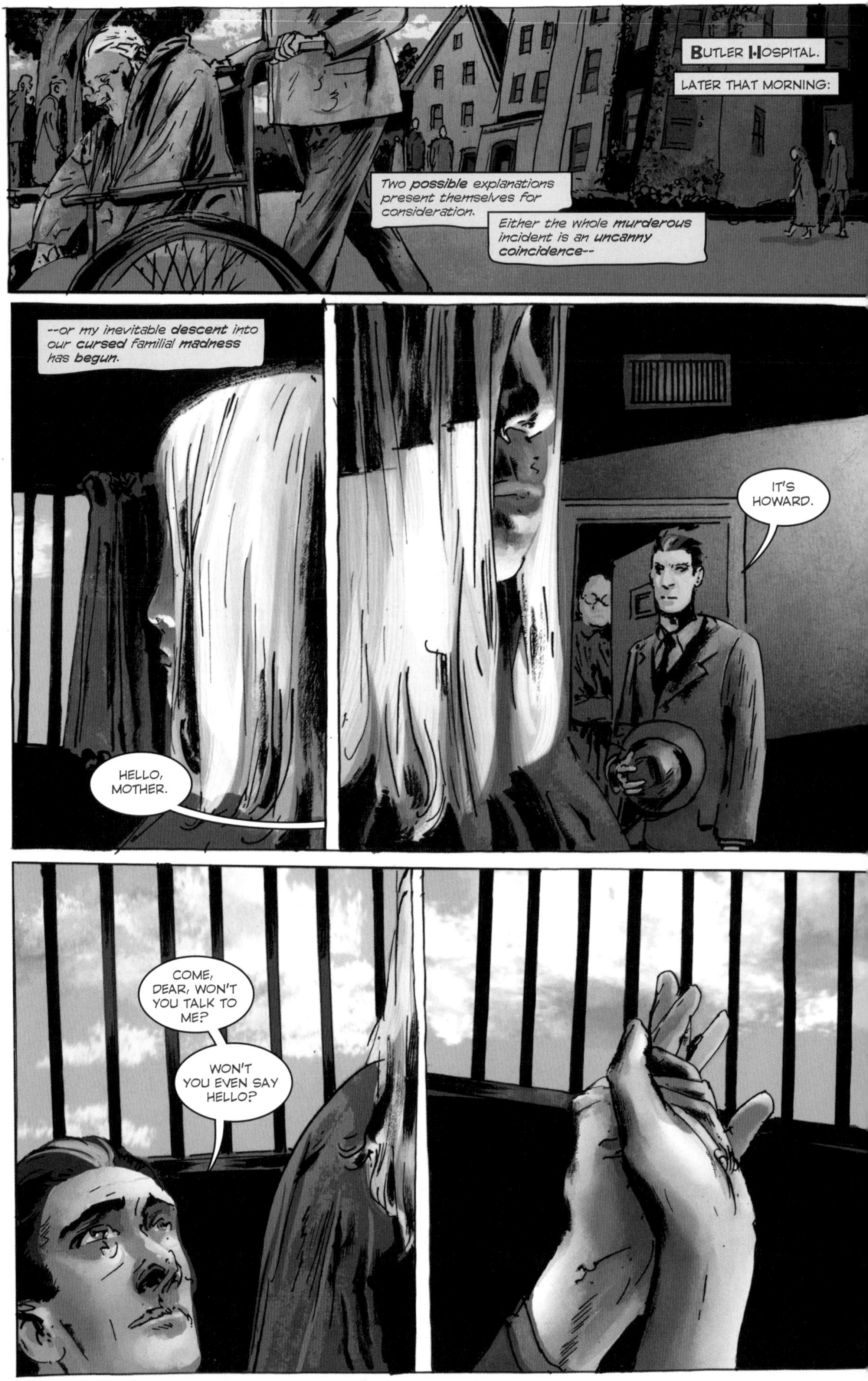
BUTLER HOSPITAL.
LATER THAT MORNING:
Two possible explanations present themselves for consideration.
Either the whole murderous incident is an uncanny coincidence--
--or my inevitable descent into our cursed familial madness has begun.
IT'S HOWARD.
HELLO, MOTHER.
COME, DEAR, WON'T YOU TALK TO ME?
WON'T YOU EVEN SAY HELLO?

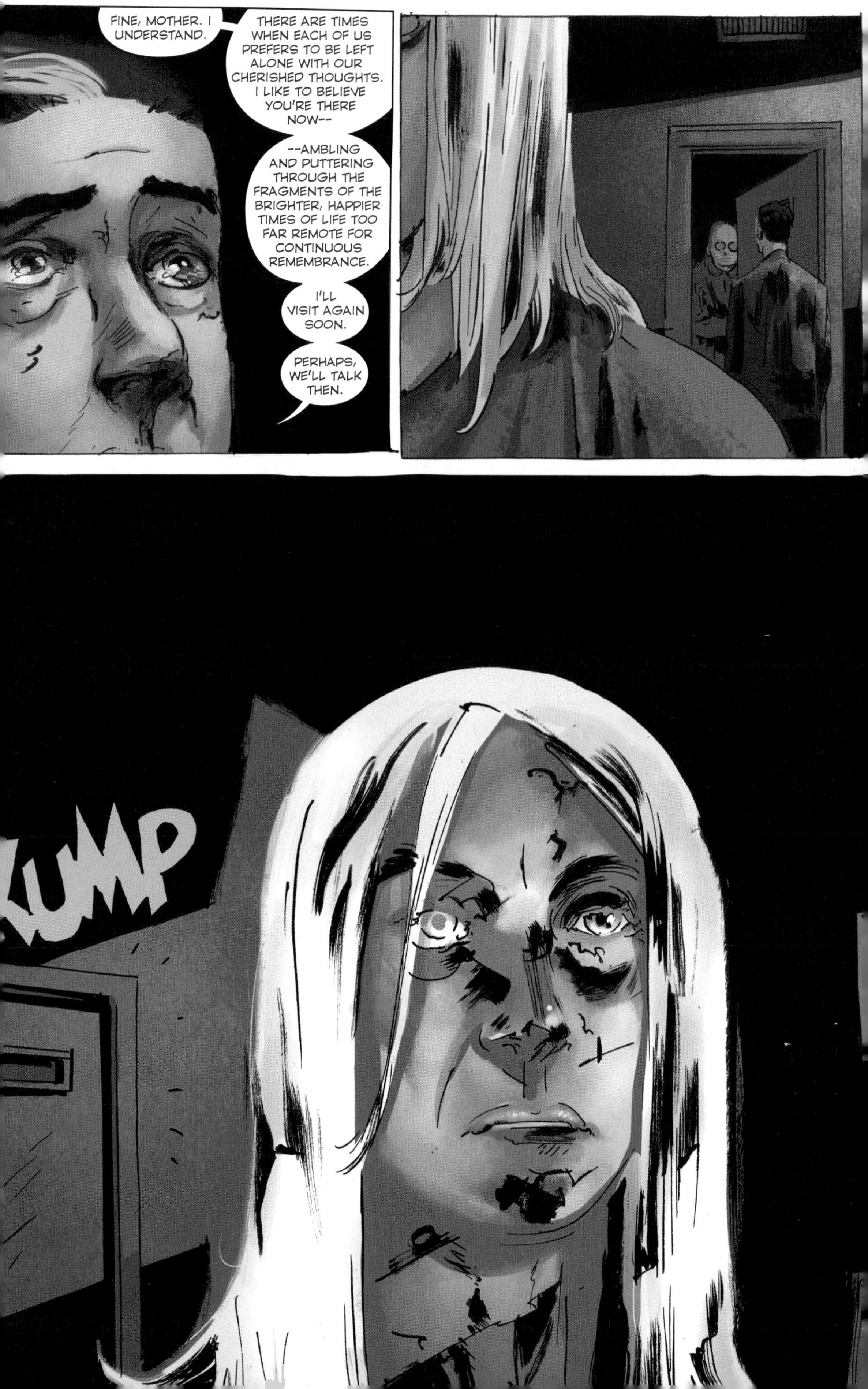
FINE, MOTHER. I UNDERSTAND.
THERE ARE TIMES WHEN EACH OF US PREFERS TO BE LEFT ALONE WITH OUR CHERISHED THOUGHTS. I LIKE TO BELIEVE YOU'RE THERE NOW--
--AMBLING AND PUTTERING THROUGH THE FRAGMENTS OF THE BRIGHTER, HAPPIER TIMES OF LIFE TOO FAR REMOTE FOR CONTINUOUS REMEMBRANCE.
I'LL VISIT AGAIN SOON.
PERHAPS, WE'LL TALK THEN.
KUMP

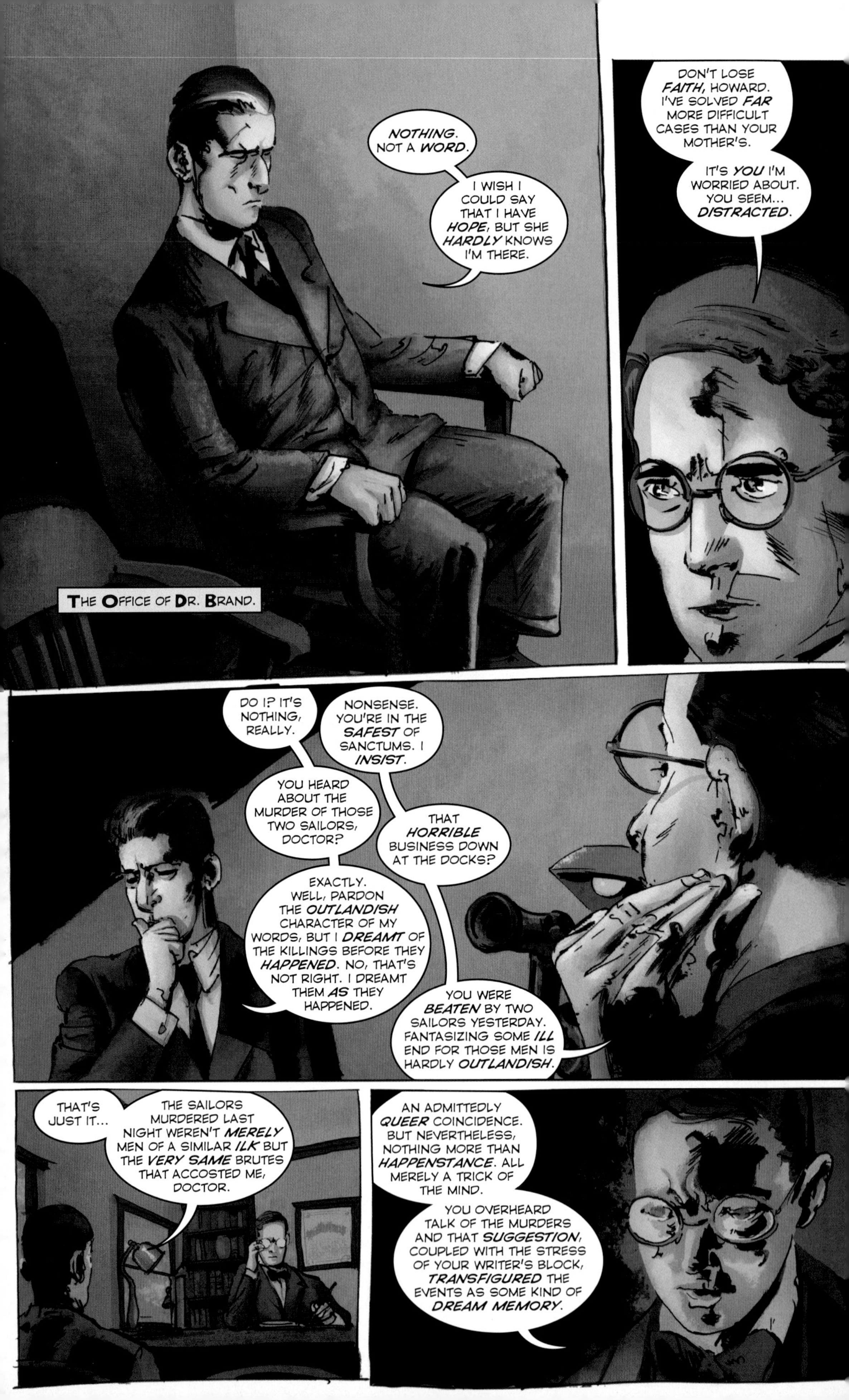
NOTHING. NOT A WORD.
I WISH I COULD SAY THAT I HAVE HOPE, BUT SHE HARDLY KNOWS I'M THERE.
THE OFFICE OF DR. BRAND.
DON'T LOSE FAITH, HOWARD. I'VE SOLVED FAR MORE DIFFICULT CASES THAN YOUR MOTHER'S.
IT'S YOU I'M WORRIED ABOUT. YOU SEEM... DISTRACTED.
DO I? IT'S NOTHING, REALLY.
NONSENSE. YOU'RE IN THE SAFEST OF SANCTUMS. I INSIST.
YOU HEARD ABOUT THE MURDER OF THOSE TWO SAILORS, DOCTOR?
THAT HORRIBLE BUSINESS DOWN AT THE DOCKS?
EXACTLY. WELL, PARDON THE OUTLANDISH CHARACTER OF MY WORDS, BUT I DREAMT OF THE KILLINGS BEFORE THEY HAPPENED. NO, THAT'S NOT RIGHT. I DREAMT THEM AS THEY HAPPENED.
YOU WERE BEATEN BY TWO SAILORS YESTERDAY. FANTASIZING SOME ILL END FOR THOSE MEN IS HARDLY OUTLANDISH.
THAT'S JUST IT...
THE SAILORS MURDERED LAST NIGHT WEREN'T MERELY MEN OF A SIMILAR ILK BUT THE VERY SAME BRUTES THAT ACCOSTED ME, DOCTOR.
AN ADMITTEDLY QUEER COINCIDENCE. BUT NEVERTHELESS, NOTHING MORE THAN HAPPENSTANCE. ALL MERELY A TRICK OF THE MIND.
YOU OVERHEARD TALK OF THE MURDERS AND THAT SUGGESTION, COUPLED WITH THE STRESS OF YOUR WRITER'S BLOCK, TRANSFIGURED THE EVENTS AS SOME KIND OF DREAM MEMORY.

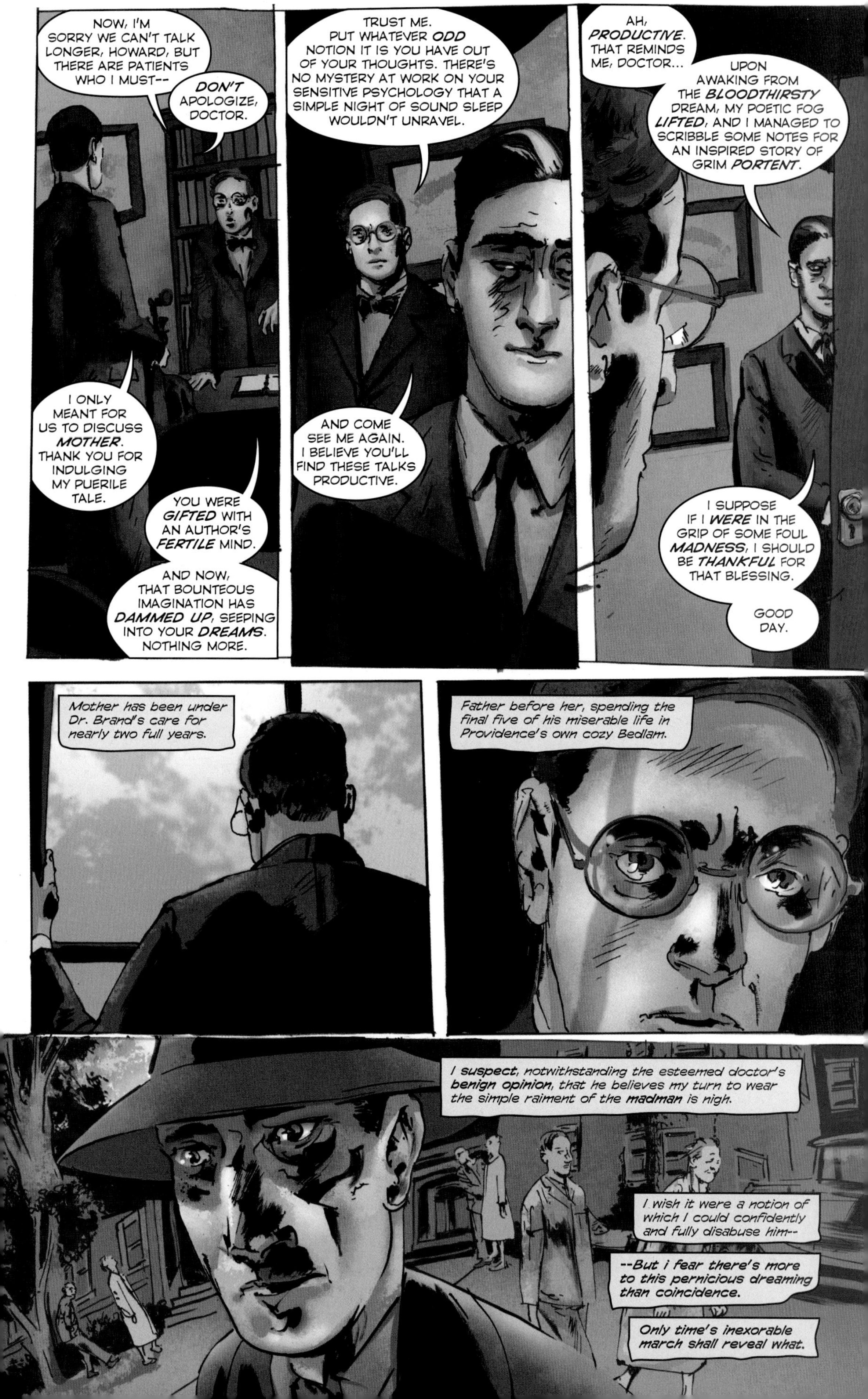
NOW, I'M SORRY WE CAN'T TALK LONGER, HOWARD, BUT THERE ARE PATIENTS WHO I MUST--
DON'T APOLOGIZE, DOCTOR.
I ONLY MEANT FOR US TO DISCUSS MOTHER. THANK YOU FOR INDULGING MY PUERILE TALE.
YOU WERE GIFTED WITH AN AUTHOR'S FERTILE MIND.
AND NOW, THAT BOUNTEOUS IMAGINATION HAS DAMMED UP, SEEPING INTO YOUR DREAMS. NOTHING MORE.
TRUST ME. PUT WHATEVER ODD NOTION IT IS YOU HAVE OUT OF YOUR THOUGHTS. THERE'S NO MYSTERY AT WORK ON YOUR SENSITIVE PSYCHOLOGY THAT A SIMPLE NIGHT OF SOUND SLEEP WOULDN'T UNRAVEL.
AND COME SEE ME AGAIN. I BELIEVE YOU'LL FIND THESE TALKS PRODUCTIVE.
AH, PRODUCTIVE. THAT REMINDS ME, DOCTOR...
UPON AWAKING FROM THE BLOODTHIRSTY DREAM, MY POETIC FOG LIFTED, AND I MANAGED TO SCRIBBLE SOME NOTES FOR AN INSPIRED STORY OF GRIM PORTENT.
I SUPPOSE IF I WERE IN THE GRIP OF SOME FOUL MADNESS, I SHOULD BE THANKFUL FOR THAT BLESSING.
GOOD DAY.
Mother has been under Dr. Brand's care for nearly two full years.
Father before her, spending the final five of his miserable life in Providence's own cozy Bedlam.
I suspect, notwithstanding the esteemed doctor's benign opinion, that he believes my turn to wear the simple raiment of the madman is nigh.
I wish it were a notion of which I could confidently and fully disabuse him--
--But i fear there's more to this pernicious dreaming than coincidence.
Only time's inexorable march shall reveal what.

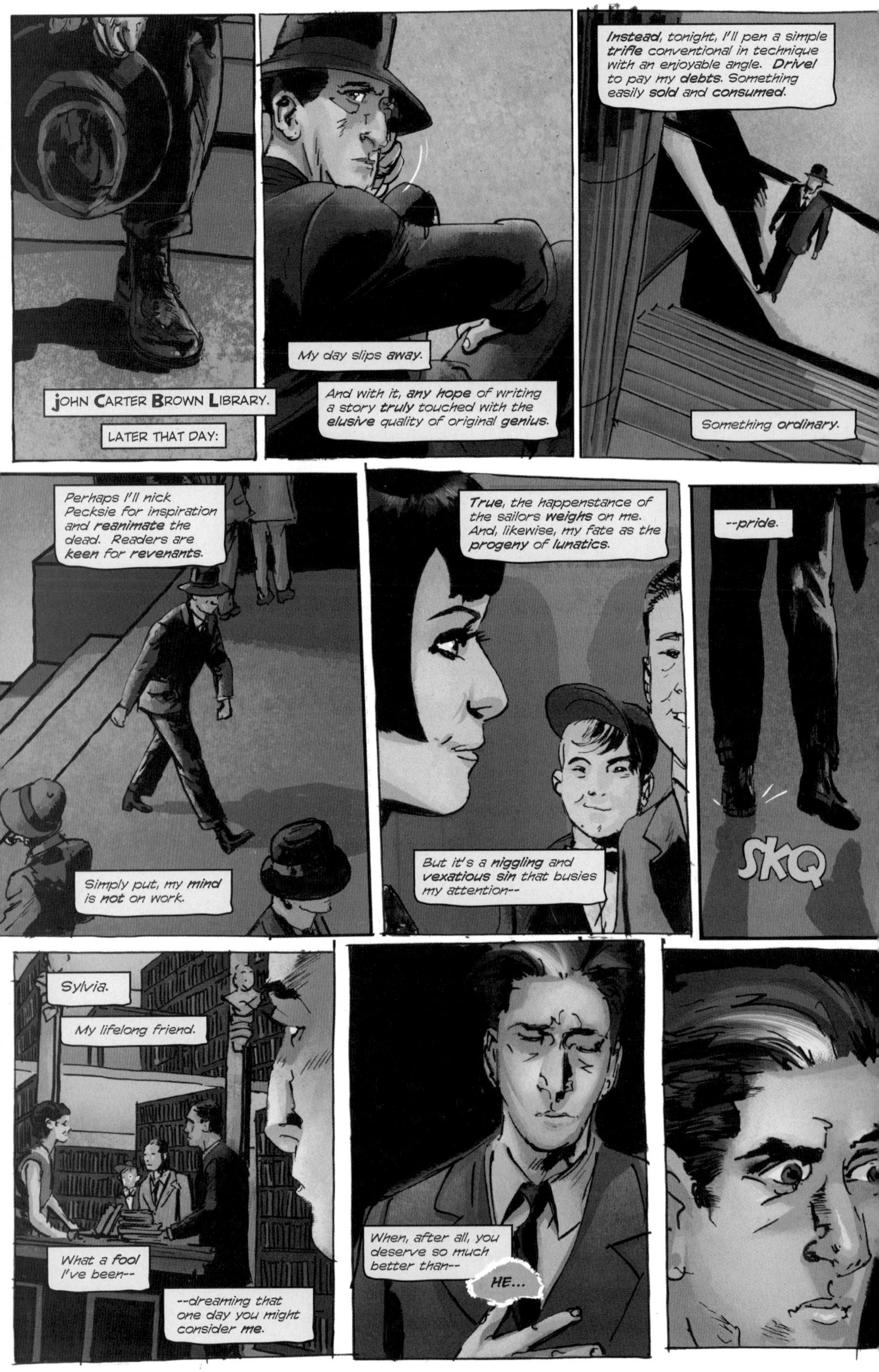
JOHN CARTER BROWN LIBRARY.
LATER THAT DAY:
My day slips away.
And with it, any hope of writing a story truly touched with the elusive quality of original genius.
Instead, tonight, I'll pen a simple trifle conventional in technique with an enjoyable angle. Drivel to pay my debts. Something easily sold and consumed.
Something ordinary.
Perhaps I'll nick Pecksie for inspiration and reanimate the dead. Readers are keen for revenants.
Simply put, my mind is not on work.
True, the happenstance of the sailors weighs on me. And, likewise, my fate as the progeny of lunatics.
But it's a niggling and vexatious sin that busies my attention--
--pride.
SKQ
Sylvia.
My lifelong friend.
What a fool I've been--
--dreaming that one day you might consider me.
When, after all, you deserve so much better than--
HE...

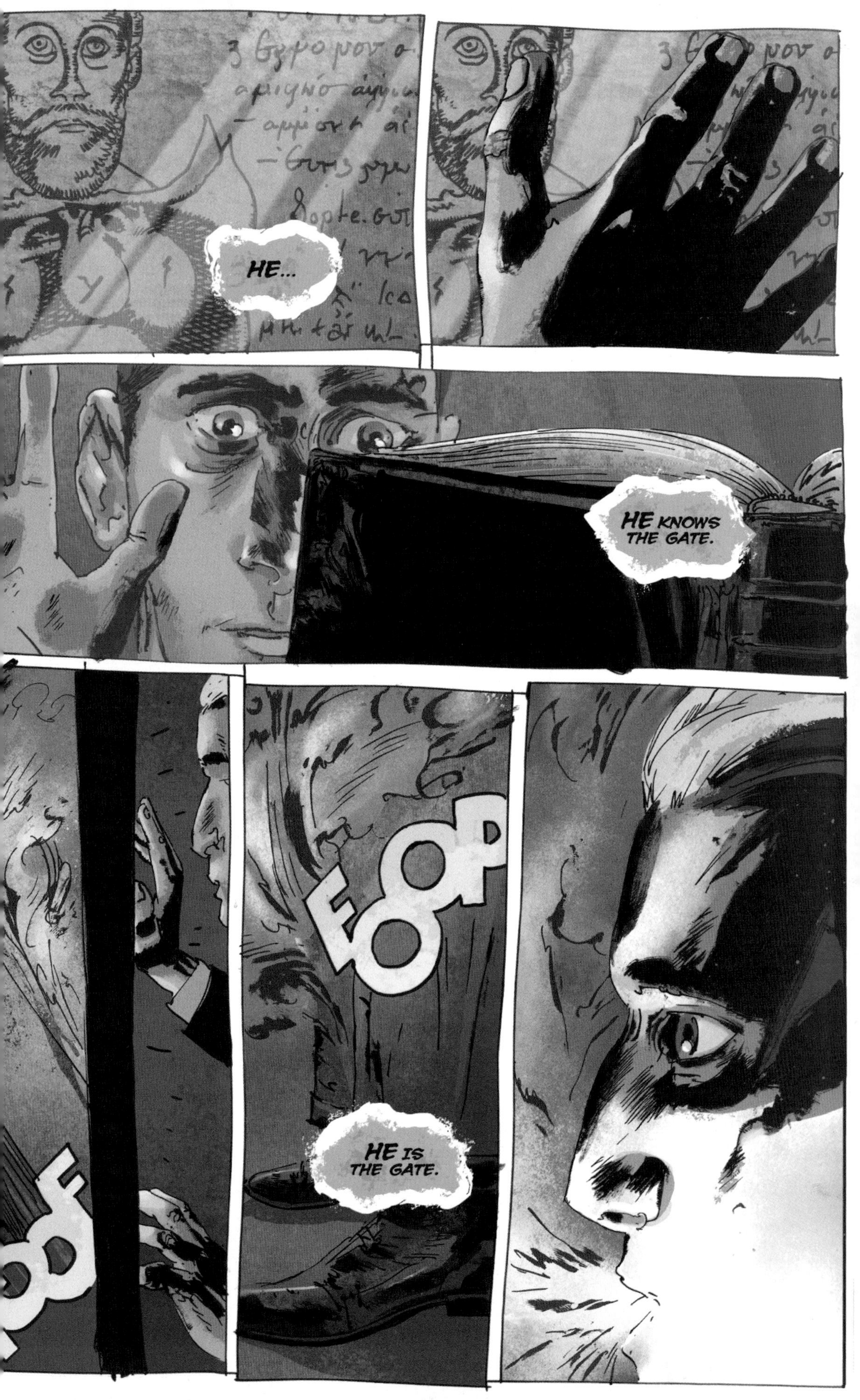
HE...
HE KNOWS THE GATE.
FOOP
HE IS THE GATE.

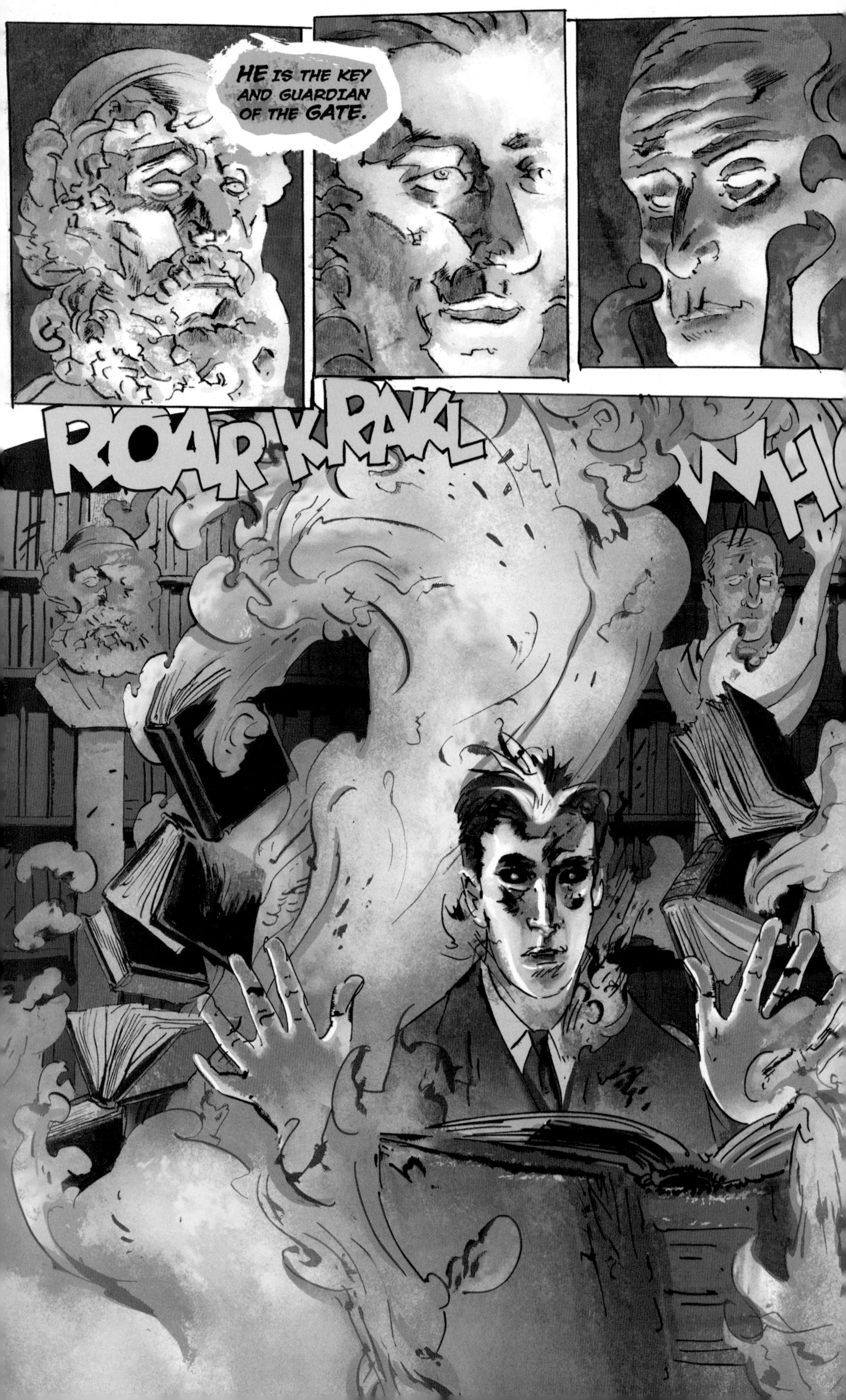
HE IS THE KEY AND GUARDIAN OF THE GATE.
RROAR
KRAKL
WHO

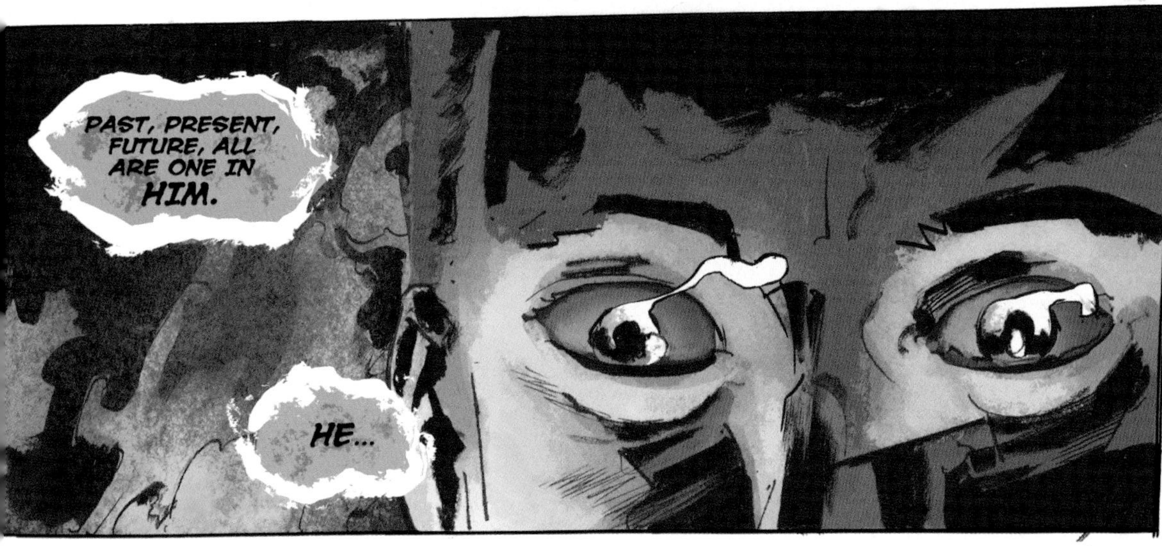
PAST, PRESENT, FUTURE, ALL ARE ONE IN HIM.
HE...
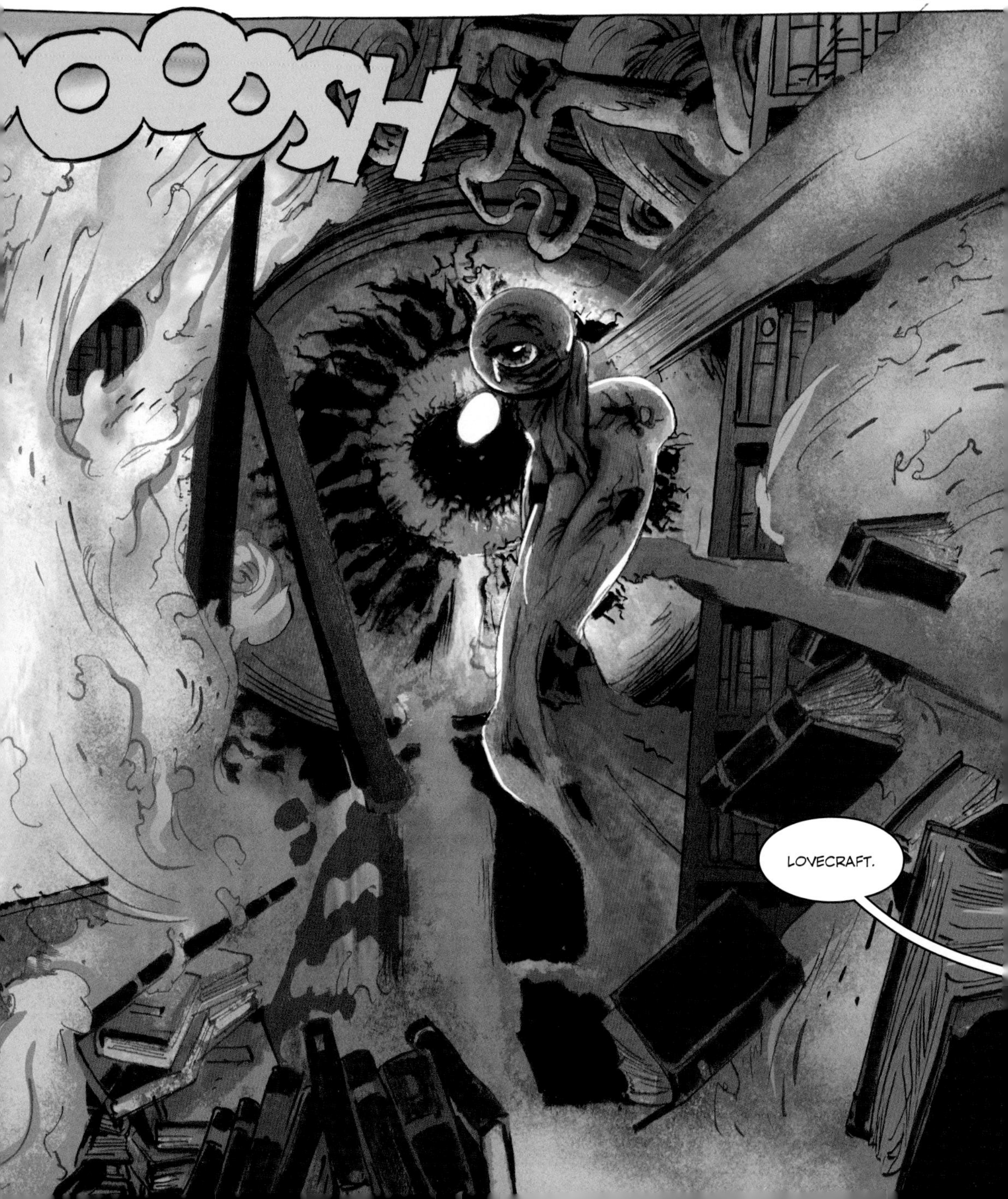
OOOOSH
LOVECRAFT.

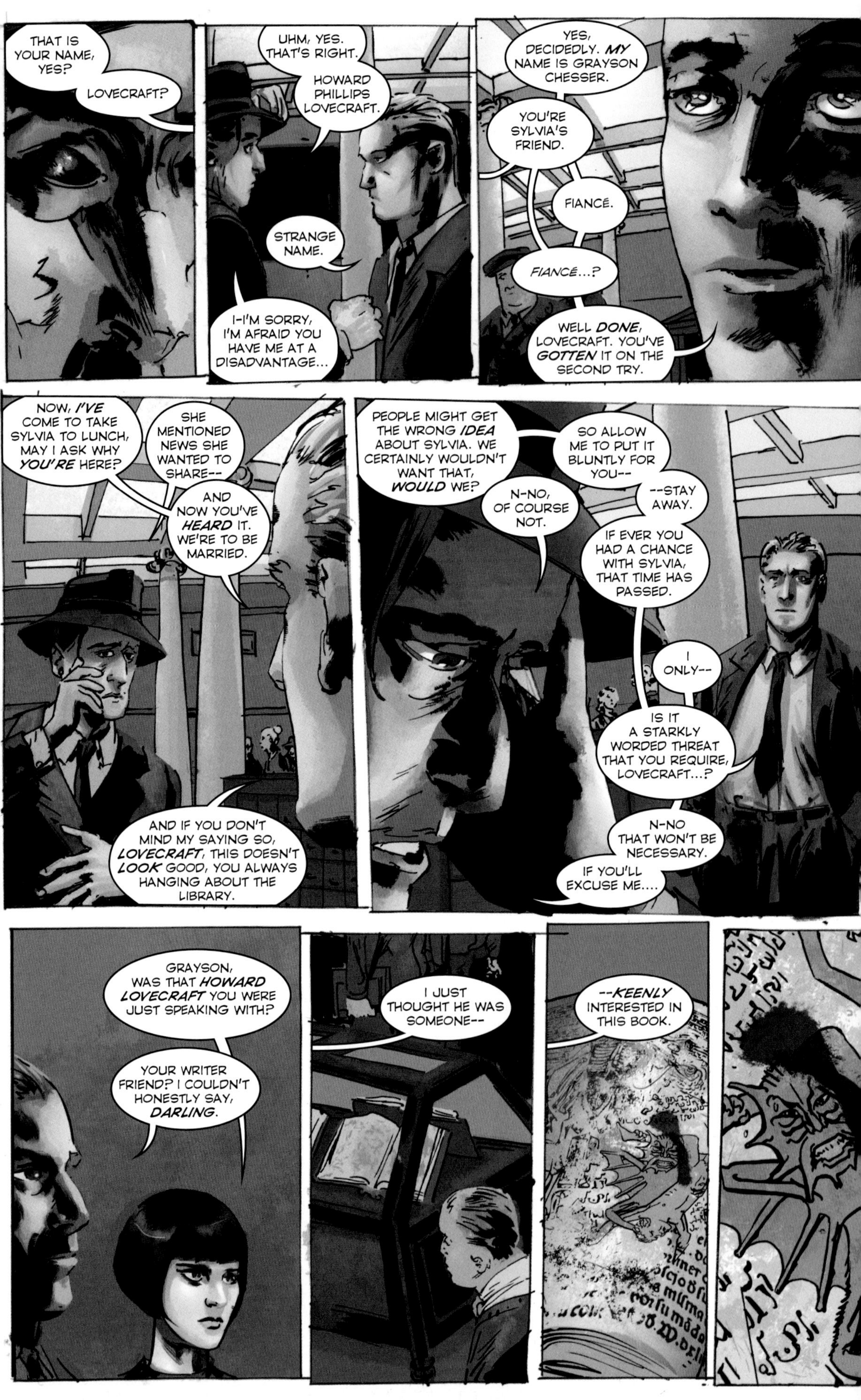

THAT IS YOUR NAME, YES?
LOVECRAFT?
UHM, YES. THAT'S RIGHT.
HOWARD PHILLIPS LOVECRAFT.
STRANGE NAME.
I-I'M SORRY, I'M AFRAID YOU HAVE ME AT A DISADVANTAGE...
YES, DECIDEDLY. MY NAME IS GRAYSON CHESSER.
YOU'RE SYLVIA'S FRIEND.
FIANCÉ.
FIANCÉ...?
WELL DONE, LOVECRAFT. YOU'VE GOTTEN IT ON THE SECOND TRY.
NOW, I'VE COME TO TAKE SYLVIA TO LUNCH, MAY I ASK WHY YOU'RE HERE?
SHE MENTIONED NEWS SHE WANTED TO SHARE--
AND NOW YOU'VE HEARD IT. WE'RE TO BE MARRIED.
AND IF YOU DON'T MIND MY SAYING SO, LOVECRAFT, THIS DOESN'T LOOK GOOD, YOU ALWAYS HANGING ABOUT THE LIBRARY.
PEOPLE MIGHT GET THE WRONG IDEA ABOUT SYLVIA. WE CERTAINLY WOULDN'T WANT THAT, WOULD WE?
N-NO, OF COURSE NOT.
SO ALLOW ME TO PUT IT BLUNTLY FOR YOU--
--STAY AWAY.
IF EVER YOU HAD A CHANCE WITH SYLVIA, THAT TIME HAS PASSED.
I ONLY--
IS IT A STARKLY WORDED THREAT THAT YOU REQUIRE, LOVECRAFT...?
N-NO THAT WON'T BE NECESSARY.
IF YOU'LL EXCUSE ME....
GRAYSON, WAS THAT HOWARD LOVECRAFT YOU WERE JUST SPEAKING WITH?
YOUR WRITER FRIEND? I COULDN'T HONESTLY SAY, DARLING.
I JUST THOUGHT HE WAS SOMEONE--
--KEENLY INTERESTED IN THIS BOOK.

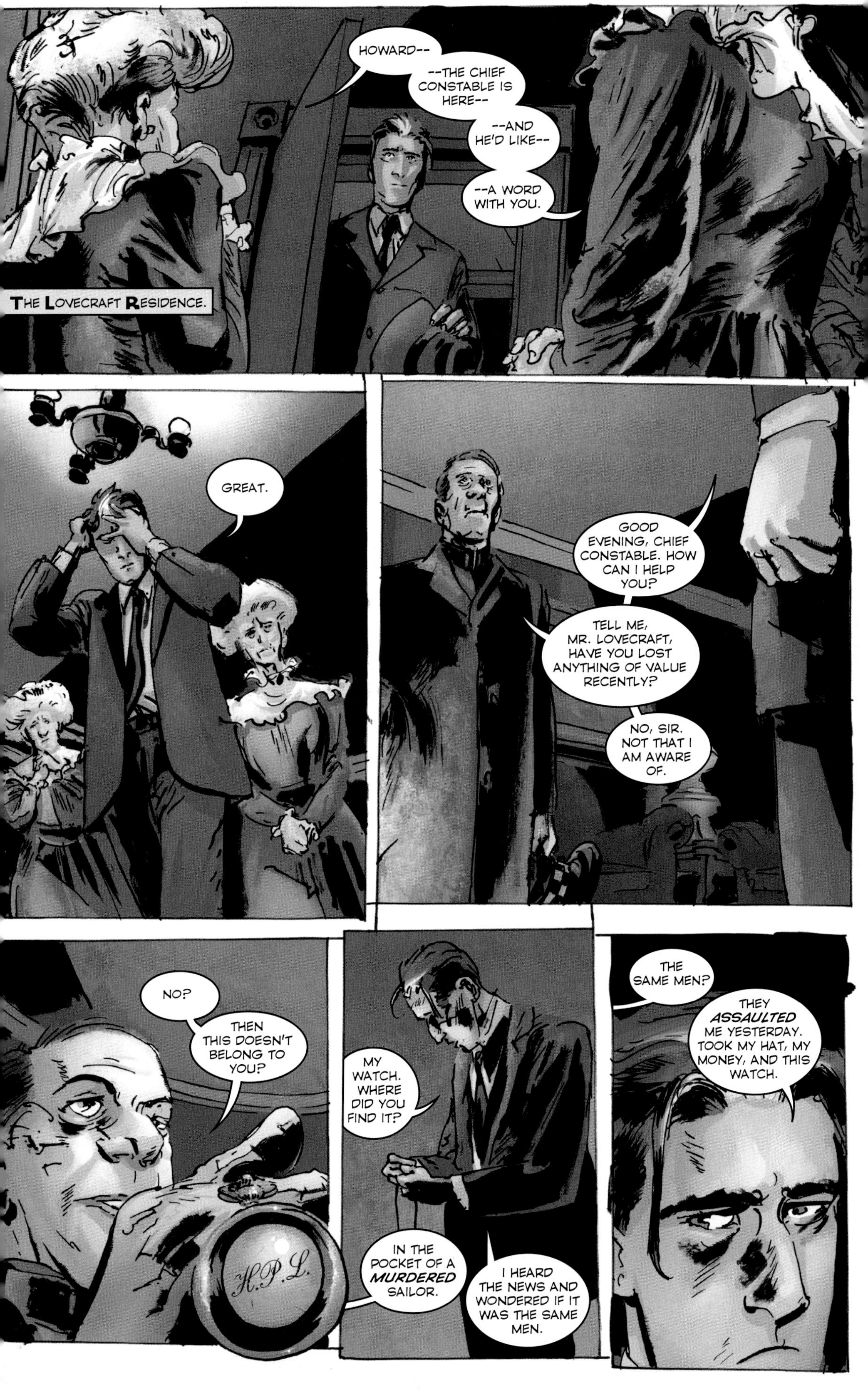
HOWARD--
--THE CHIEF CONSTABLE IS HERE--
--AND HE'D LIKE--
--A WORD WITH YOU.
THE LOVECRAFT RESIDENCE.
GREAT.
GOOD EVENING, CHIEF CONSTABLE. HOW CAN I HELP YOU?
TELL ME, MR. LOVECRAFT, HAVE YOU LOST ANYTHING OF VALUE RECENTLY?
NO, SIR. NOT THAT I AM AWARE OF.
NO?
THEN THIS DOESN'T BELONG TO YOU?
H.P.L.
MY WATCH. WHERE DID YOU FIND IT?
IN THE POCKET OF A MURDERED SAILOR.
I HEARD THE NEWS AND WONDERED IF IT WAS THE SAME MEN.
THE SAME MEN?
THEY ASSAULTED ME YESTERDAY. TOOK MY HAT, MY MONEY, AND THIS WATCH.

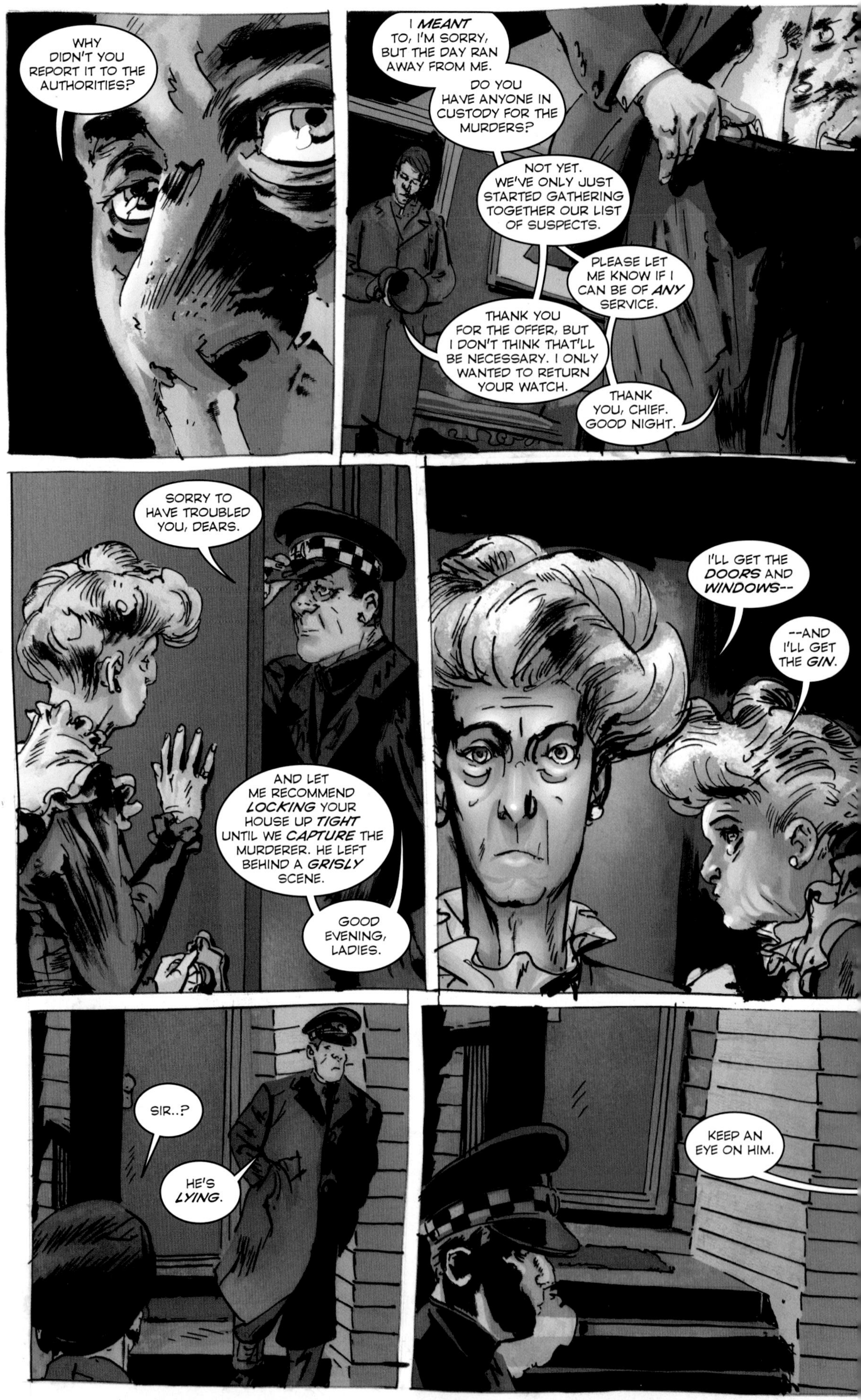
WHY DIDN'T YOU REPORT IT TO THE AUTHORITIES?
I MEANT TO, I'M SORRY, BUT THE DAY RAN AWAY FROM ME.
DO YOU HAVE ANYONE IN CUSTODY FOR THE MURDERS?
NOT YET. WE'VE ONLY JUST STARTED GATHERING TOGETHER OUR LIST OF SUSPECTS.
PLEASE LET ME KNOW IF I CAN BE OF ANY SERVICE.
THANK YOU FOR THE OFFER, BUT I DON'T THINK THAT'LL BE NECESSARY. I ONLY WANTED TO RETURN YOUR WATCH.
THANK YOU, CHIEF. GOOD NIGHT.
SORRY TO HAVE TROUBLED YOU, DEARS.
AND LET ME RECOMMEND LOCKING YOUR HOUSE UP TIGHT UNTIL WE CAPTURE THE MURDERER. HE LEFT BEHIND A GRISLY SCENE.
GOOD EVENING, LADIES.
I'LL GET THE DOORS AND WINDOWS--
--AND I'LL GET THE GIN.
SIR..?
HE'S LYING.
KEEP AN EYE ON HIM.

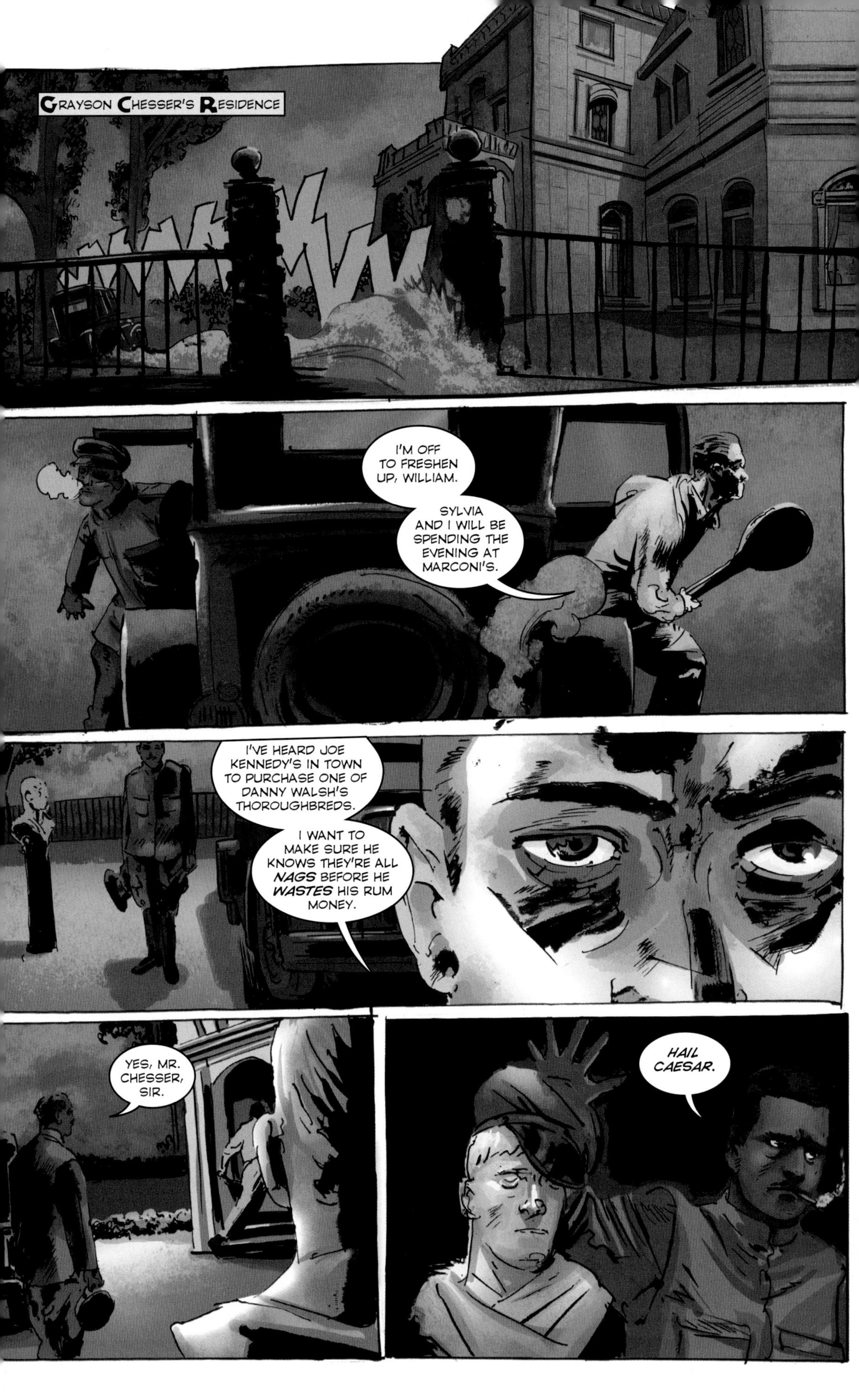
GRAYSON CHESSER'S RESIDENCE
I'M OFF TO FRESHEN UP, WILLIAM.
SYLVIA AND I WILL BE SPENDING THE EVENING AT MARCONI'S.
I'VE HEARD JOE KENNEDY'S IN TOWN TO PURCHASE ONE OF DANNY WALSH'S THOROUGHBREDS.
I WANT TO MAKE SURE HE KNOWS THEY'RE ALL NAGS BEFORE HE WASTES HIS RUM MONEY.
YES, MR. CHESSER, SIR.
HAIL CAESAR.

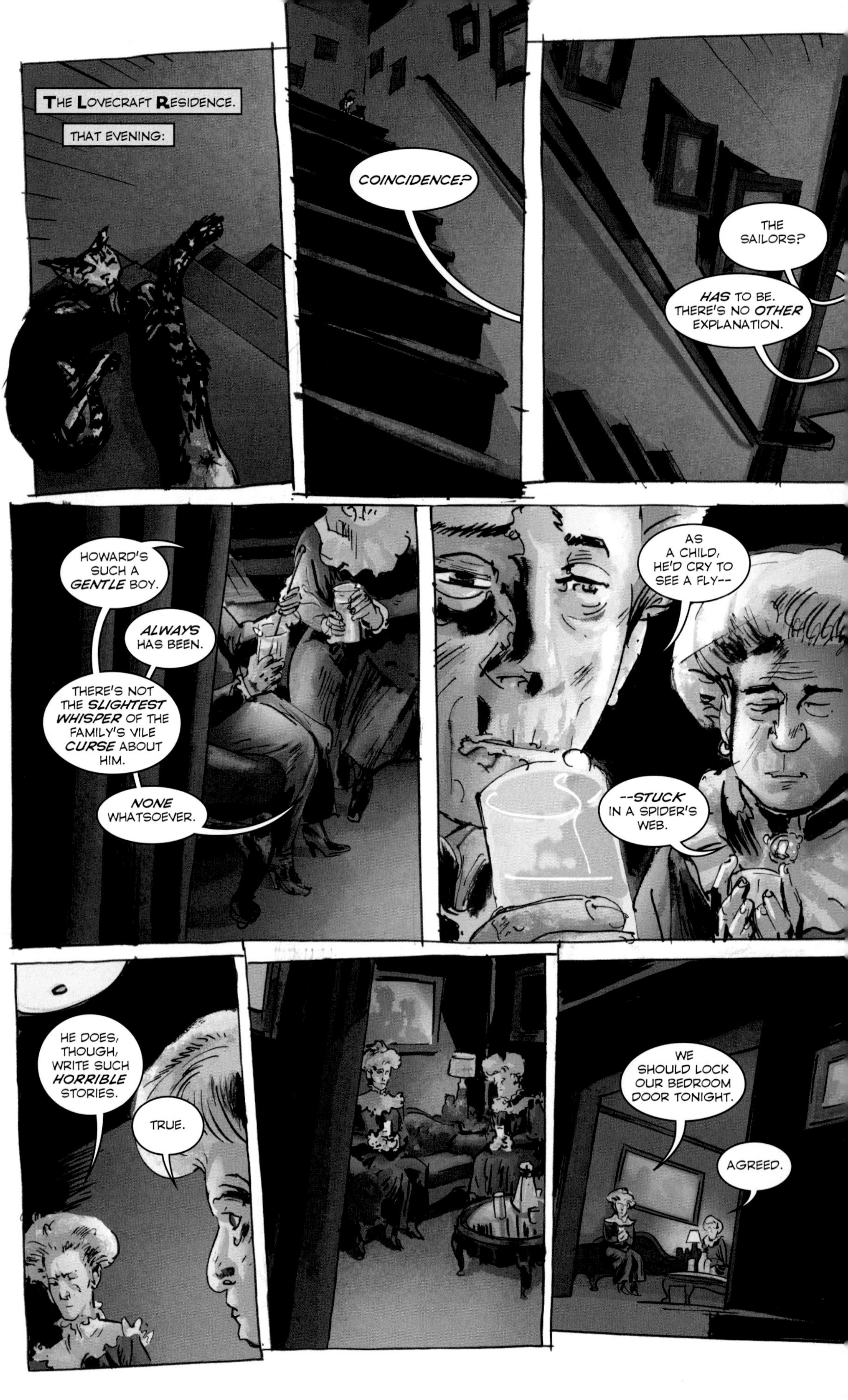

THE LOVECRAFT RESIDENCE.
THAT EVENING:
COINCIDENCE?
THE SAILORS?
HAS TO BE. THERE'S NO OTHER EXPLANATION.
HOWARD'S SUCH A GENTLE BOY.
ALWAYS HAS BEEN.
THERE'S NOT THE SLIGHTEST WHISPER OF THE FAMILY'S VILE CURSE ABOUT HIM.
NONE WHATSOEVER.
AS A CHILD, HE'D CRY TO SEE A FLY--
--STUCK IN A SPIDER'S WEB.
HE DOES, THOUGH, WRITE SUCH HORRIBLE STORIES.
TRUE.
WE SHOULD LOCK OUR BEDROOM DOOR TONIGHT.
AGREED.

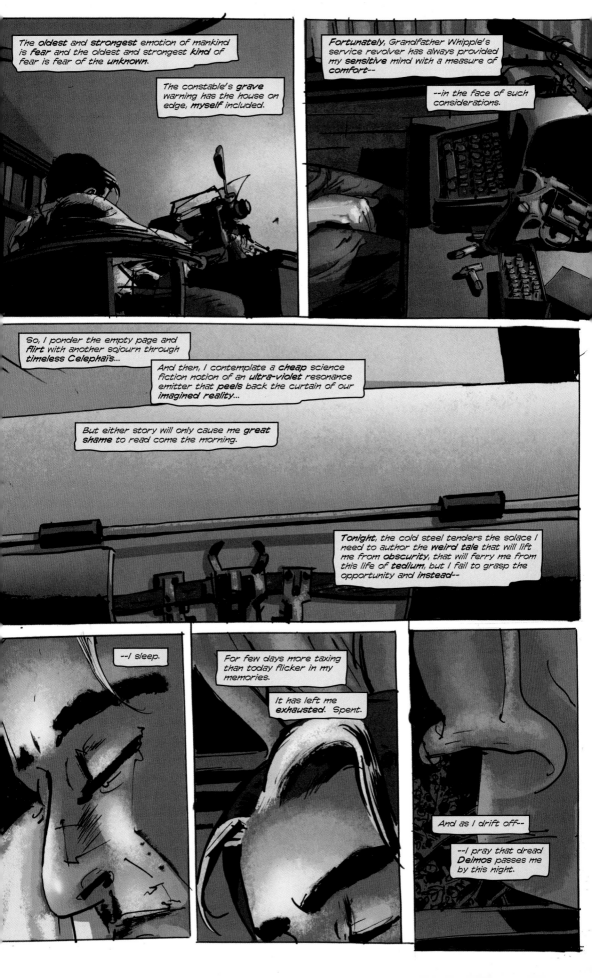

The oldest and strongest emotion of mankind is fear and the oldest and strongest kind of fear is fear of the unknown.

The constable's grave warning has the house on edge, myself included.

Fortunately, Grandfather Whipple's service revolver has always provided my sensitive mind with a measure of comfort--

--in the face of such considerations.

So, I ponder the empty page and flirt with another sojourn through timeless Celephaïs...

And then, I contemplate a cheap science fiction notion of an ultra-violet resonance emitter that peels back the curtain of our imagined reality...

But either story will only cause me great shame to read come the morning.

Tonight, the cold steel tenders the solace I need to author the weird tale that will lift me from obscurity, that will ferry me from this life of tedium, but I fail to grasp the opportunity and instead--

--I sleep.

For few days more taxing than today flicker in my memories.

It has left me exhausted. Spent.

And as I drift off--

--I pray that dread Deimos passes me by this night.

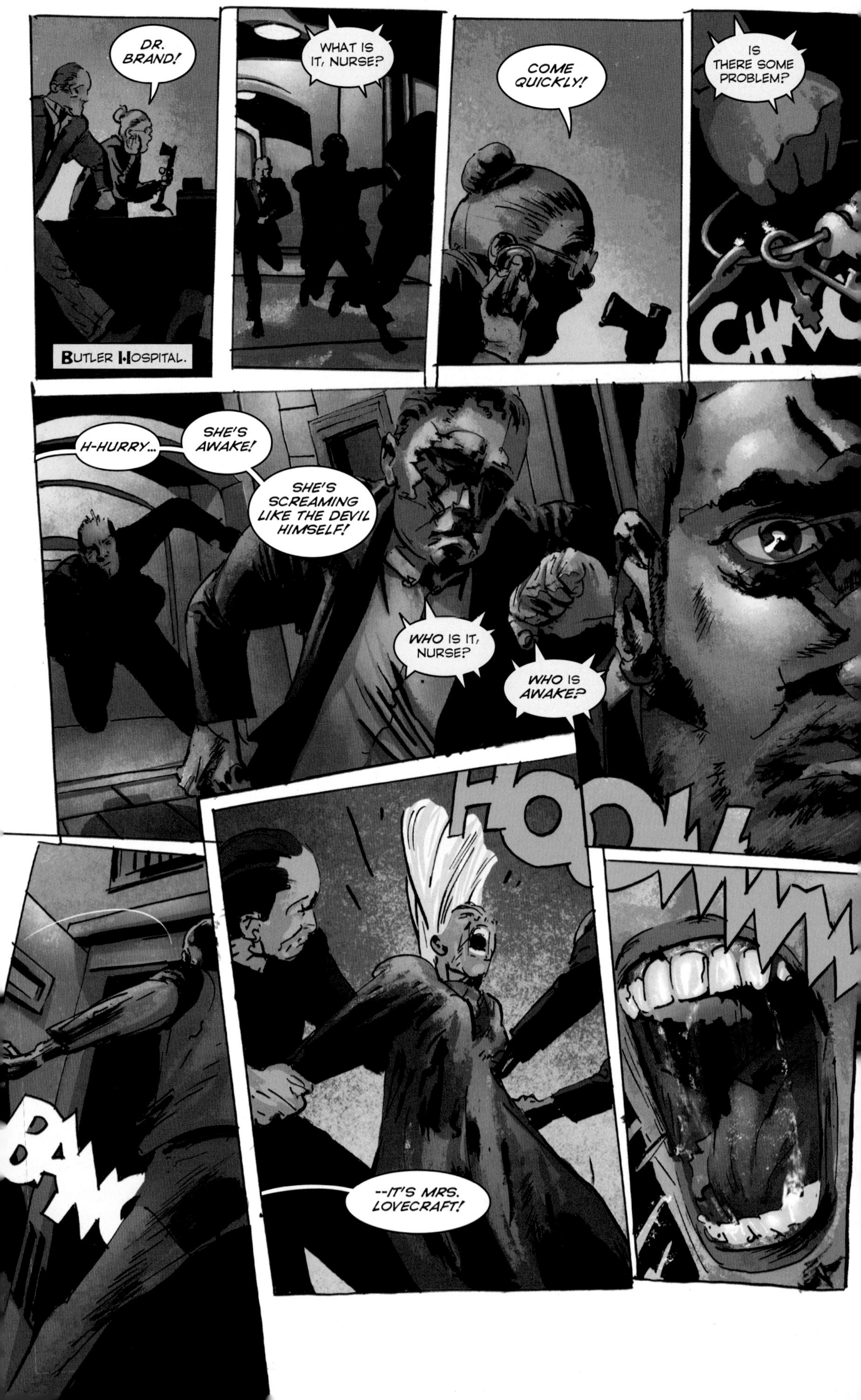
DR. BRAND!
BUTLER HOSPITAL.
WHAT IS IT, NURSE?
COME QUICKLY!
IS THERE SOME PROBLEM?
CHU
H-HURRY...
SHE'S AWAKE!
SHE'S SCREAMING LIKE THE DEVIL HIMSELF!
WHO IS IT, NURSE?
WHO IS AWAKE?
HOO
BAM
--IT'S MRS. LOVECRAFT!

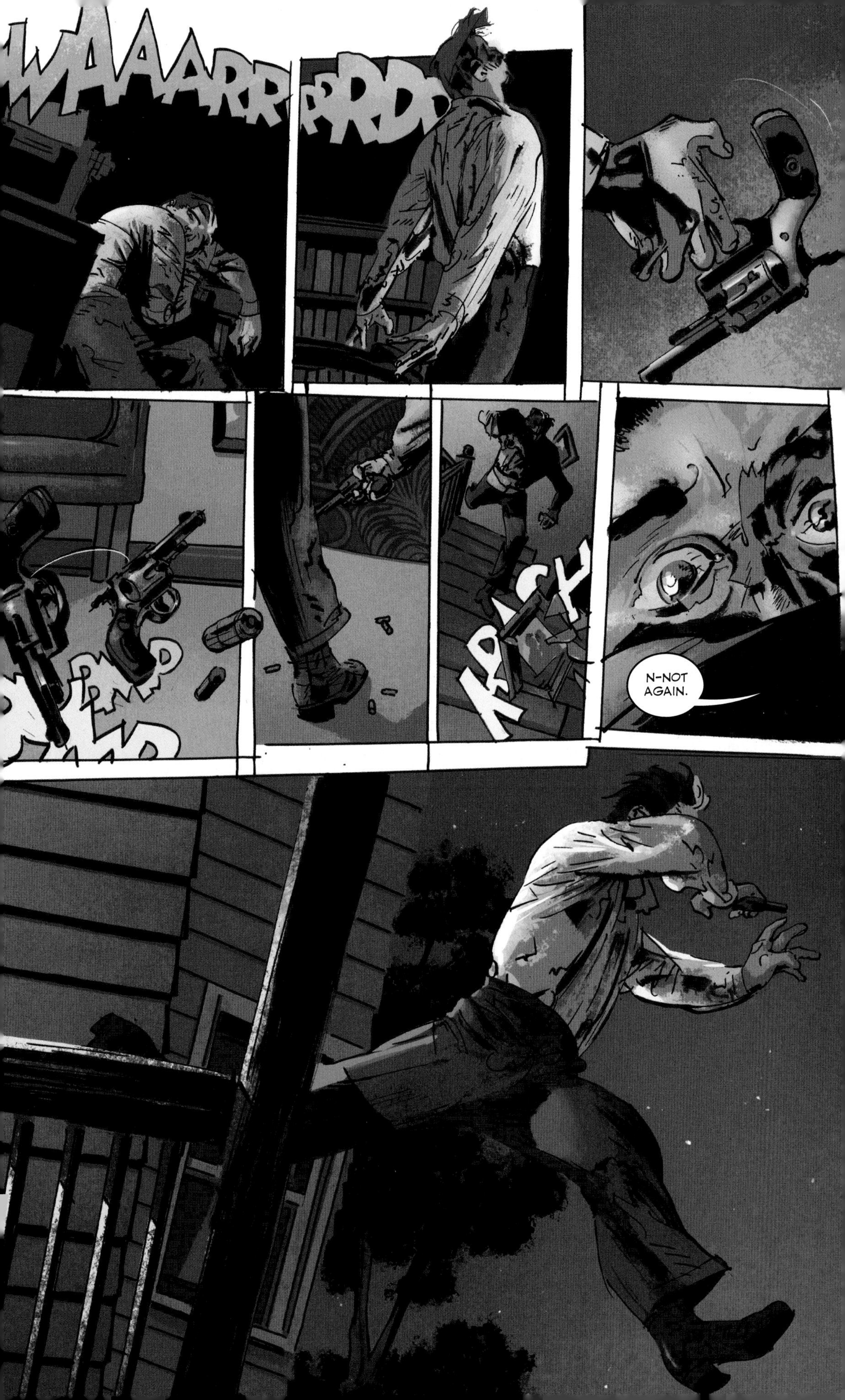
WAAARRRRRDD
N-NOT AGAIN.

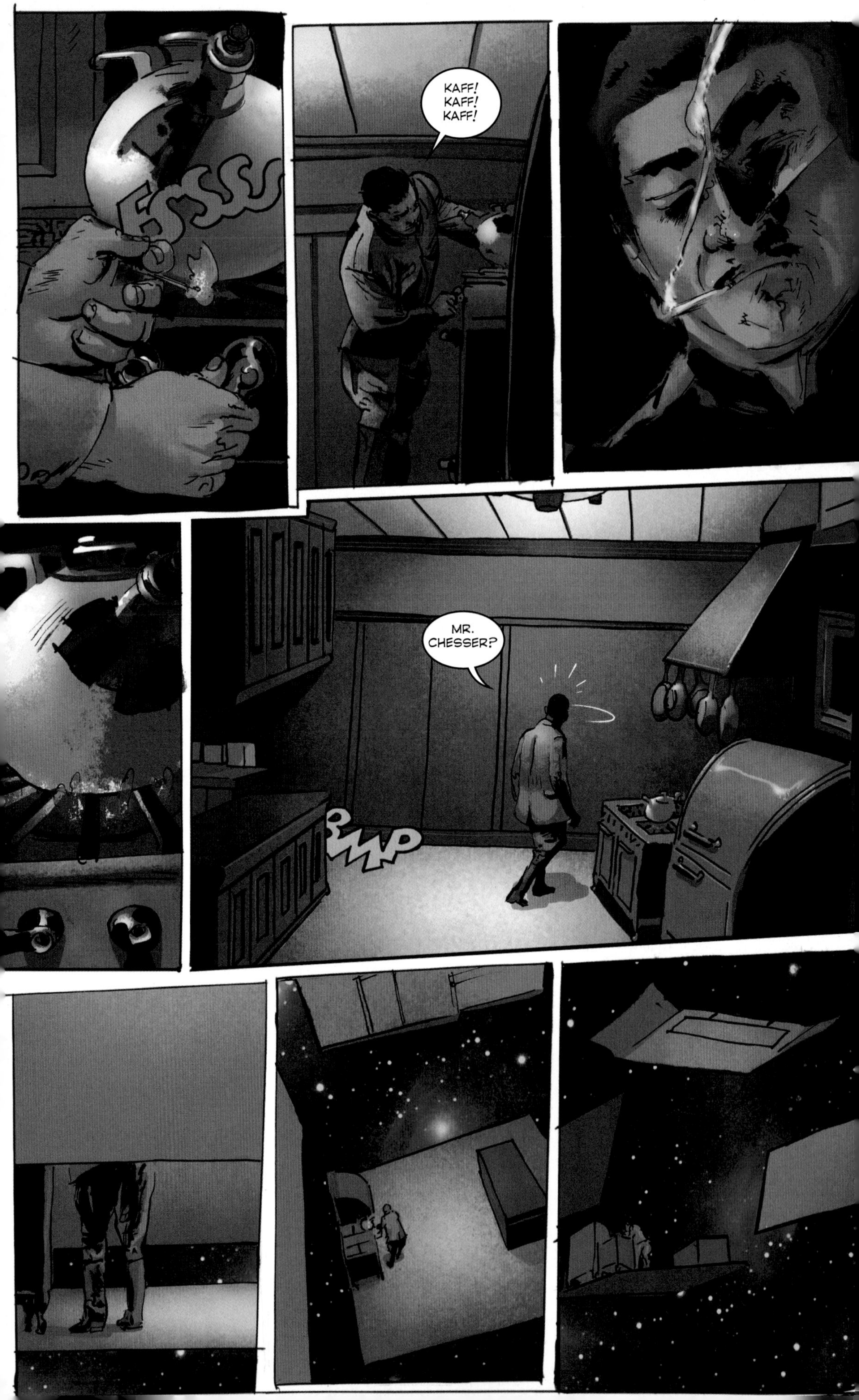
FSSSS
KAFF! KAFF! KAFF!
MR. CHESSER?

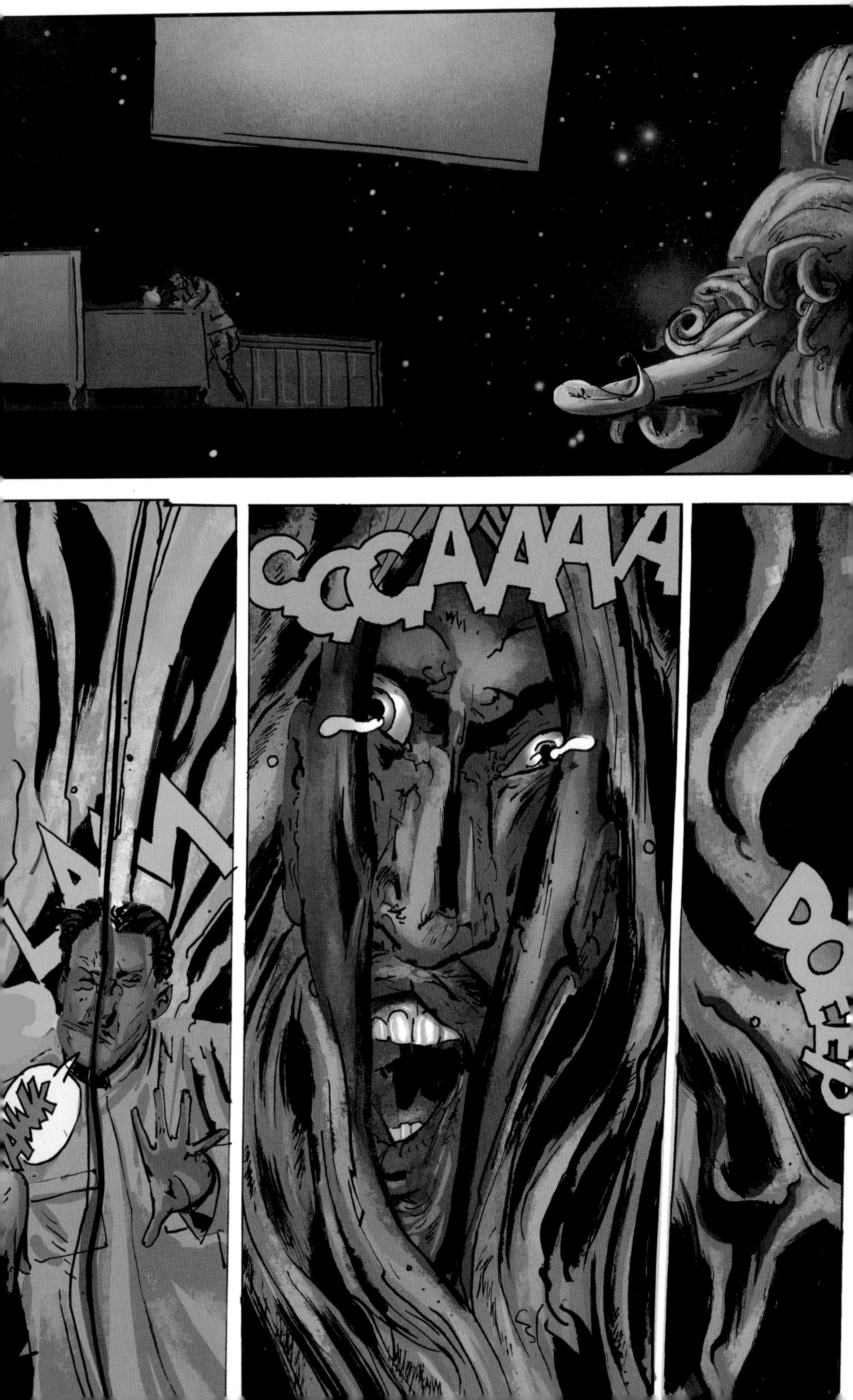
CCCAAAAA

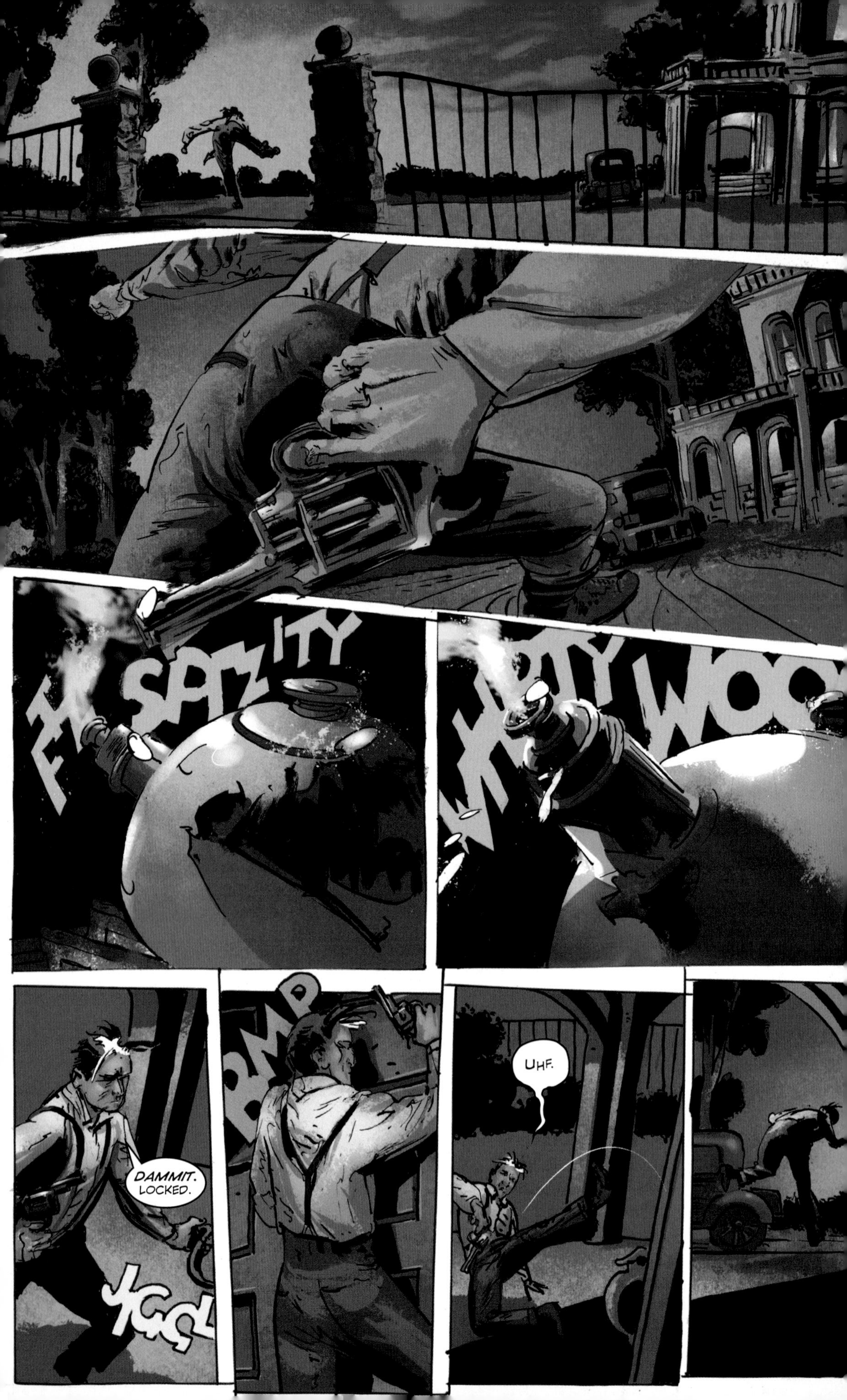
DAMMIT. LOCKED.
UHF.

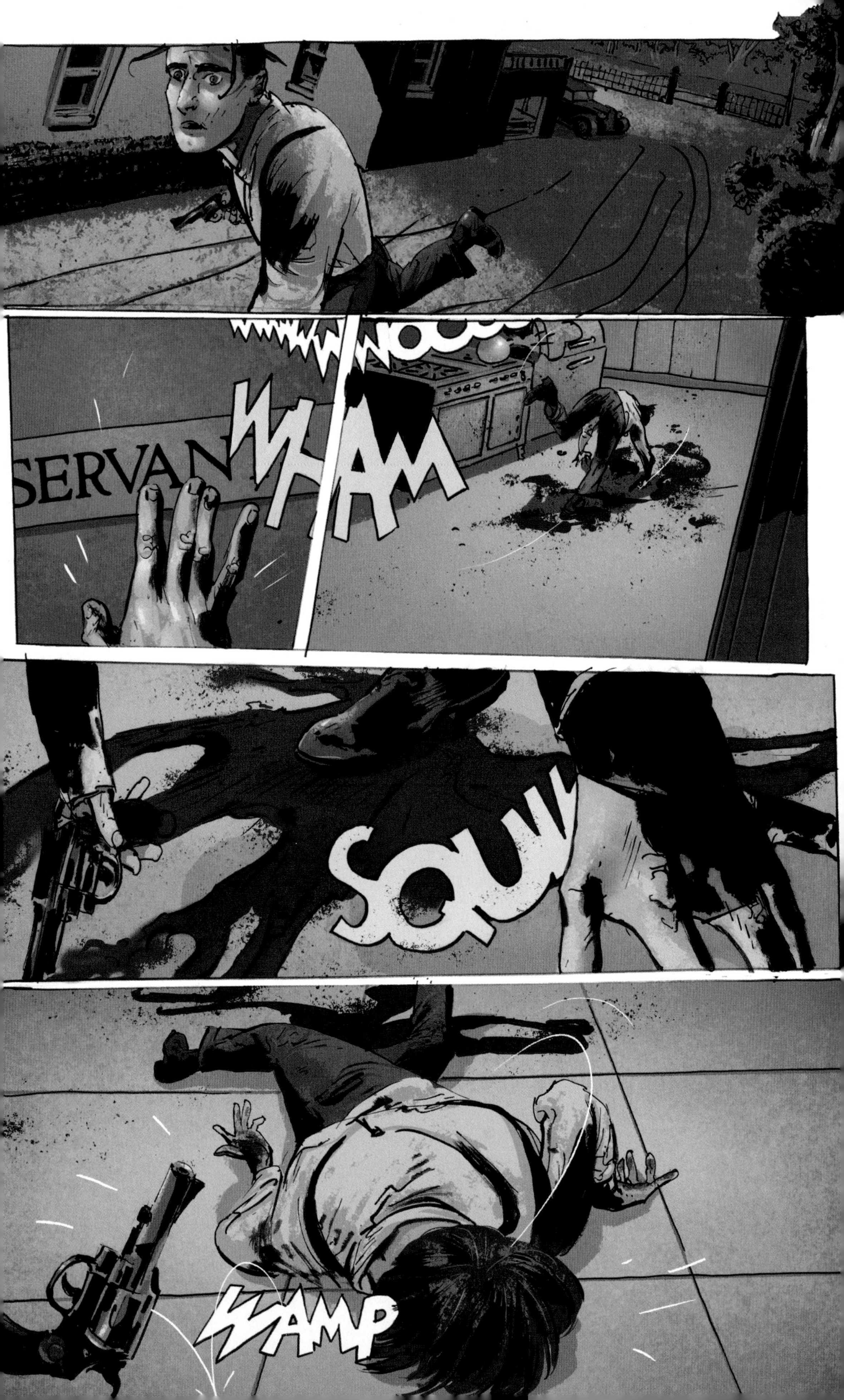
WHAM
WAMP

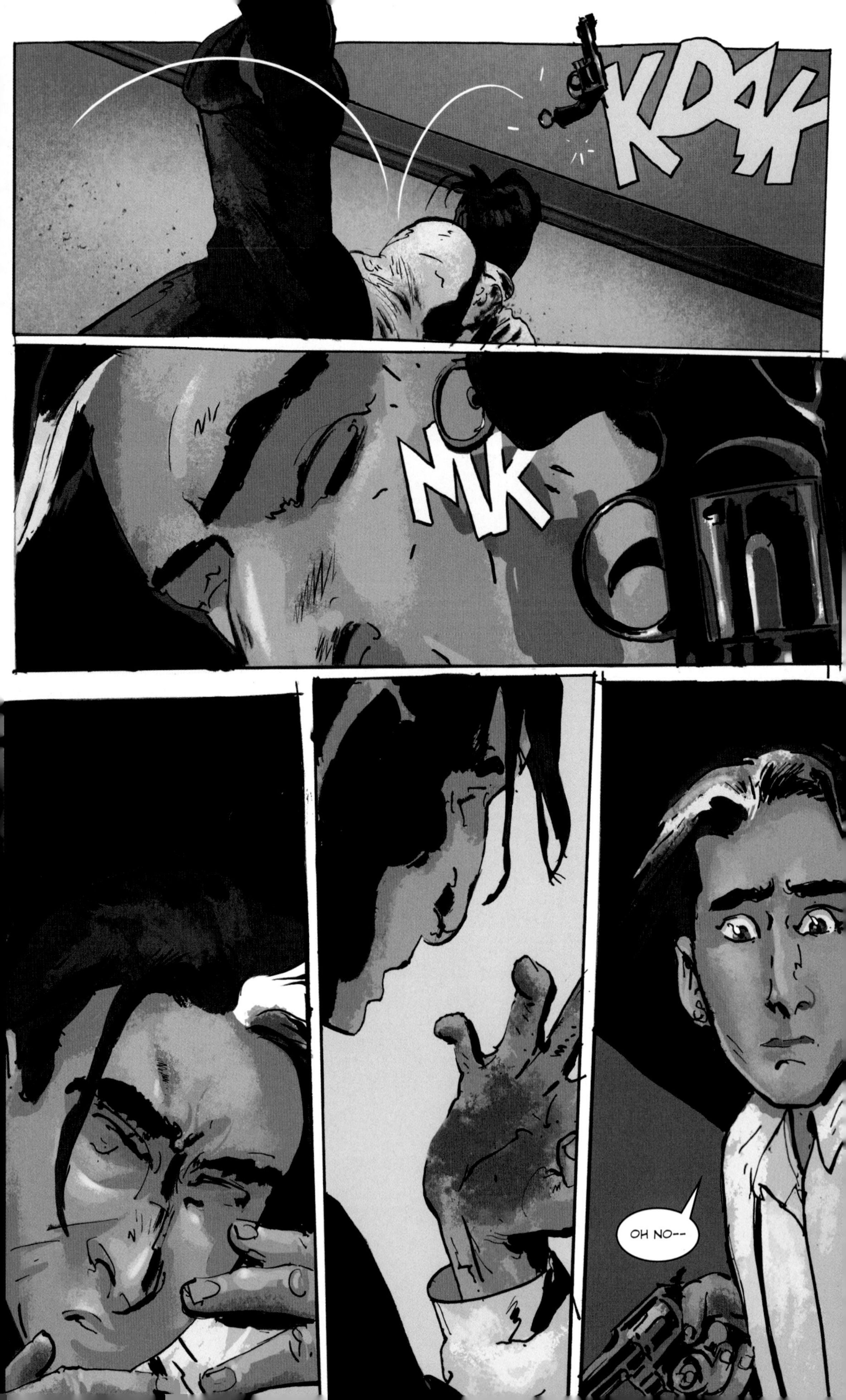
KDAK
NIK
OH NO--

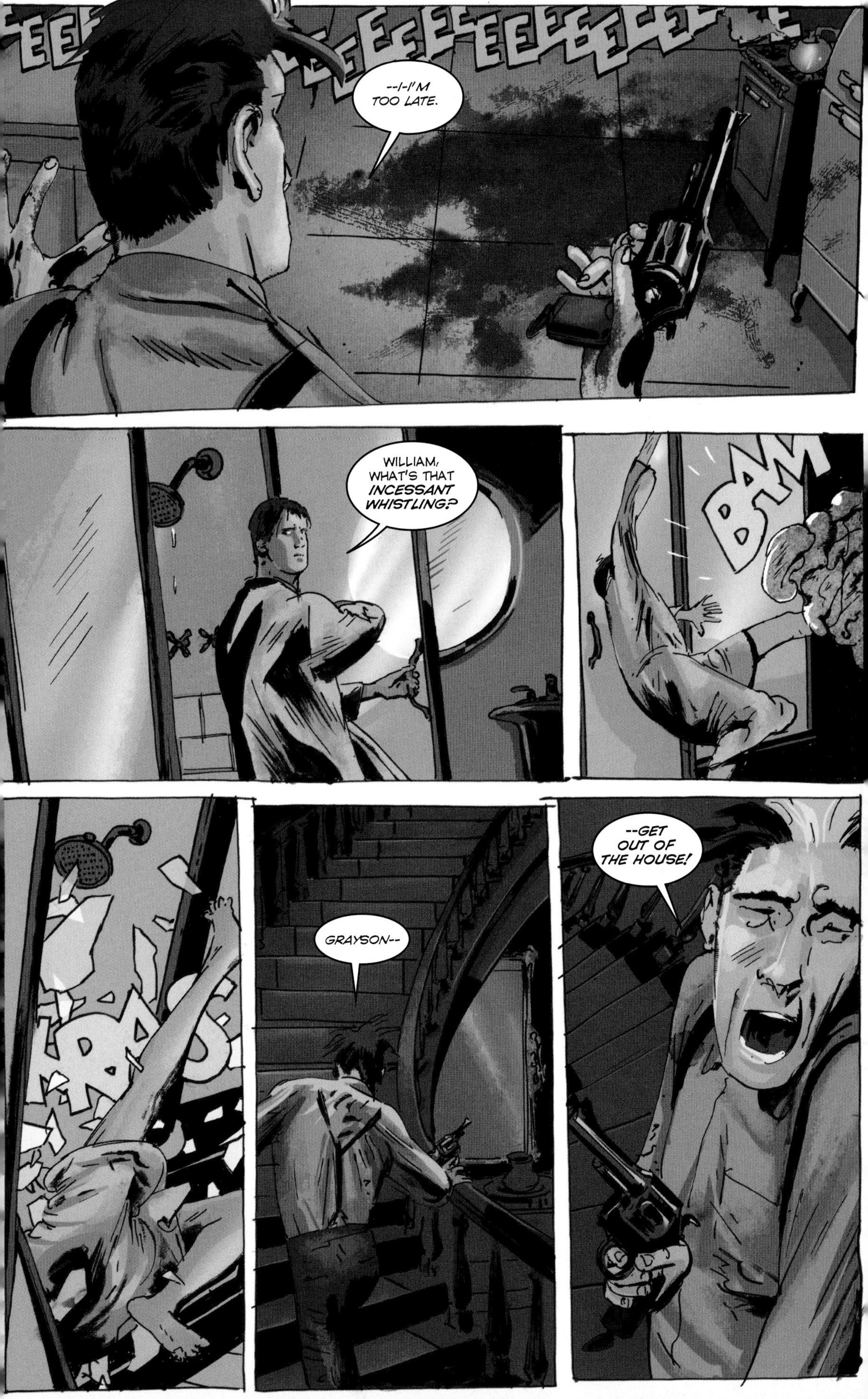
EEEEEEEEEEEEEEEEEEE
--I-I'M TOO LATE.
WILLIAM, WHAT'S THAT *INCESSANT WHISTLING?*
BAM
GRAYSON--
--GET OUT OF THE HOUSE!

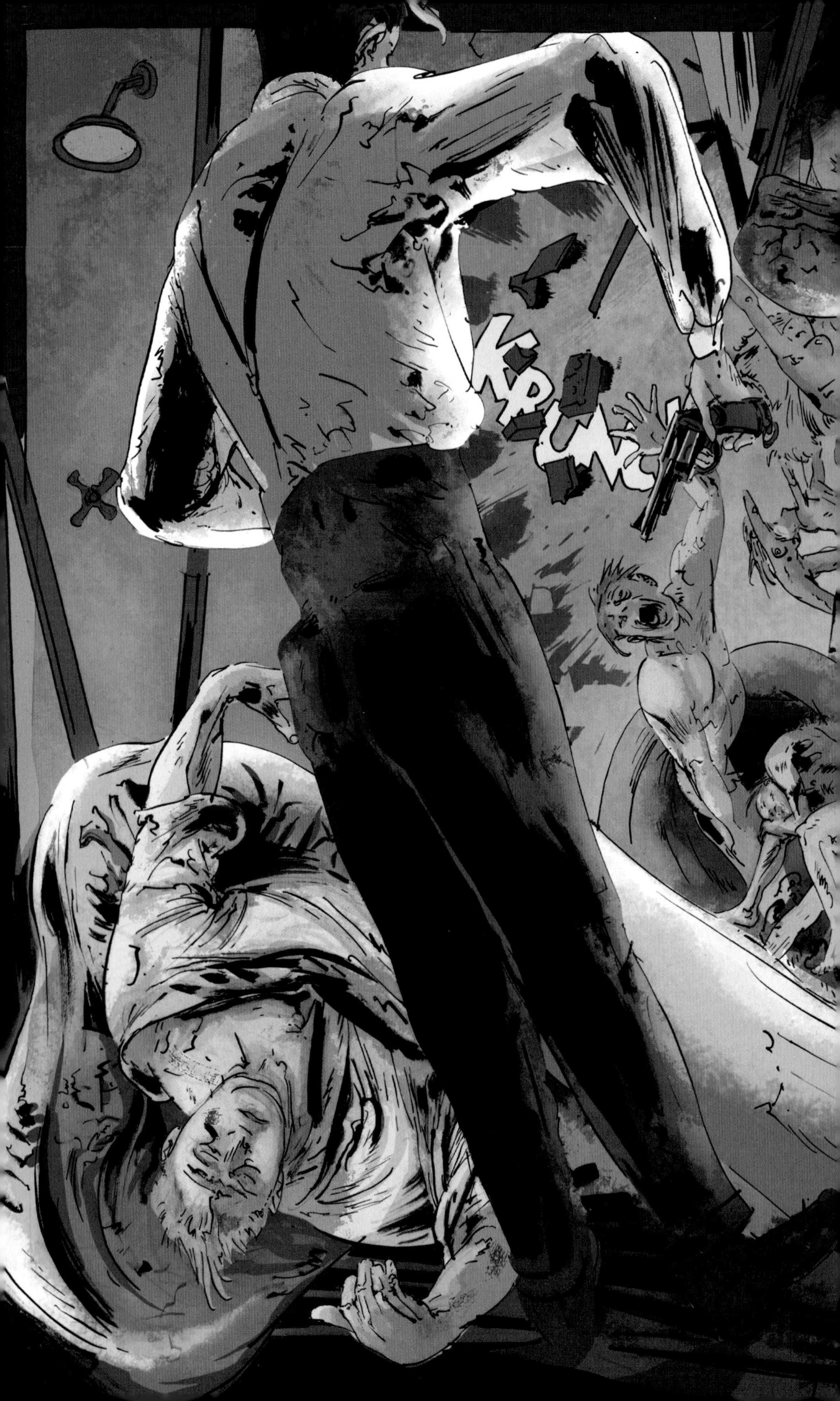
KRUNC

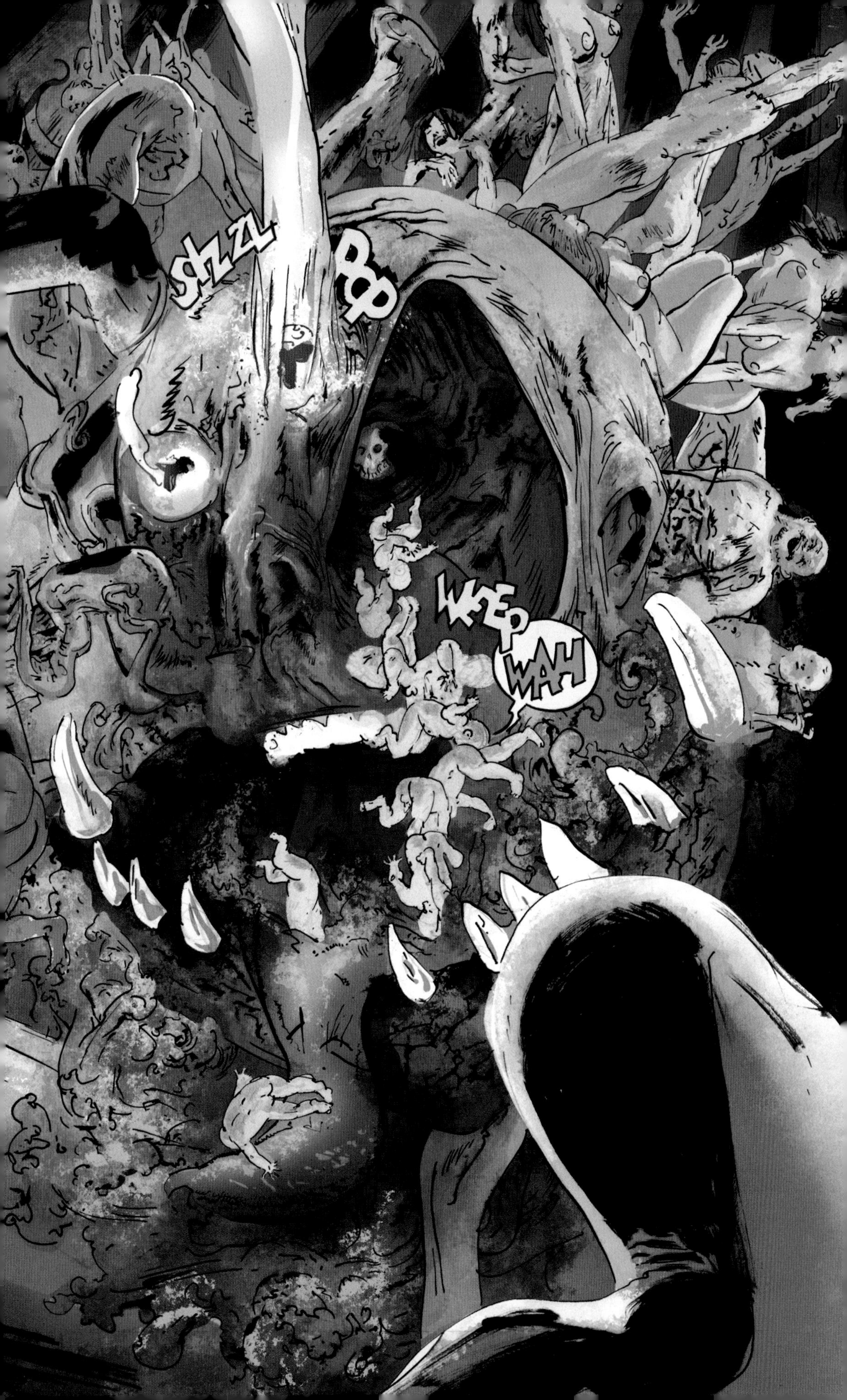
SHZZL
POP
WEEP
WAH

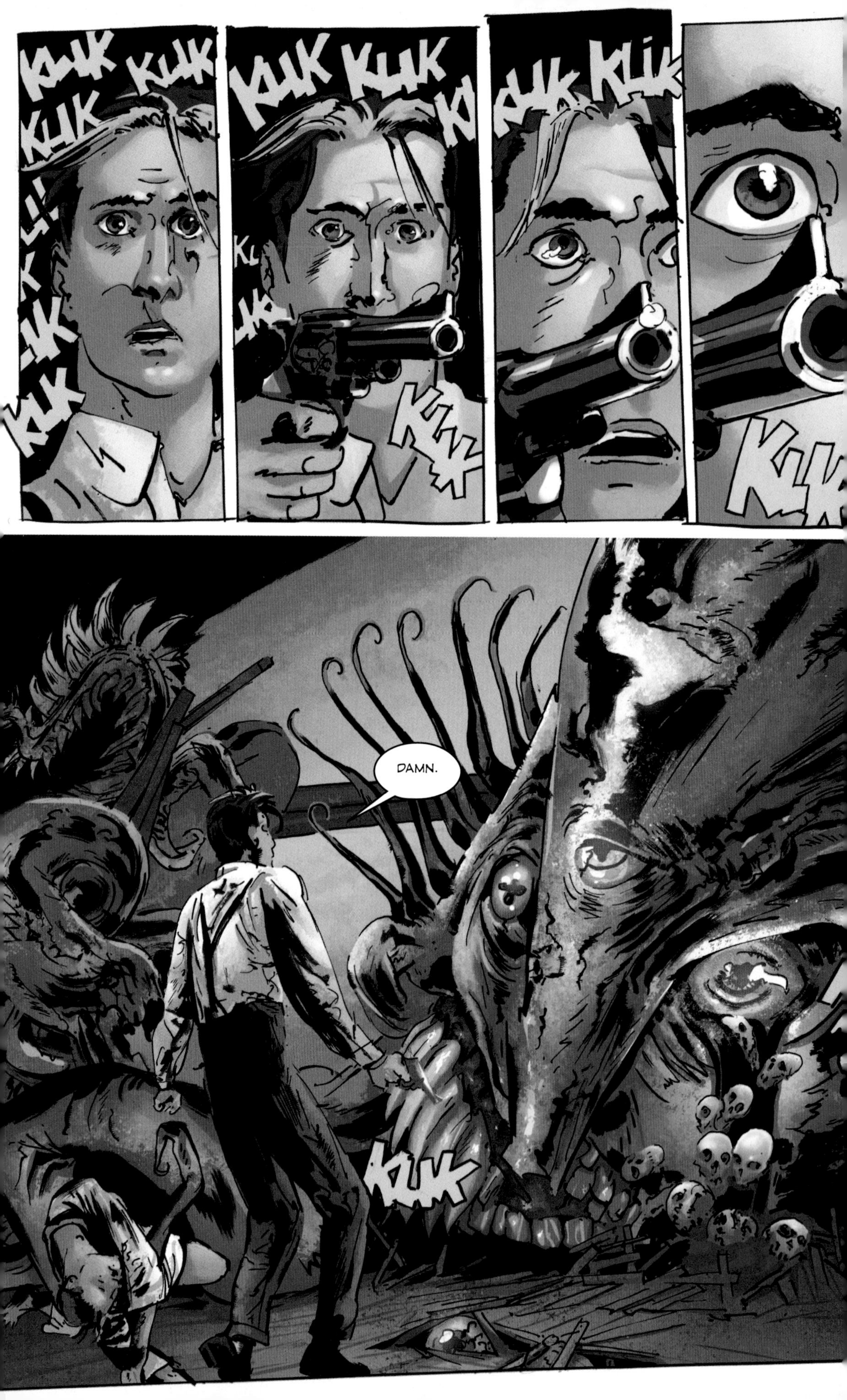
KLIK
KLIK
KLIK
KLIK
KLIK
KLIK
KLIK
KLIK
KLIK
DAMN.
KLIK

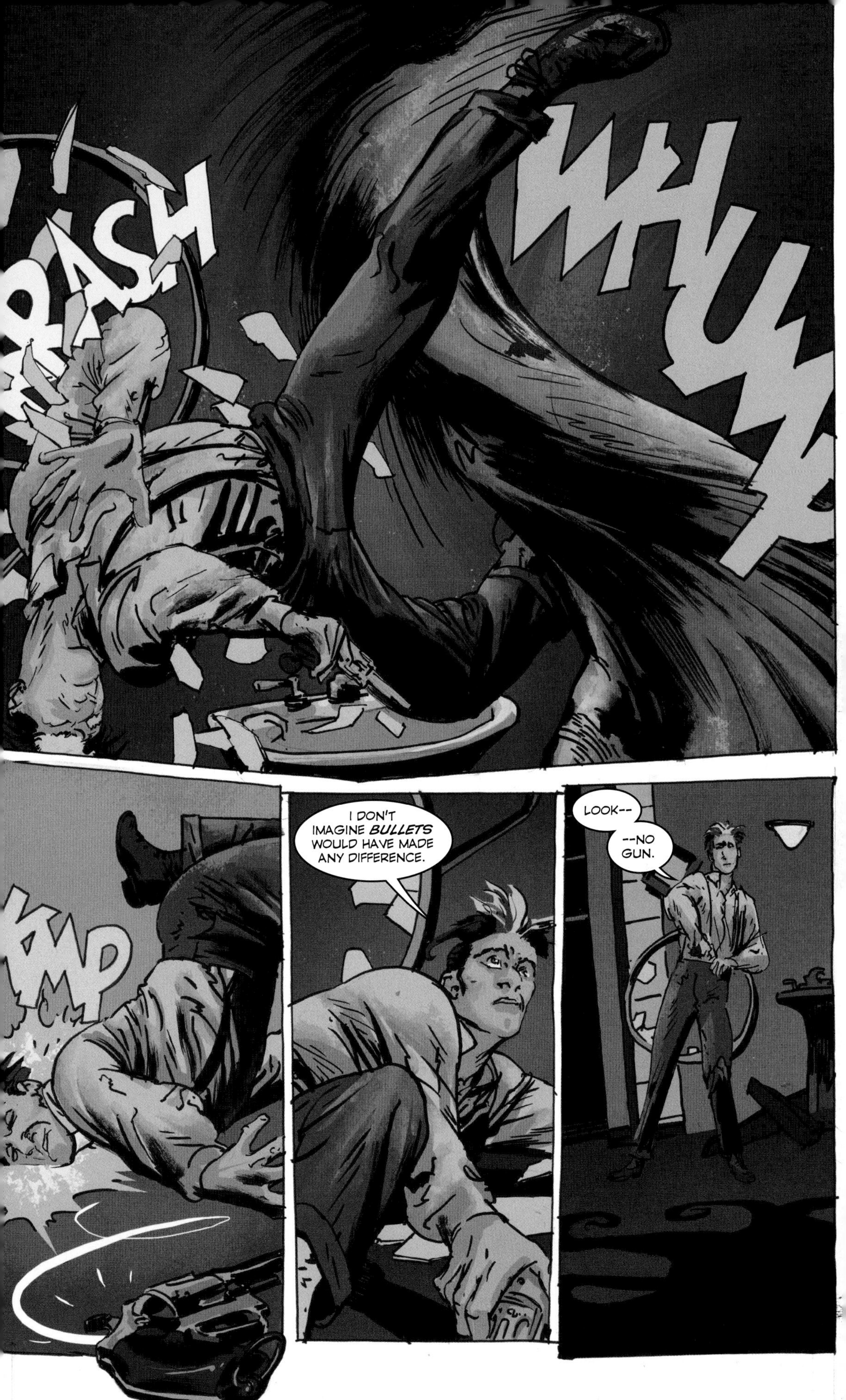
I DON'T IMAGINE *BULLETS* WOULD HAVE MADE ANY DIFFERENCE.
LOOK--
--NO GUN.

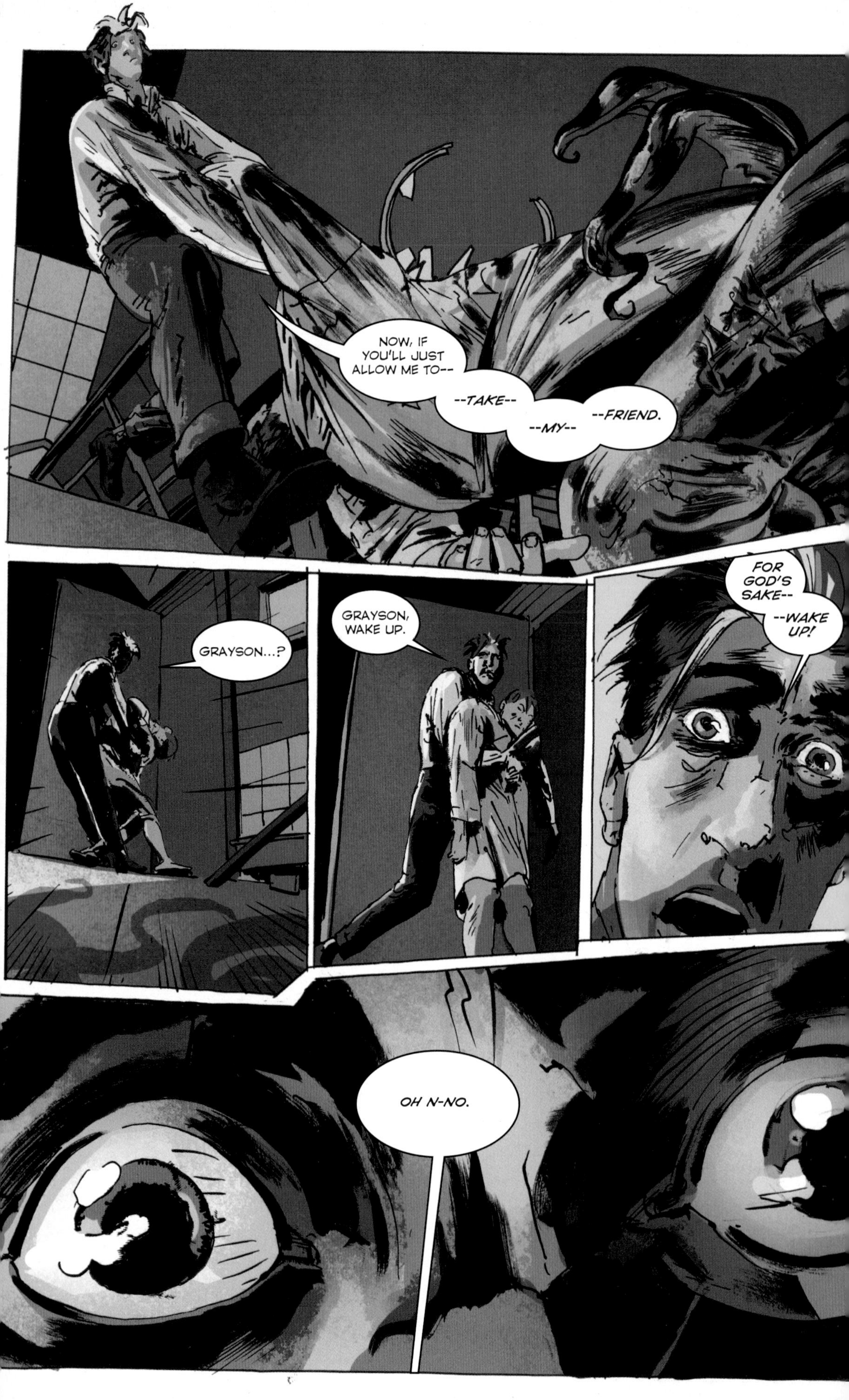
NOW, IF YOU'LL JUST ALLOW ME TO--
--TAKE--
--MY--
--FRIEND.
GRAYSON...?
GRAYSON, WAKE UP.
FOR GOD'S SAKE--
--WAKE UP!
OH N-NO.

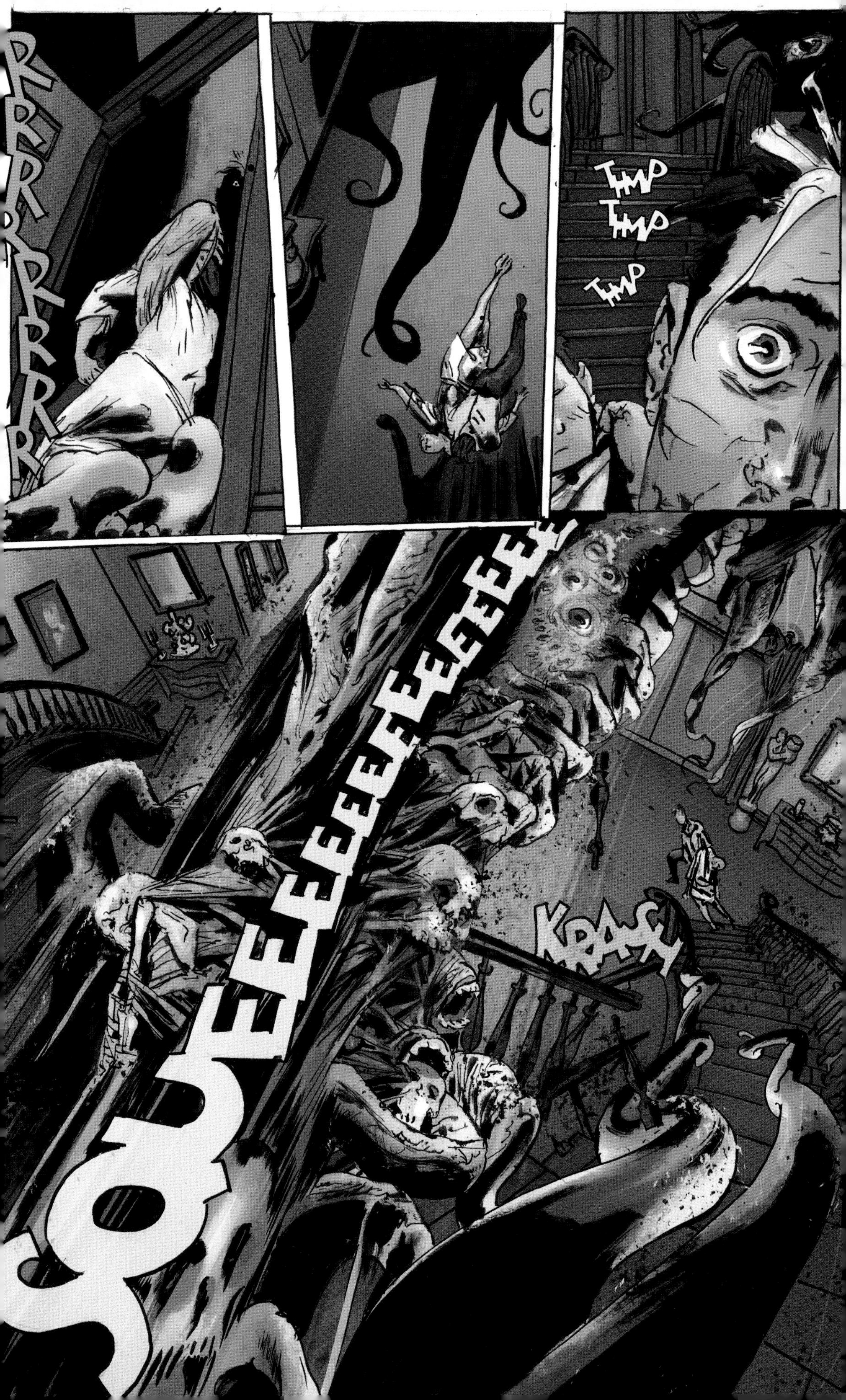
RRRRRRRRR
THMP
THMP
THMP
QUEEEEEEEEEEEEEE
KRASH

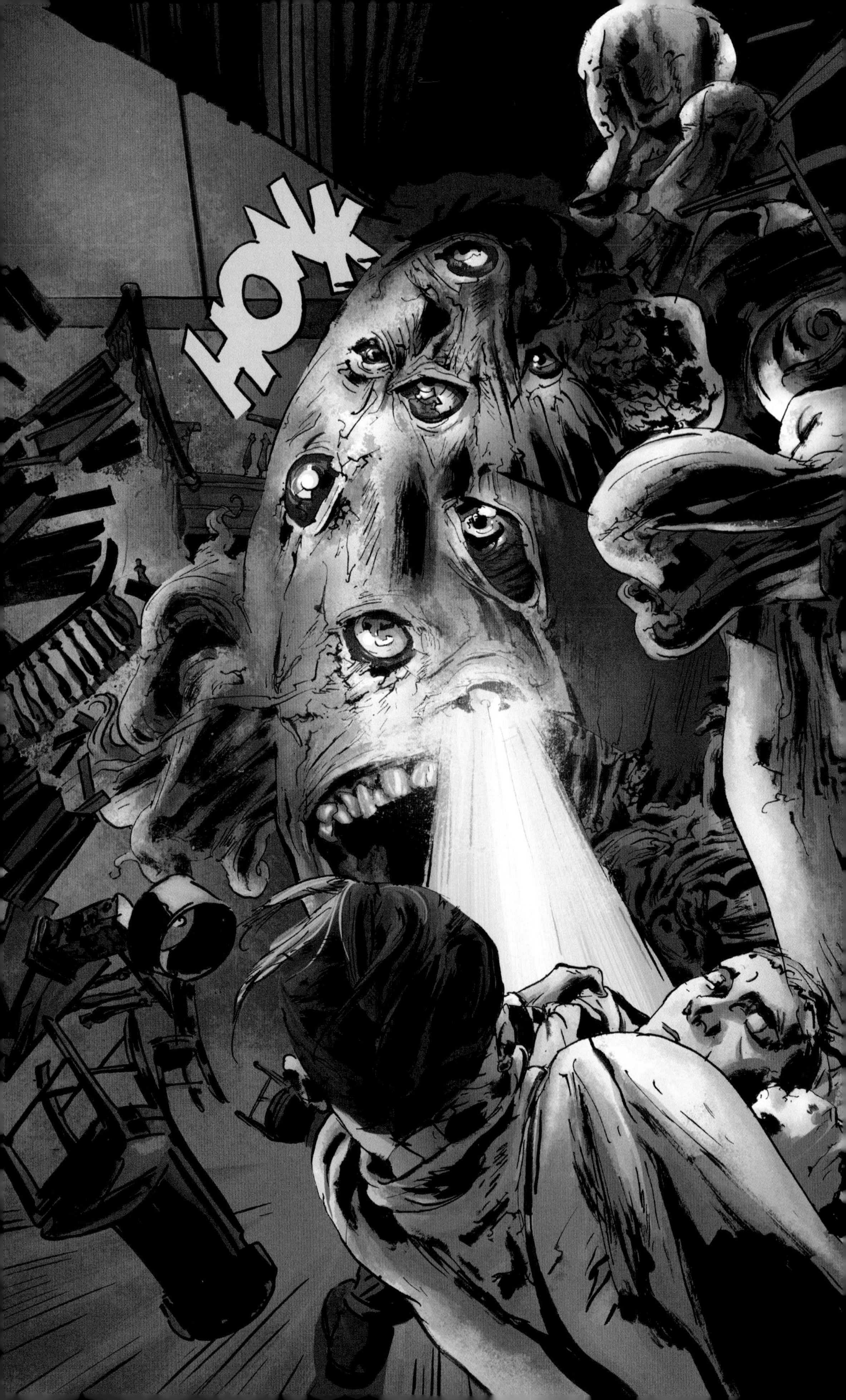
HOK

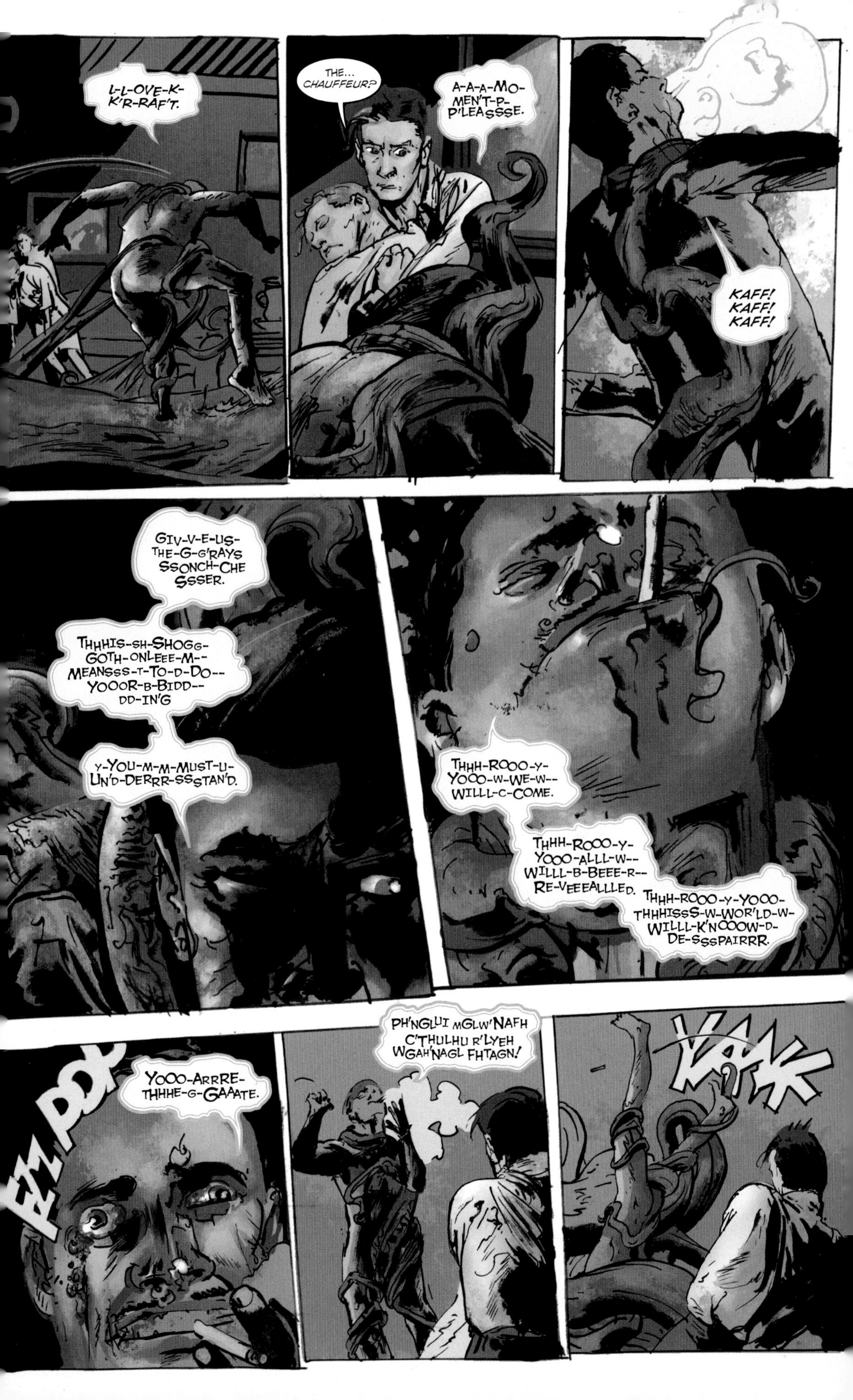
L-L-OVE-K-K'R-RAF'T.
THE... CHAUFFEUR?
A-A-A-MO-MEN'T-P-P'LEASSSE.
KAFF! KAFF! KAFF!
GIV-V-E-US-THE-G-G'RAYS SSONCH-CHE SSSER.
THHHIS-SH-SHOGG-GOTH-ONLEEE-M-MEANSSS-T-TO-D-DO--YOOOR-B-BIDD--DD-IN'G
Y-YOU-M-M-MUST-U-UN'D-DERRR-SSSTAN'D.
THHH-ROOO-Y-YOOO-W-WE-W--WILLL-C-COME.
THHH-ROOO-Y-YOOO-ALLL-W--WILLL-B-BEEE-R--RE-VEEEALLLED.
THHH-ROOO-Y-YOOO-THHHISSS-W-WOR'LD-W-WILLL-K'NOOOW-D-DE-SSSPAIRRR.
YOOO-ARRRE-THHHE-G-GAAATE.
PH'NGLUI MGLW'NAFH C'THULHU R'LYEH WGAH'NAGL FHTAGN!

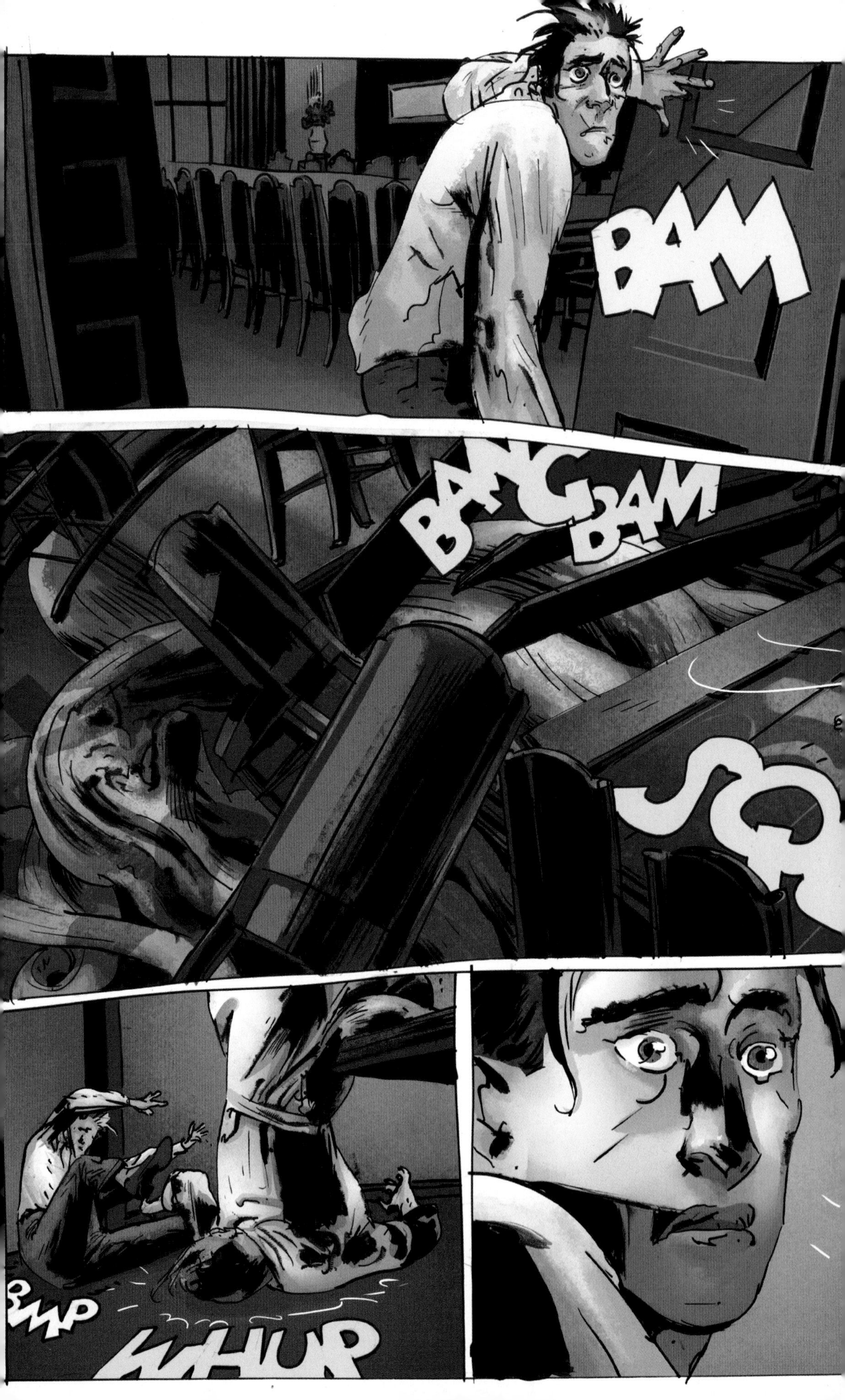
BAM
BANG
BAM
SQ
WHUR

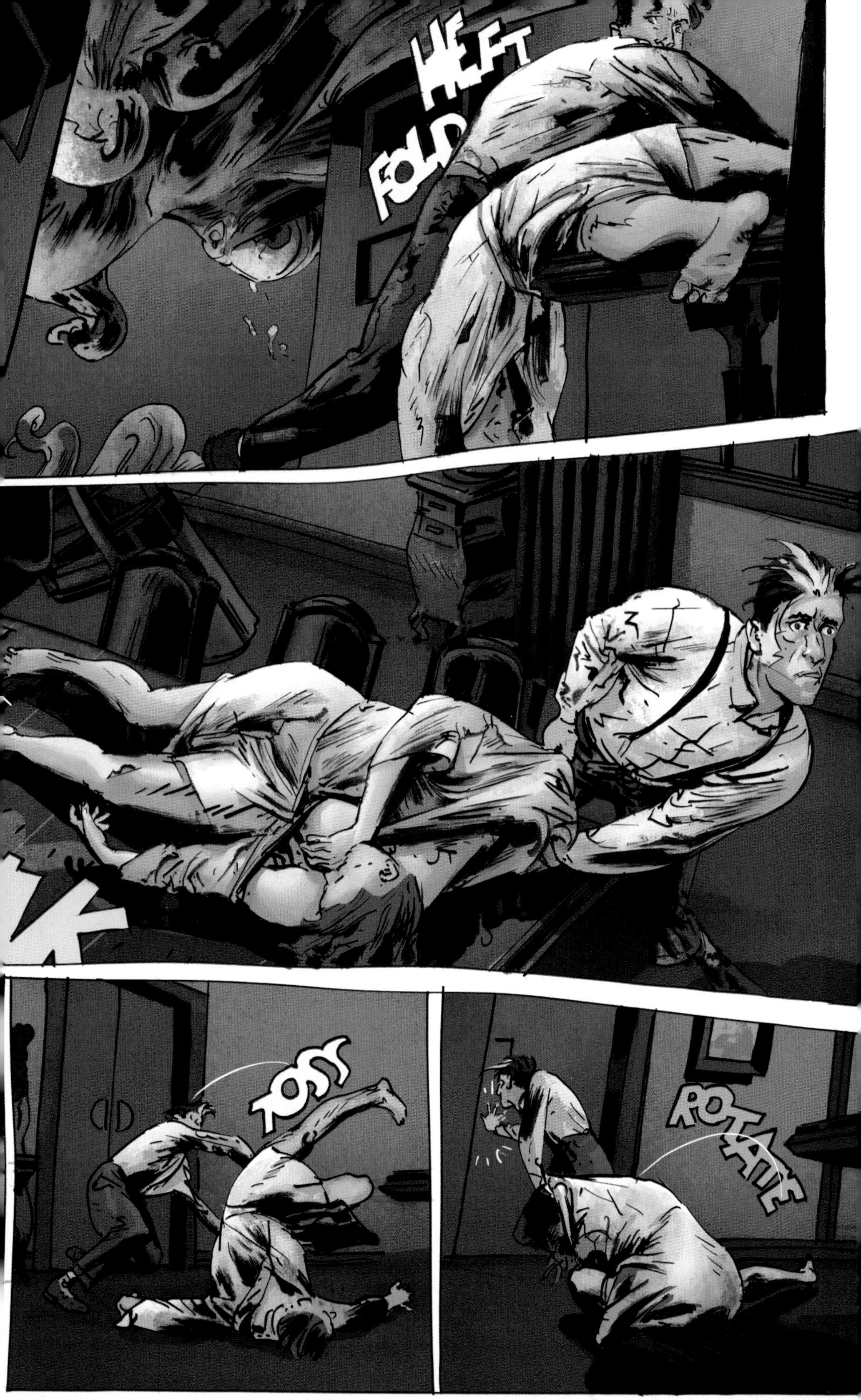
HEFT
FOLD
TOSS
ROTATE

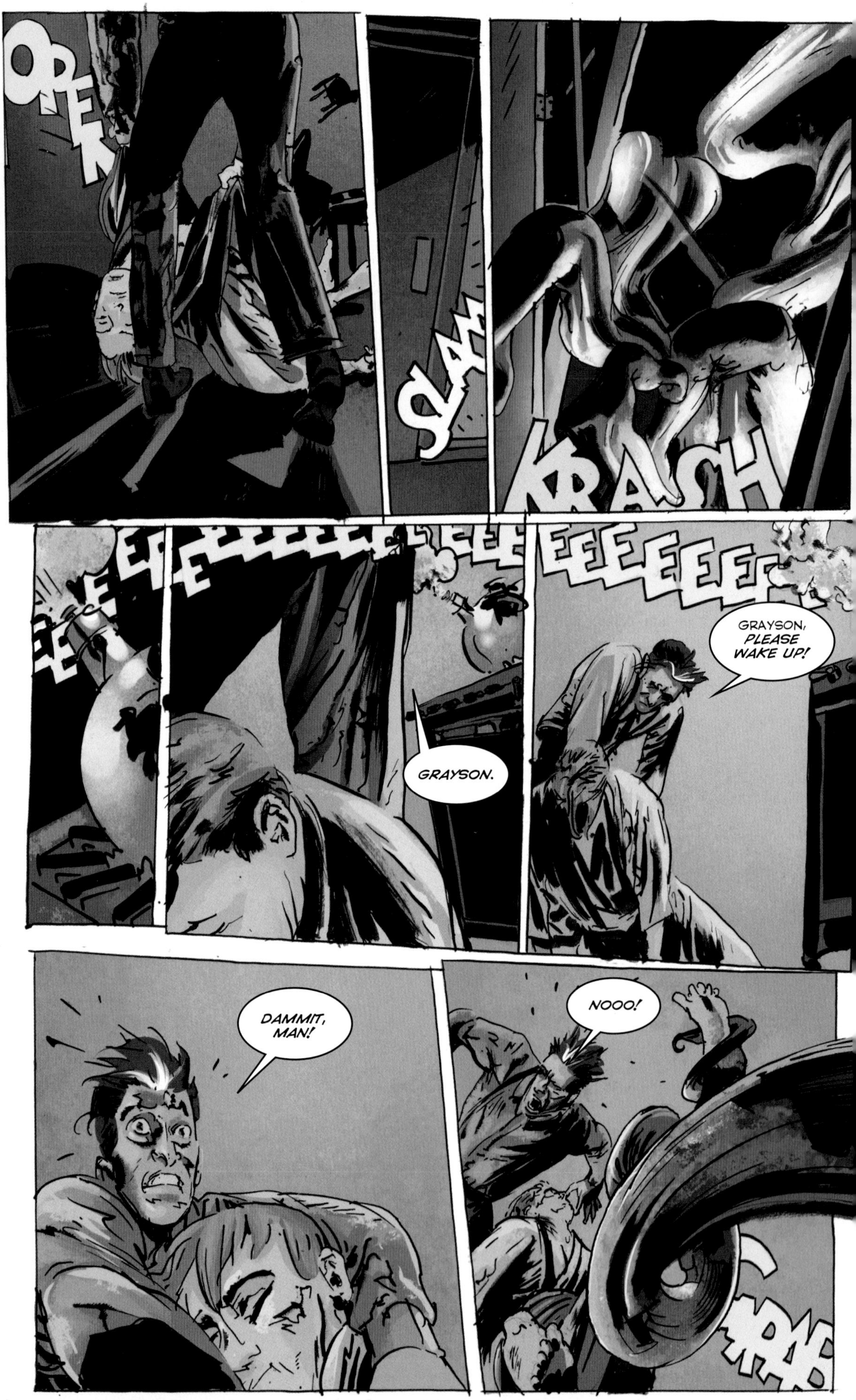

KRASH
GRAYSON.
GRAYSON, PLEASE WAKE UP!
DAMMIT, MAN!
NOOO!

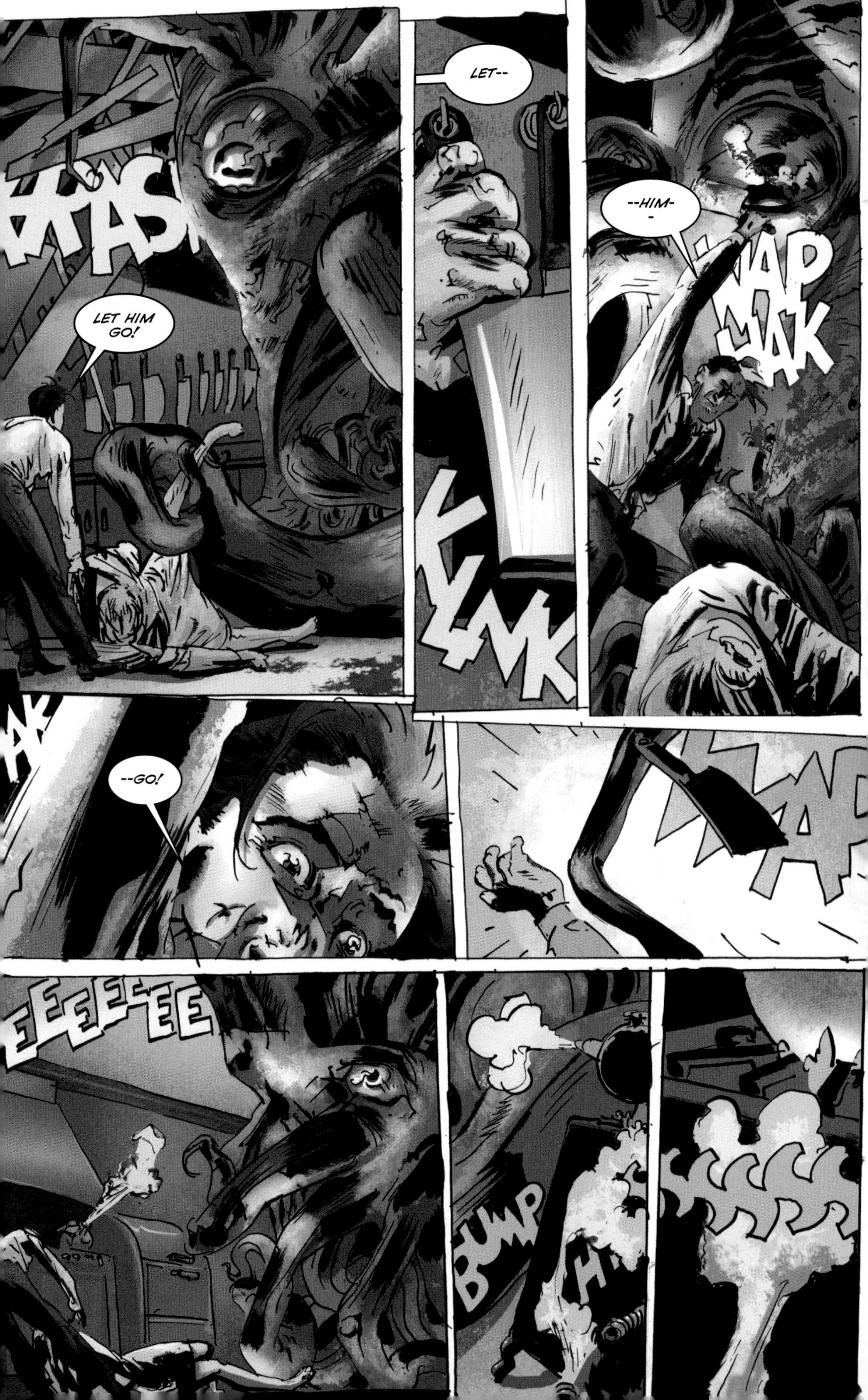
LET HIM GO!
LET--
--HIM--
--GO!
BUMP

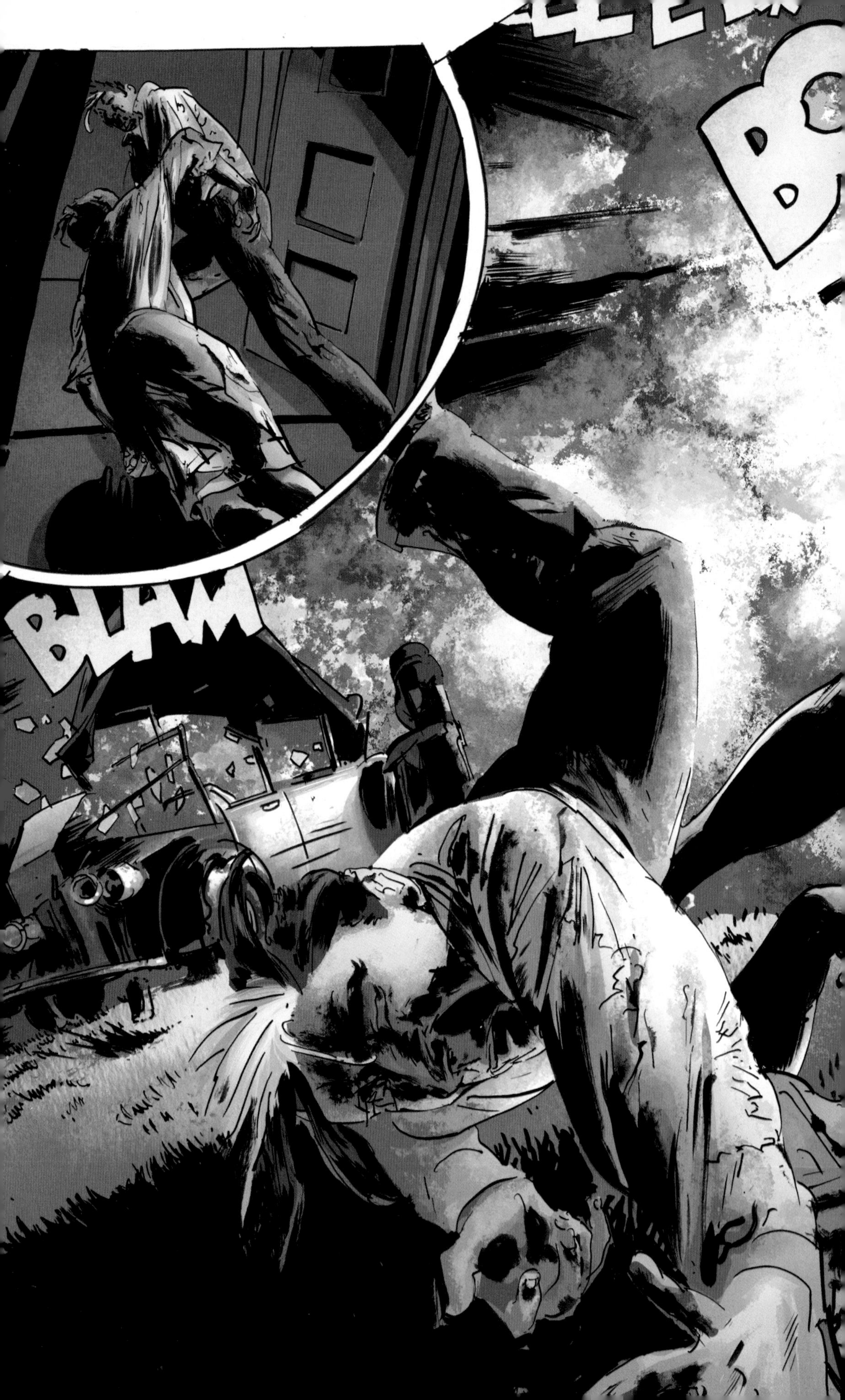
BLAM

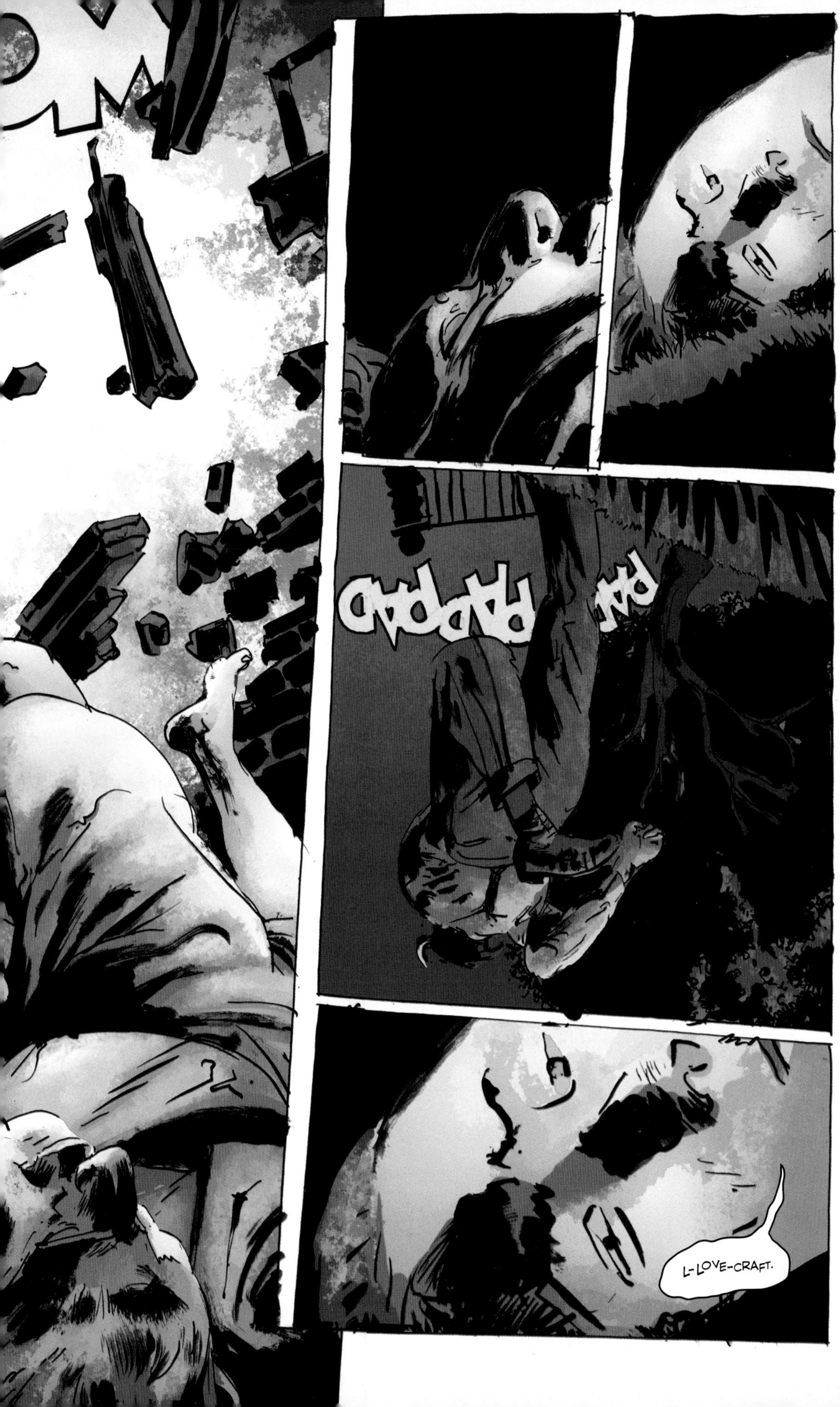
L-LOVE-CRAFT.

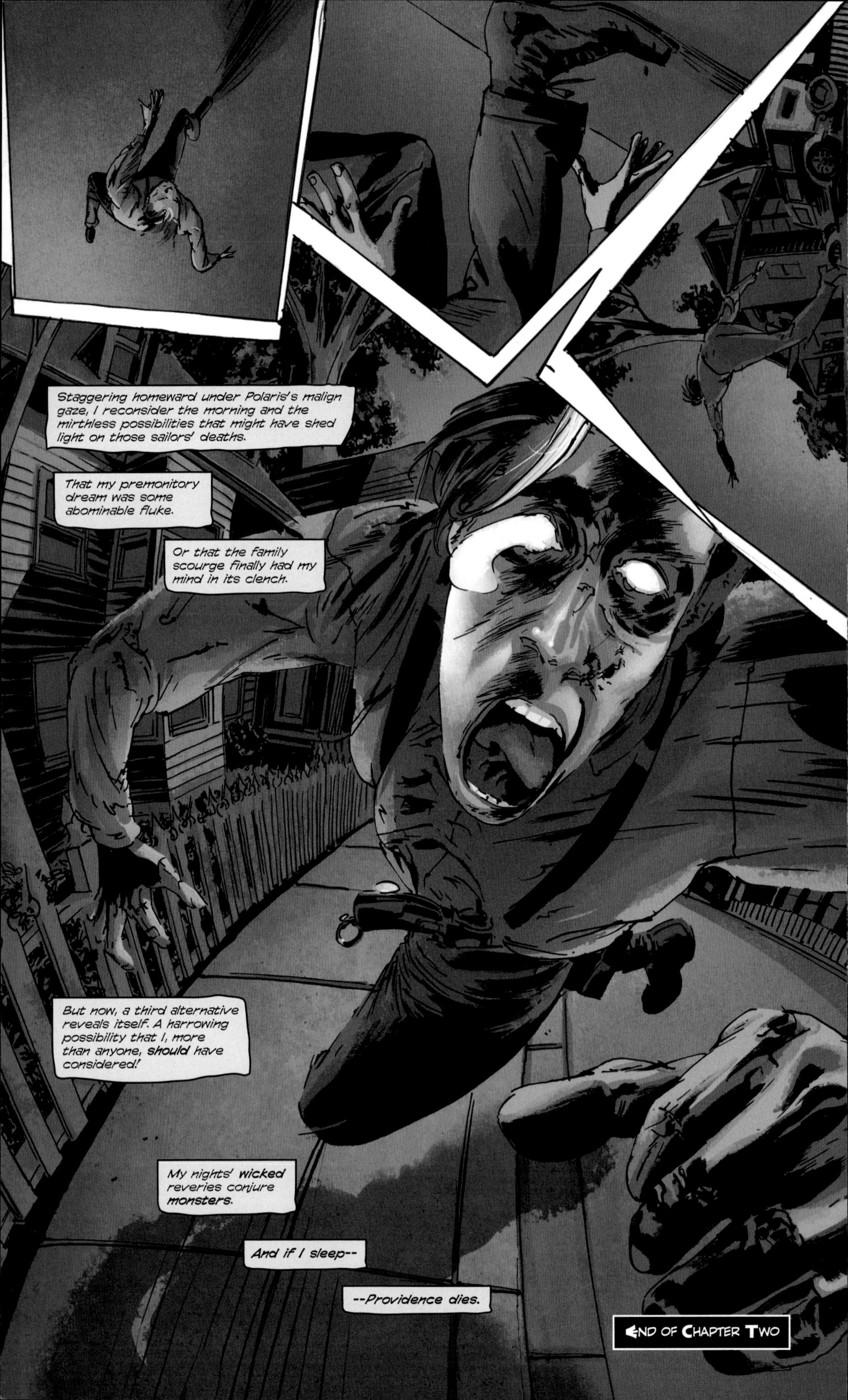
Staggering homeward under Polaris's malign gaze, I reconsider the morning and the mirthless possibilities that might have shed light on those sailors' deaths.
That my premonitory dream was some abominable fluke.
Or that the family scourge finally had my mind in its clench.
But now, a third alternative reveals itself. A harrowing possibility that I, more than anyone, should have considered!
My nights' wicked reveries conjure monsters.
And if I sleep--
--Providence dies.
End of Chapter Two

Obviously one must hold oneself responsible for the evil impulses of one's dreams. In what other way can one deal with them? Unless the content of the dream rightly understood is inspired by alien spirits, it is part of my own being.

No one who, like me, conjures up the most evil of those half-tamed demons that inhabit the human breast, and seeks to wrestle with them, can expect to come through the struggle unscathed.

— SIGMUND FREUD

CHAPTER THREE:
NEVER AGAIN TO SLEEP

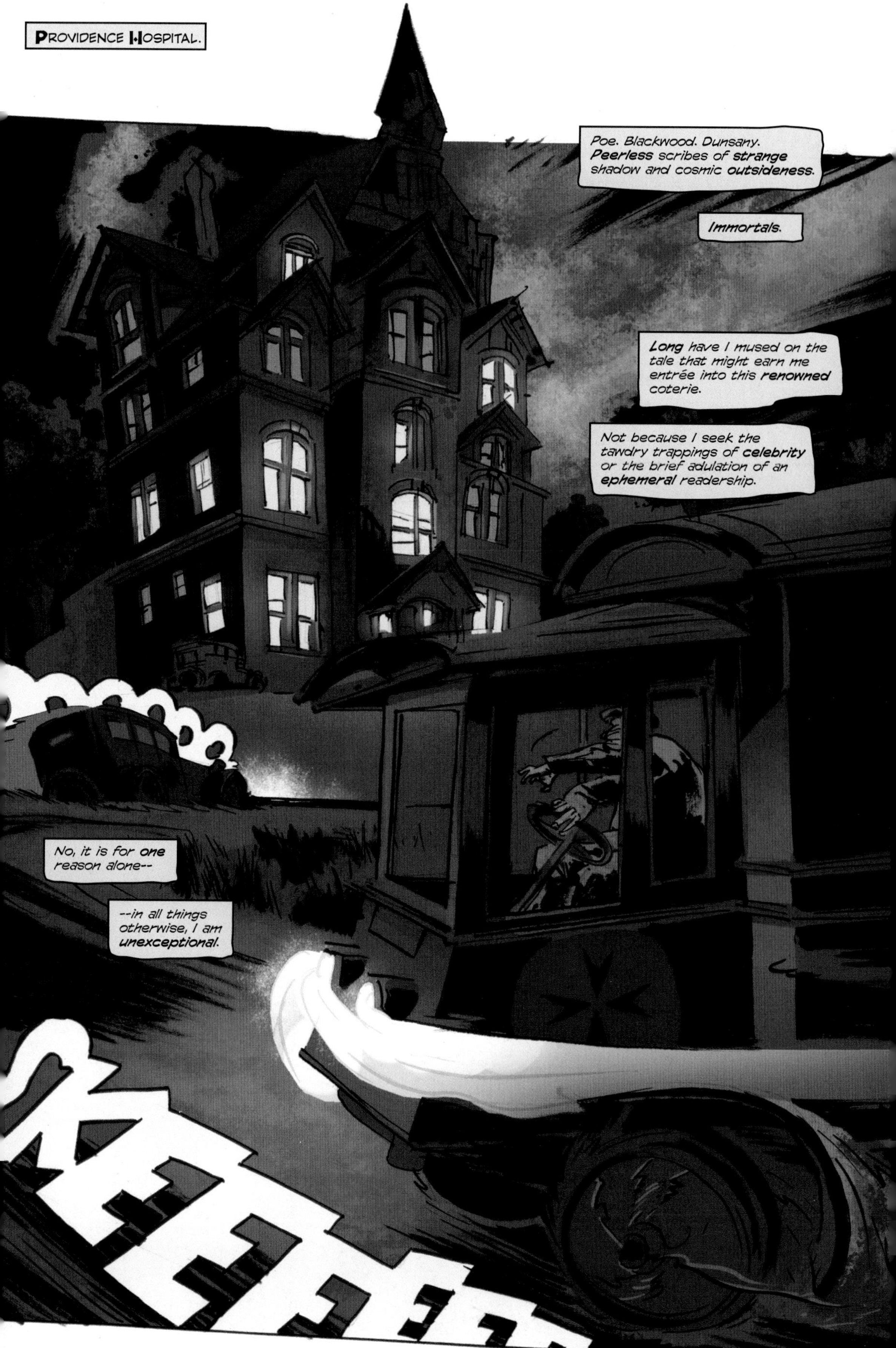
PROVIDENCE HOSPITAL.
Poe. Blackwood. Dunsany. Peerless scribes of strange shadow and cosmic outsideness.
Immortals.
Long have I mused on the tale that might earn me entrée into this renowned coterie.
Not because I seek the tawdry trappings of celebrity or the brief adulation of an ephemeral readership.
No, it is for one reason alone--
--in all things otherwise, I am unexceptional.

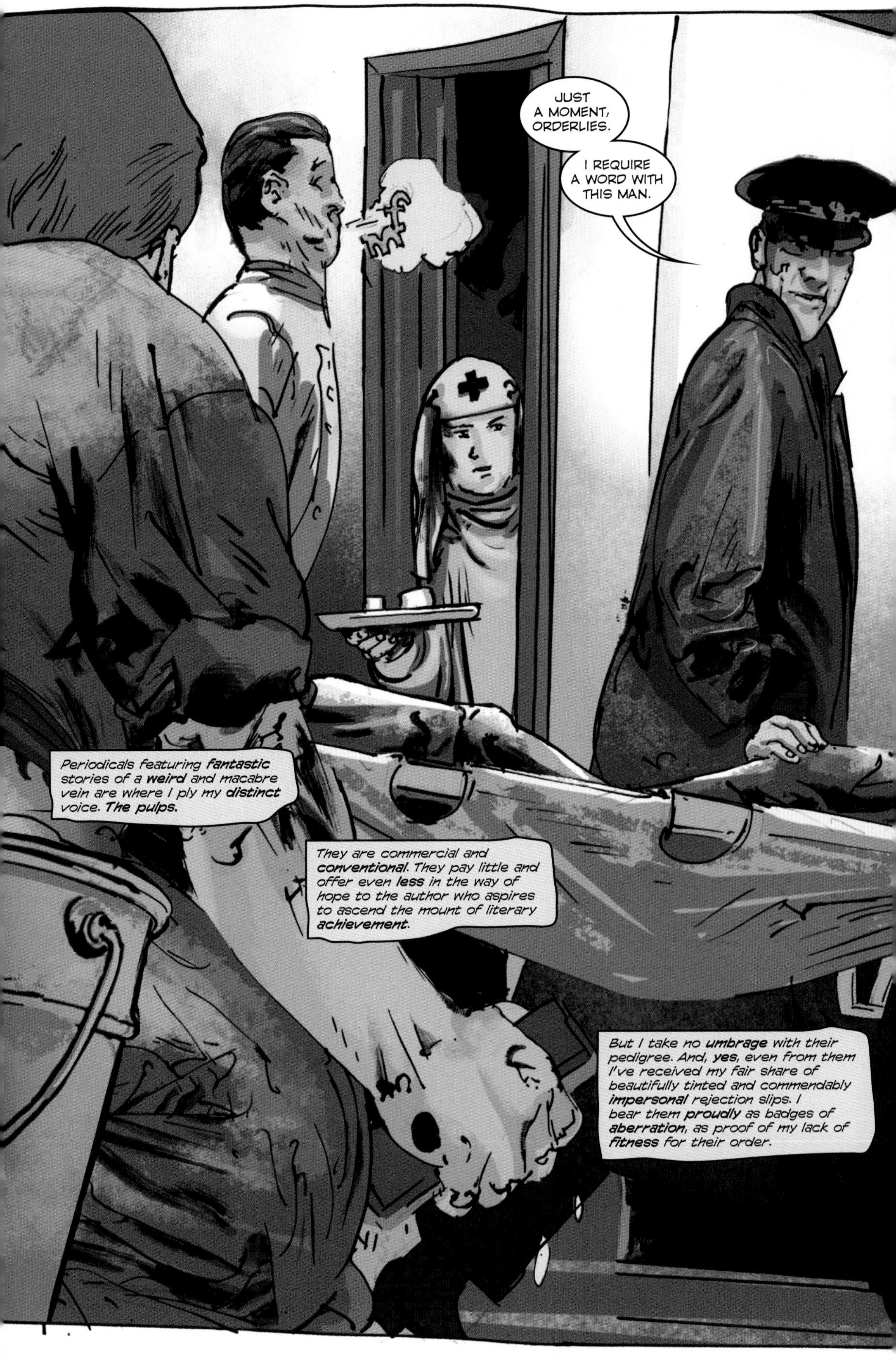
JUST A MOMENT, ORDERLIES.
I REQUIRE A WORD WITH THIS MAN.
Periodicals featuring fantastic stories of a weird and macabre vein are where I ply my distinct voice. The pulps.
They are commercial and conventional. They pay little and offer even less in the way of hope to the author who aspires to ascend the mount of literary achievement.
But I take no umbrage with their pedigree. And, yes, even from them I've received my fair share of beautifully tinted and commendably impersonal rejection slips. I bear them proudly as badges of aberration, as proof of my lack of fitness for their order.

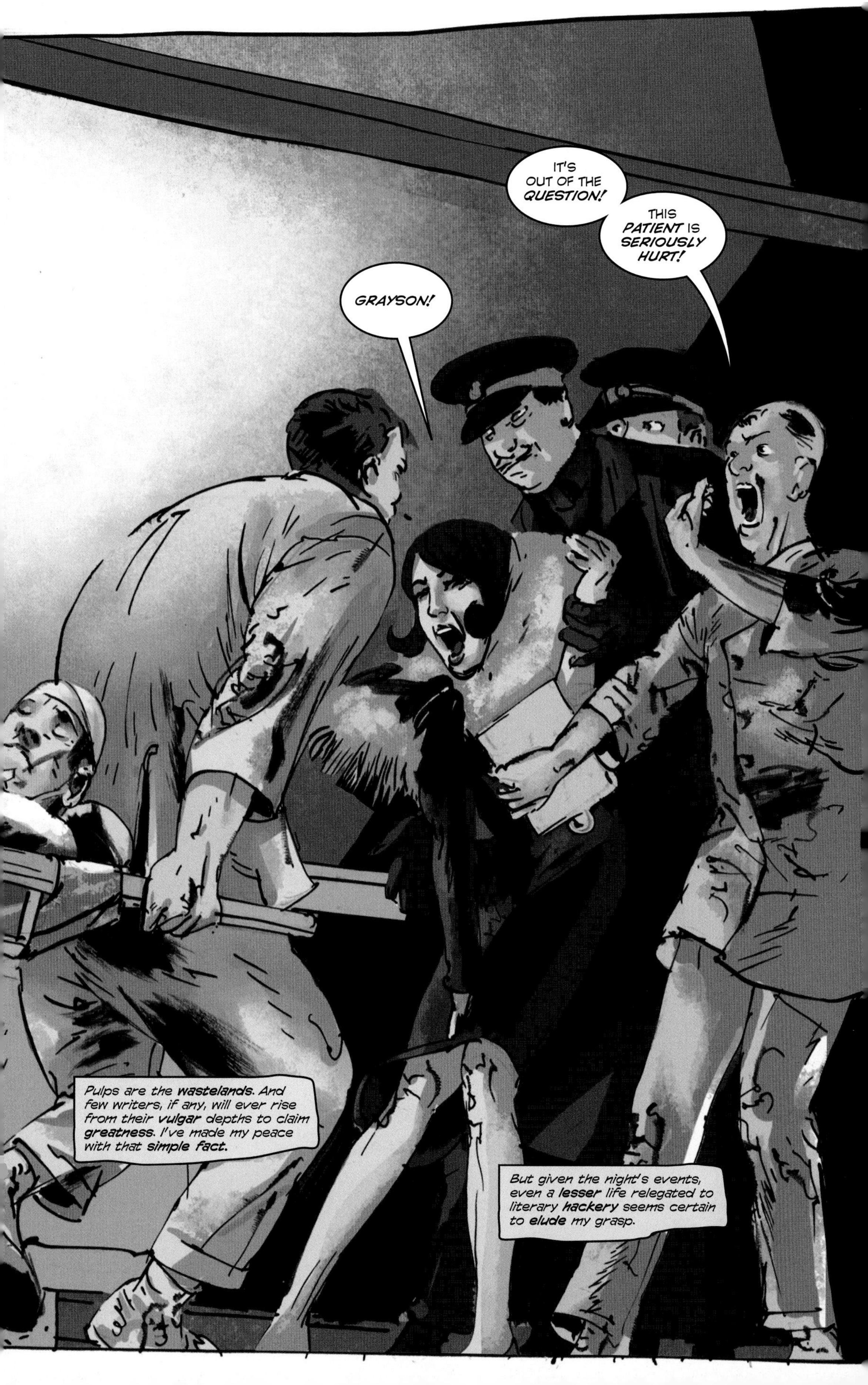

IT'S OUT OF THE QUESTION!
THIS PATIENT IS SERIOUSLY HURT!
GRAYSON!
Pulps are the wastelands. And few writers, if any, will ever rise from their vulgar depths to claim greatness. I've made my peace with that simple fact.
But given the night's events, even a lesser life relegated to literary hackery seems certain to elude my grasp.

Soon, here in Providence and perhaps *beyond*, I will be remembered *eternally* for a *darker accomplishment*.

Over the past two nights, *monsters* have *slithered* out from my dreams to murder *three* and nearly claim a *fourth*.

NO, DOCTOR. YOUR CARE WILL HAVE TO WAIT.

I BELIEVE YOUR PATIENT MAY KNOW THE IDENTITY OF A KILLER.

MR. CHESSER?

COME, MAN. WHO DID THIS? WHO'S RESPONSIBLE?

GIVE ME A NAME.

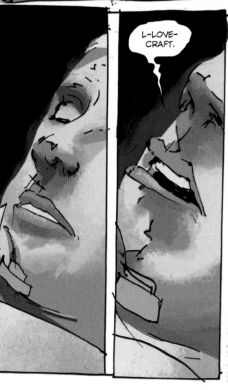

L-LOVE-CRAFT.

My name will *never* be linked to that *writers pantheon*, to those *renowned* conjurers of the *uncanny*--

--but my *fame*... or rather, my *infamy* is secure.

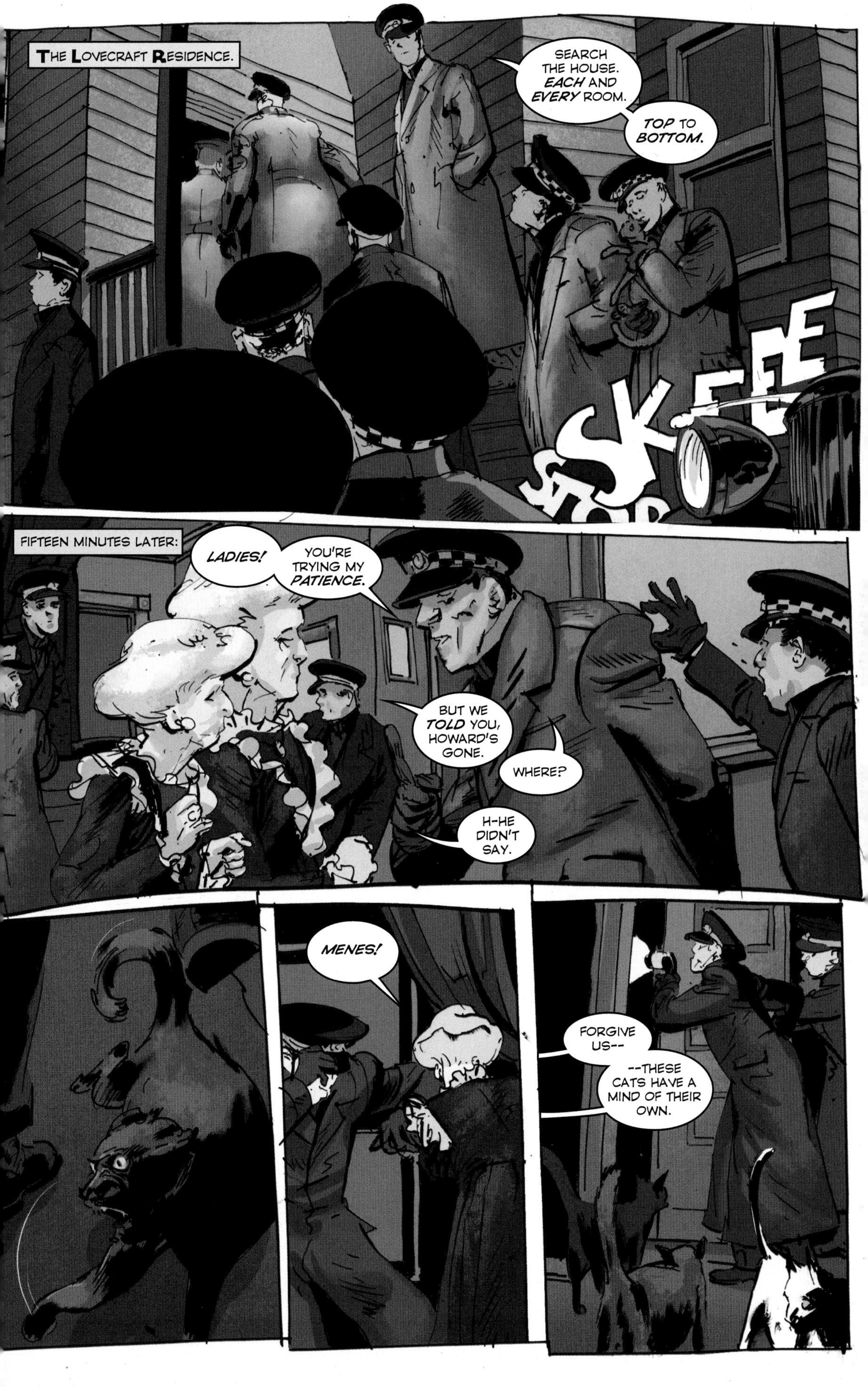
THE LOVECRAFT RESIDENCE.
SEARCH THE HOUSE. EACH AND EVERY ROOM.
TOP TO BOTTOM.
FIFTEEN MINUTES LATER:
LADIES!
YOU'RE TRYING MY PATIENCE.
BUT WE TOLD YOU, HOWARD'S GONE.
WHERE?
H-HE DIDN'T SAY.
MENES!
FORGIVE US--
--THESE CATS HAVE A MIND OF THEIR OWN.

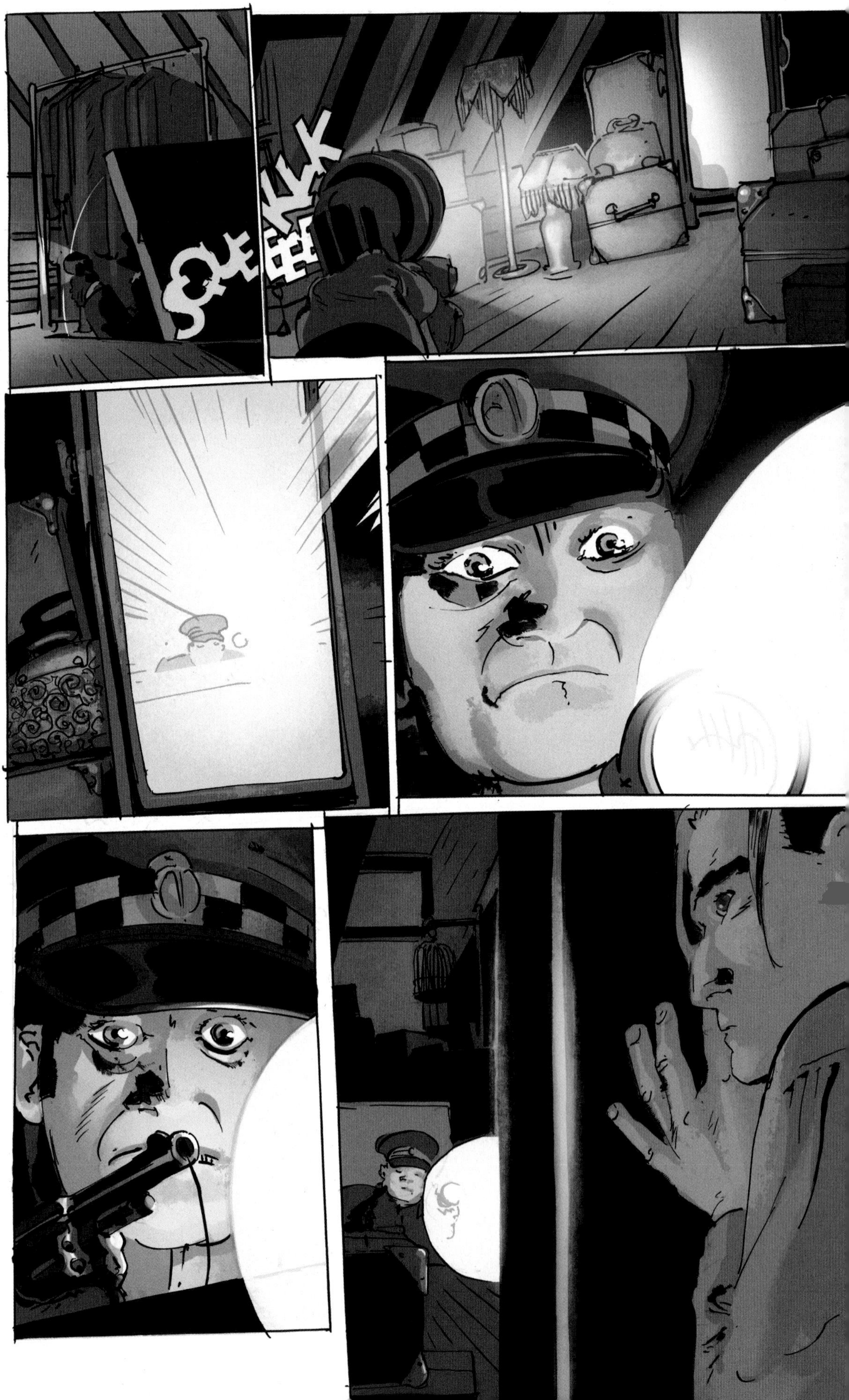
SQUEEEEKKK

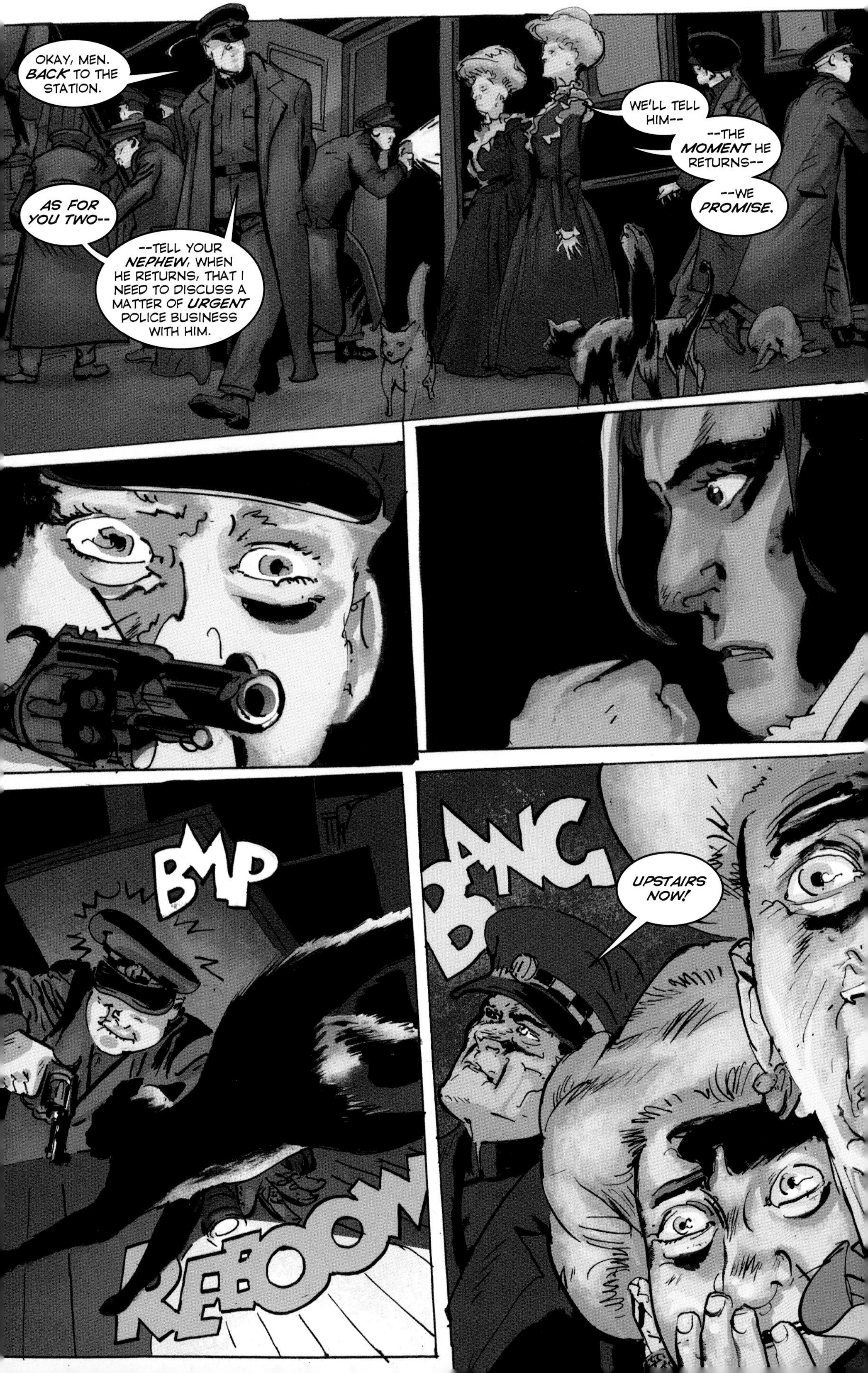
OKAY, MEN. BACK TO THE STATION.
AS FOR YOU TWO--
--TELL YOUR NEPHEW, WHEN HE RETURNS, THAT I NEED TO DISCUSS A MATTER OF URGENT POLICE BUSINESS WITH HIM.
WE'LL TELL HIM--
--THE MOMENT HE RETURNS--
--WE PROMISE.
BMP
KEBOOM
BANG
UPSTAIRS NOW!

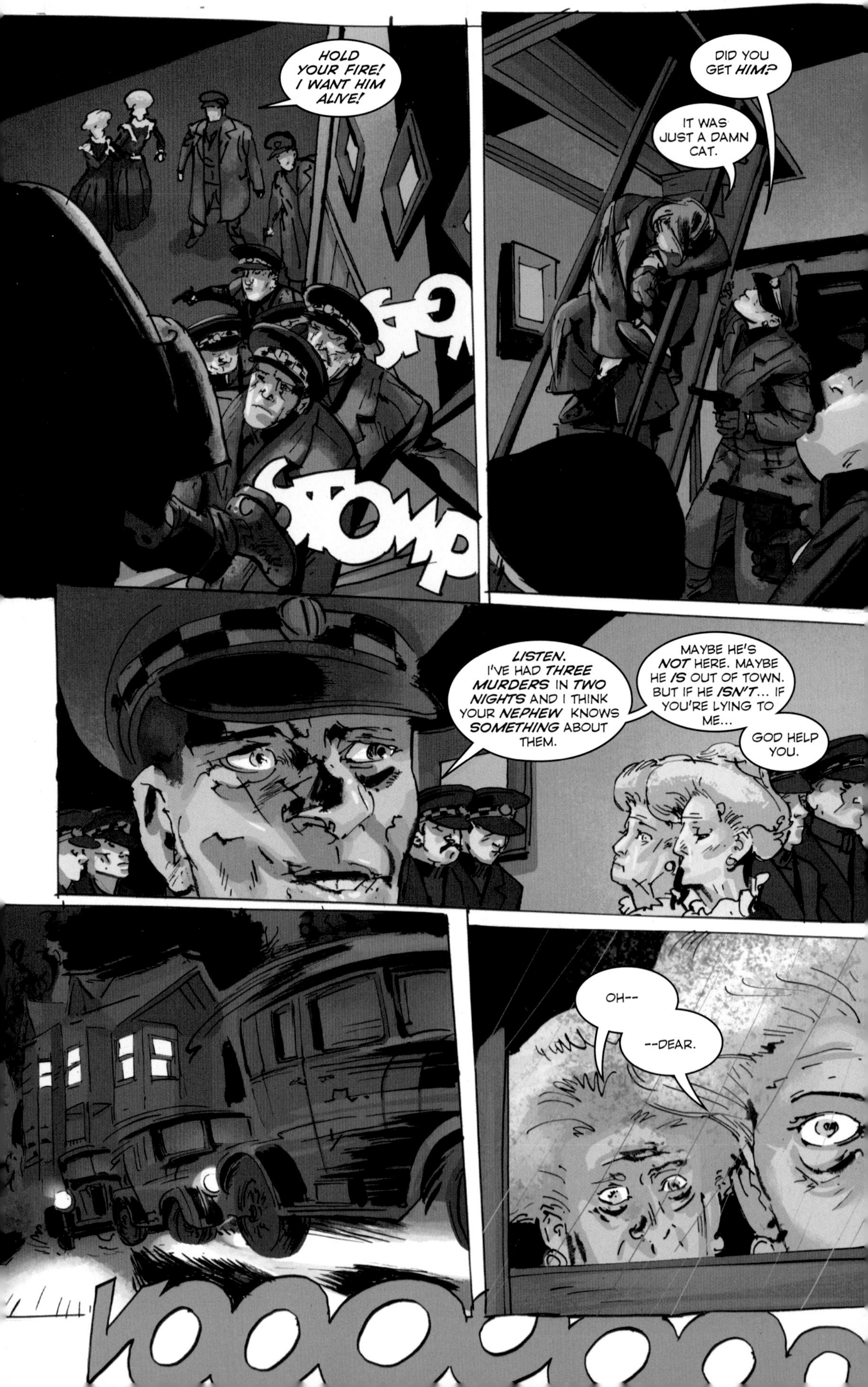
HOLD YOUR FIRE! I WANT HIM ALIVE!
STOMP
DID YOU GET HIM?
IT WAS JUST A DAMN CAT.
LISTEN. I'VE HAD THREE MURDERS IN TWO NIGHTS AND I THINK YOUR NEPHEW KNOWS SOMETHING ABOUT THEM.
MAYBE HE'S NOT HERE. MAYBE HE IS OUT OF TOWN. BUT IF HE ISN'T... IF YOU'RE LYING TO ME...
GOD HELP YOU.
OH--
--DEAR.

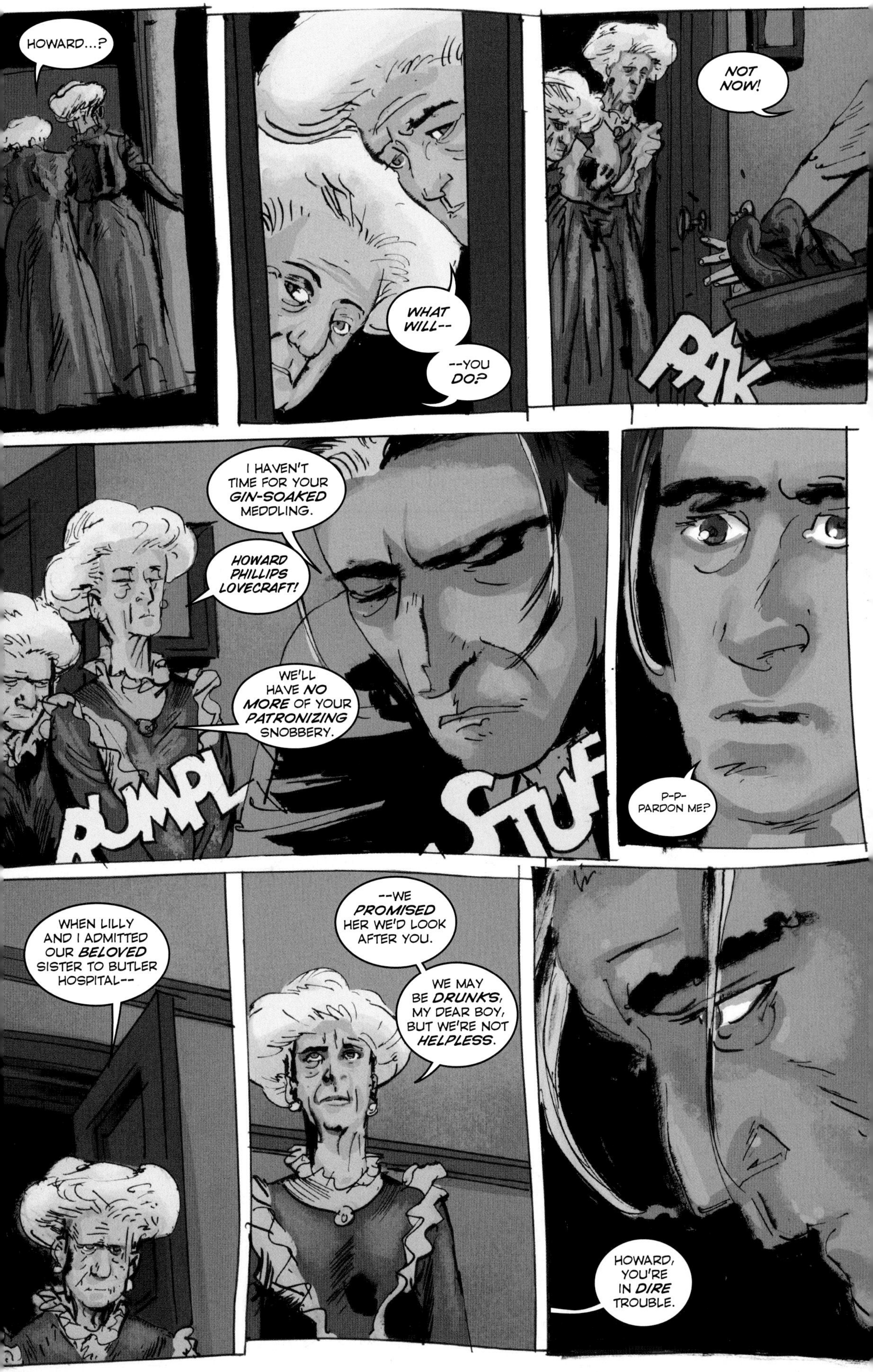
HOWARD...?
WHAT WILL--
--YOU DO?
NOT NOW!
PAK
I HAVEN'T TIME FOR YOUR GIN-SOAKED MEDDLING.
HOWARD PHILLIPS LOVECRAFT!
WE'LL HAVE NO MORE OF YOUR PATRONIZING SNOBBERY.
RUMPL
STUF
P-P-PARDON ME?
WHEN LILLY AND I ADMITTED OUR BELOVED SISTER TO BUTLER HOSPITAL--
--WE PROMISED HER WE'D LOOK AFTER YOU.
WE MAY BE DRUNKS, MY DEAR BOY, BUT WE'RE NOT HELPLESS.
HOWARD, YOU'RE IN DIRE TROUBLE.

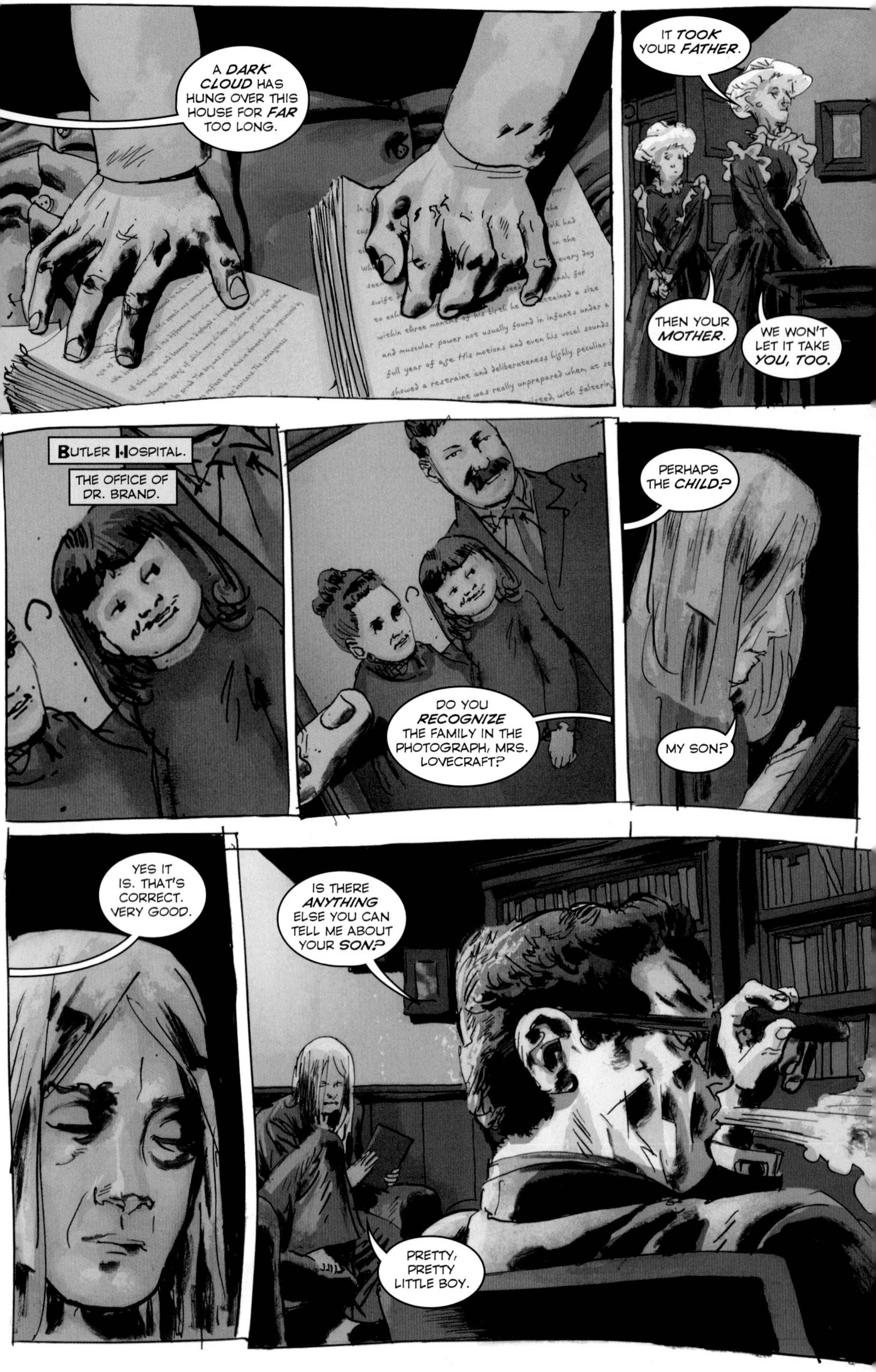

A DARK CLOUD HAS HUNG OVER THIS HOUSE FOR FAR TOO LONG.
IT TOOK YOUR FATHER.
THEN YOUR MOTHER.
WE WON'T LET IT TAKE YOU, TOO.
BUTLER HOSPITAL.
THE OFFICE OF DR. BRAND.
DO YOU RECOGNIZE THE FAMILY IN THE PHOTOGRAPH, MRS. LOVECRAFT?
PERHAPS THE CHILD?
MY SON?
YES IT IS. THAT'S CORRECT. VERY GOOD.
IS THERE ANYTHING ELSE YOU CAN TELL ME ABOUT YOUR SON?
PRETTY, PRETTY LITTLE BOY.

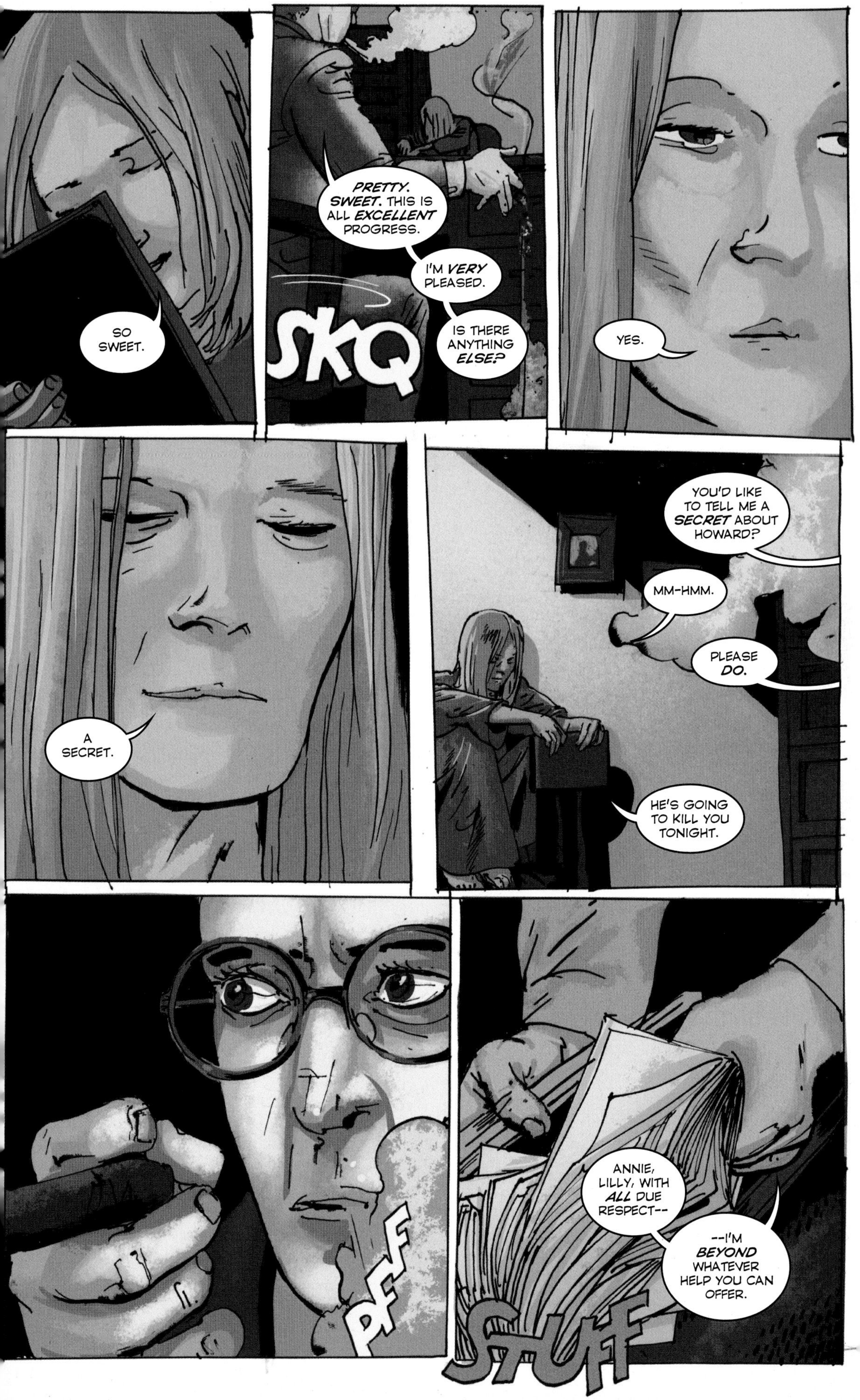
SO SWEET.
PRETTY. SWEET. THIS IS ALL EXCELLENT PROGRESS.
I'M VERY PLEASED.
SKQ
IS THERE ANYTHING ELSE?
YES.
A SECRET.
YOU'D LIKE TO TELL ME A SECRET ABOUT HOWARD?
MM-HMM.
PLEASE DO.
HE'S GOING TO KILL YOU TONIGHT.
PFF
ANNIE, LILLY, WITH ALL DUE RESPECT--
--I'M BEYOND WHATEVER HELP YOU CAN OFFER.
STUFF

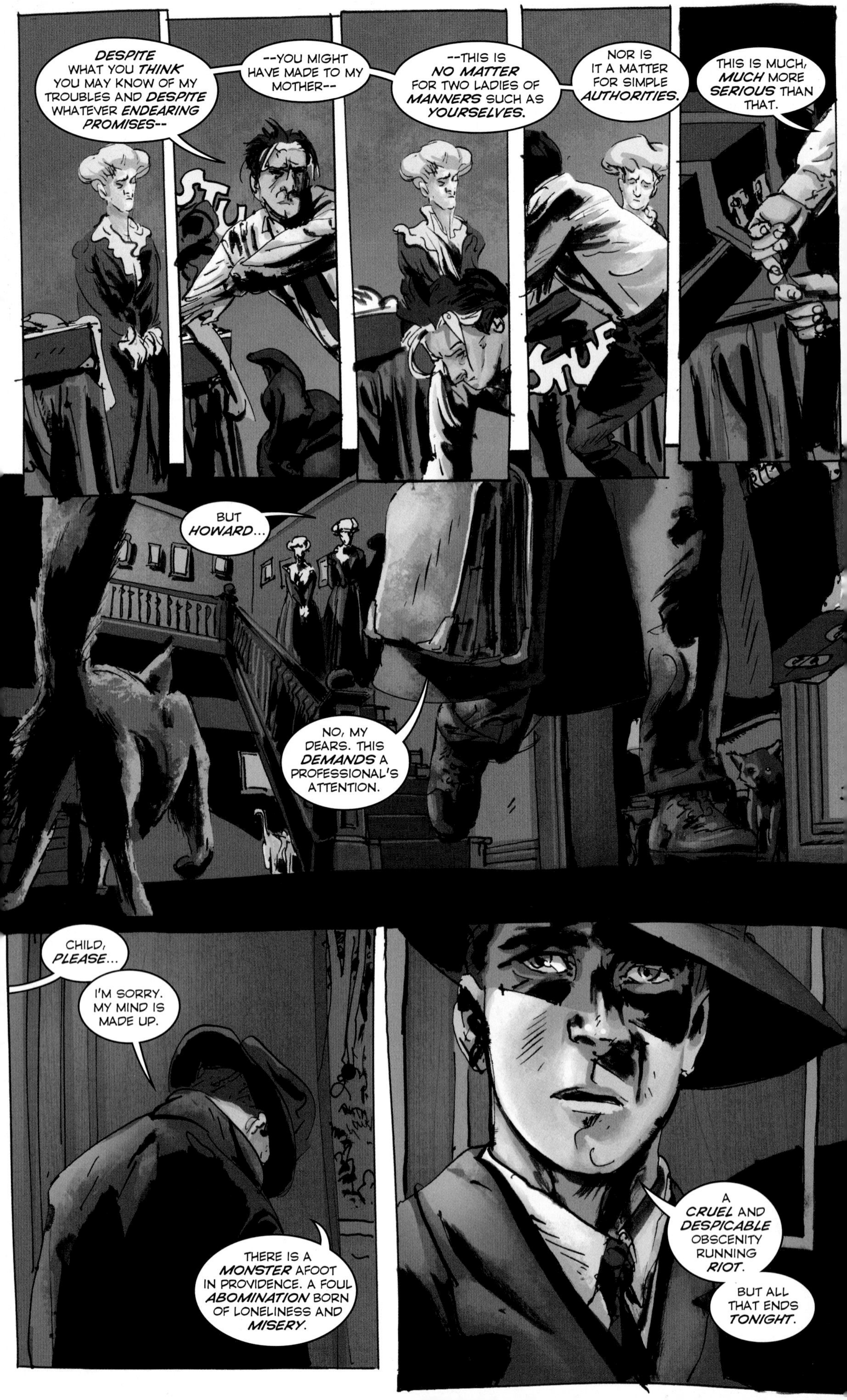
DESPITE WHAT YOU THINK YOU MAY KNOW OF MY TROUBLES AND DESPITE WHATEVER ENDEARING PROMISES--
--YOU MIGHT HAVE MADE TO MY MOTHER--
STU
--THIS IS NO MATTER FOR TWO LADIES OF MANNERS SUCH AS YOURSELVES.
NOR IS IT A MATTER FOR SIMPLE AUTHORITIES.
STUF
THIS IS MUCH, MUCH MORE SERIOUS THAN THAT.
BUT HOWARD...
NO, MY DEARS. THIS DEMANDS A PROFESSIONAL'S ATTENTION.
CHILD, PLEASE...
I'M SORRY. MY MIND IS MADE UP.
THERE IS A MONSTER AFOOT IN PROVIDENCE. A FOUL ABOMINATION BORN OF LONELINESS AND MISERY.
A CRUEL AND DESPICABLE OBSCENITY RUNNING RIOT.
BUT ALL THAT ENDS TONIGHT.

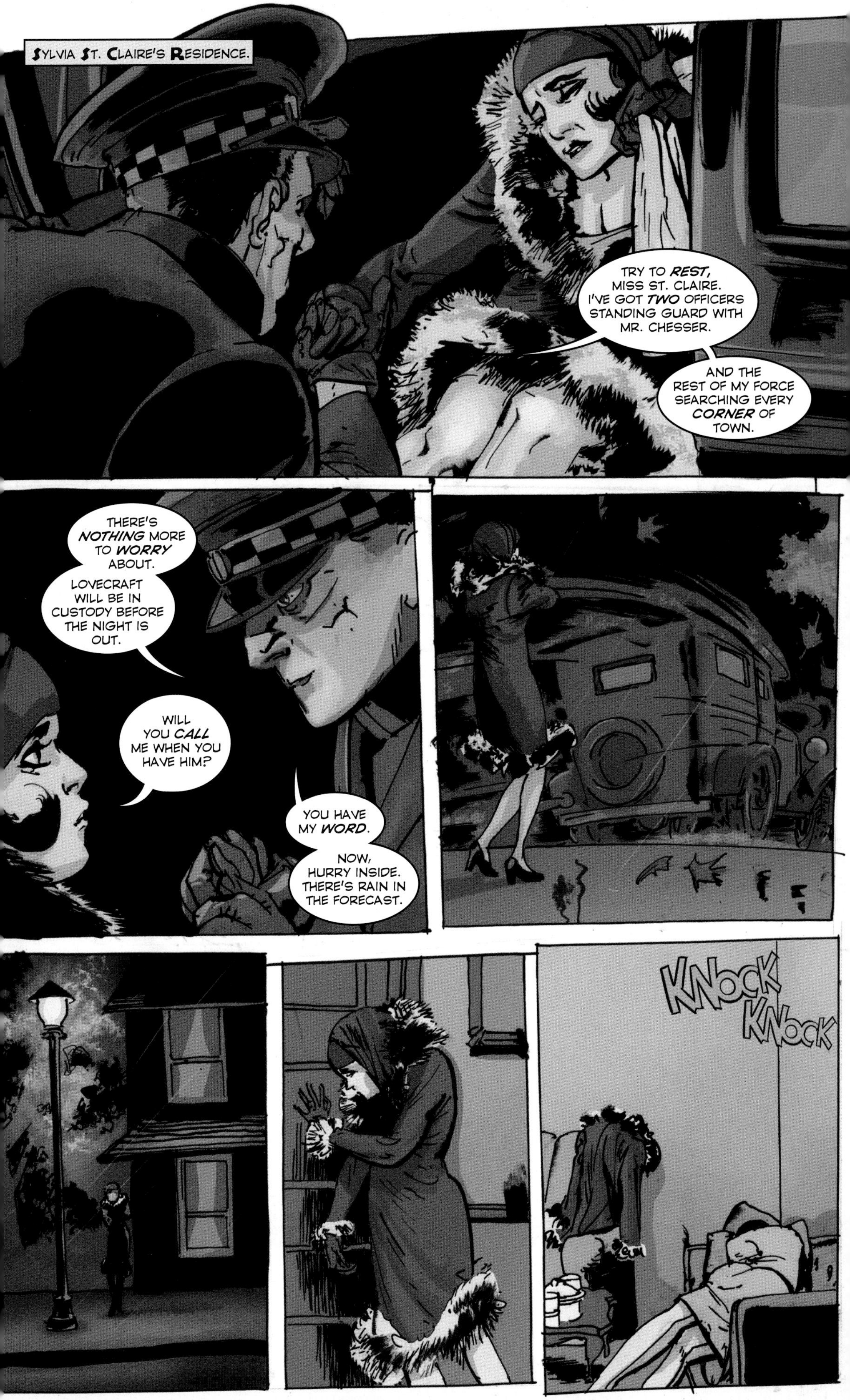
SYLVIA ST. CLAIRE'S RESIDENCE.
TRY TO REST, MISS ST. CLAIRE. I'VE GOT TWO OFFICERS STANDING GUARD WITH MR. CHESSER.
AND THE REST OF MY FORCE SEARCHING EVERY CORNER OF TOWN.
THERE'S NOTHING MORE TO WORRY ABOUT.
LOVECRAFT WILL BE IN CUSTODY BEFORE THE NIGHT IS OUT.
WILL YOU CALL ME WHEN YOU HAVE HIM?
YOU HAVE MY WORD.
NOW, HURRY INSIDE. THERE'S RAIN IN THE FORECAST.
KNOCK KNOCK

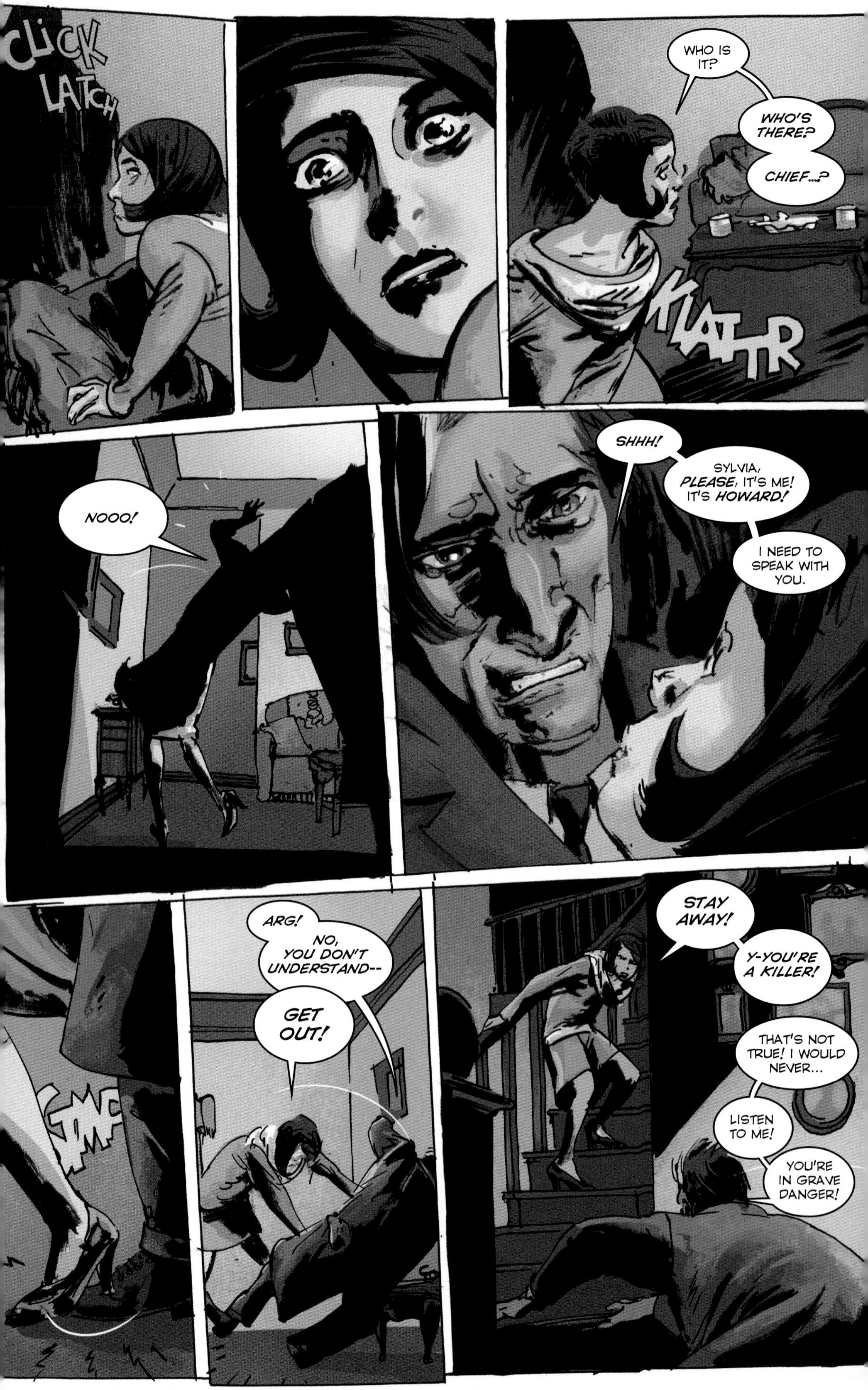
CLICK
LATCH
WHO IS IT?
WHO'S THERE?
CHIEF...?
KLATTR
NOOO!
SHHH!
SYLVIA, PLEASE, IT'S ME! IT'S HOWARD!
I NEED TO SPEAK WITH YOU.
ARG!
NO, YOU DON'T UNDERSTAND--
GET OUT!
STAY AWAY!
Y-YOU'RE A KILLER!
THAT'S NOT TRUE! I WOULD NEVER...
LISTEN TO ME!
YOU'RE IN GRAVE DANGER!

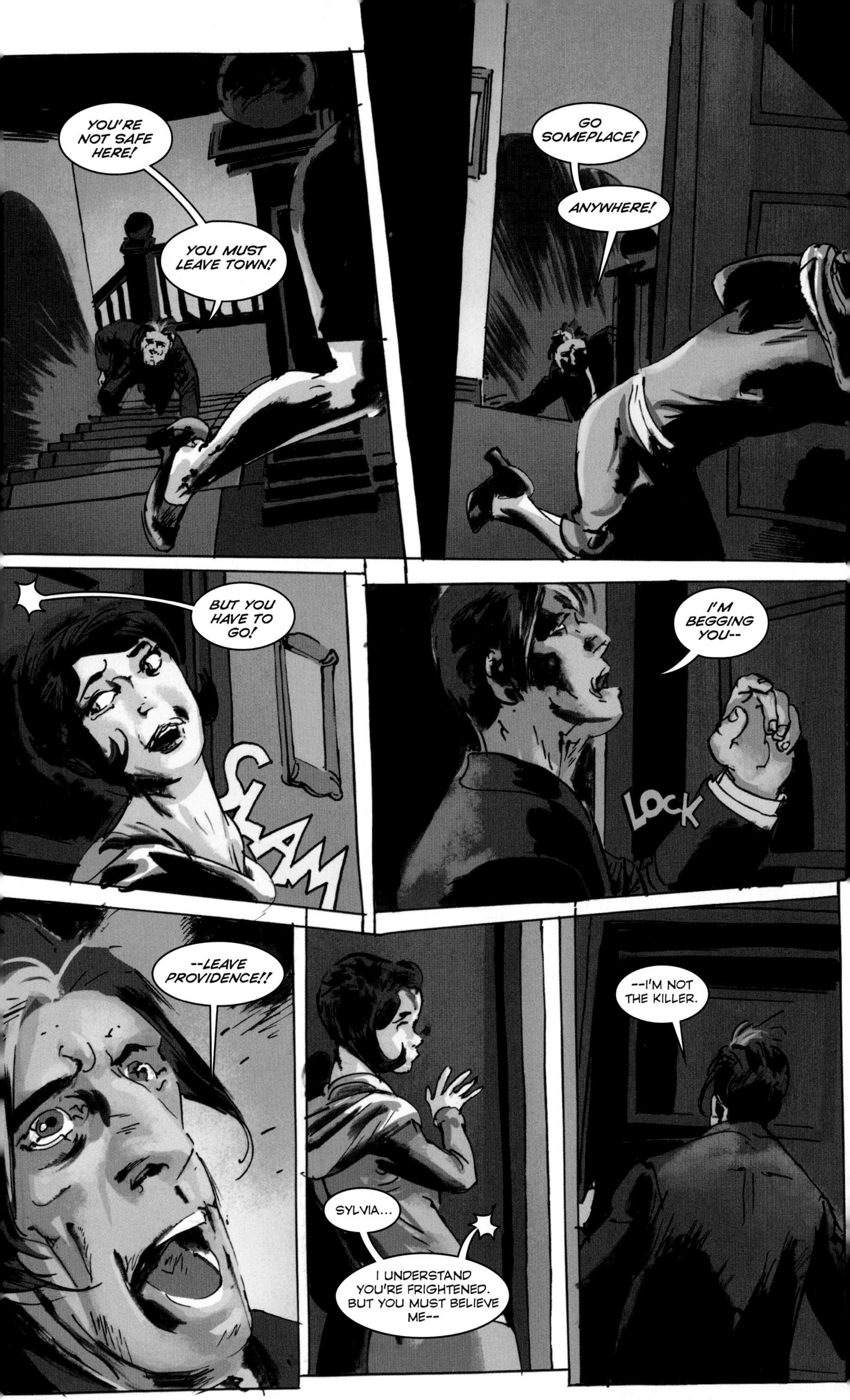
YOU'RE NOT SAFE HERE!
YOU MUST LEAVE TOWN!
GO SOMEPLACE!
ANYWHERE!
BUT YOU HAVE TO GO!
SLAM
I'M BEGGING YOU--
LOCK
--LEAVE PROVIDENCE!!
SYLVIA...
I UNDERSTAND YOU'RE FRIGHTENED. BUT YOU MUST BELIEVE ME--
--I'M NOT THE KILLER.

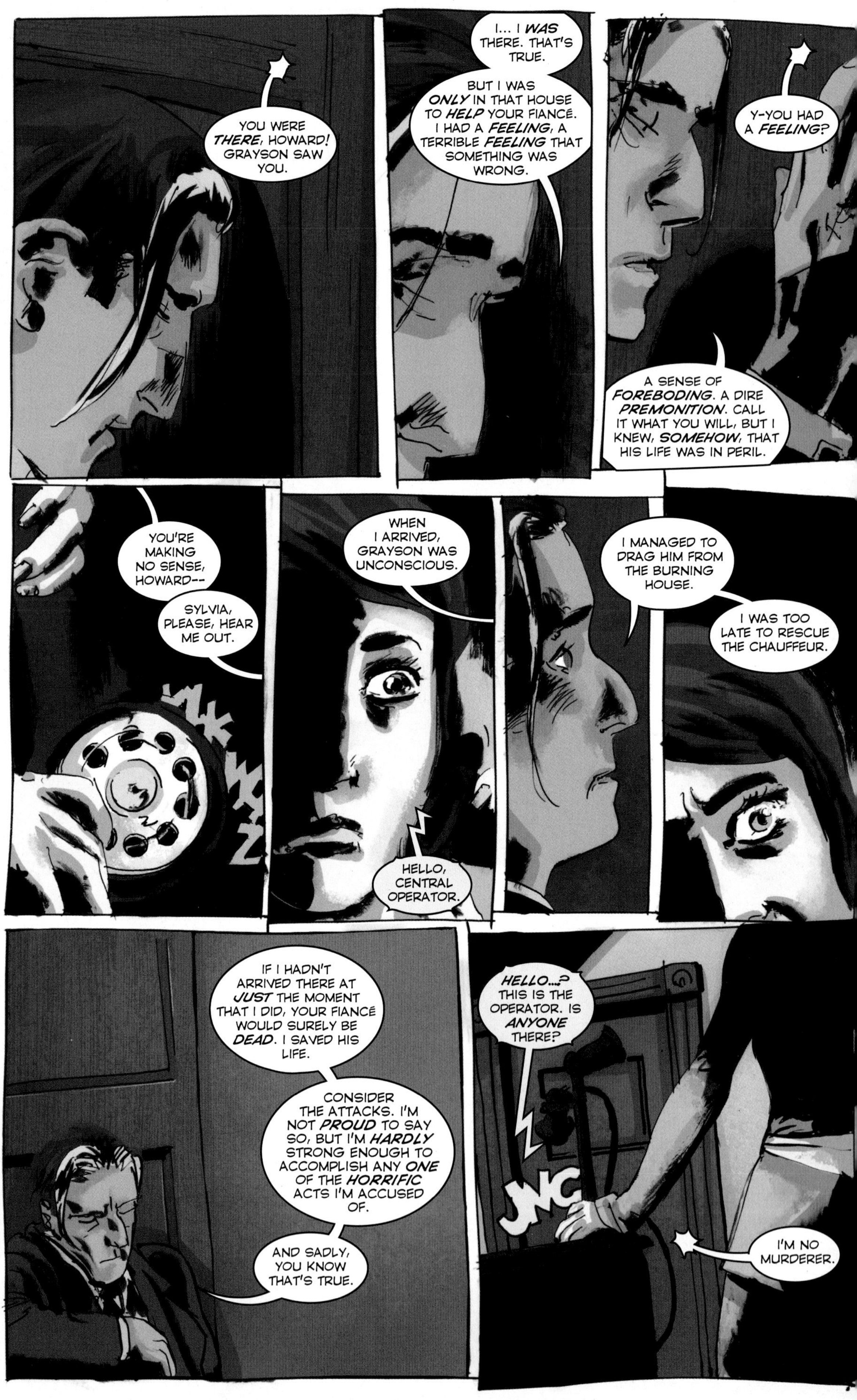
YOU WERE THERE, HOWARD! GRAYSON SAW YOU.
I... I WAS THERE. THAT'S TRUE.
BUT I WAS ONLY IN THAT HOUSE TO HELP YOUR FIANCÉ. I HAD A FEELING, A TERRIBLE FEELING THAT SOMETHING WAS WRONG.
Y-YOU HAD A FEELING?
A SENSE OF FOREBODING. A DIRE PREMONITION. CALL IT WHAT YOU WILL, BUT I KNEW, SOMEHOW, THAT HIS LIFE WAS IN PERIL.
YOU'RE MAKING NO SENSE, HOWARD--
SYLVIA, PLEASE, HEAR ME OUT.
WHEN I ARRIVED, GRAYSON WAS UNCONSCIOUS.
HELLO, CENTRAL OPERATOR.
I MANAGED TO DRAG HIM FROM THE BURNING HOUSE.
I WAS TOO LATE TO RESCUE THE CHAUFFEUR.
IF I HADN'T ARRIVED THERE AT JUST THE MOMENT THAT I DID, YOUR FIANCÉ WOULD SURELY BE DEAD. I SAVED HIS LIFE.
CONSIDER THE ATTACKS. I'M NOT PROUD TO SAY SO, BUT I'M HARDLY STRONG ENOUGH TO ACCOMPLISH ANY ONE OF THE HORRIFIC ACTS I'M ACCUSED OF.
AND SADLY, YOU KNOW THAT'S TRUE.
HELLO...? THIS IS THE OPERATOR. IS ANYONE THERE?
JNG
I'M NO MURDERER.

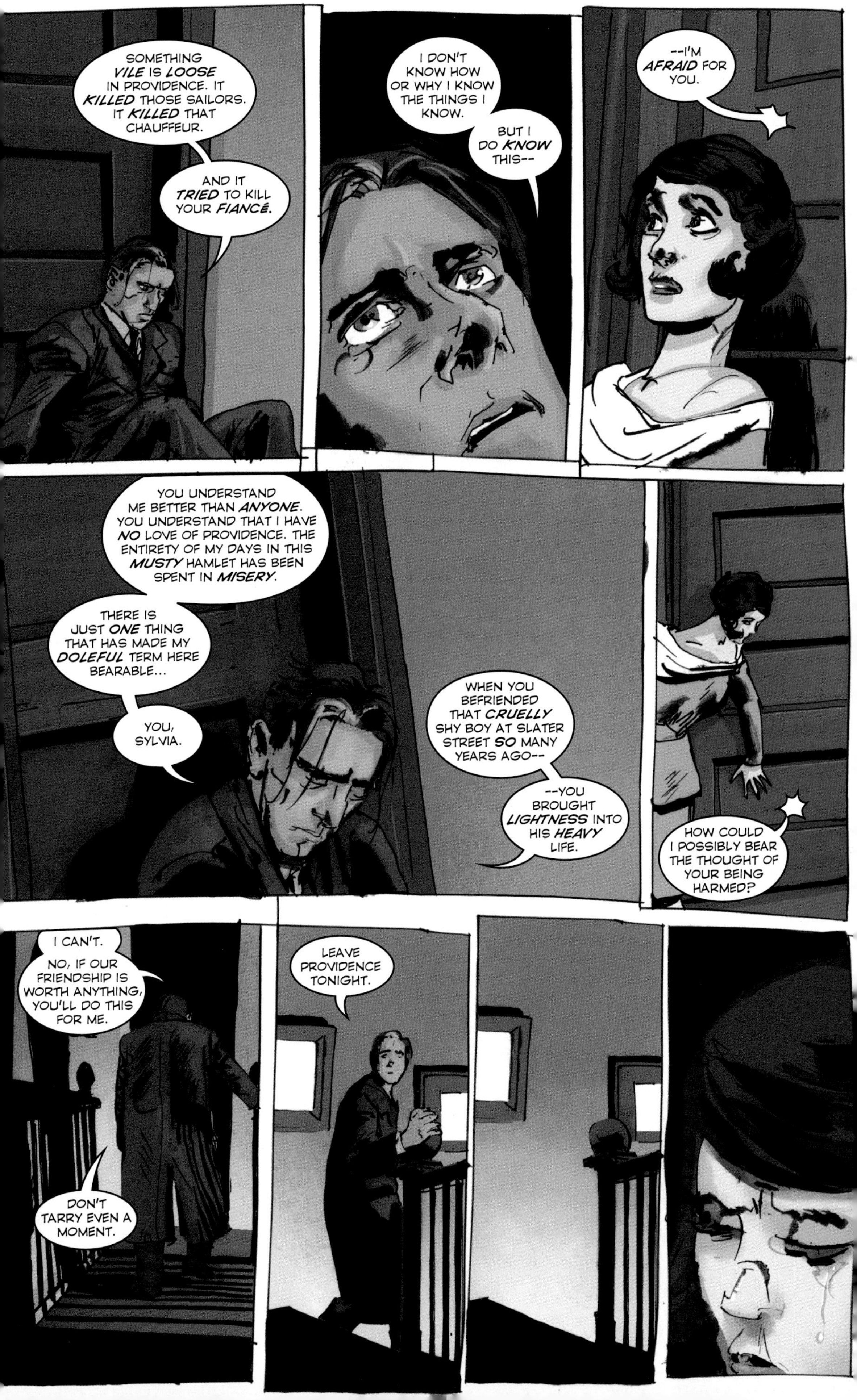
SOMETHING VILE IS LOOSE IN PROVIDENCE. IT KILLED THOSE SAILORS. IT KILLED THAT CHAUFFEUR.
AND IT TRIED TO KILL YOUR FIANCÉ.
I DON'T KNOW HOW OR WHY I KNOW THE THINGS I KNOW.
BUT I DO KNOW THIS--
--I'M AFRAID FOR YOU.
YOU UNDERSTAND ME BETTER THAN ANYONE. YOU UNDERSTAND THAT I HAVE NO LOVE OF PROVIDENCE. THE ENTIRETY OF MY DAYS IN THIS MUSTY HAMLET HAS BEEN SPENT IN MISERY.
THERE IS JUST ONE THING THAT HAS MADE MY DOLEFUL TERM HERE BEARABLE...
YOU, SYLVIA.
WHEN YOU BEFRIENDED THAT CRUELLY SHY BOY AT SLATER STREET SO MANY YEARS AGO--
--YOU BROUGHT LIGHTNESS INTO HIS HEAVY LIFE.
HOW COULD I POSSIBLY BEAR THE THOUGHT OF YOUR BEING HARMED?
I CAN'T.
NO, IF OUR FRIENDSHIP IS WORTH ANYTHING, YOU'LL DO THIS FOR ME.
DON'T TARRY EVEN A MOMENT.
LEAVE PROVIDENCE TONIGHT.

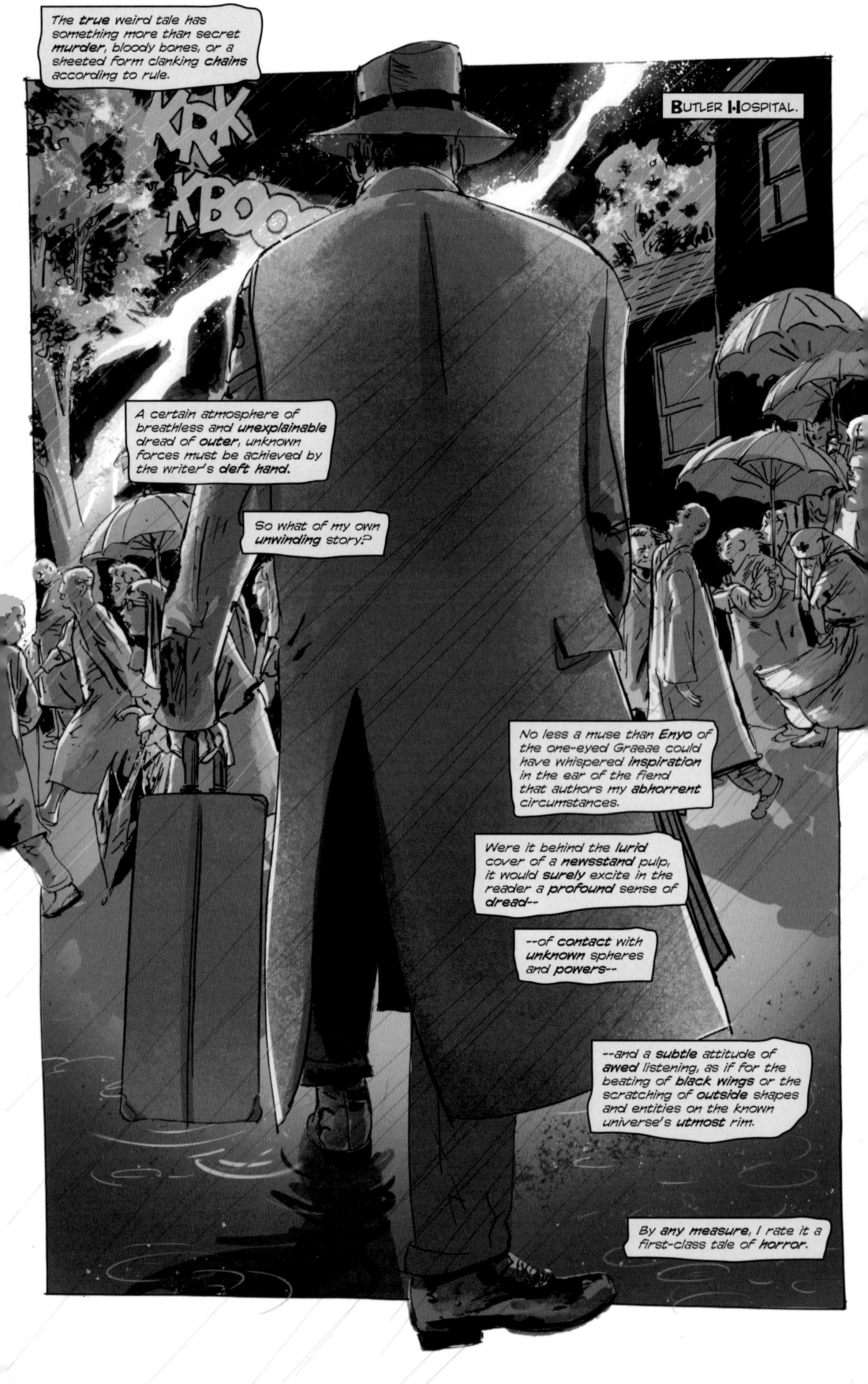

The true weird tale has something more than secret murder, bloody bones, or a sheeted form clanking chains according to rule.
Butler Hospital.
A certain atmosphere of breathless and unexplainable dread of outer, unknown forces must be achieved by the writer's deft hand.
So what of my own unwinding story?
No less a muse than Enyo of the one-eyed Graeae could have whispered inspiration in the ear of the fiend that authors my abhorrent circumstances.
Were it behind the lurid cover of a newsstand pulp, it would surely excite in the reader a profound sense of dread--
--of contact with unknown spheres and powers--
--and a subtle attitude of awed listening, as if for the beating of black wings or the scratching of outside shapes and entities on the known universe's utmost rim.
By any measure, I rate it a first-class tale of horror.

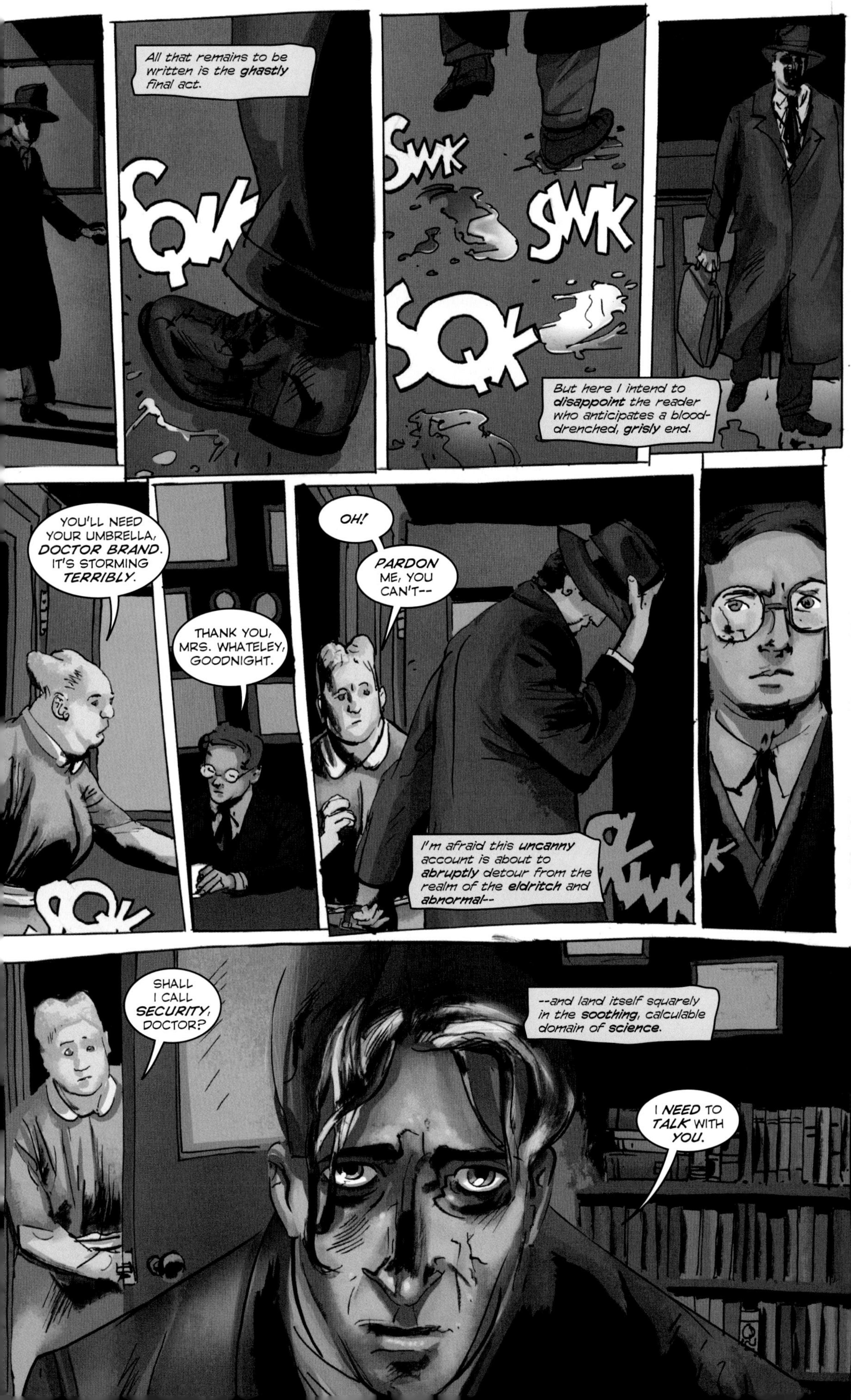

All that remains to be written is the ghastly final act.
SQK
SWK
SWK
SQK
But here I intend to disappoint the reader who anticipates a blood-drenched, grisly end.
YOU'LL NEED YOUR UMBRELLA, DOCTOR BRAND. IT'S STORMING TERRIBLY.
SQK
THANK YOU, MRS. WHATELEY, GOODNIGHT.
OH!
PARDON ME, YOU CAN'T--
I'm afraid this uncanny account is about to abruptly detour from the realm of the eldritch and abnormal--
SHALL I CALL SECURITY, DOCTOR?
--and land itself squarely in the soothing, calculable domain of science.
I NEED TO TALK WITH YOU.

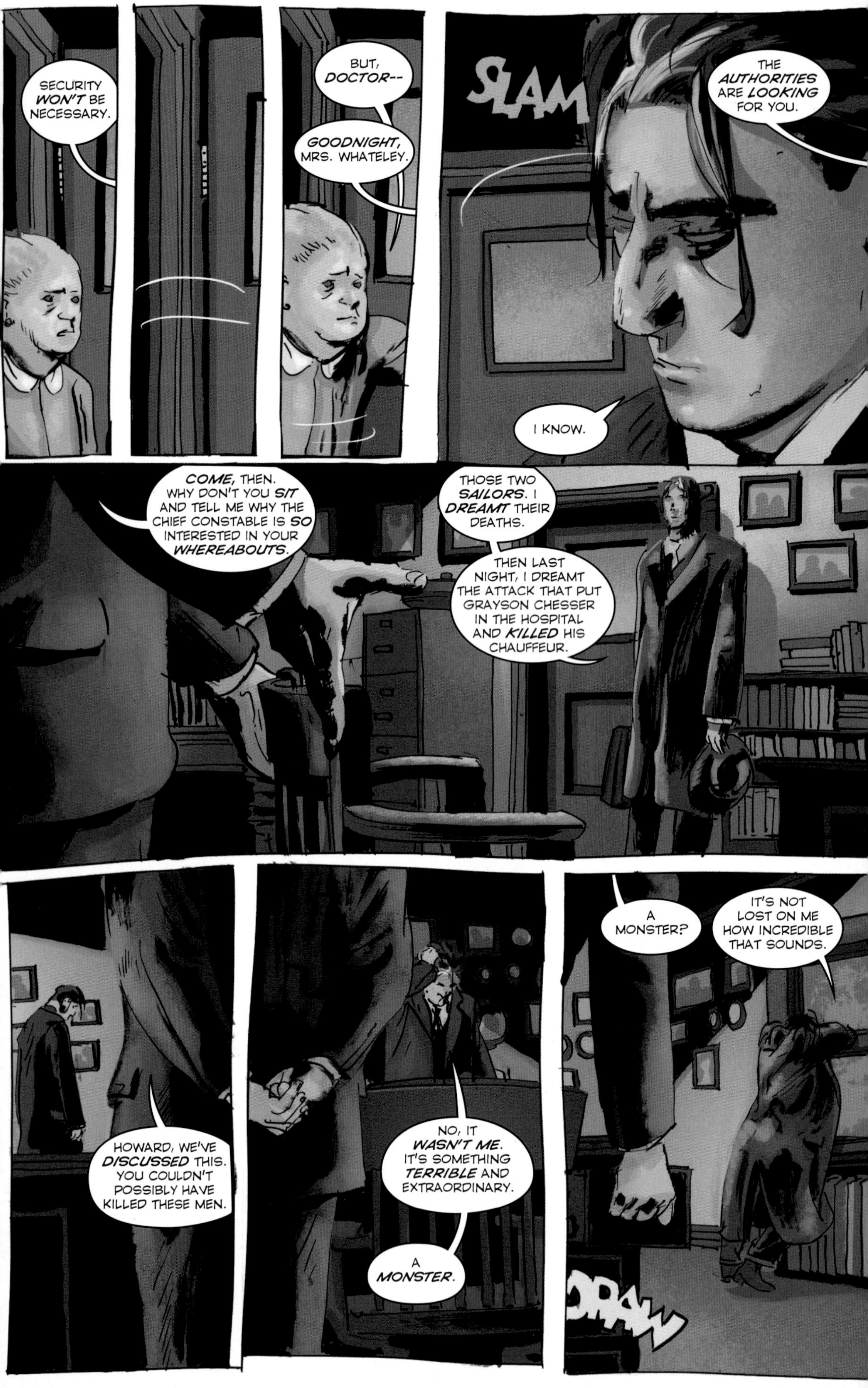
SECURITY WON'T BE NECESSARY.
BUT, DOCTOR--
GOODNIGHT, MRS. WHATELEY.
SLAM
THE AUTHORITIES ARE LOOKING FOR YOU.
I KNOW.
COME, THEN. WHY DON'T YOU SIT AND TELL ME WHY THE CHIEF CONSTABLE IS SO INTERESTED IN YOUR WHEREABOUTS.
THOSE TWO SAILORS. I DREAMT THEIR DEATHS.
THEN LAST NIGHT, I DREAMT THE ATTACK THAT PUT GRAYSON CHESSER IN THE HOSPITAL AND KILLED HIS CHAUFFEUR.
HOWARD, WE'VE DISCUSSED THIS. YOU COULDN'T POSSIBLY HAVE KILLED THESE MEN.
NO, IT WASN'T ME. IT'S SOMETHING TERRIBLE AND EXTRAORDINARY.
A MONSTER.
A MONSTER?
IT'S NOT LOST ON ME HOW INCREDIBLE THAT SOUNDS.

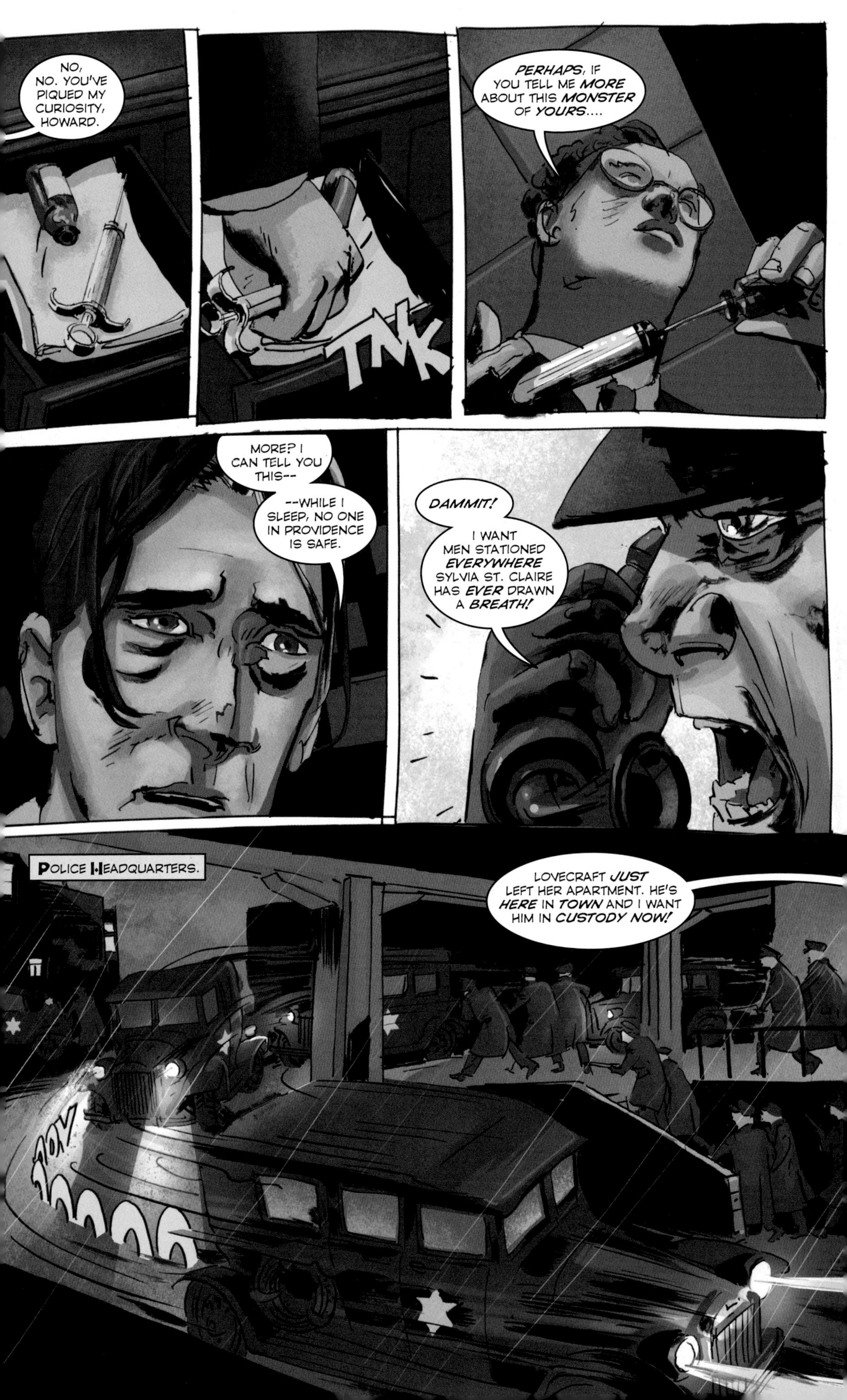
NO, NO. YOU'VE PIQUED MY CURIOSITY, HOWARD.
TNK
PERHAPS, IF YOU TELL ME MORE ABOUT THIS MONSTER OF YOURS....
MORE? I CAN TELL YOU THIS--
--WHILE I SLEEP, NO ONE IN PROVIDENCE IS SAFE.
DAMMIT!
I WANT MEN STATIONED EVERYWHERE SYLVIA ST. CLAIRE HAS EVER DRAWN A BREATH!
POLICE HEADQUARTERS.
LOVECRAFT JUST LEFT HER APARTMENT. HE'S HERE IN TOWN AND I WANT HIM IN CUSTODY NOW!

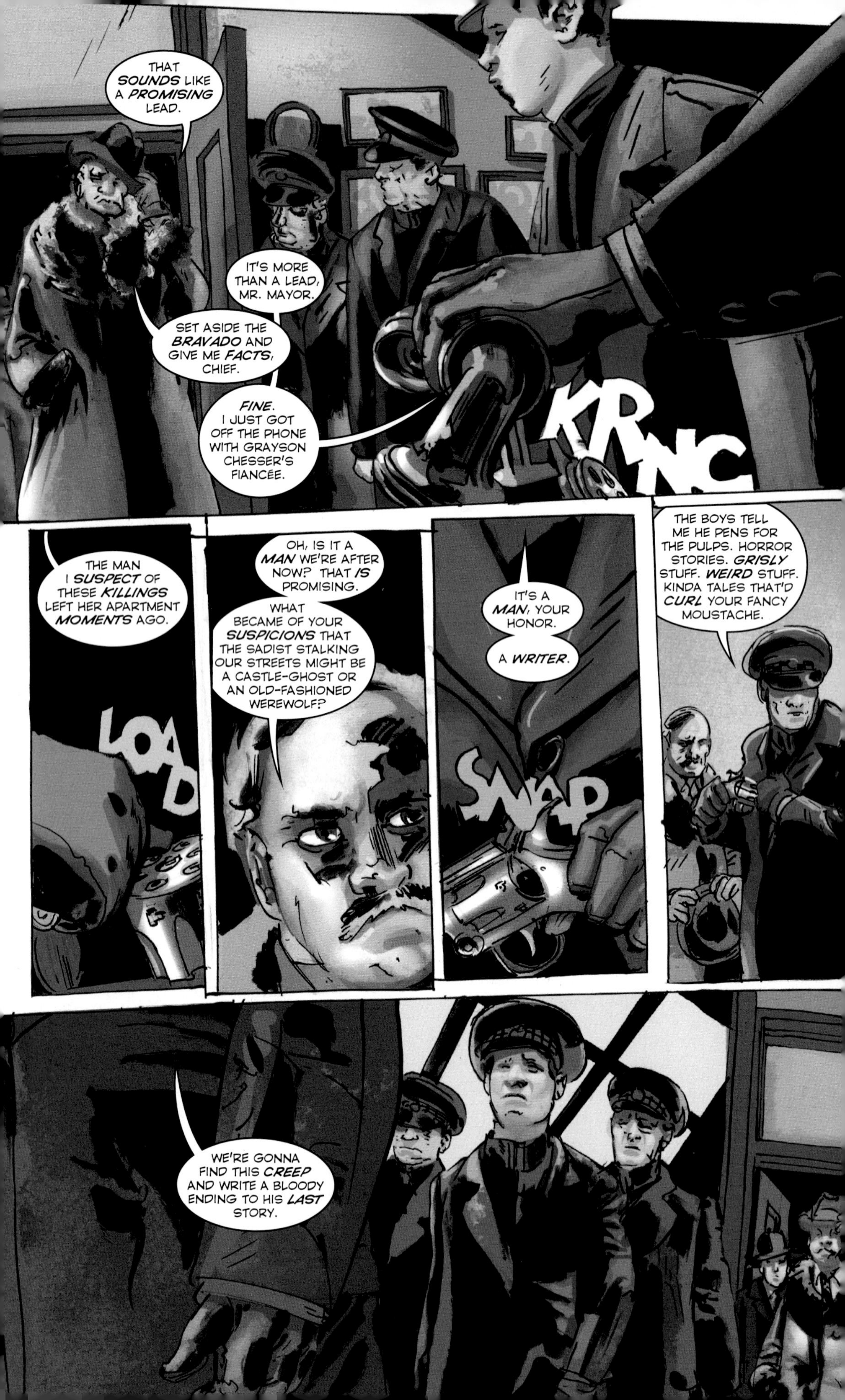
THAT SOUNDS LIKE A PROMISING LEAD.
IT'S MORE THAN A LEAD, MR. MAYOR.
SET ASIDE THE BRAVADO AND GIVE ME FACTS, CHIEF.
FINE. I JUST GOT OFF THE PHONE WITH GRAYSON CHESSER'S FIANCÉE.
KRNC
THE MAN I SUSPECT OF THESE KILLINGS LEFT HER APARTMENT MOMENTS AGO.
LOAD
OH, IS IT A MAN WE'RE AFTER NOW? THAT IS PROMISING.
WHAT BECAME OF YOUR SUSPICIONS THAT THE SADIST STALKING OUR STREETS MIGHT BE A CASTLE-GHOST OR AN OLD-FASHIONED WEREWOLF?
IT'S A MAN, YOUR HONOR.
A WRITER.
SNAP
THE BOYS TELL ME HE PENS FOR THE PULPS. HORROR STORIES. GRISLY STUFF. WEIRD STUFF. KINDA TALES THAT'D CURL YOUR FANCY MOUSTACHE.
WE'RE GONNA FIND THIS CREEP AND WRITE A BLOODY ENDING TO HIS LAST STORY.

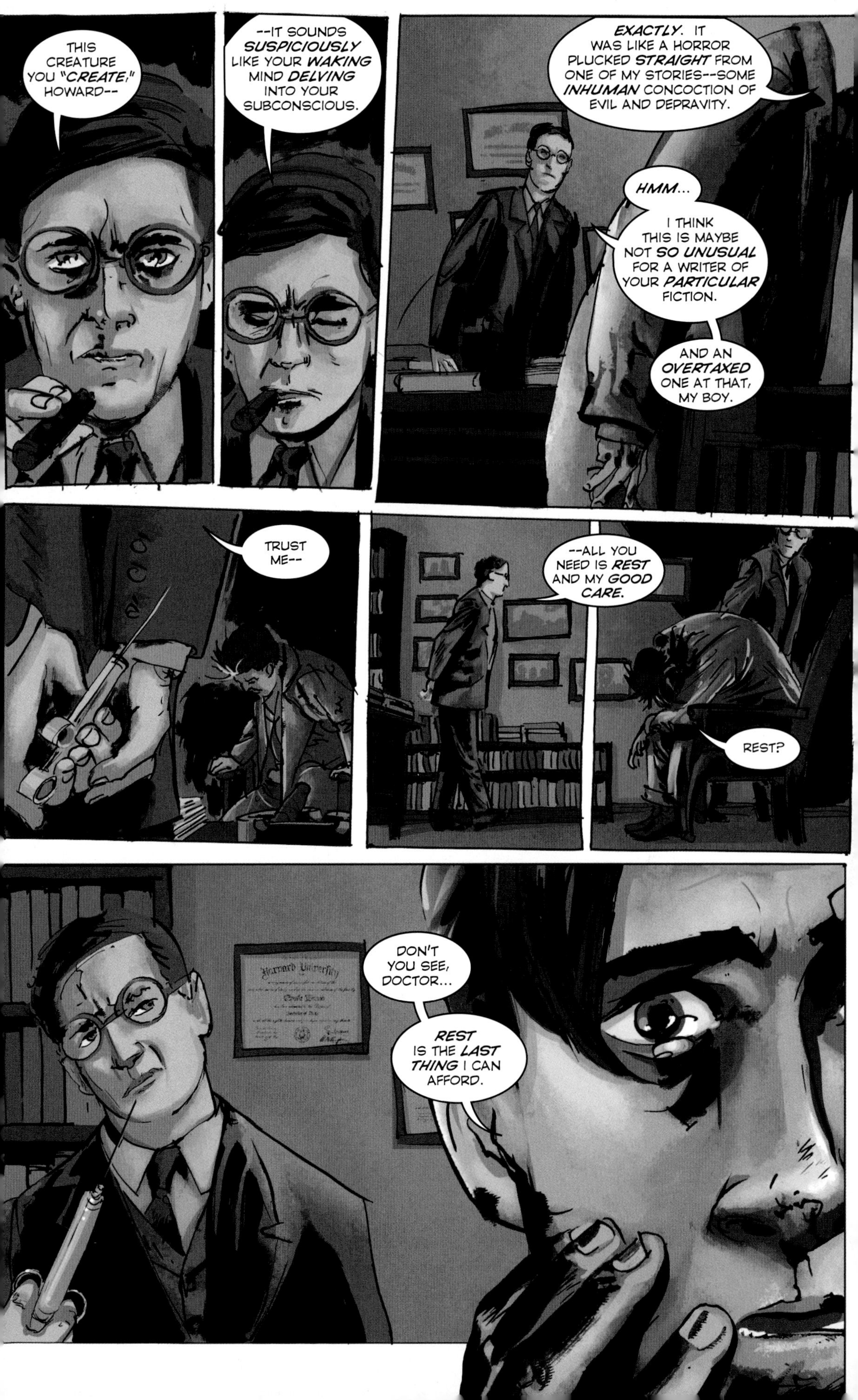
THIS CREATURE YOU "CREATE," HOWARD--
--IT SOUNDS SUSPICIOUSLY LIKE YOUR WAKING MIND DELVING INTO YOUR SUBCONSCIOUS.
EXACTLY. IT WAS LIKE A HORROR PLUCKED STRAIGHT FROM ONE OF MY STORIES--SOME INHUMAN CONCOCTION OF EVIL AND DEPRAVITY.
HMM...
I THINK THIS IS MAYBE NOT SO UNUSUAL FOR A WRITER OF YOUR PARTICULAR FICTION.
AND AN OVERTAXED ONE AT THAT, MY BOY.
TRUST ME--
--ALL YOU NEED IS REST AND MY GOOD CARE.
REST?
DON'T YOU SEE, DOCTOR...
REST IS THE LAST THING I CAN AFFORD.

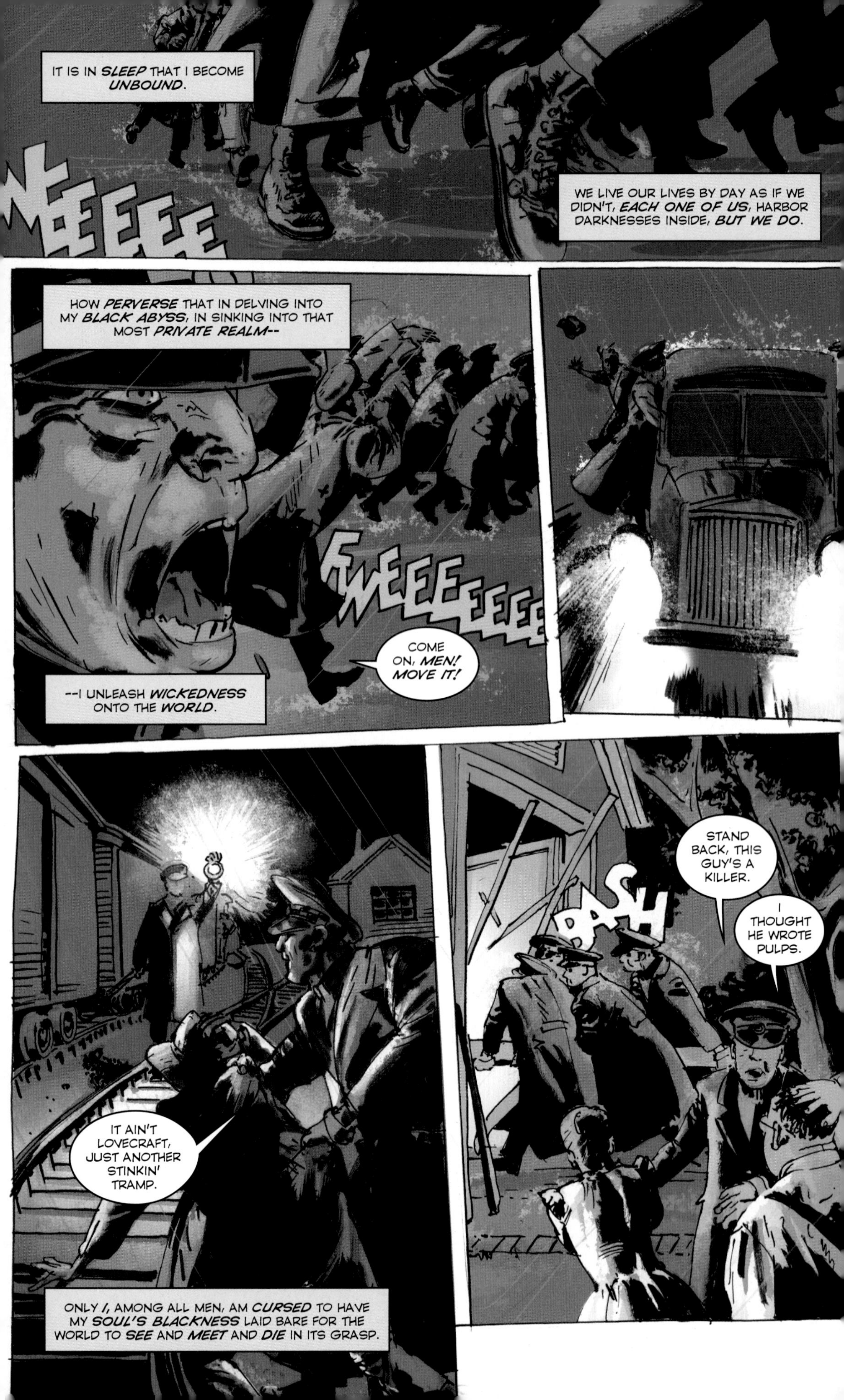

IT IS IN SLEEP THAT I BECOME UNBOUND.
WEEEEE
WE LIVE OUR LIVES BY DAY AS IF WE DIDN'T, EACH ONE OF US, HARBOR DARKNESSES INSIDE, BUT WE DO.
HOW PERVERSE THAT IN DELVING INTO MY BLACK ABYSS, IN SINKING INTO THAT MOST PRIVATE REALM--
FWEEEEEEE
COME ON, MEN! MOVE IT!
--I UNLEASH WICKEDNESS ONTO THE WORLD.
IT AIN'T LOVECRAFT, JUST ANOTHER STINKIN' TRAMP.
ONLY I, AMONG ALL MEN, AM CURSED TO HAVE MY SOUL'S BLACKNESS LAID BARE FOR THE WORLD TO SEE AND MEET AND DIE IN ITS GRASP.
BASH
STAND BACK, THIS GUY'S A KILLER.
I THOUGHT HE WROTE PULPS.

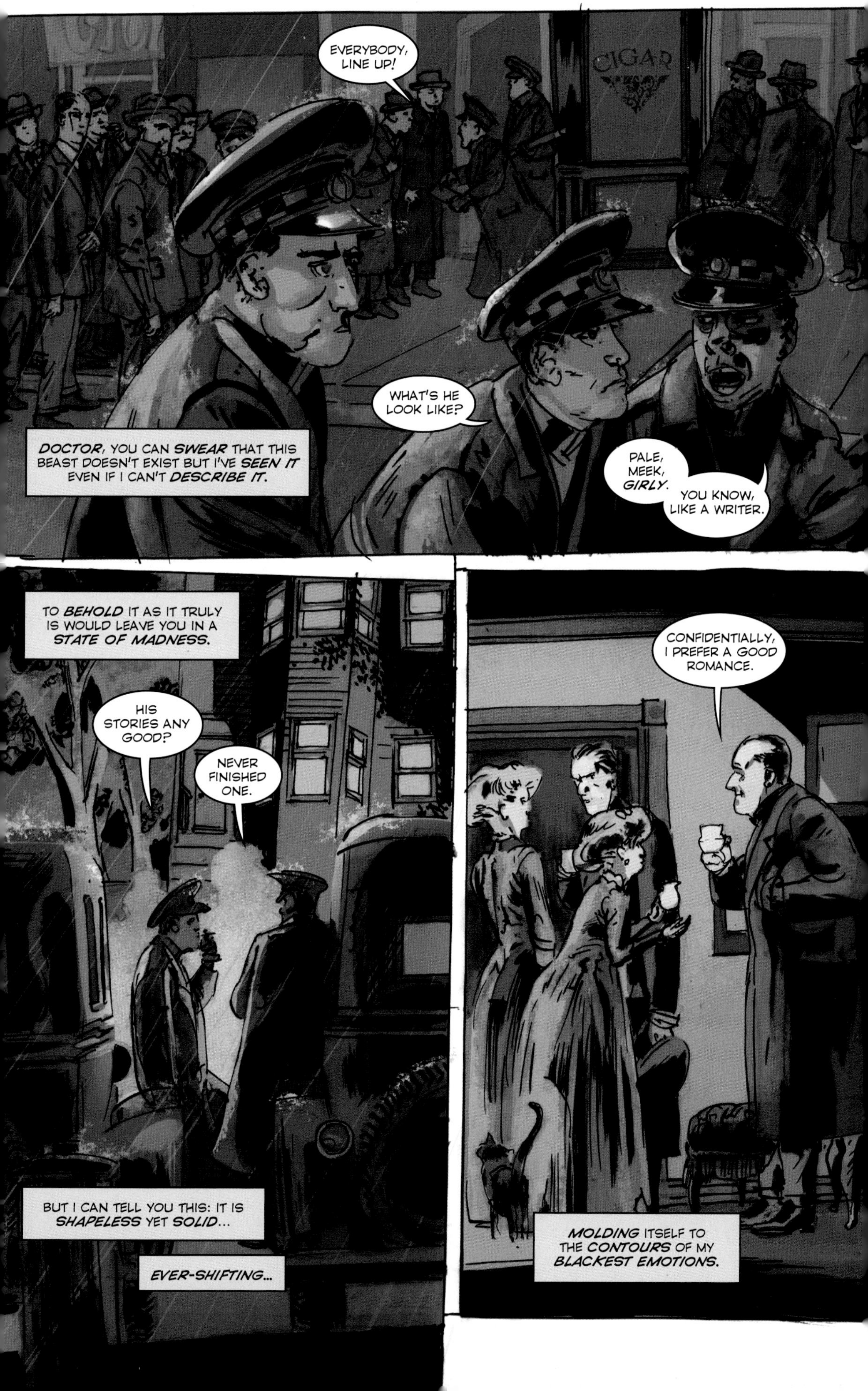

EVERYBODY, LINE UP!
WHAT'S HE LOOK LIKE?
DOCTOR, YOU CAN SWEAR THAT THIS BEAST DOESN'T EXIST BUT I'VE SEEN IT EVEN IF I CAN'T DESCRIBE IT.
PALE, MEEK, GIRLY.
YOU KNOW, LIKE A WRITER.
CIGAR
TO BEHOLD IT AS IT TRULY IS WOULD LEAVE YOU IN A STATE OF MADNESS.
HIS STORIES ANY GOOD?
NEVER FINISHED ONE.
BUT I CAN TELL YOU THIS: IT IS SHAPELESS YET SOLID...
EVER-SHIFTING...
CONFIDENTIALLY, I PREFER A GOOD ROMANCE.
MOLDING ITSELF TO THE CONTOURS OF MY BLACKEST EMOTIONS.

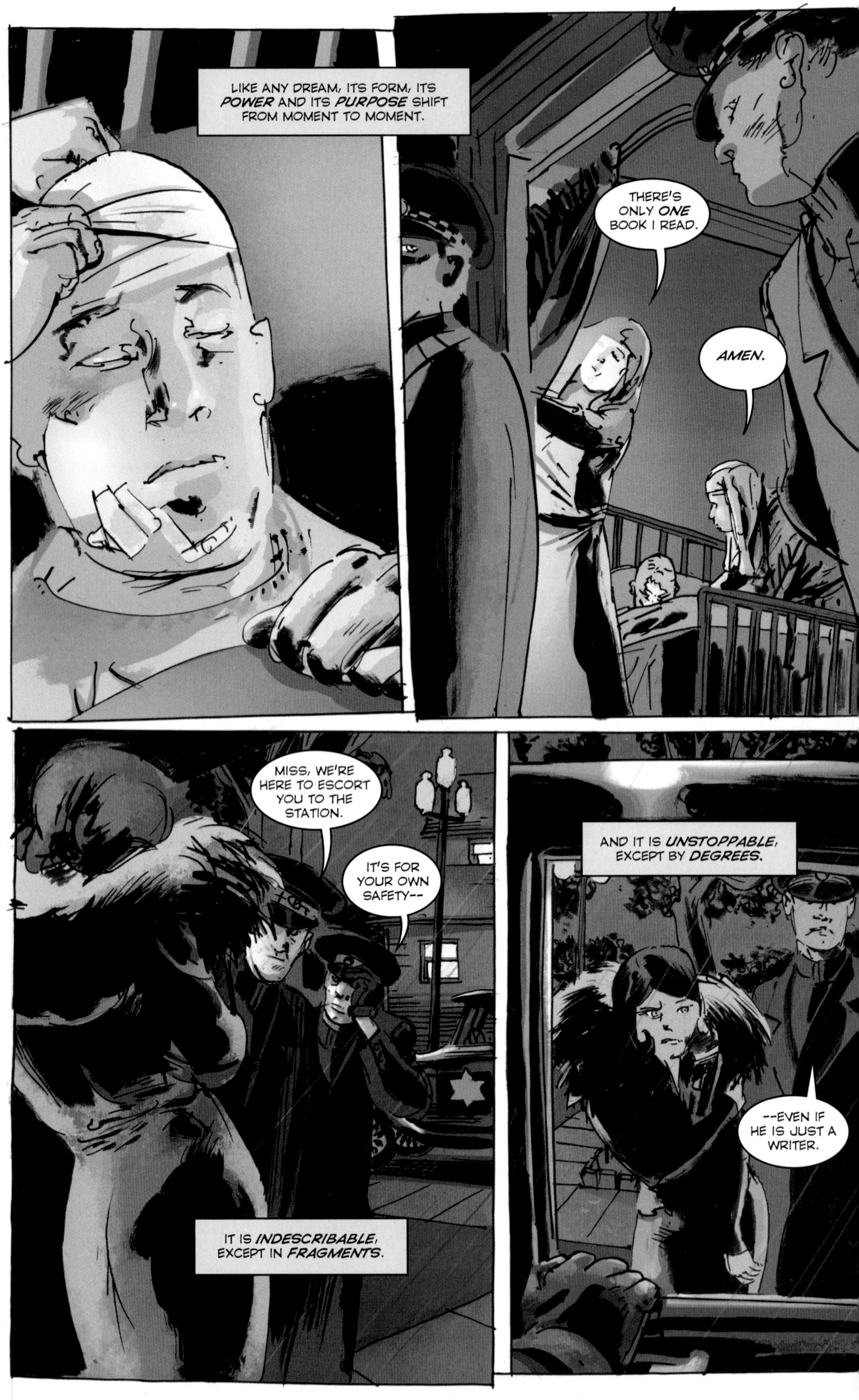
LIKE ANY DREAM, ITS FORM, ITS *POWER* AND ITS *PURPOSE* SHIFT FROM MOMENT TO MOMENT.
THERE'S ONLY *ONE* BOOK I READ.
AMEN.
MISS, WE'RE HERE TO ESCORT YOU TO THE STATION.
IT'S FOR YOUR OWN SAFETY--
IT IS *INDESCRIBABLE*, EXCEPT IN *FRAGMENTS*.
AND IT IS *UNSTOPPABLE*, EXCEPT BY *DEGREES*.
--EVEN IF HE IS JUST A WRITER.

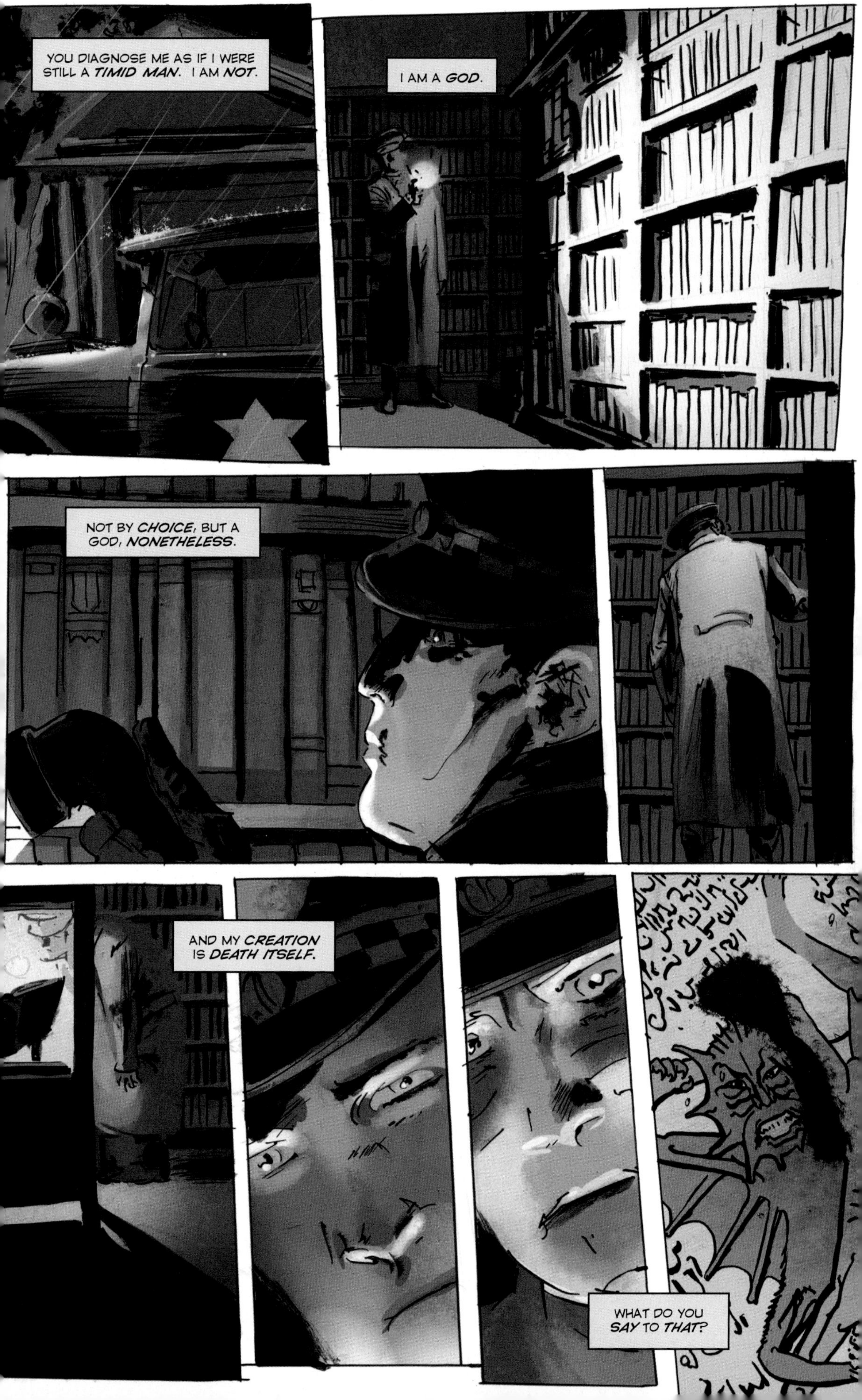
YOU DIAGNOSE ME AS IF I WERE STILL A *TIMID MAN*. I AM *NOT*.
I AM A *GOD*.
NOT BY *CHOICE*, BUT A GOD, *NONETHELESS*.
AND MY *CREATION* IS *DEATH ITSELF*.
WHAT DO YOU *SAY* TO *THAT*?

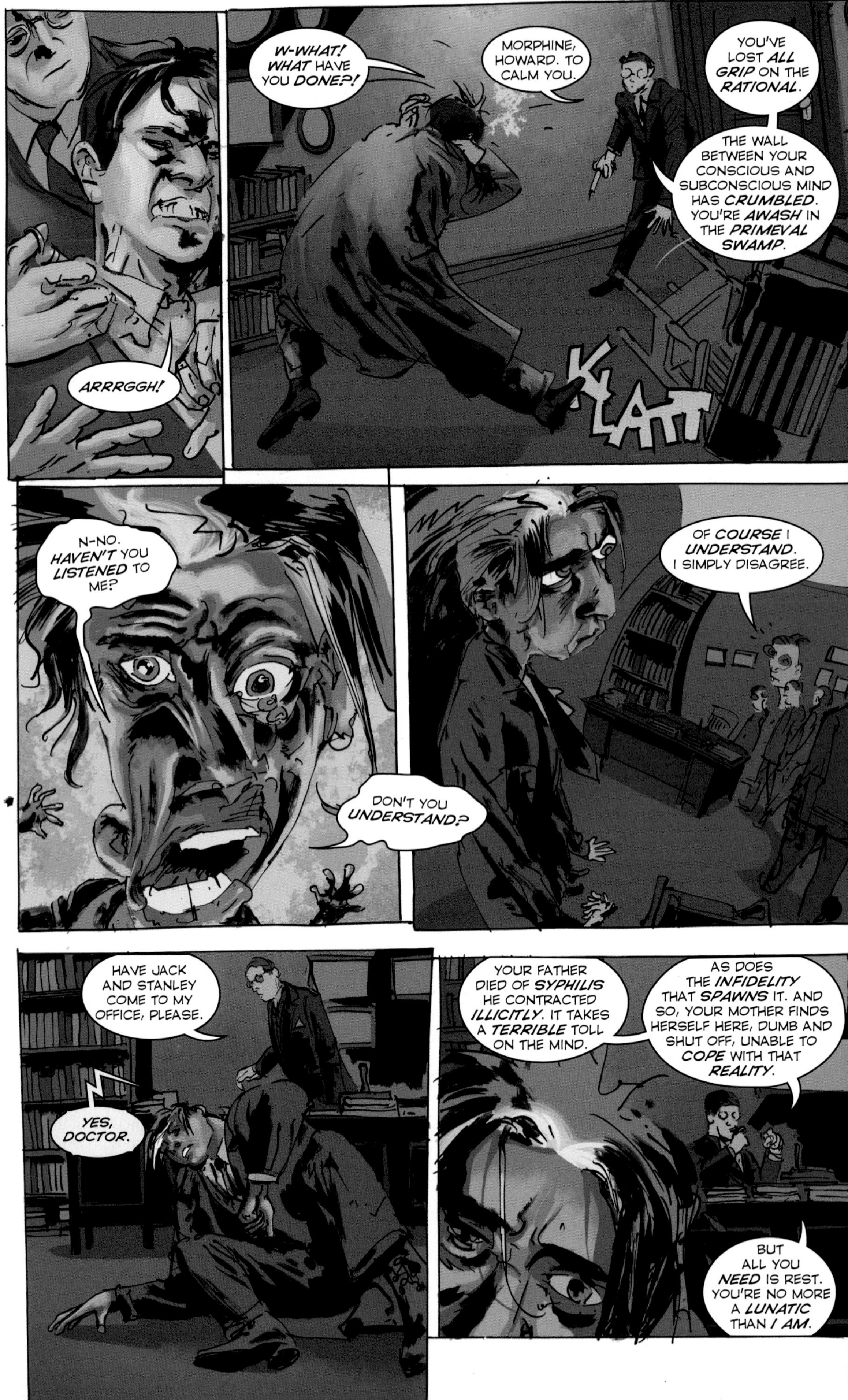
ARRRGGH!
W-WHAT! WHAT HAVE YOU DONE?!
MORPHINE, HOWARD. TO CALM YOU.
YOU'VE LOST ALL GRIP ON THE RATIONAL.
THE WALL BETWEEN YOUR CONSCIOUS AND SUBCONSCIOUS MIND HAS CRUMBLED. YOU'RE AWASH IN THE PRIMEVAL SWAMP.
KLATT
N-NO. HAVEN'T YOU LISTENED TO ME?
DON'T YOU UNDERSTAND?
OF COURSE I UNDERSTAND. I SIMPLY DISAGREE.
HAVE JACK AND STANLEY COME TO MY OFFICE, PLEASE.
YES, DOCTOR.
YOUR FATHER DIED OF SYPHILIS HE CONTRACTED ILLICITLY. IT TAKES A TERRIBLE TOLL ON THE MIND.
AS DOES THE INFIDELITY THAT SPAWNS IT. AND SO, YOUR MOTHER FINDS HERSELF HERE, DUMB AND SHUT OFF, UNABLE TO COPE WITH THAT REALITY.
BUT ALL YOU NEED IS REST. YOU'RE NO MORE A LUNATIC THAN I AM.

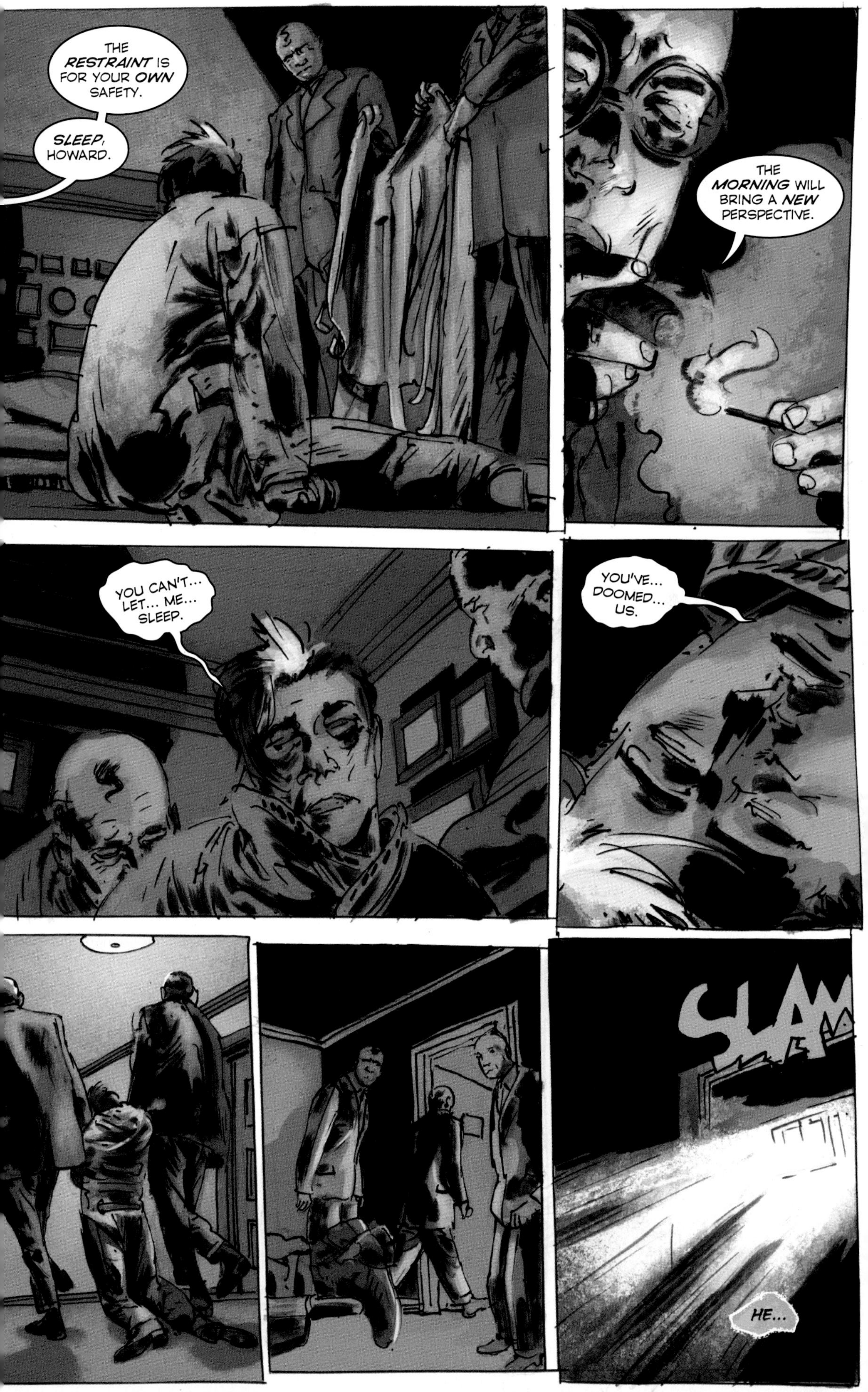
THE RESTRAINT IS FOR YOUR OWN SAFETY.
SLEEP, HOWARD.
THE MORNING WILL BRING A NEW PERSPECTIVE.
YOU CAN'T... LET... ME... SLEEP.
YOU'VE... DOOMED... US.
SLAM
HE...

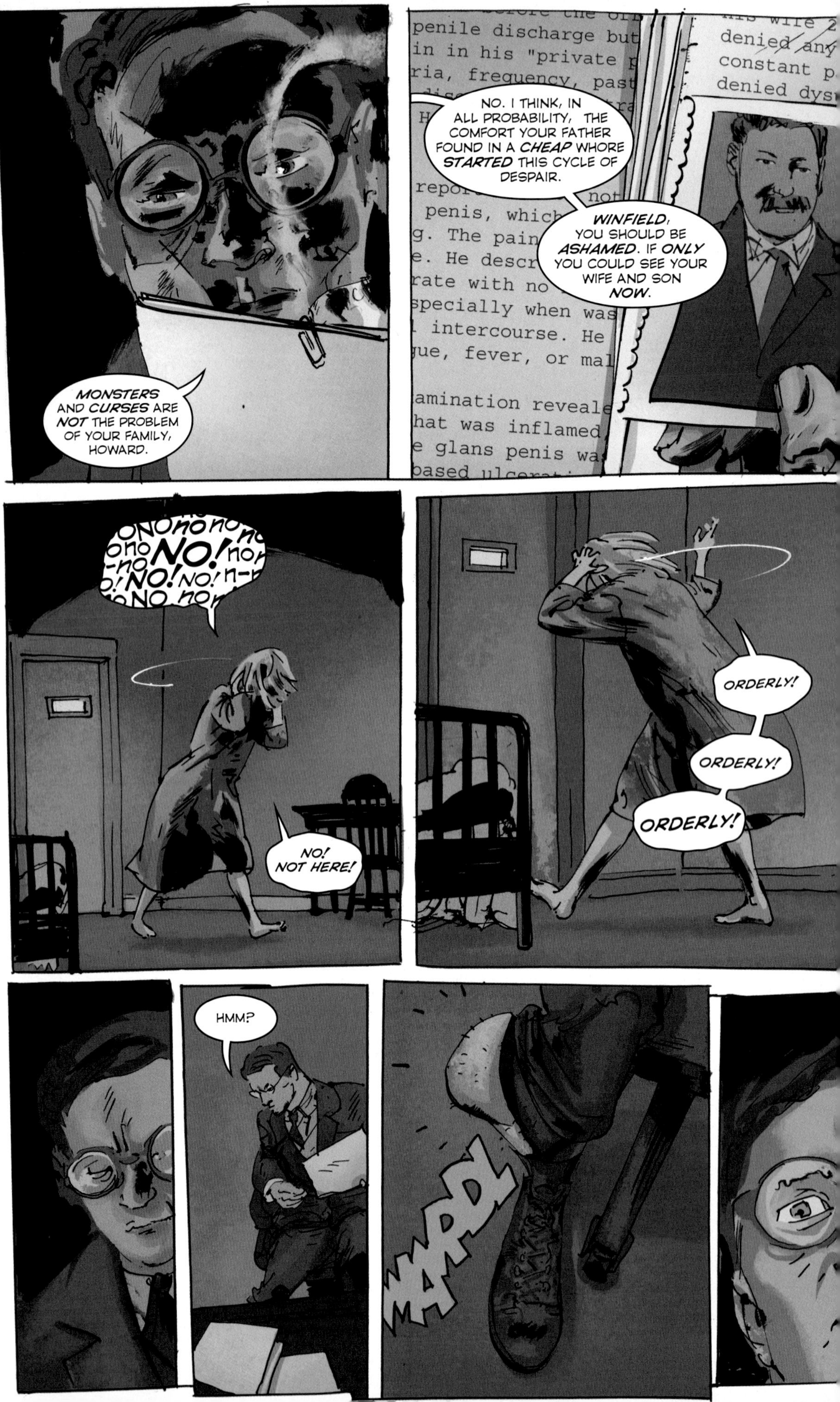
MONSTERS AND CURSES ARE NOT THE PROBLEM OF YOUR FAMILY, HOWARD.
NO. I THINK, IN ALL PROBABILITY, THE COMFORT YOUR FATHER FOUND IN A CHEAP WHORE STARTED THIS CYCLE OF DESPAIR.
WINFIELD, YOU SHOULD BE ASHAMED. IF ONLY YOU COULD SEE YOUR WIFE AND SON NOW.
NONONONONO NO! NO! NO! NONO
NO! NOT HERE!
ORDERLY!
ORDERLY!
ORDERLY!
HMM?

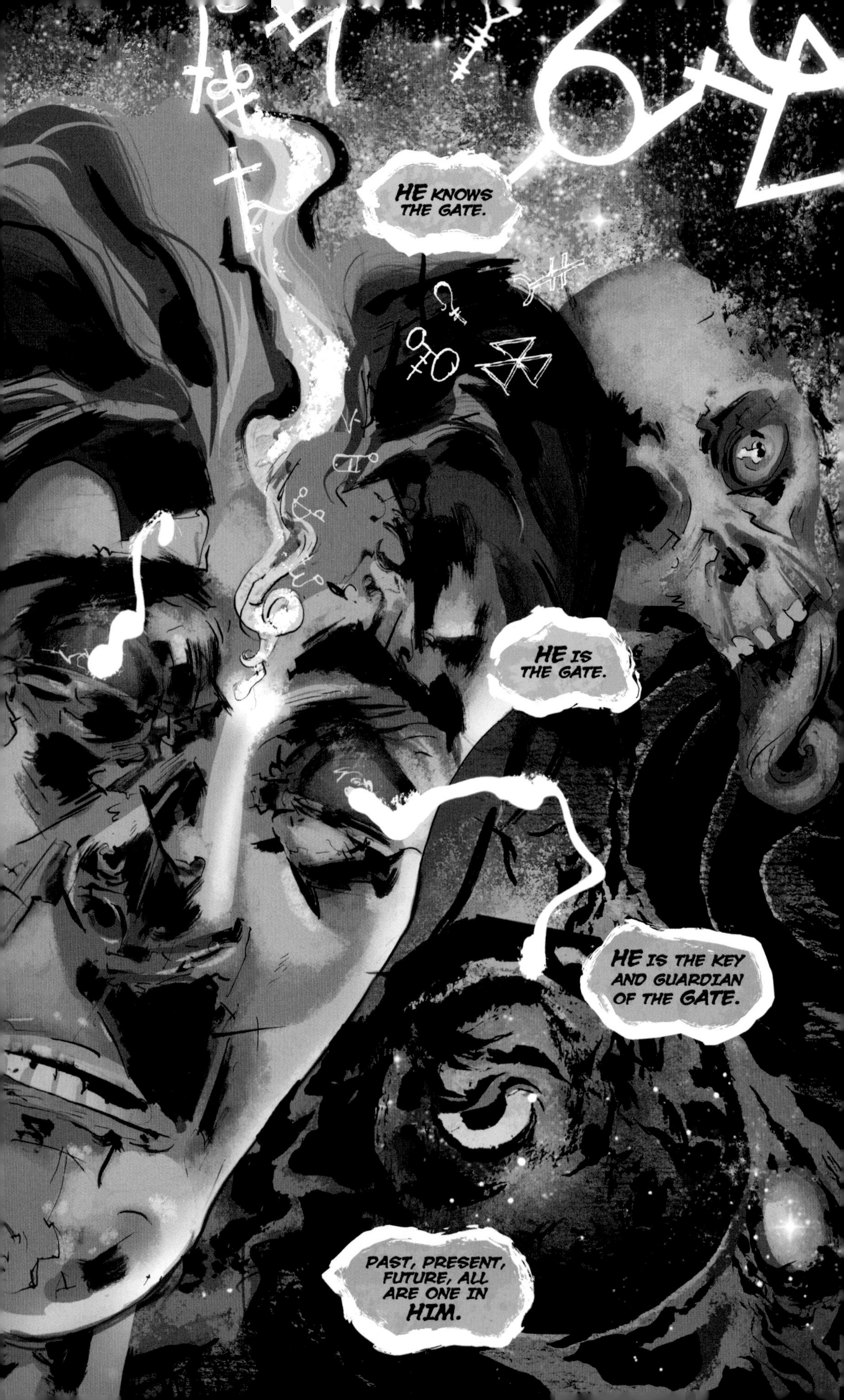
HE KNOWS THE GATE.
HE IS THE GATE.
HE IS THE KEY AND GUARDIAN OF THE GATE.
PAST, PRESENT, FUTURE, ALL ARE ONE IN HIM.

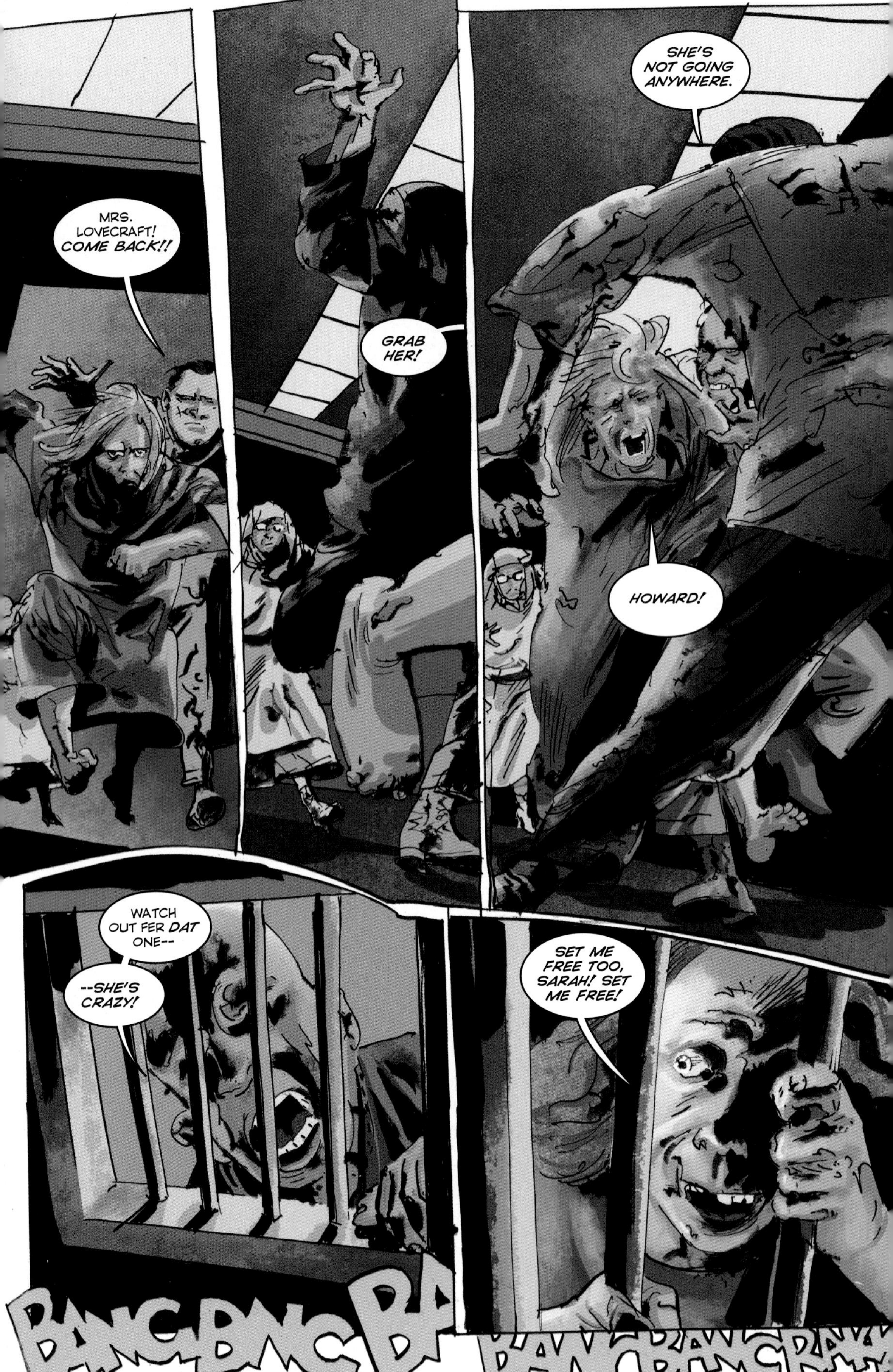
MRS. LOVECRAFT! COME BACK!!
GRAB HER!
SHE'S NOT GOING ANYWHERE.
HOWARD!
WATCH OUT FER DAT ONE--
--SHE'S CRAZY!
SET ME FREE TOO, SARAH! SET ME FREE!

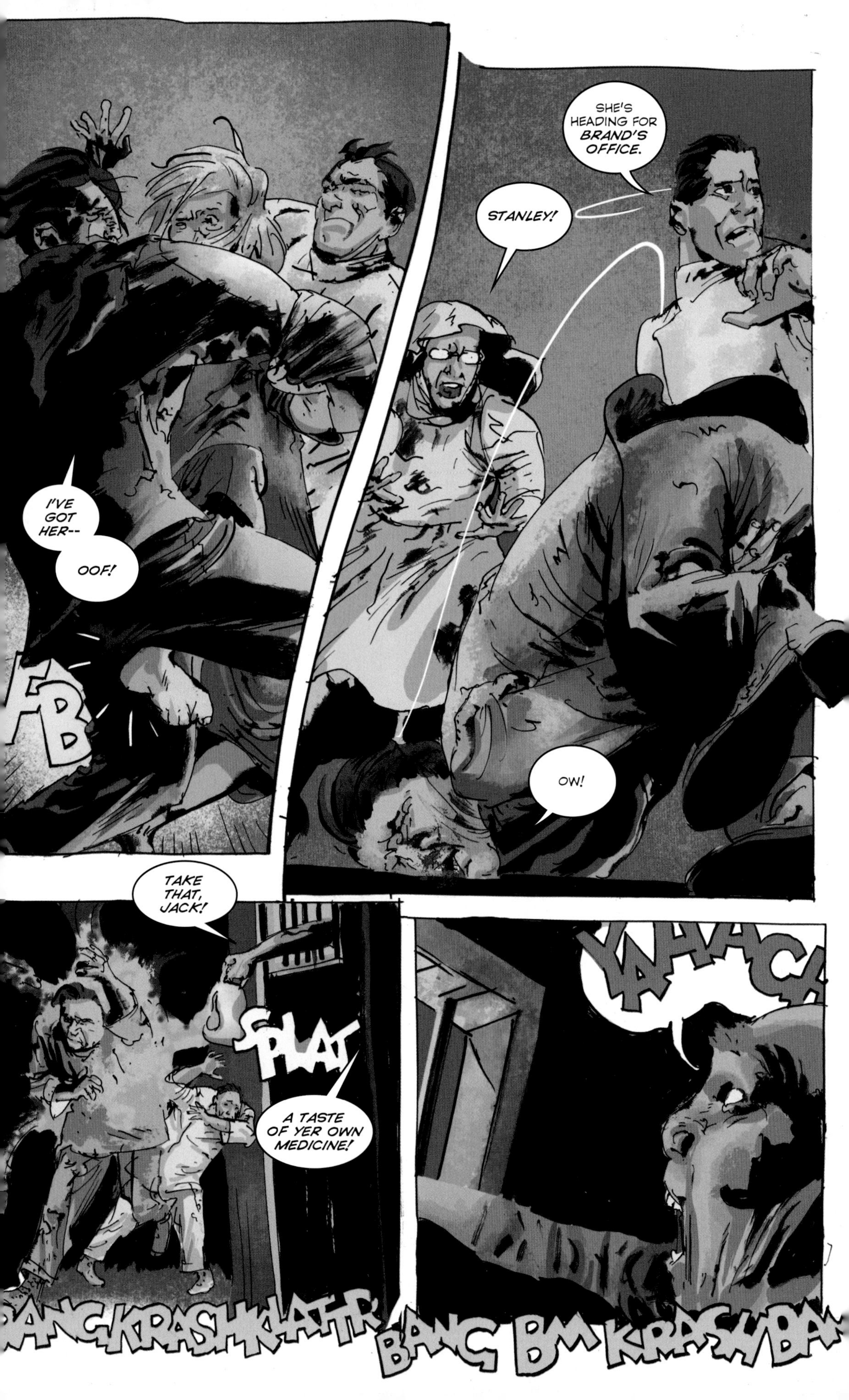
I'VE GOT HER--
OOF!
FB
STANLEY!
SHE'S HEADING FOR BRAND'S OFFICE.
OW!
TAKE THAT, JACK!
SPLAT
A TASTE OF YER OWN MEDICINE!
YAAACK
ANG KRASH KLATTR
BANG BM KRASH BA

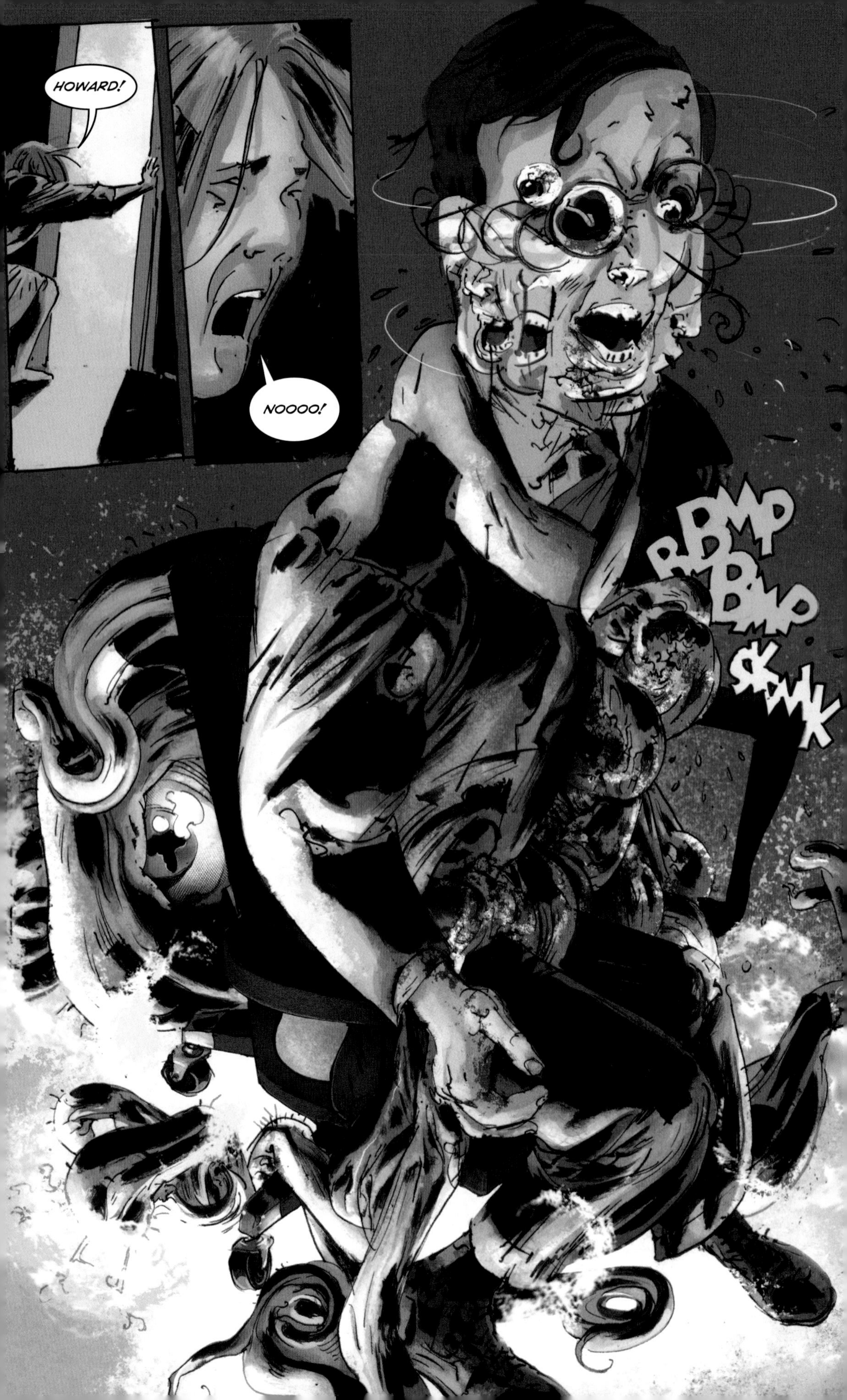
HOWARD!
NOOOO!
BDMP
BDMP
SKWK

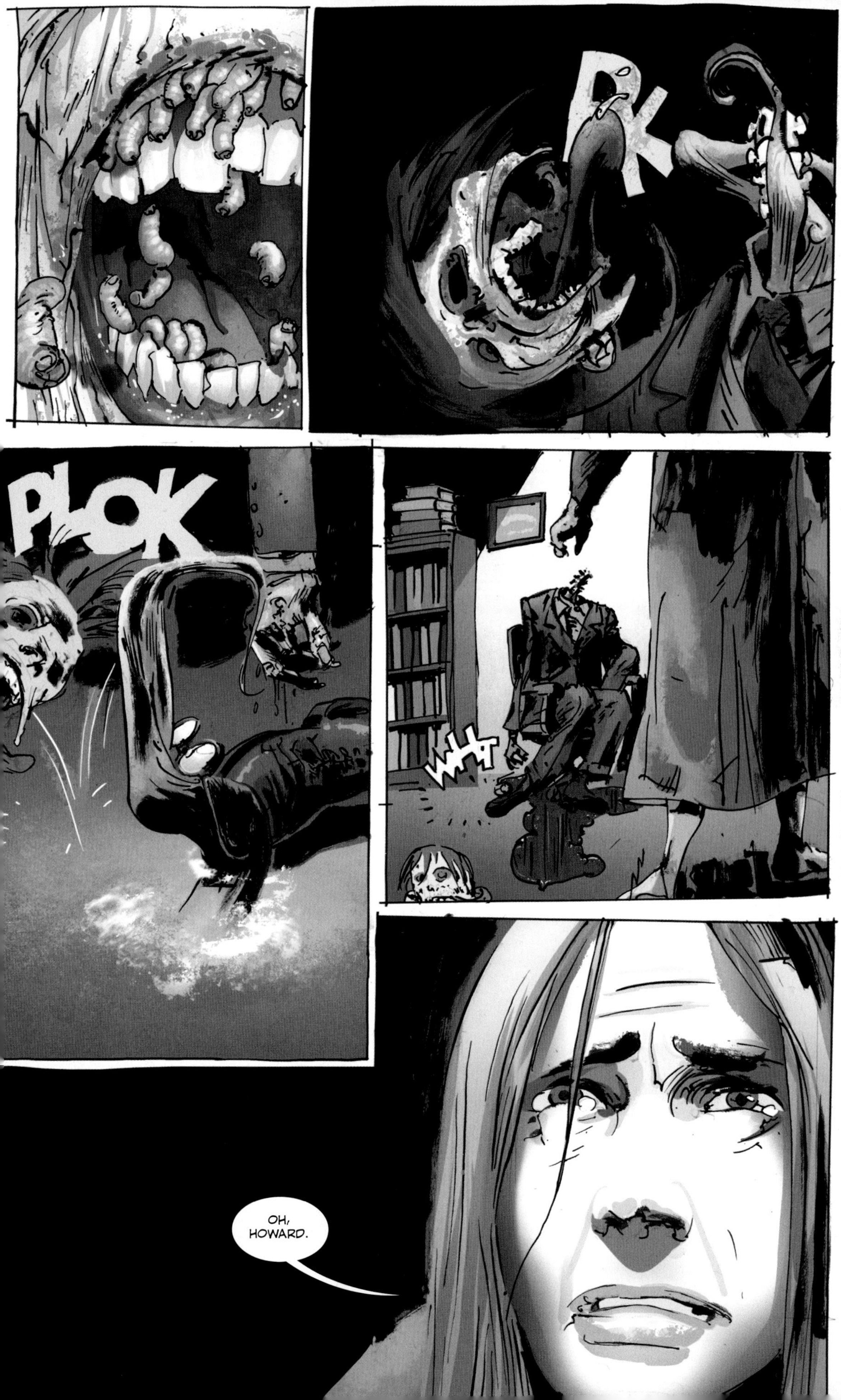
PLOK
OH, HOWARD.

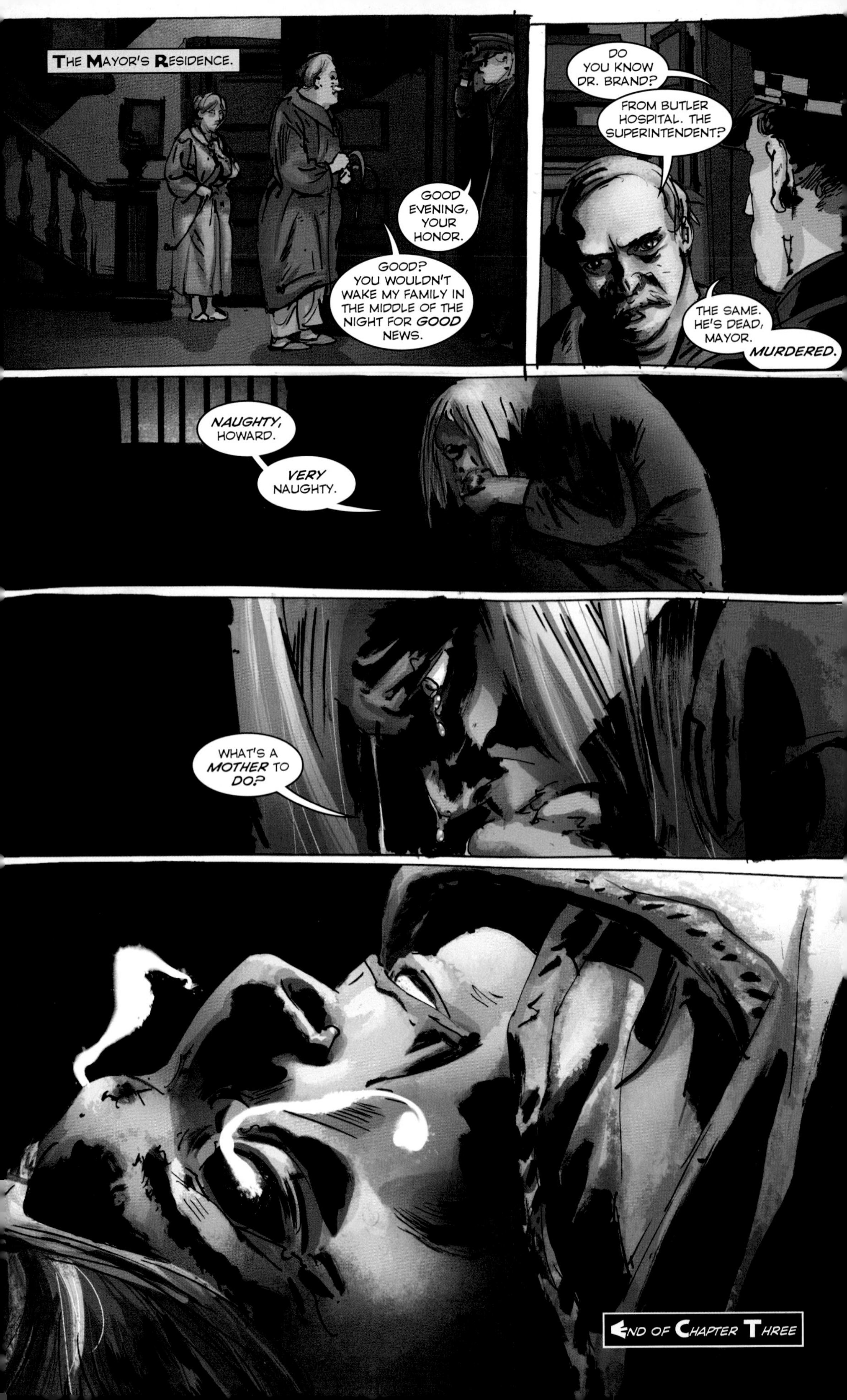
THE MAYOR'S RESIDENCE.
GOOD EVENING, YOUR HONOR.
GOOD? YOU WOULDN'T WAKE MY FAMILY IN THE MIDDLE OF THE NIGHT FOR *GOOD* NEWS.
DO YOU KNOW DR. BRAND?
FROM BUTLER HOSPITAL. THE SUPERINTENDENT?
THE SAME. HE'S DEAD, MAYOR. *MURDERED.*
NAUGHTY, HOWARD.
VERY NAUGHTY.
WHAT'S A *MOTHER* TO *DO?*
END OF CHAPTER THREE

While I was musing, writing-tablets in hand,
The house seemed brighter than it was before.
Then suddenly, sacred and marvellous, Janus,
In two-headed form, showed his twin faces to my eyes.
Terrified, I felt my hair grow stiff with fear
And my heart was frozen with sudden cold.
Holding his stick in his right hand, his key in the left,
He spoke these words to me from his forward looking face:
'Learn, without fear, what you seek, poet who labours
Over the days, and remember my speech.
The ancients called me Chaos.

— **OVID**

CHAPTER FOUR:
OF HOPE AND THE ABYSS

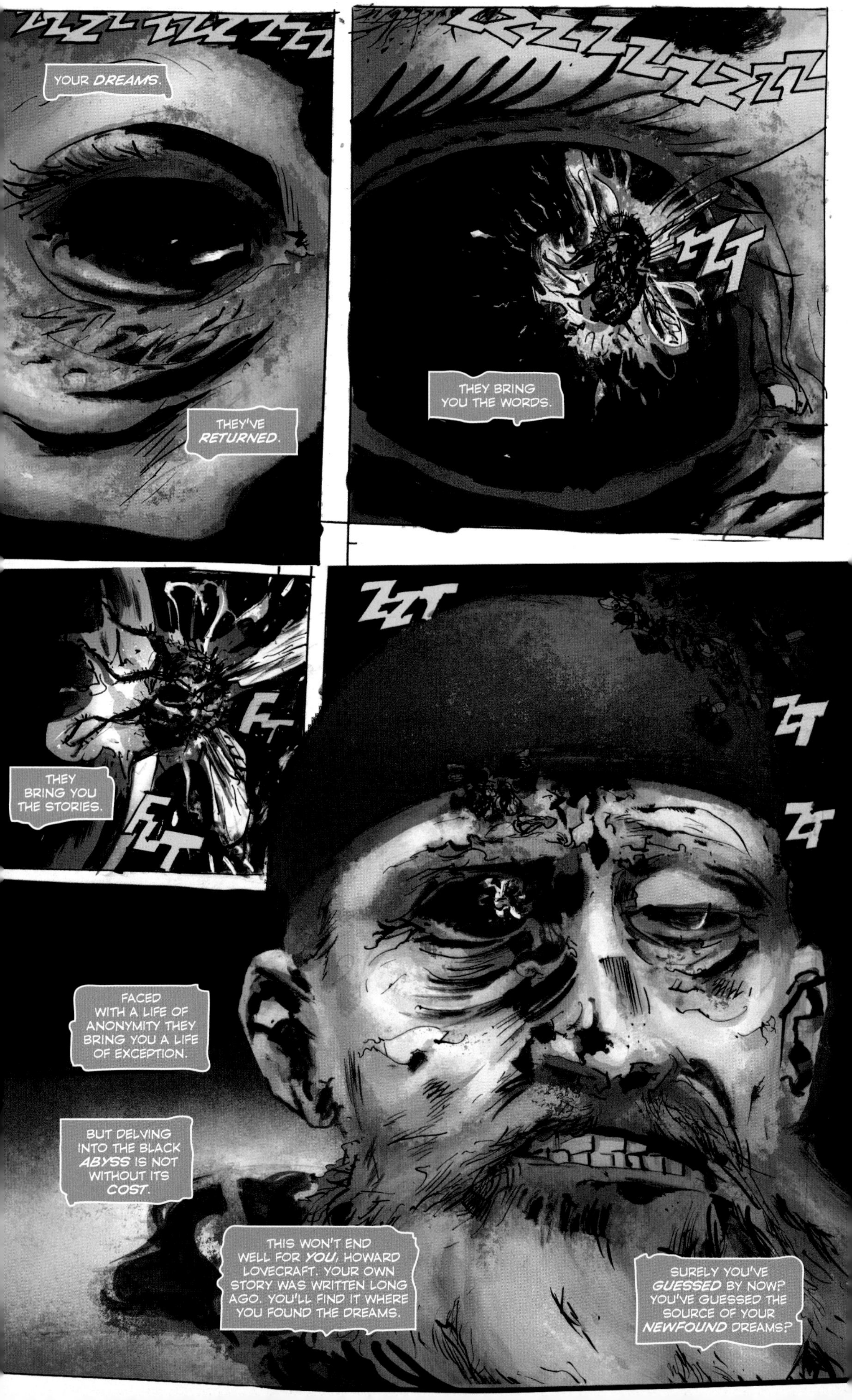

ZZZT ZZZZZZ
YOUR *DREAMS*.
THEY'VE *RETURNED*.
ZZZZZZZZZT
ZZT
THEY BRING YOU THE WORDS.
FZT
THEY BRING YOU THE STORIES.
FZZT
ZZT
ZZT
ZZT
FACED WITH A LIFE OF ANONYMITY THEY BRING YOU A LIFE OF EXCEPTION.
BUT DELVING INTO THE BLACK *ABYSS* IS NOT WITHOUT ITS *COST*.
THIS WON'T END WELL FOR *YOU*, HOWARD LOVECRAFT. YOUR OWN STORY WAS WRITTEN LONG AGO. YOU'LL FIND IT WHERE YOU FOUND THE DREAMS.
SURELY YOU'VE *GUESSED* BY NOW? YOU'VE GUESSED THE SOURCE OF YOUR *NEWFOUND* DREAMS?

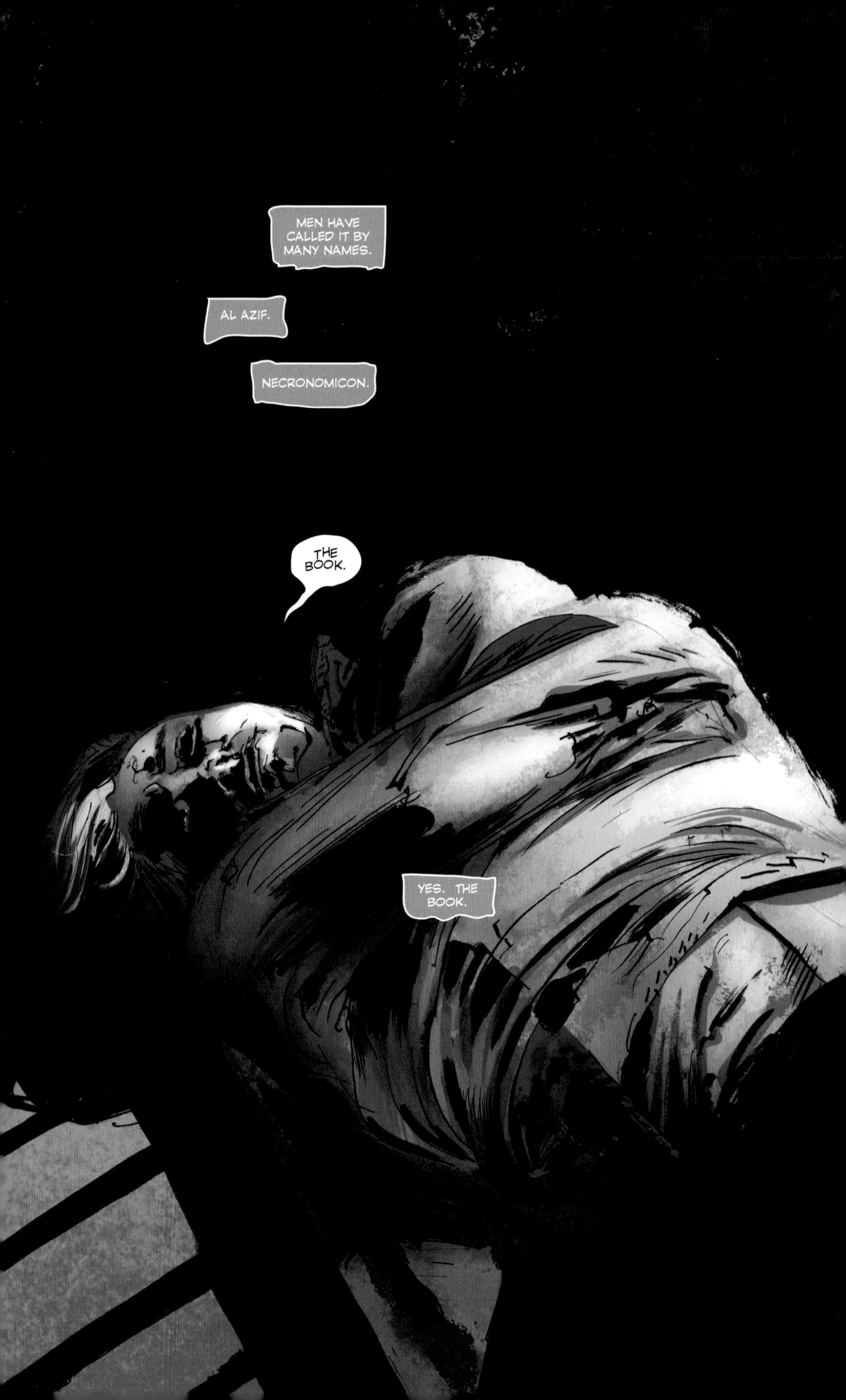
MEN HAVE CALLED IT BY MANY NAMES.
AL AZIF.
NECRONOMICON.
THE BOOK.
YES. THE BOOK.

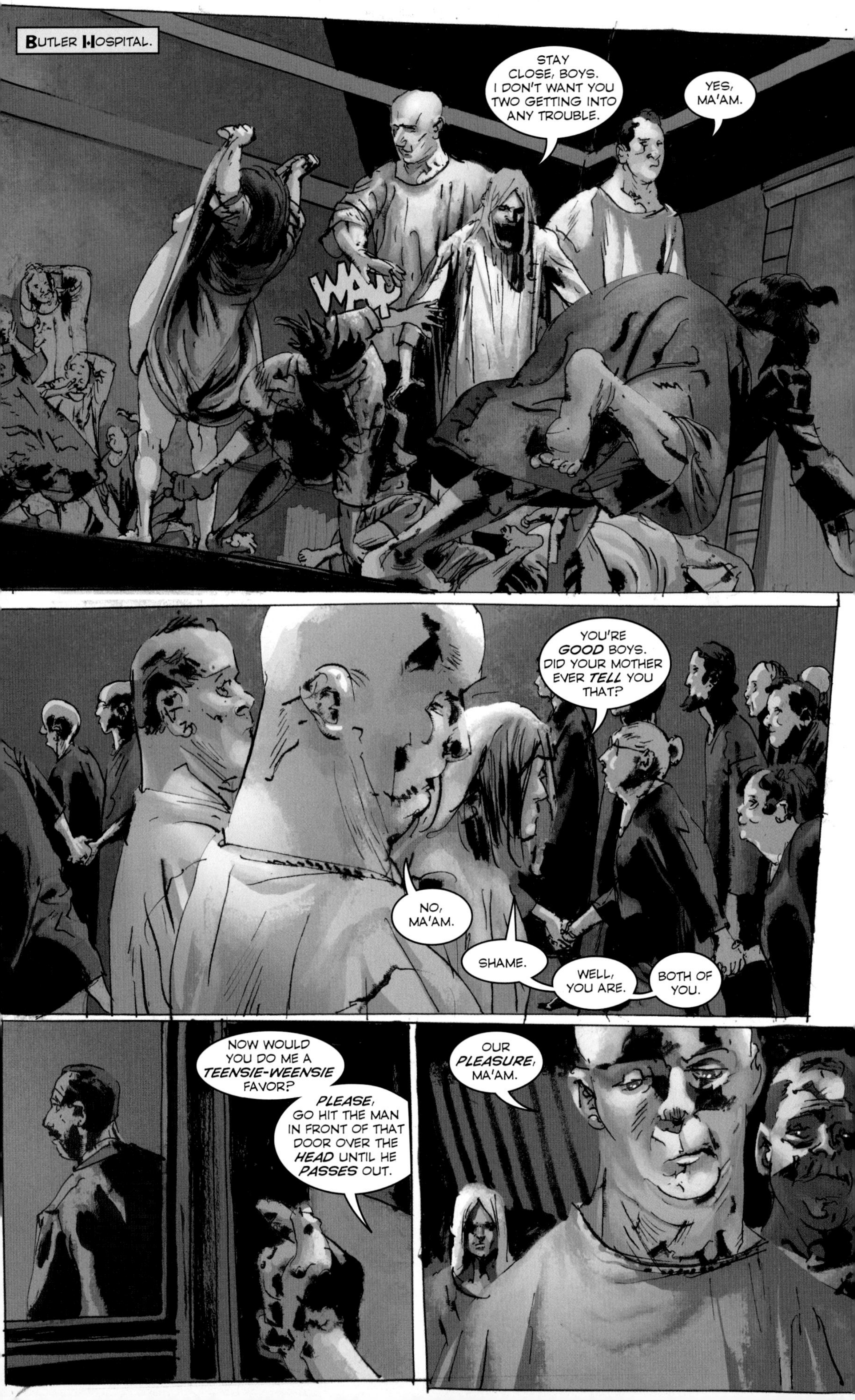
BUTLER HOSPITAL.
STAY CLOSE, BOYS. I DON'T WANT YOU TWO GETTING INTO ANY TROUBLE.
YES, MA'AM.
YOU'RE GOOD BOYS. DID YOUR MOTHER EVER TELL YOU THAT?
NO, MA'AM.
SHAME.
WELL, YOU ARE.
BOTH OF YOU.
NOW WOULD YOU DO ME A TEENSIE-WEENSIE FAVOR?
PLEASE, GO HIT THE MAN IN FRONT OF THAT DOOR OVER THE HEAD UNTIL HE PASSES OUT.
OUR PLEASURE, MA'AM.

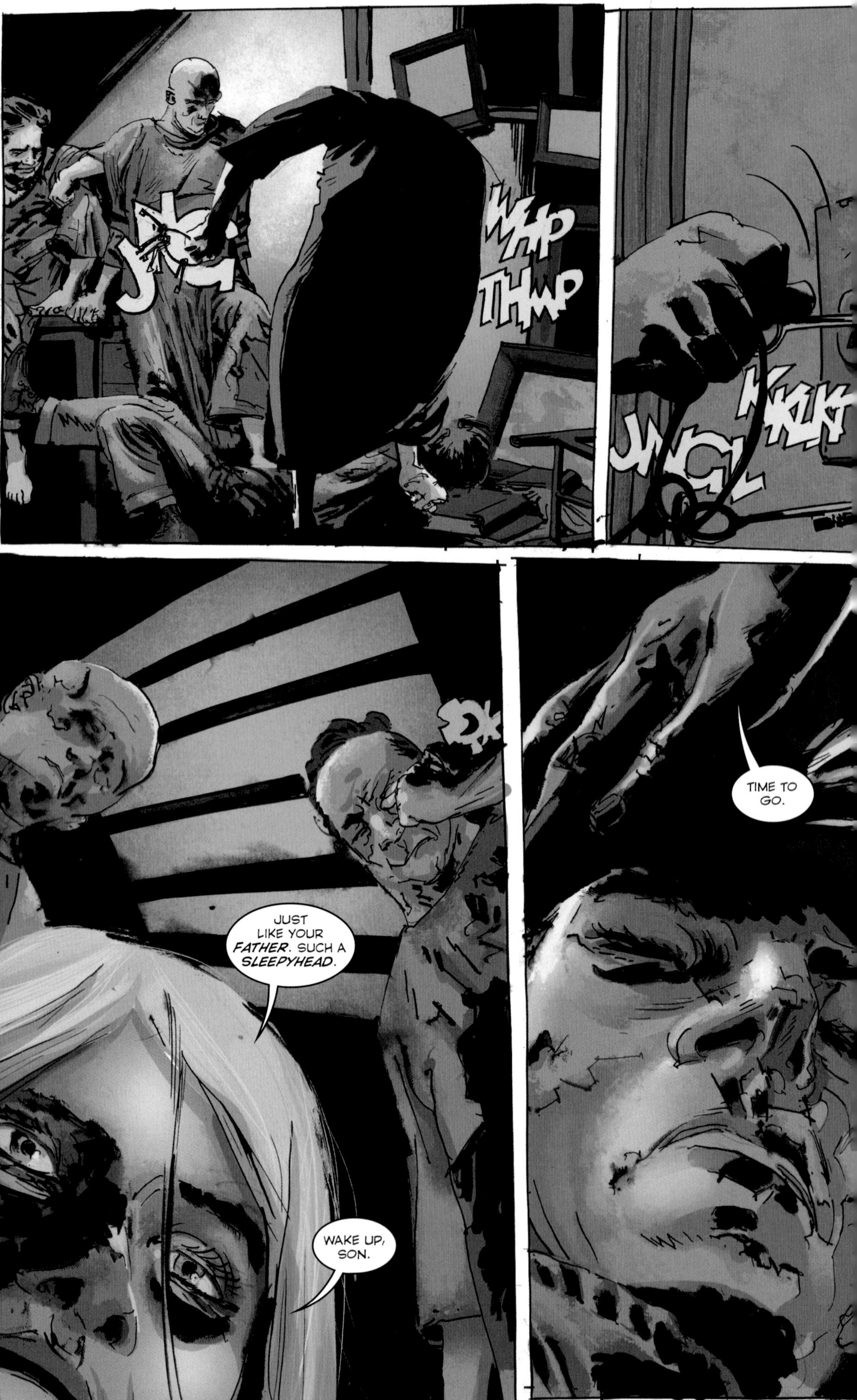
WHIP
THMP
JNGL
KLIK
JUST LIKE YOUR FATHER. SUCH A SLEEPYHEAD.
WAKE UP, SON.
TIME TO GO.

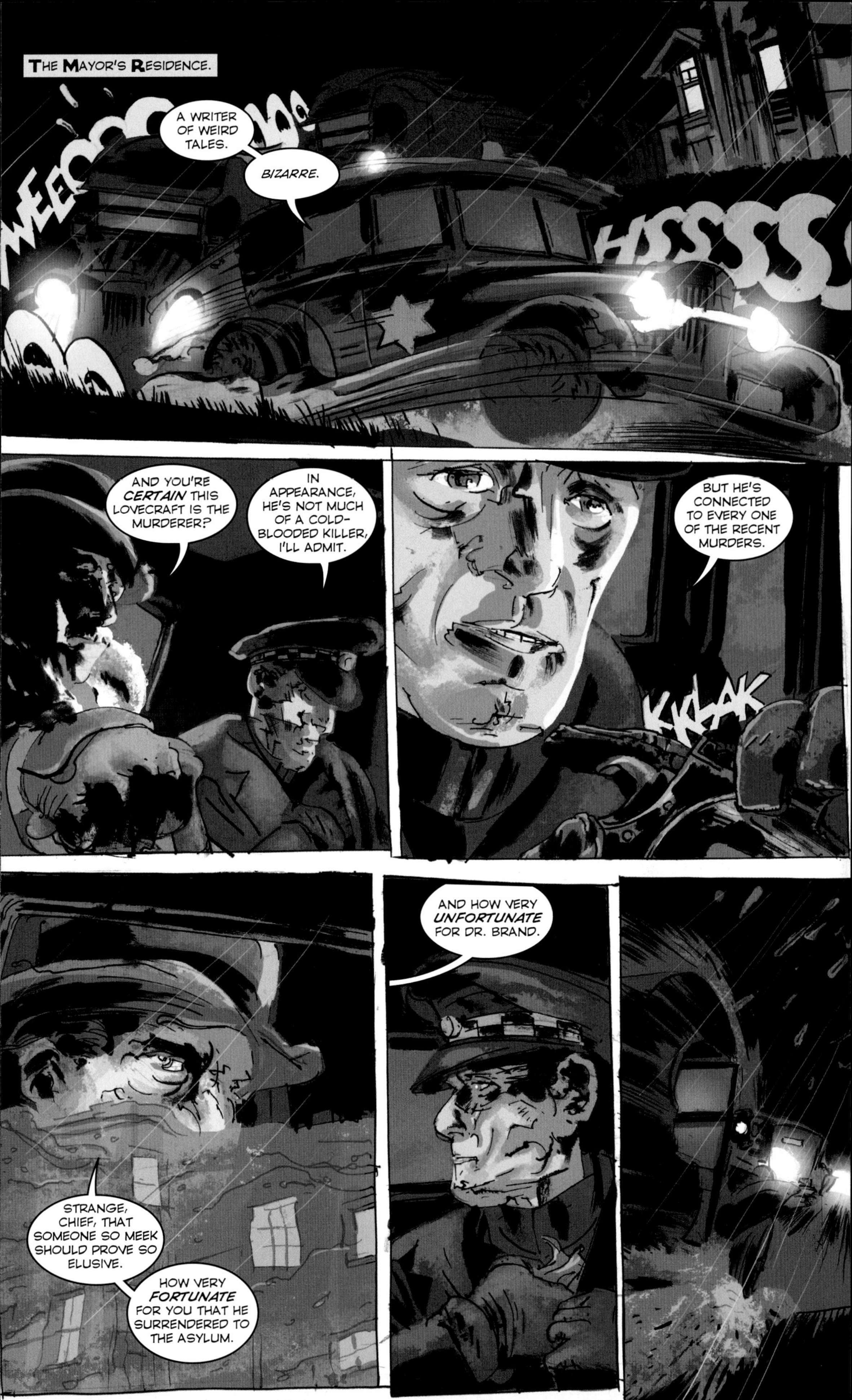
THE MAYOR'S RESIDENCE.
WEEOOOOOO
A WRITER OF WEIRD TALES.
BIZARRE.
HISSSS
AND YOU'RE CERTAIN THIS LOVECRAFT IS THE MURDERER?
IN APPEARANCE, HE'S NOT MUCH OF A COLD-BLOODED KILLER, I'LL ADMIT.
BUT HE'S CONNECTED TO EVERY ONE OF THE RECENT MURDERS.
KLAK
STRANGE, CHIEF, THAT SOMEONE SO MEEK SHOULD PROVE SO ELUSIVE.
HOW VERY FORTUNATE FOR YOU THAT HE SURRENDERED TO THE ASYLUM.
AND HOW VERY UNFORTUNATE FOR DR. BRAND.

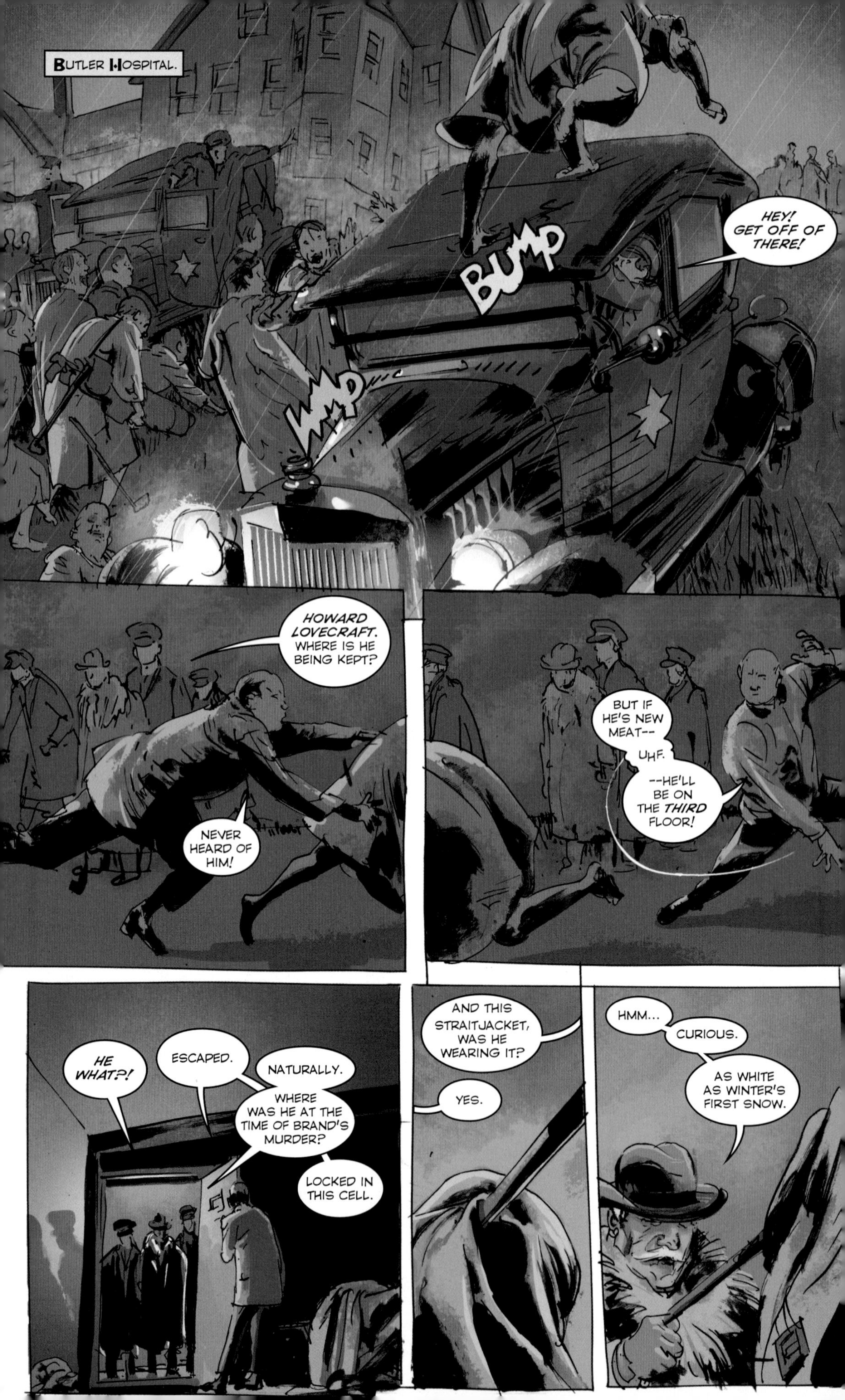

BUTLER HOSPITAL.
HEY! GET OFF OF THERE!
BUMP
WMP
HOWARD LOVECRAFT. WHERE IS HE BEING KEPT?
NEVER HEARD OF HIM!
BUT IF HE'S NEW MEAT--
UHF.
--HE'LL BE ON THE THIRD FLOOR!
HE WHAT?!
ESCAPED.
NATURALLY.
WHERE WAS HE AT THE TIME OF BRAND'S MURDER?
LOCKED IN THIS CELL.
AND THIS STRAITJACKET, WAS HE WEARING IT?
YES.
HMM...
CURIOUS.
AS WHITE AS WINTER'S FIRST SNOW.

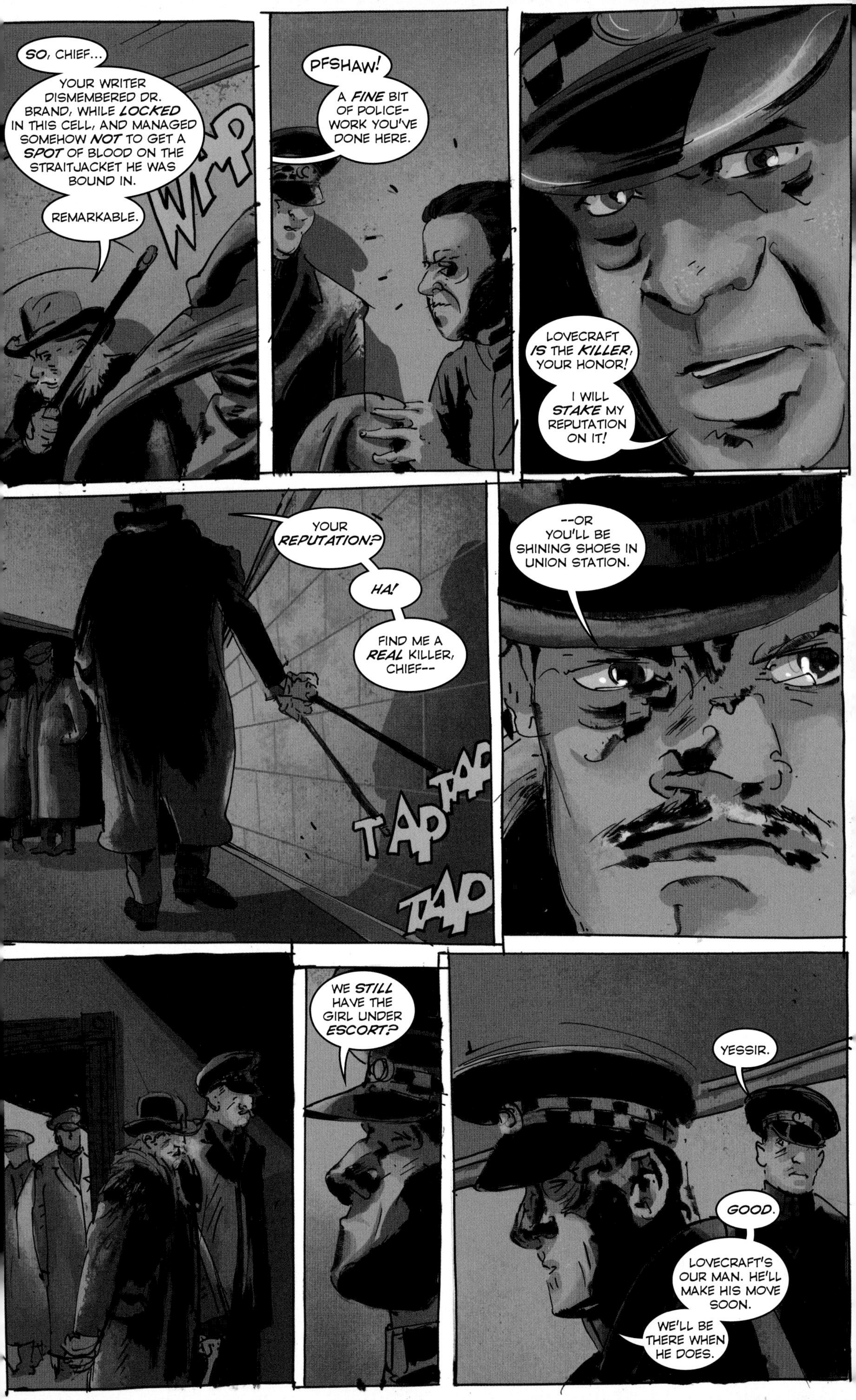
SO, CHIEF...
YOUR WRITER DISMEMBERED DR. BRAND, WHILE LOCKED IN THIS CELL, AND MANAGED SOMEHOW NOT TO GET A SPOT OF BLOOD ON THE STRAITJACKET HE WAS BOUND IN.
REMARKABLE.
WIP
PFSHAW!
A FINE BIT OF POLICE-WORK YOU'VE DONE HERE.
LOVECRAFT IS THE KILLER, YOUR HONOR!
I WILL STAKE MY REPUTATION ON IT!
YOUR REPUTATION?
HA!
FIND ME A REAL KILLER, CHIEF--
TAP TAP
TAP
--OR YOU'LL BE SHINING SHOES IN UNION STATION.
WE STILL HAVE THE GIRL UNDER ESCORT?
YESSIR.
GOOD.
LOVECRAFT'S OUR MAN. HE'LL MAKE HIS MOVE SOON.
WE'LL BE THERE WHEN HE DOES.

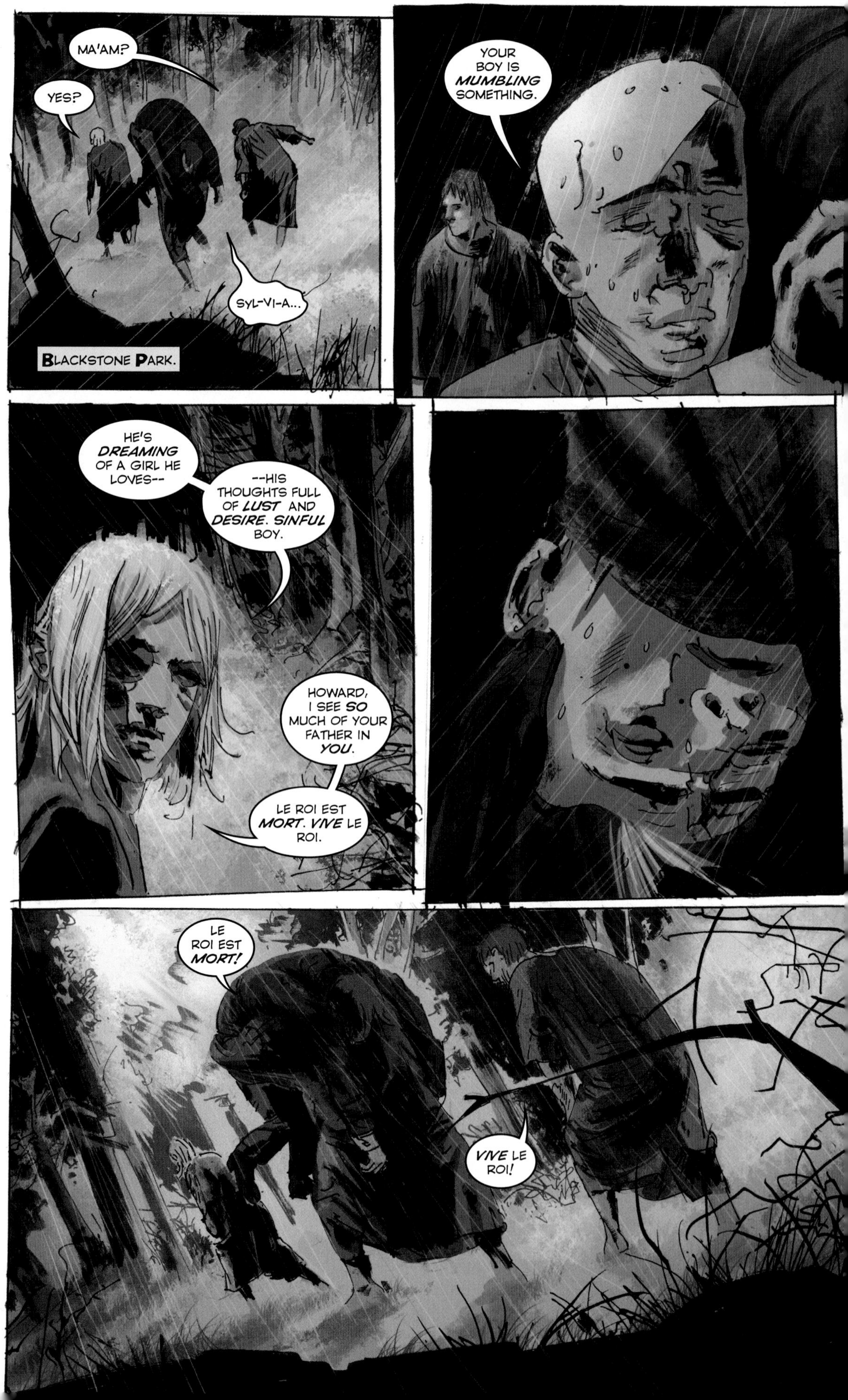
MA'AM?
YES?
SYL-VI-A...
BLACKSTONE PARK.
YOUR BOY IS MUMBLING SOMETHING.
HE'S DREAMING OF A GIRL HE LOVES--
--HIS THOUGHTS FULL OF LUST AND DESIRE. SINFUL BOY.
HOWARD, I SEE SO MUCH OF YOUR FATHER IN YOU.
LE ROI EST MORT. VIVE LE ROI.
LE ROI EST MORT!
VIVE LE ROI!

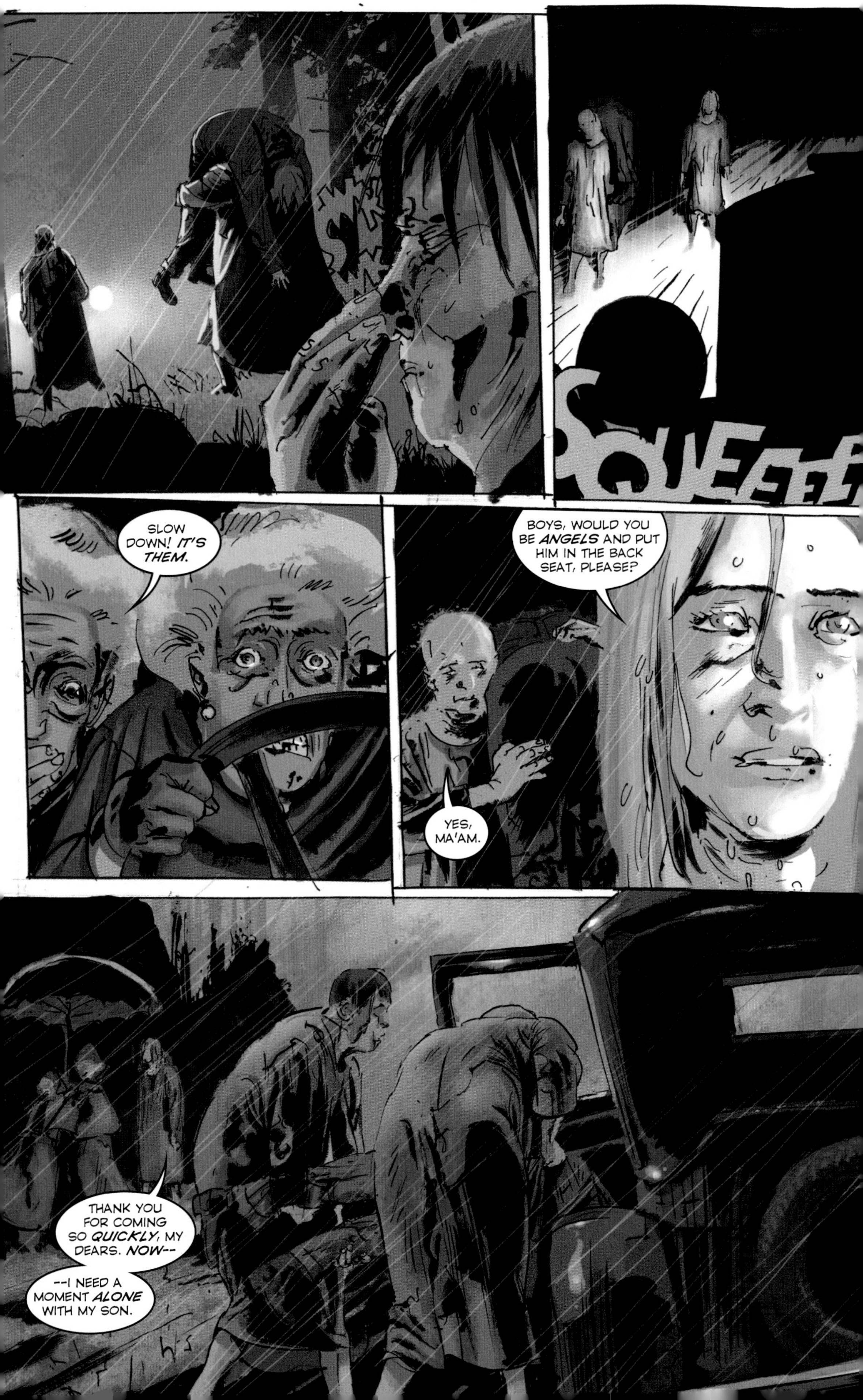

SQUEEE
SLOW DOWN! IT'S THEM.
BOYS, WOULD YOU BE ANGELS AND PUT HIM IN THE BACK SEAT, PLEASE?
YES, MA'AM.
THANK YOU FOR COMING SO QUICKLY, MY DEARS. NOW--
--I NEED A MOMENT ALONE WITH MY SON.

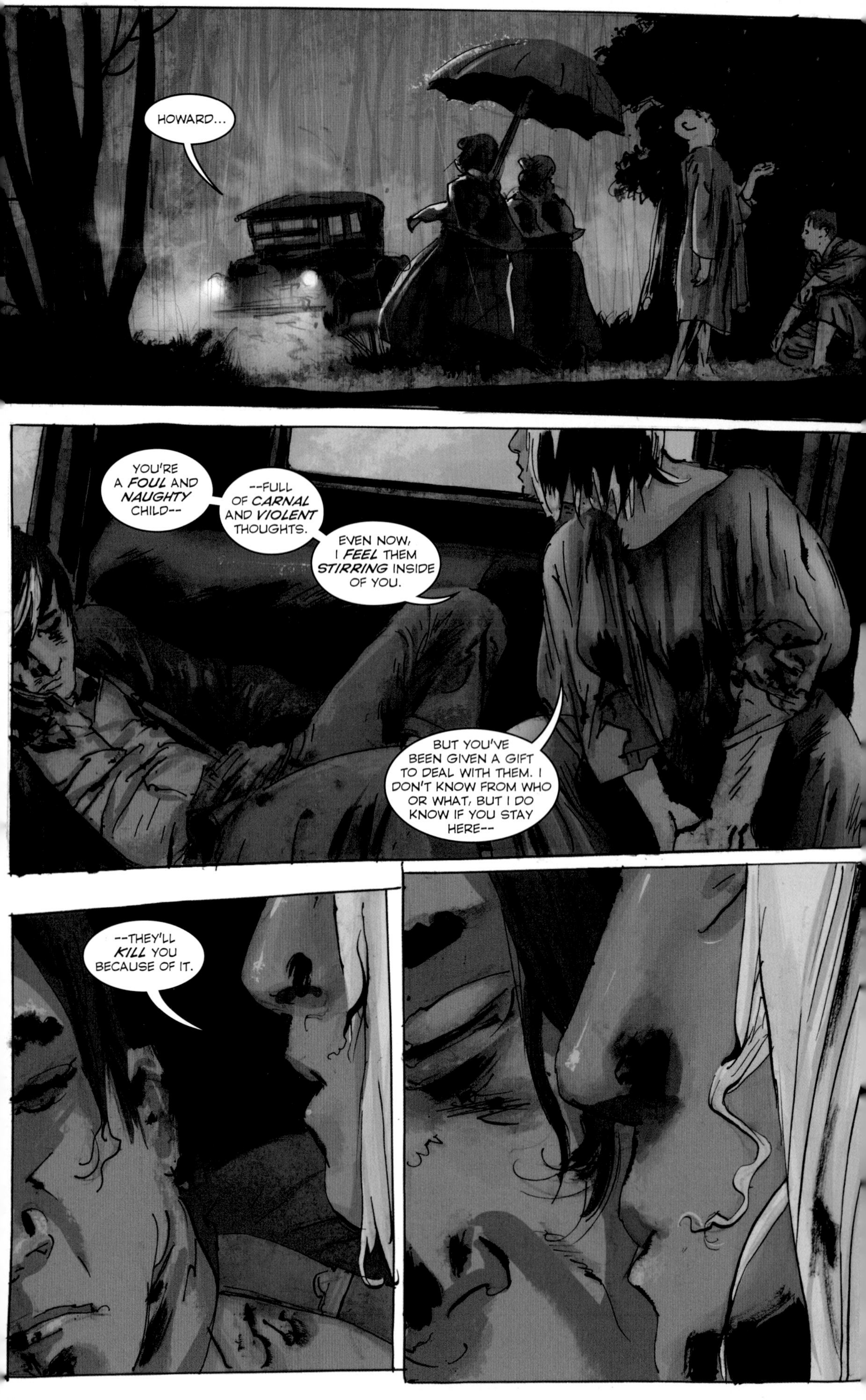
HOWARD...
YOU'RE A *FOUL* AND *NAUGHTY* CHILD--
--FULL OF *CARNAL* AND *VIOLENT* THOUGHTS.
EVEN NOW, I *FEEL* THEM *STIRRING* INSIDE OF YOU.
BUT YOU'VE BEEN GIVEN A GIFT TO DEAL WITH THEM. I DON'T KNOW FROM WHO OR WHAT, BUT I DO KNOW IF YOU STAY HERE--
--THEY'LL *KILL* YOU BECAUSE OF IT.

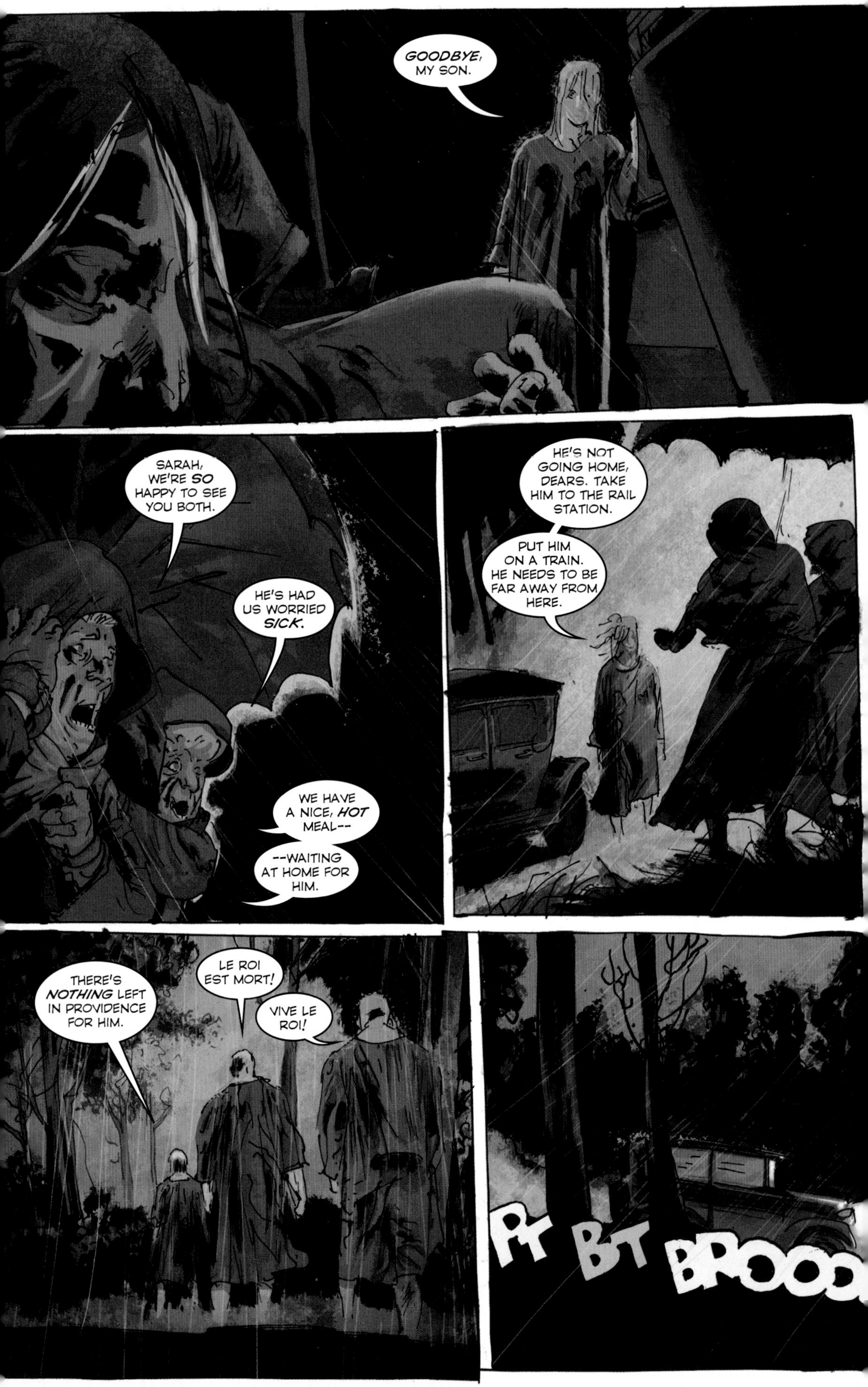
GOODBYE, MY SON.
SARAH, WE'RE SO HAPPY TO SEE YOU BOTH.
HE'S HAD US WORRIED SICK.
WE HAVE A NICE, HOT MEAL--
--WAITING AT HOME FOR HIM.
HE'S NOT GOING HOME, DEARS. TAKE HIM TO THE RAIL STATION.
PUT HIM ON A TRAIN. HE NEEDS TO BE FAR AWAY FROM HERE.
THERE'S NOTHING LEFT IN PROVIDENCE FOR HIM.
LE ROI EST MORT!
VIVE LE ROI!
PT BT BROOO

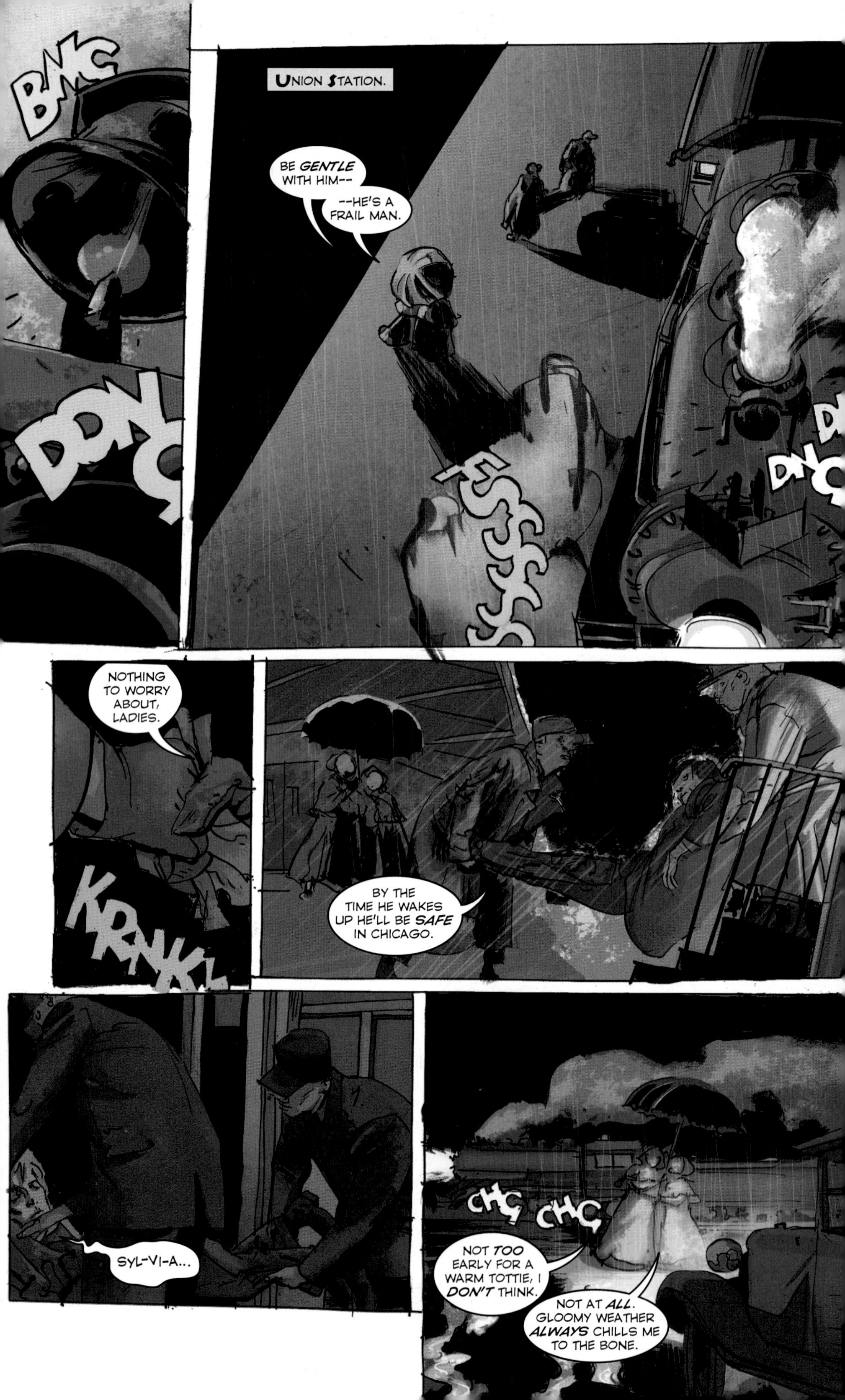
BNG
DONG
UNION STATION.
BE GENTLE WITH HIM--
--HE'S A FRAIL MAN.
FSSSSS
NOTHING TO WORRY ABOUT, LADIES.
KRNKL
BY THE TIME HE WAKES UP HE'LL BE SAFE IN CHICAGO.
SYL-VI-A...
CHG CHG
NOT TOO EARLY FOR A WARM TOTTIE, I DON'T THINK.
NOT AT ALL. GLOOMY WEATHER ALWAYS CHILLS ME TO THE BONE.

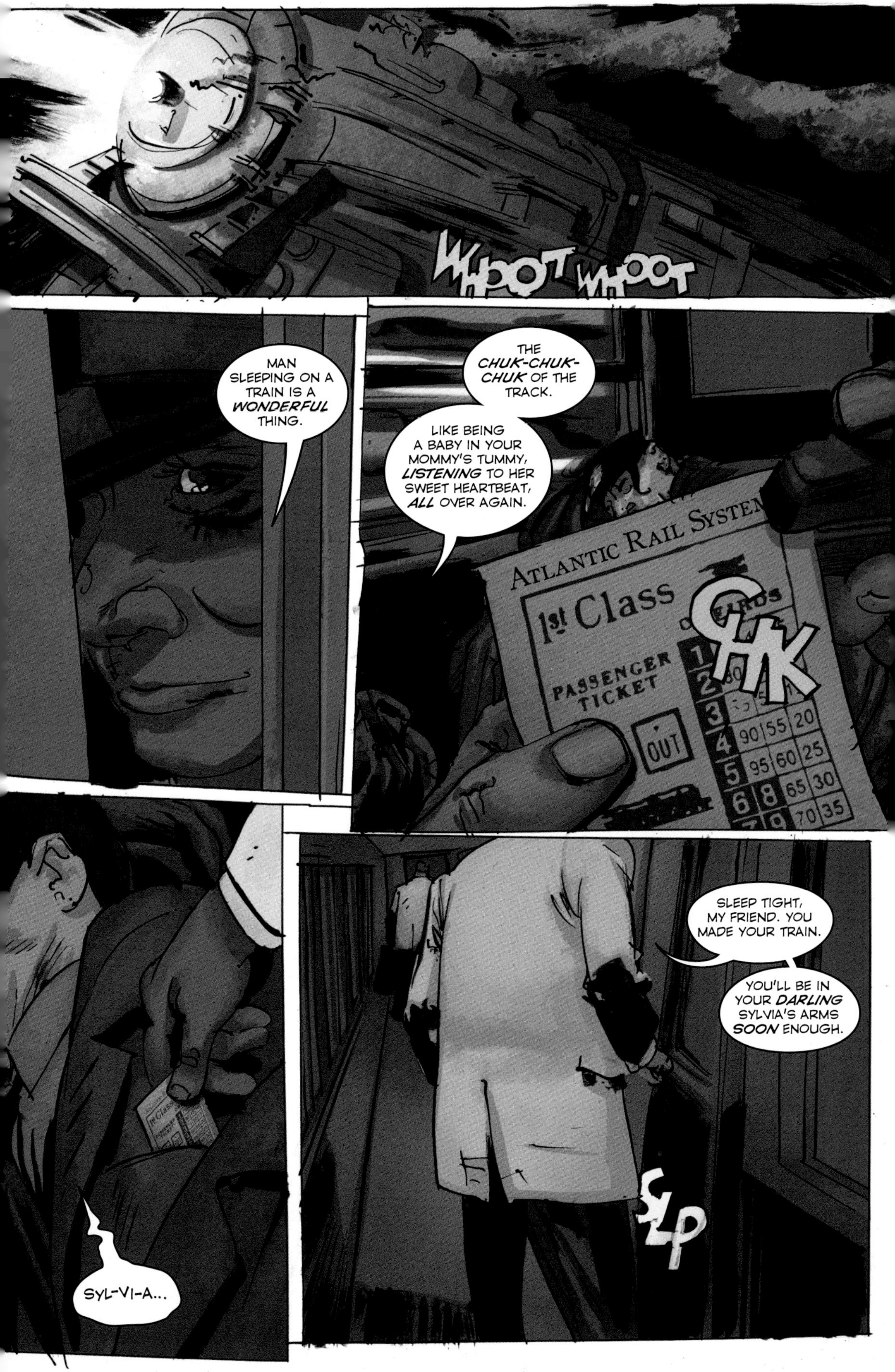
WHOOT WHOOT
MAN SLEEPING ON A TRAIN IS A WONDERFUL THING.
THE CHUK-CHUK-CHUK OF THE TRACK.
LIKE BEING A BABY IN YOUR MOMMY'S TUMMY, LISTENING TO HER SWEET HEARTBEAT, ALL OVER AGAIN.
ATLANTIC RAIL SYSTEM
1st Class
PASSENGER TICKET
OUT
CHK
SYL-VI-A...
SLEEP TIGHT, MY FRIEND. YOU MADE YOUR TRAIN.
YOU'LL BE IN YOUR DARLING SYLVIA'S ARMS SOON ENOUGH.
SLP

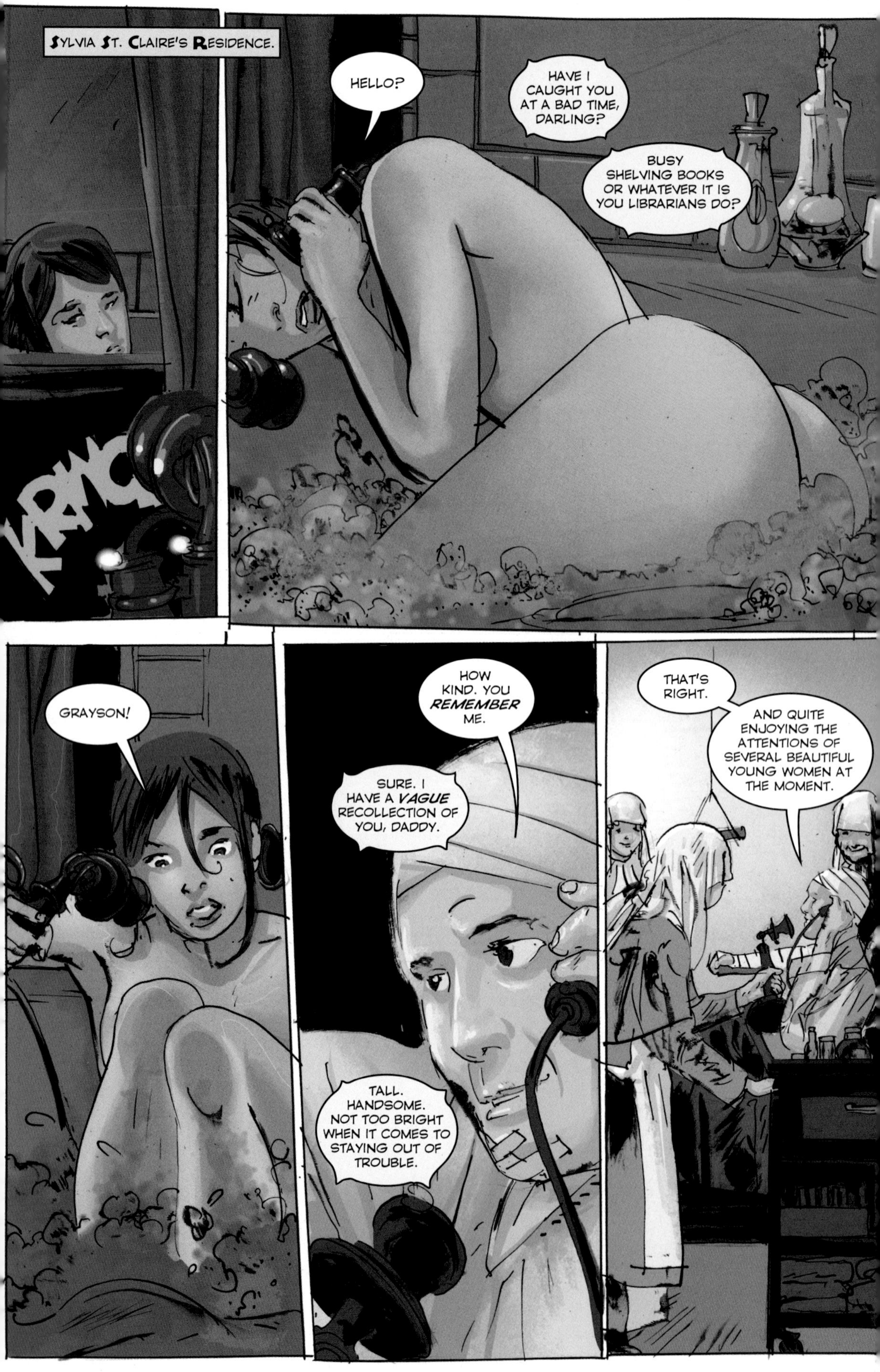
SYLVIA ST. CLAIRE'S RESIDENCE.
KRAC
HELLO?
HAVE I CAUGHT YOU AT A BAD TIME, DARLING?
BUSY SHELVING BOOKS OR WHATEVER IT IS YOU LIBRARIANS DO?
GRAYSON!
HOW KIND. YOU REMEMBER ME.
SURE. I HAVE A VAGUE RECOLLECTION OF YOU, DADDY.
TALL. HANDSOME. NOT TOO BRIGHT WHEN IT COMES TO STAYING OUT OF TROUBLE.
THAT'S RIGHT.
AND QUITE ENJOYING THE ATTENTIONS OF SEVERAL BEAUTIFUL YOUNG WOMEN AT THE MOMENT.

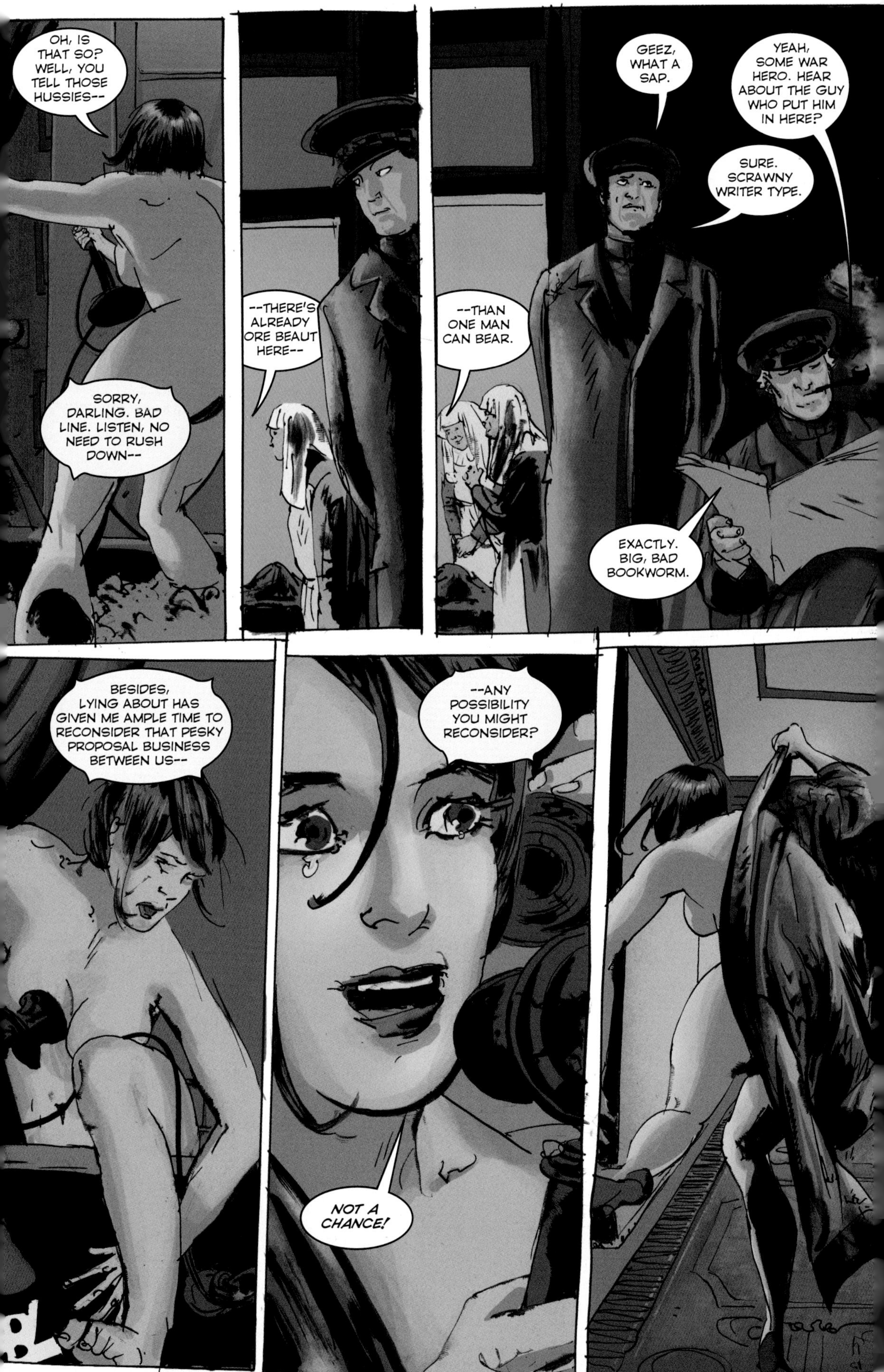
OH, IS THAT SO? WELL, YOU TELL THOSE HUSSIES--
SORRY, DARLING. BAD LINE. LISTEN, NO NEED TO RUSH DOWN--
--THERE'S ALREADY ORE BEAUT HERE--
--THAN ONE MAN CAN BEAR.
GEEZ, WHAT A SAP.
YEAH, SOME WAR HERO. HEAR ABOUT THE GUY WHO PUT HIM IN HERE?
SURE. SCRAWNY WRITER TYPE.
EXACTLY. BIG, BAD BOOKWORM.
BESIDES, LYING ABOUT HAS GIVEN ME AMPLE TIME TO RECONSIDER THAT PESKY PROPOSAL BUSINESS BETWEEN US--
--ANY POSSIBILITY YOU MIGHT RECONSIDER?
NOT A CHANCE!

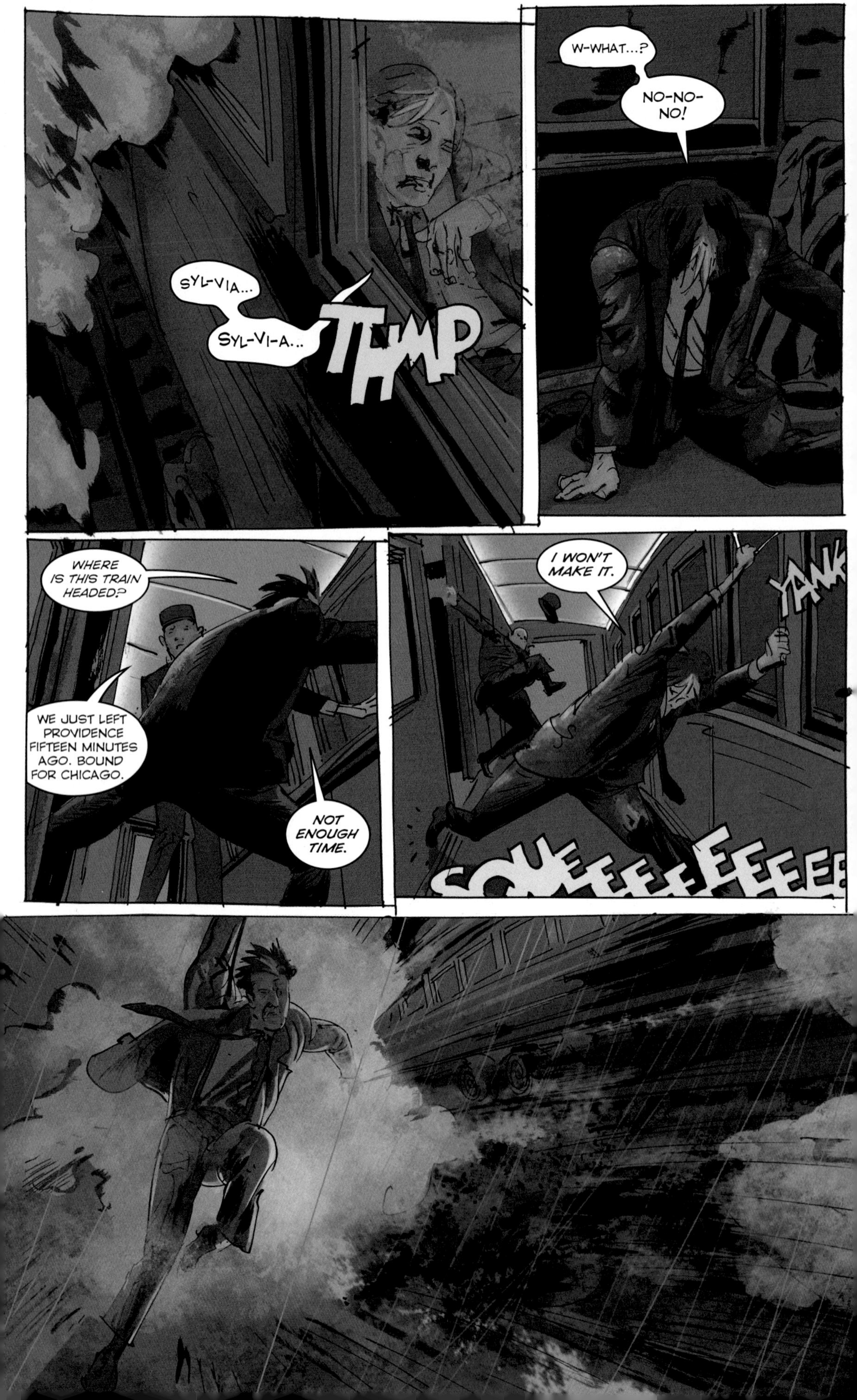
SYL-VIA...
SYL-VI-A...
THMP
W-WHAT...?
NO-NO-NO!
WHERE IS THIS TRAIN HEADED?
WE JUST LEFT PROVIDENCE FIFTEEN MINUTES AGO. BOUND FOR CHICAGO.
NOT ENOUGH TIME.
I WON'T MAKE IT.
YANK

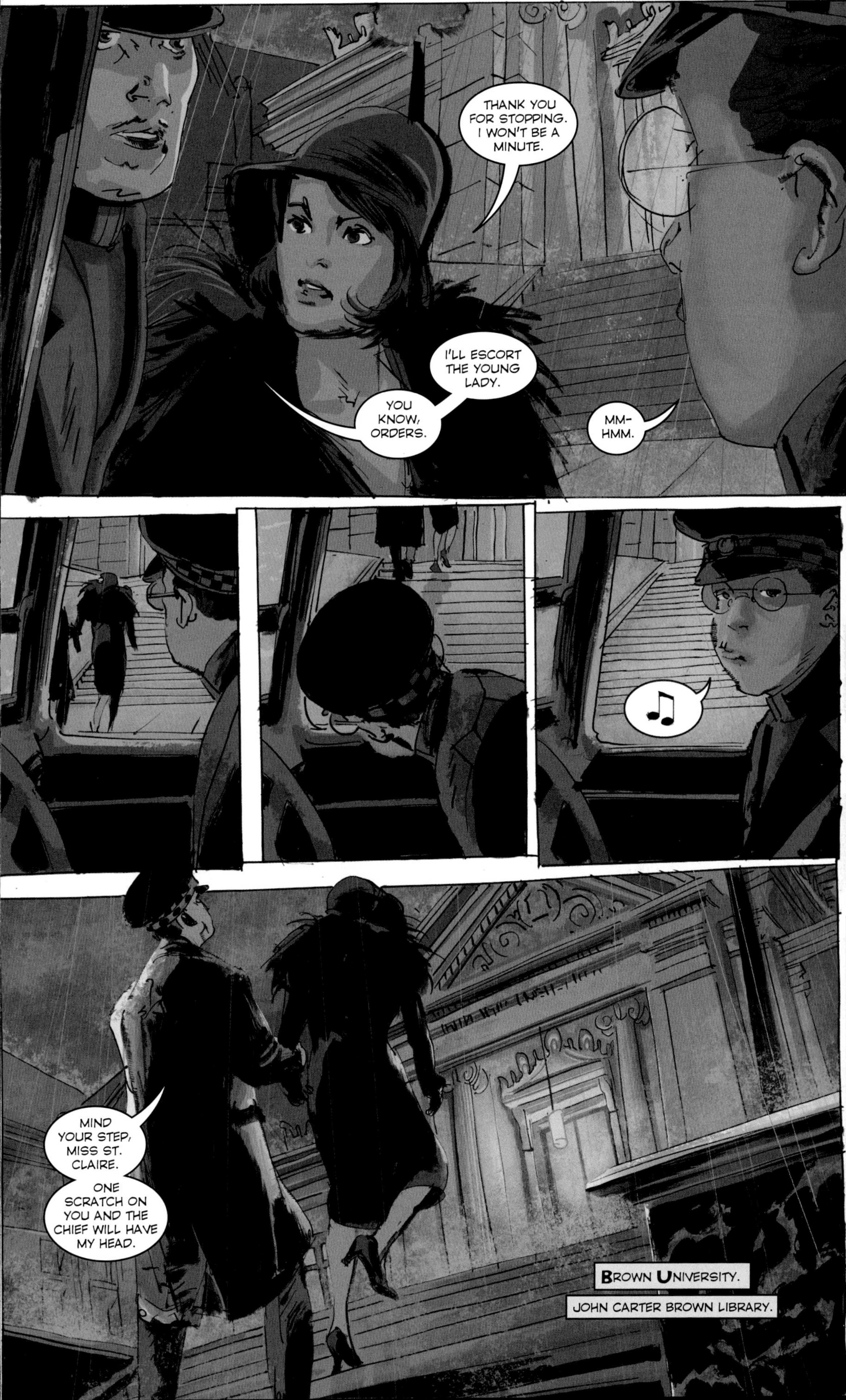
THANK YOU FOR STOPPING. I WON'T BE A MINUTE.
I'LL ESCORT THE YOUNG LADY.
YOU KNOW, ORDERS.
MM-HMM.
♫
MIND YOUR STEP, MISS ST. CLAIRE.
ONE SCRATCH ON YOU AND THE CHIEF WILL HAVE MY HEAD.
BROWN UNIVERSITY.
JOHN CARTER BROWN LIBRARY.

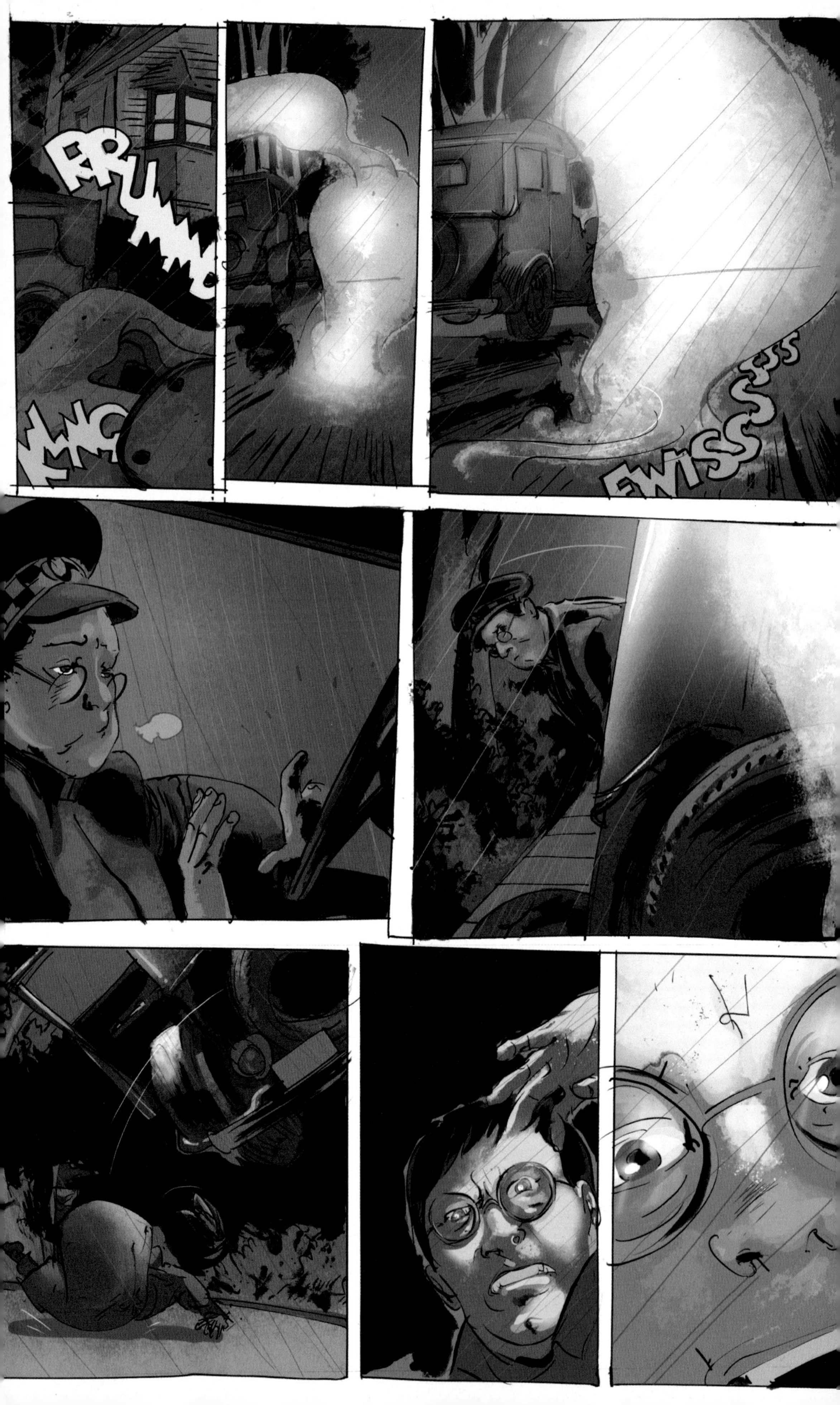
FWISSSSSS

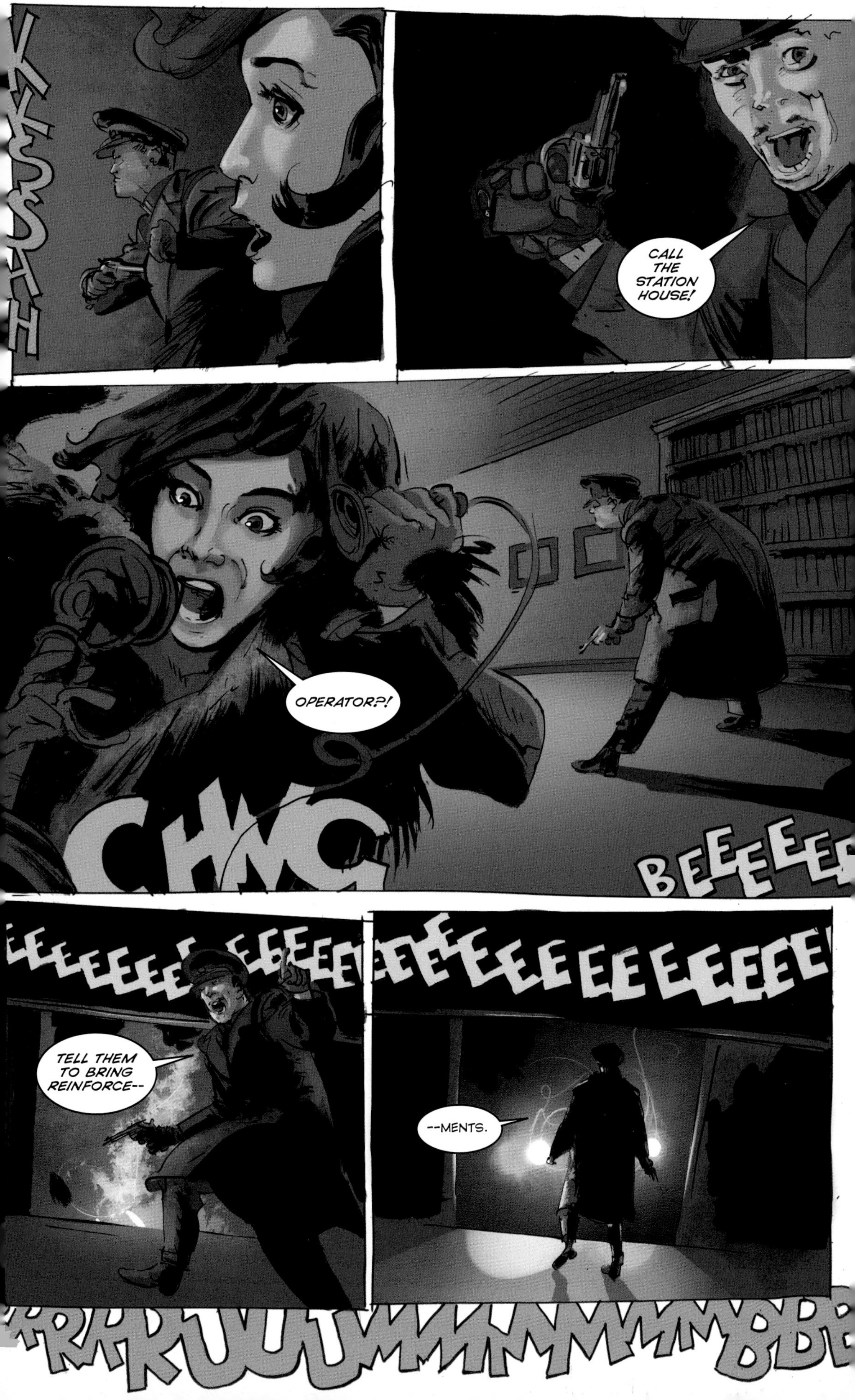
CALL THE STATION HOUSE!
OPERATOR?!
TELL THEM TO BRING REINFORCE--
--MENTS.

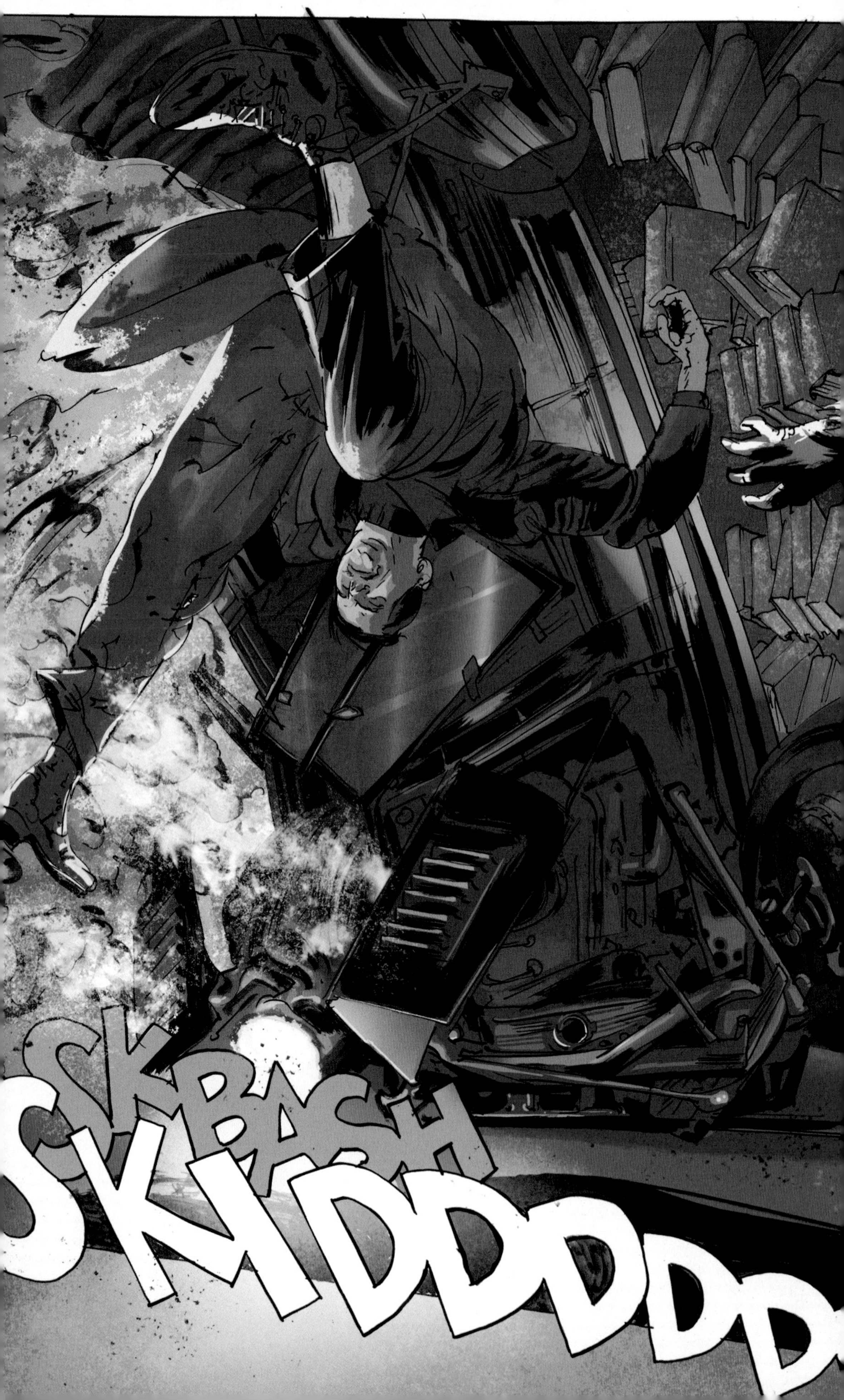
SKRASH
SKIDDDDDD

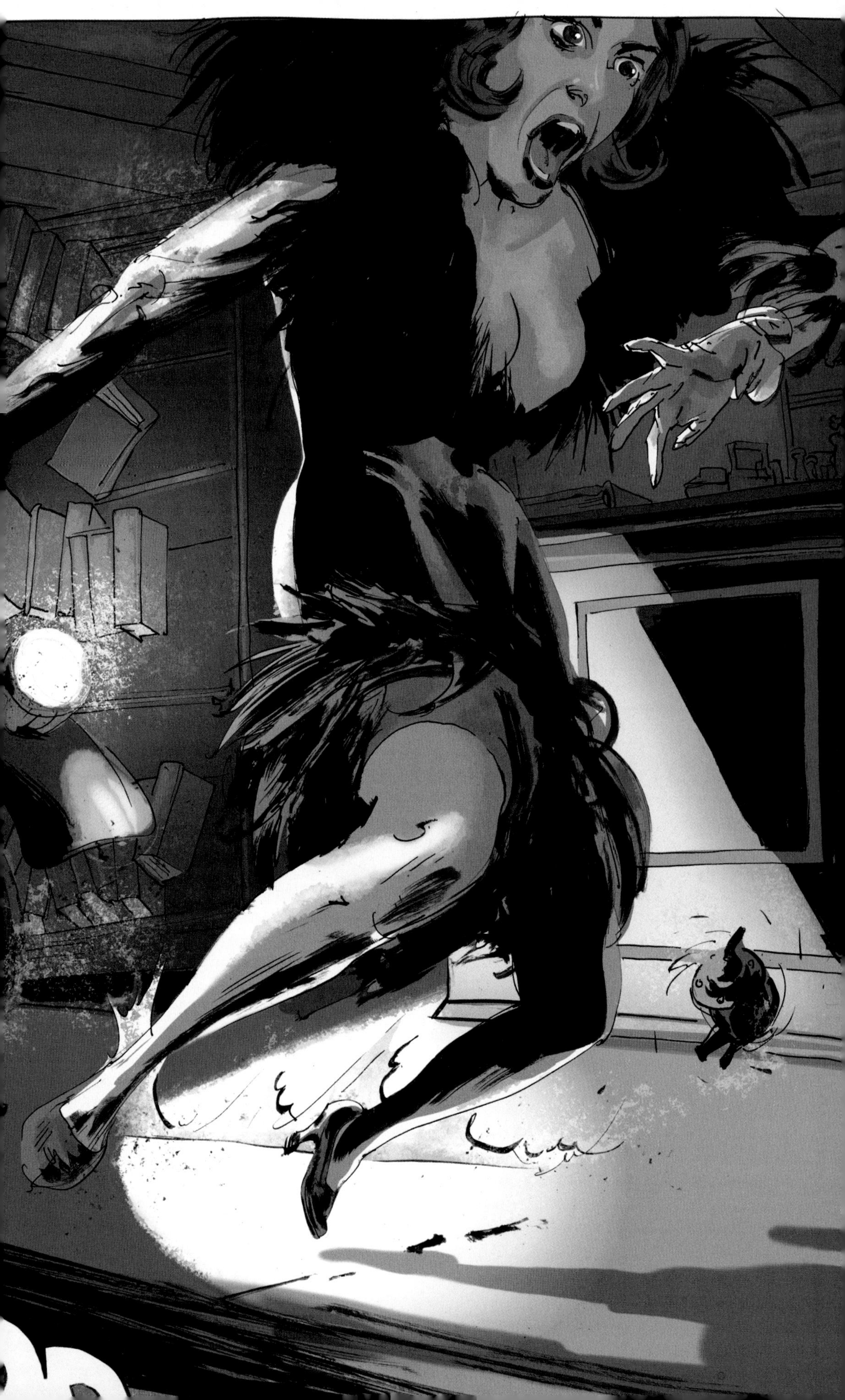

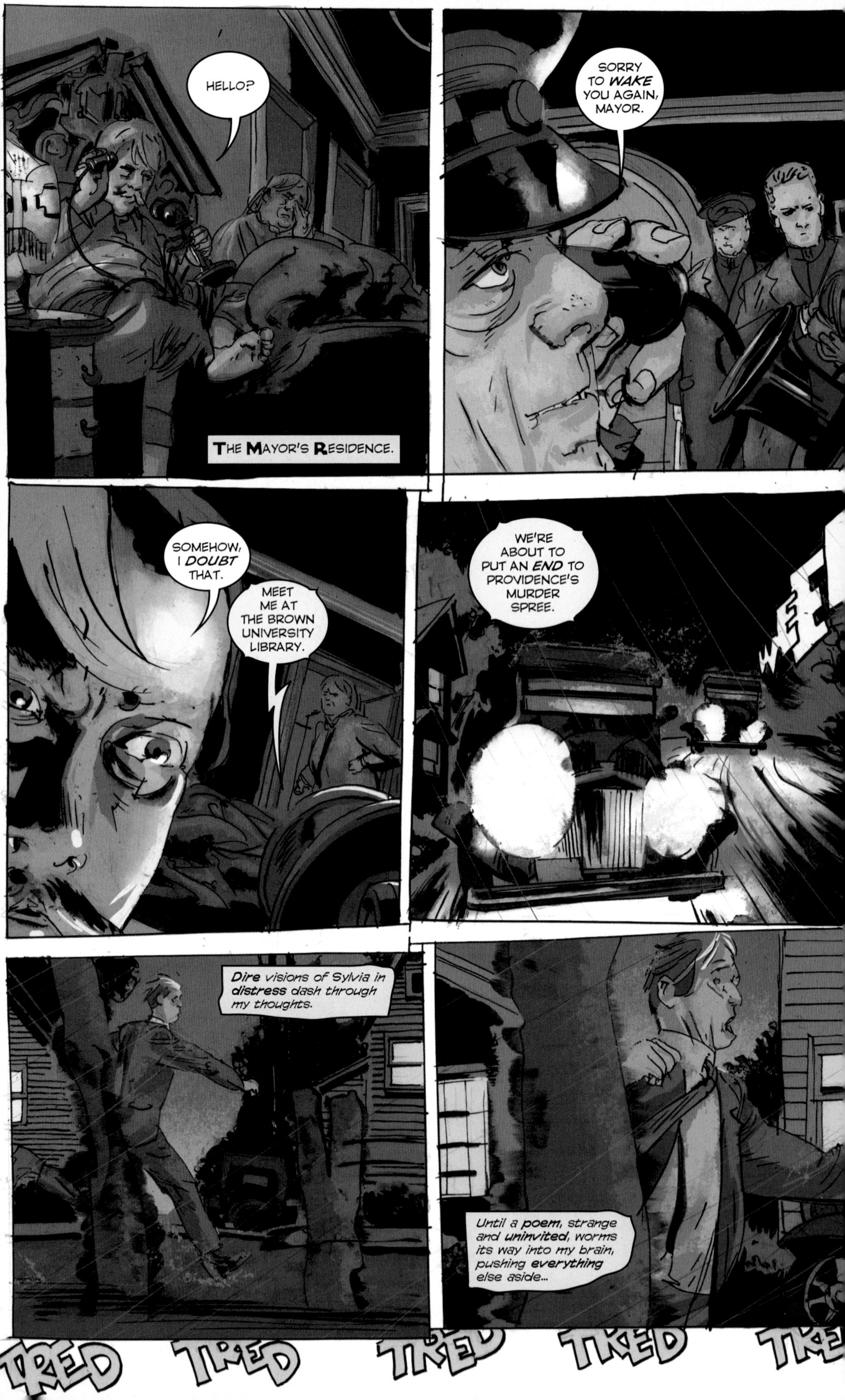
HELLO?
THE MAYOR'S RESIDENCE.
SORRY TO WAKE YOU AGAIN, MAYOR.
SOMEHOW, I DOUBT THAT.
MEET ME AT THE BROWN UNIVERSITY LIBRARY.
WE'RE ABOUT TO PUT AN END TO PROVIDENCE'S MURDER SPREE.
Dire visions of Sylvia in distress dash through my thoughts.
Until a poem, strange and uninvited, worms its way into my brain, pushing everything else aside...
TRED TRED TRED TRED

The Old Ones *were*,

The Old Ones *are*,

And the Old Ones *shall* be.

They wait *stoic* and *strong*, for *here* shall They reign again.

The words are his-- the *mad Arab's*.

A vile affirmation from his accursed book.

Their portent is *obvious*.

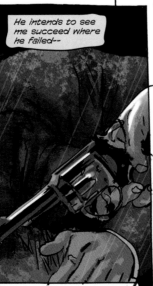

He intends to see me succeed where he failed--

--and *loose* the foulness of the *Old Ones* upon my world.

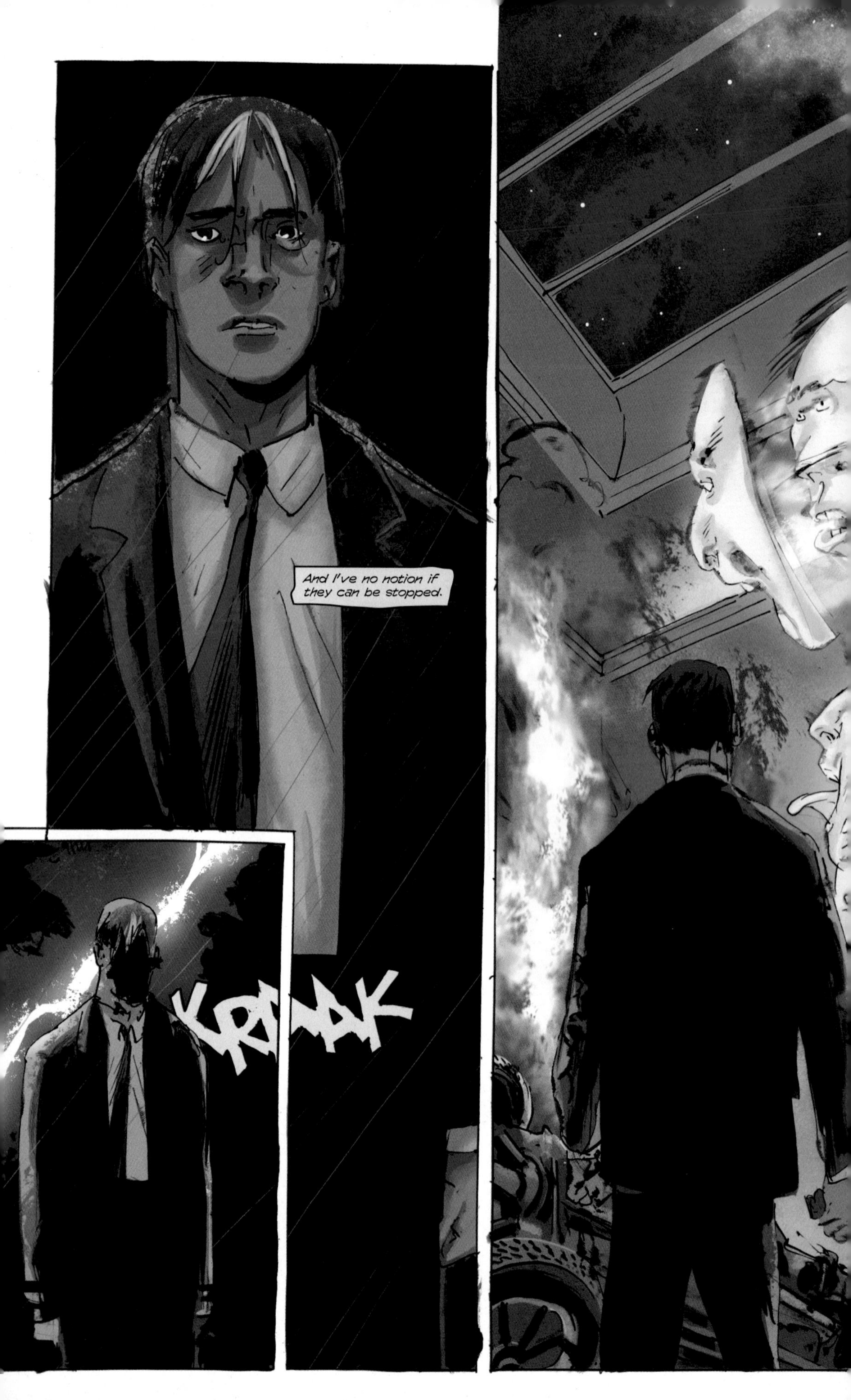
And I've no notion if they can be stopped.
KRAAK

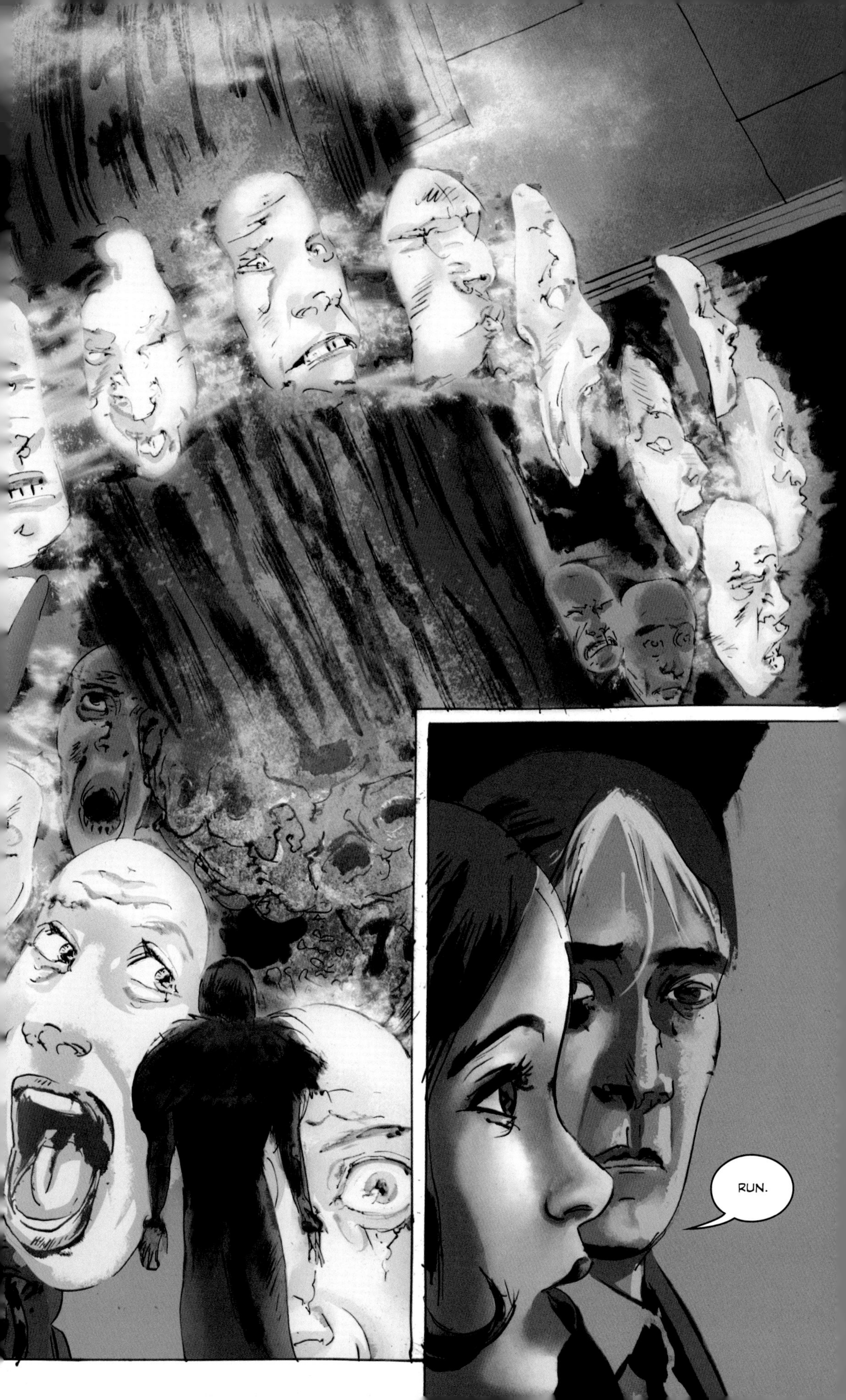
RUN.

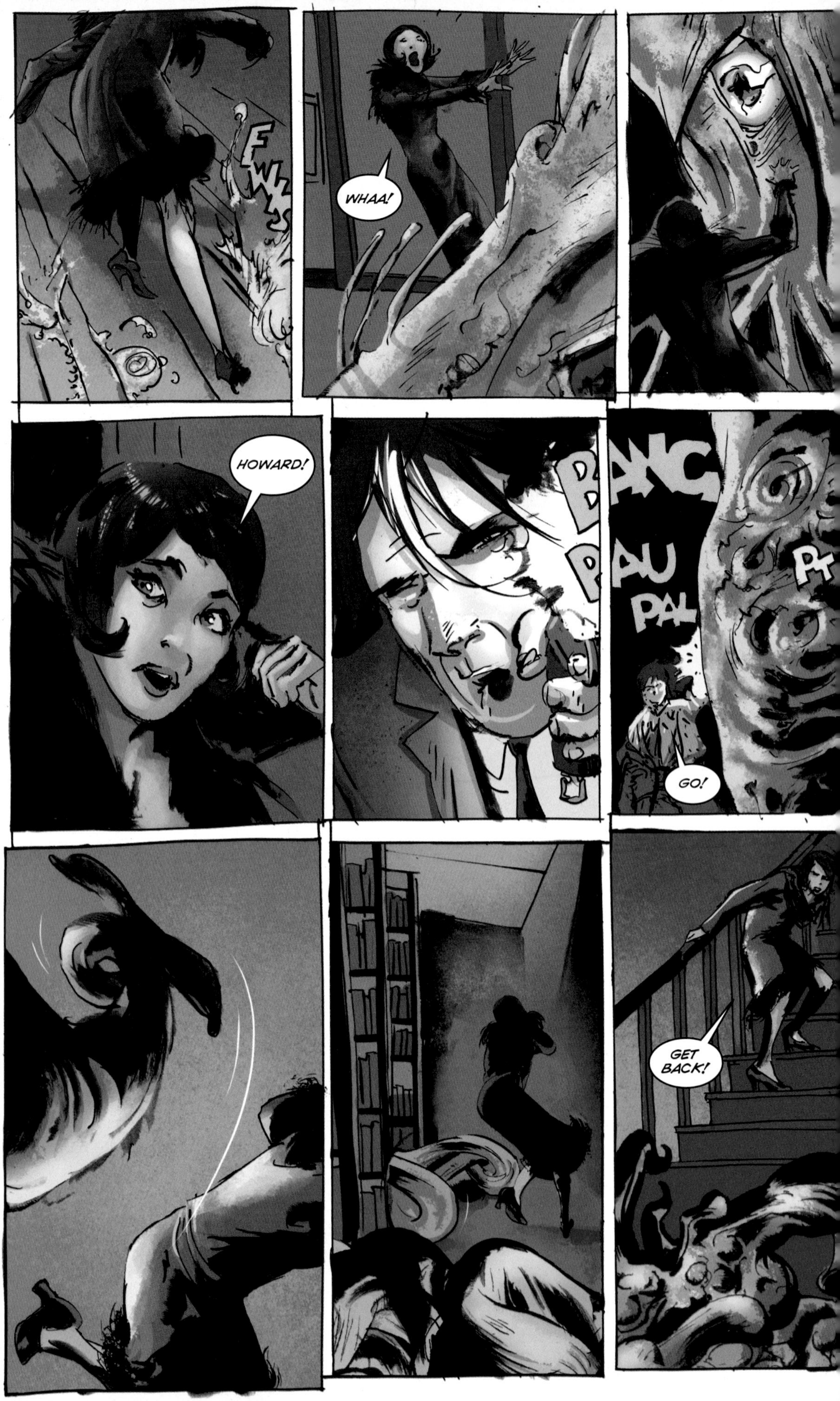
WHAA!
HOWARD!
BANG
PAU
PAL
GO!
GET BACK!

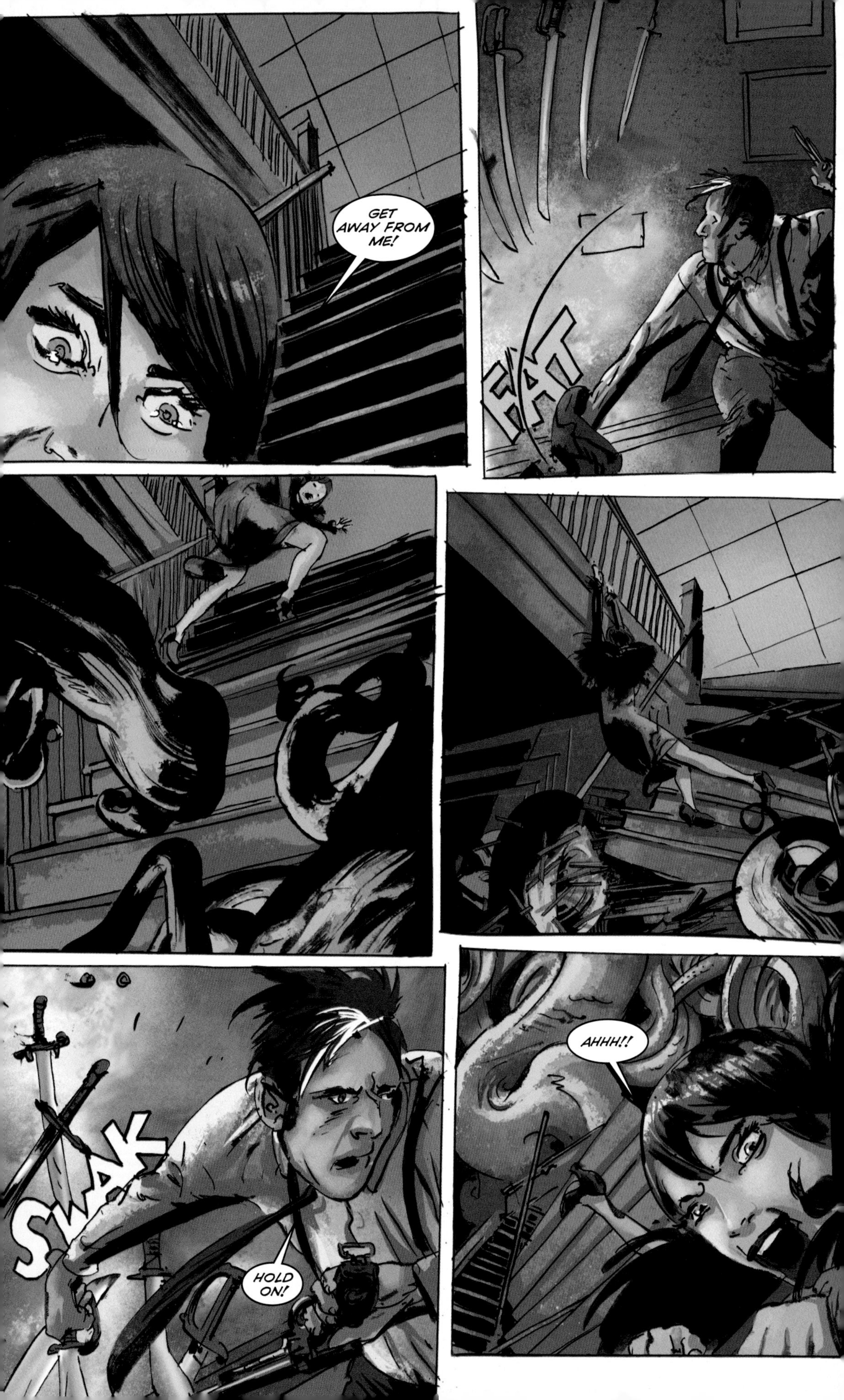
GET AWAY FROM ME!
SWAK
HOLD ON!
AHHH!!

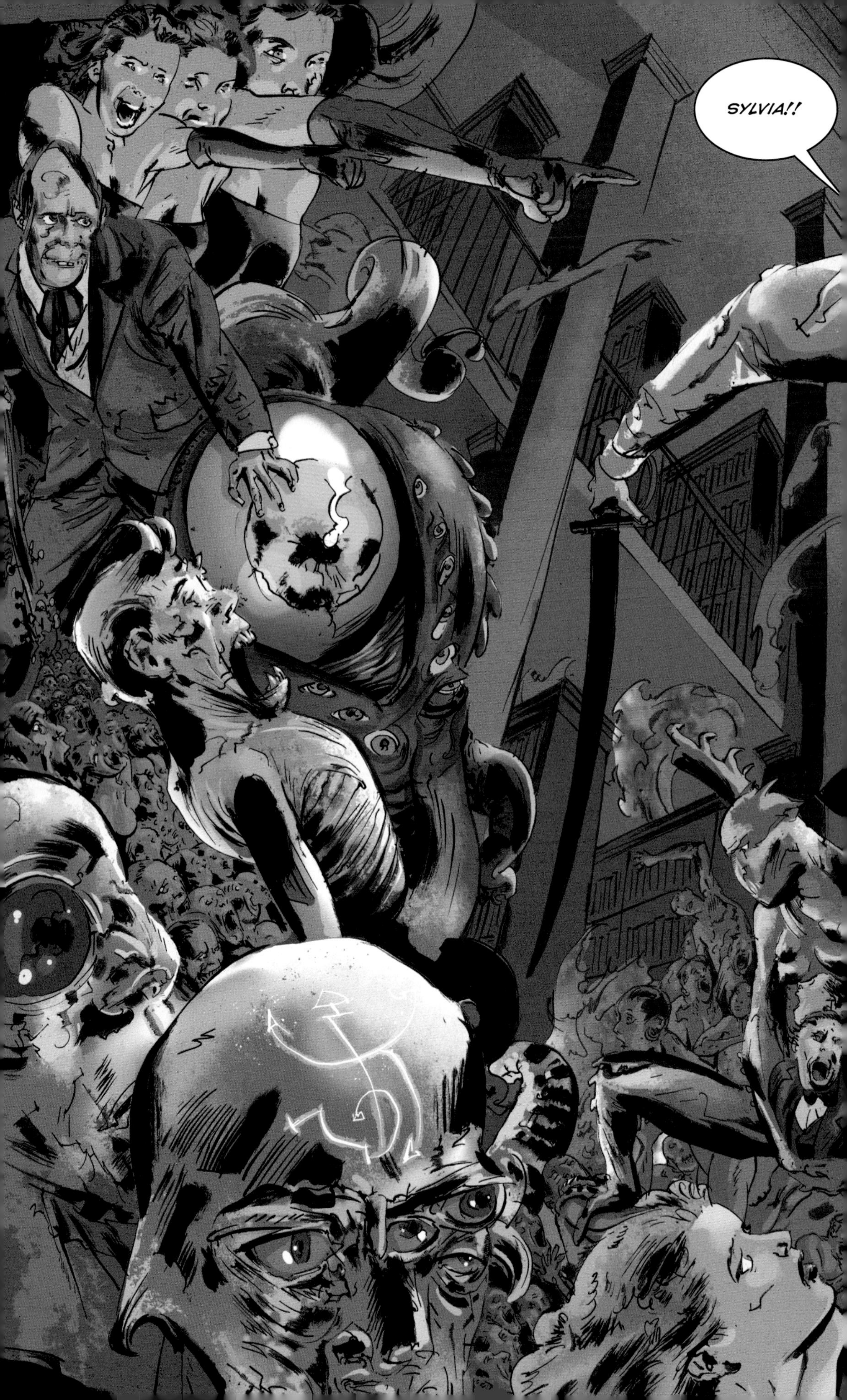
SYLVIA!!

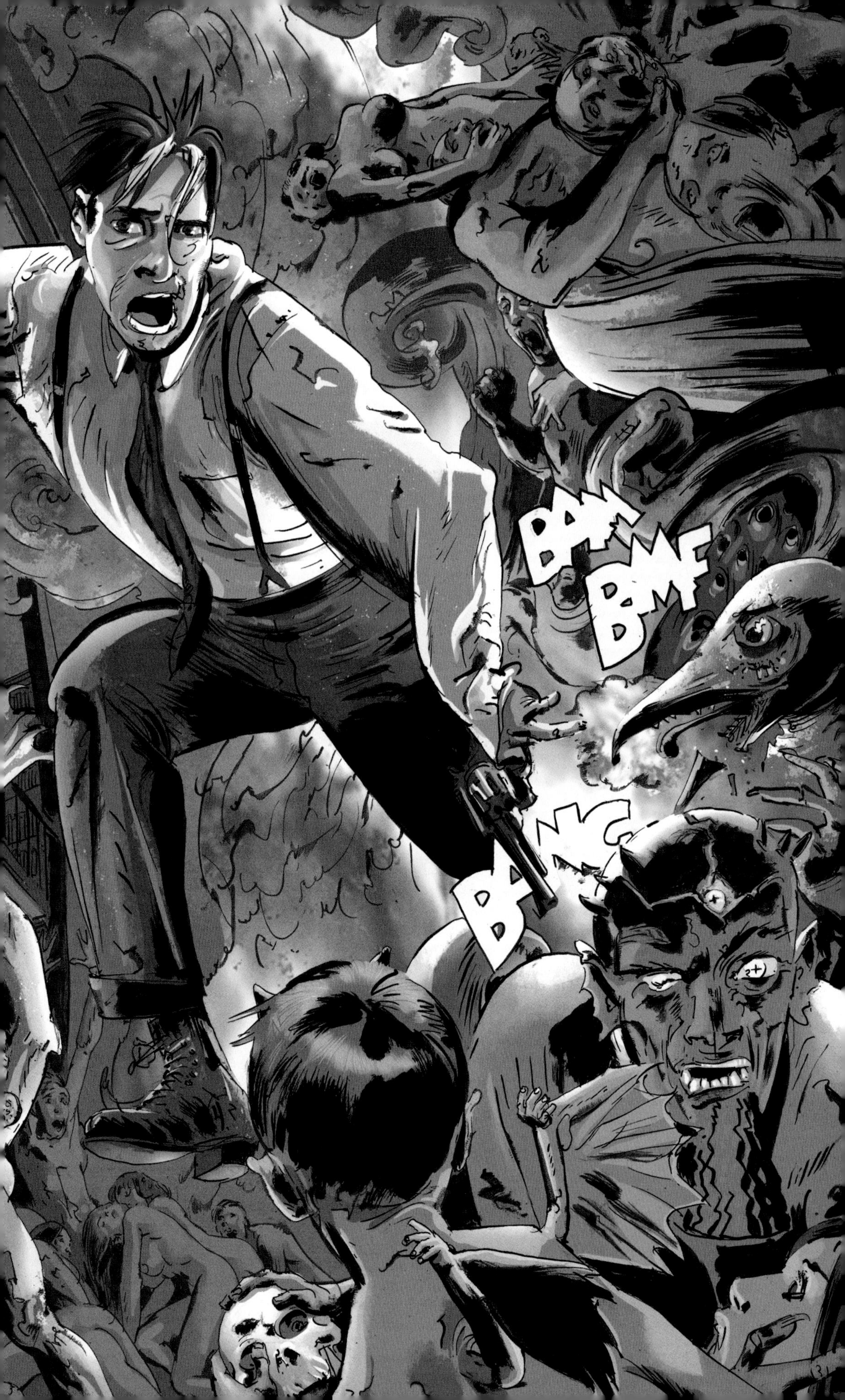
BAMF
BAMF
BANG

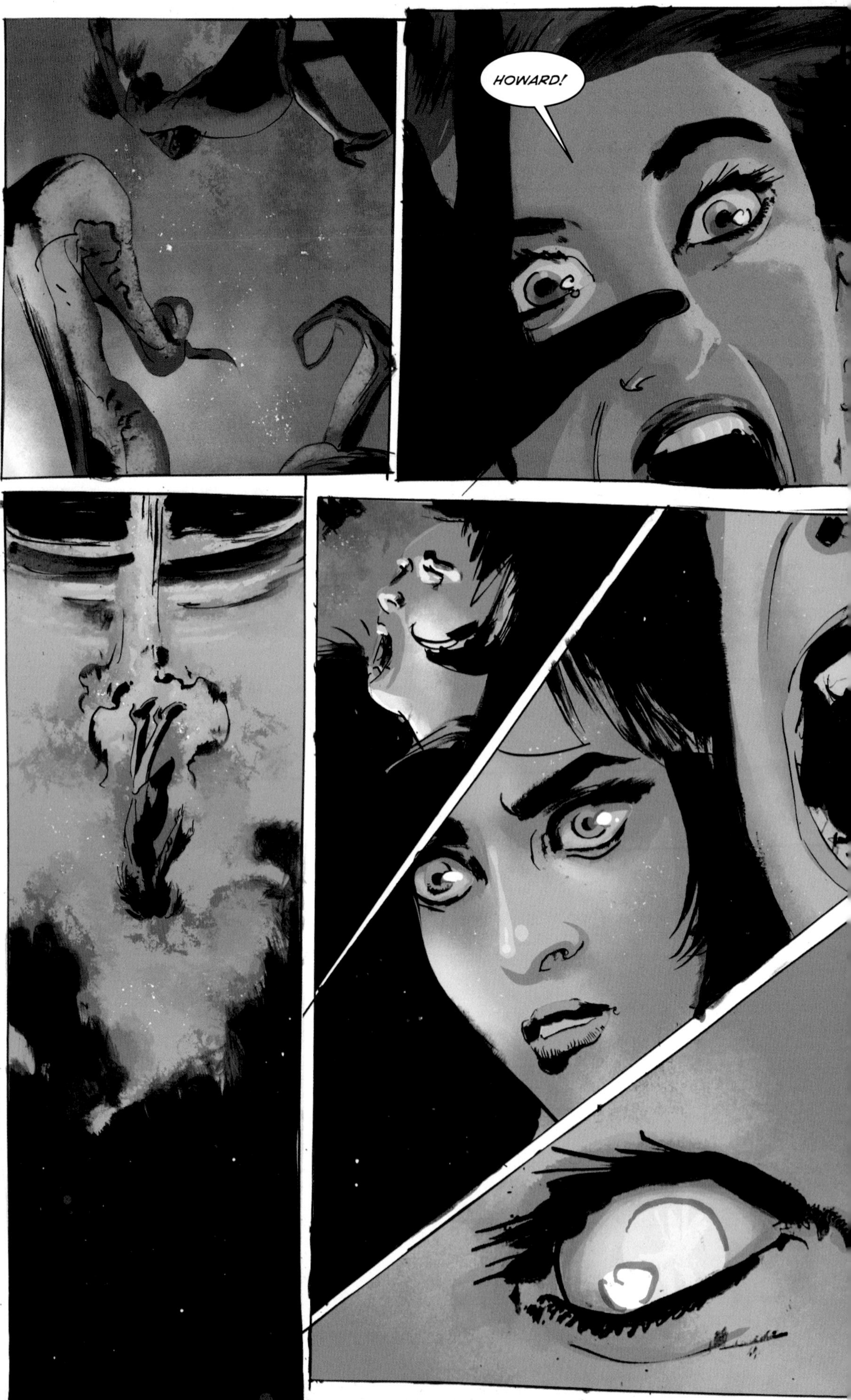
HOWARD!

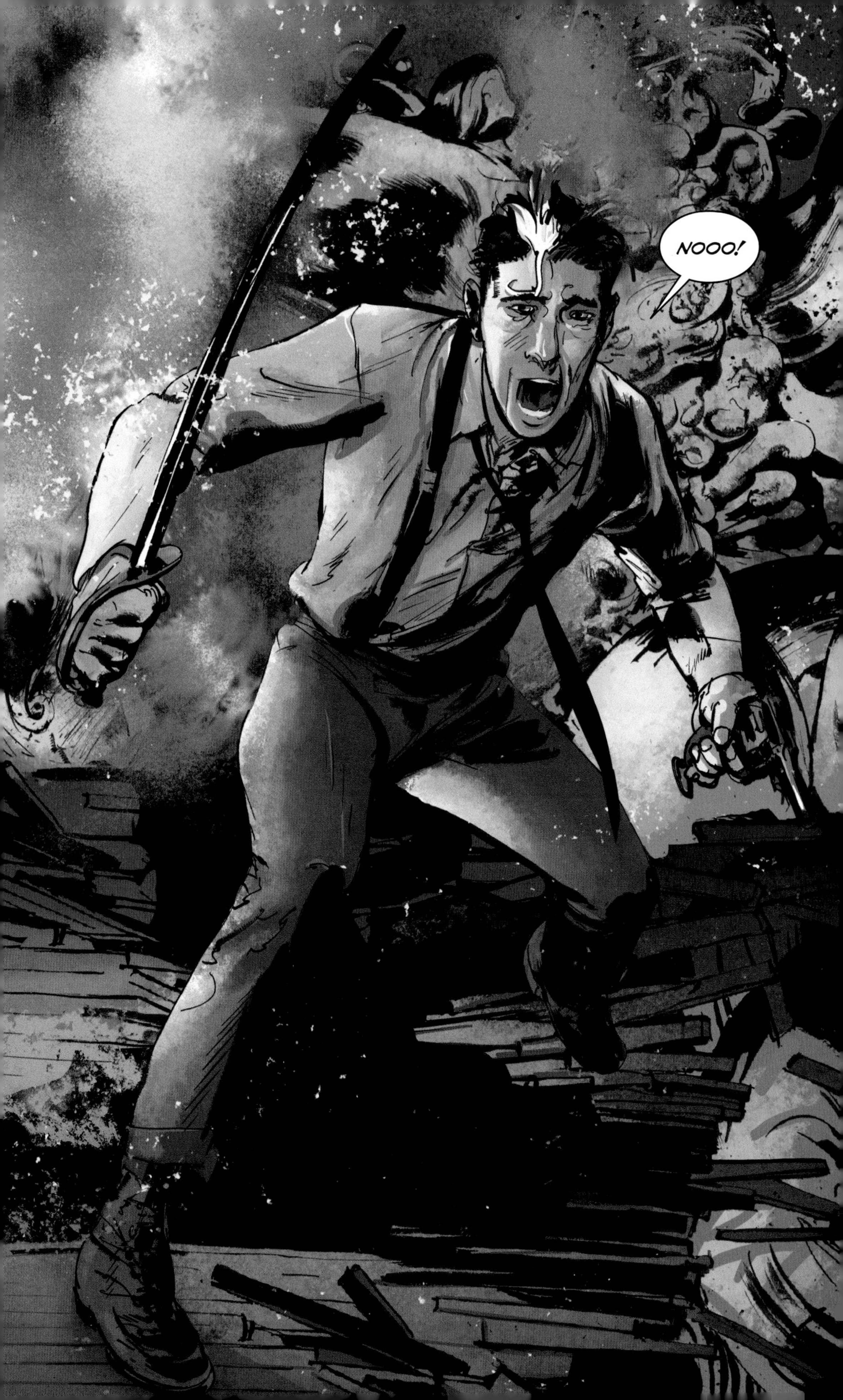
NOOO!

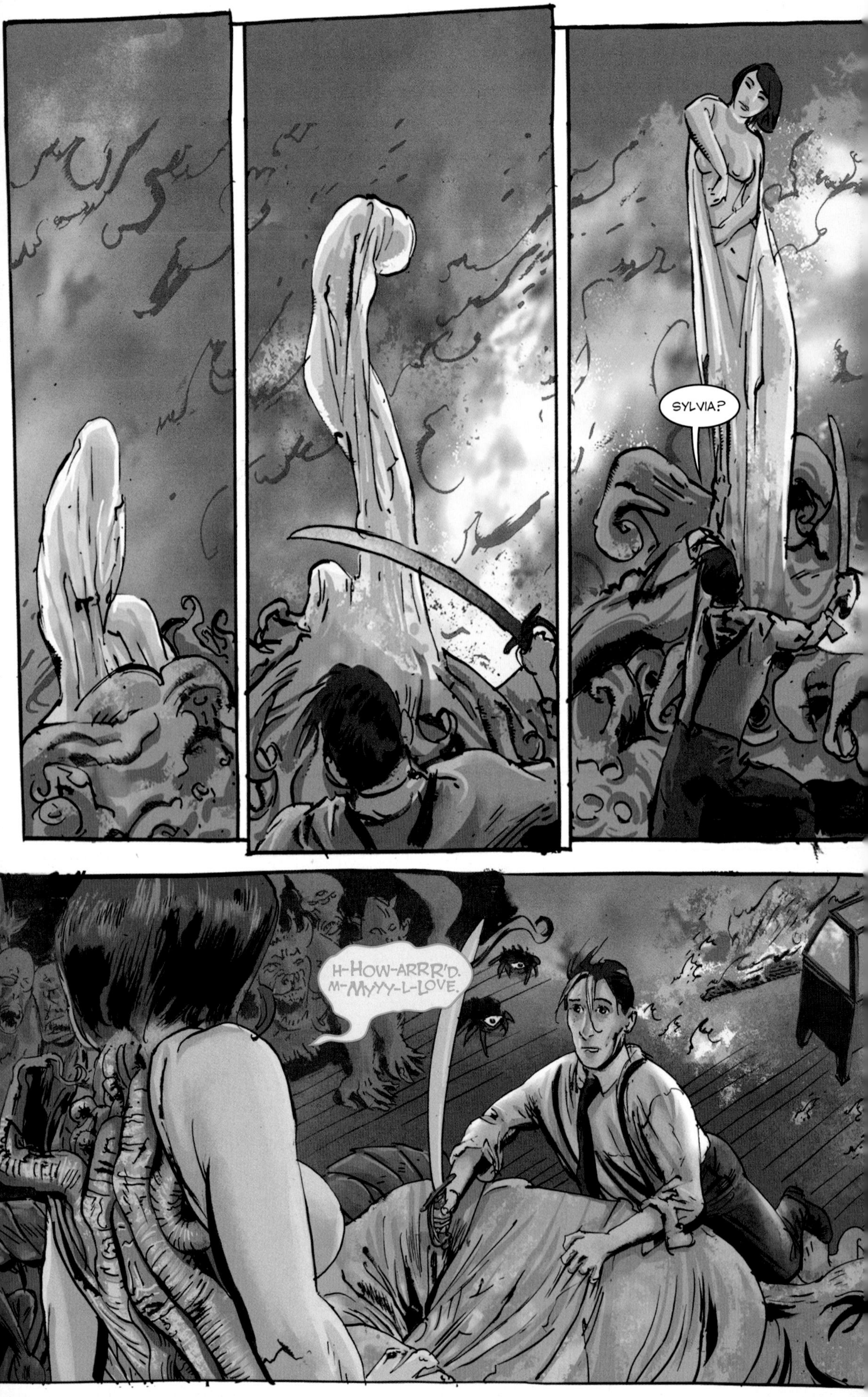
SYLVIA?
H-HOW-ARRR'D. M-MYYY-L-LOVE.

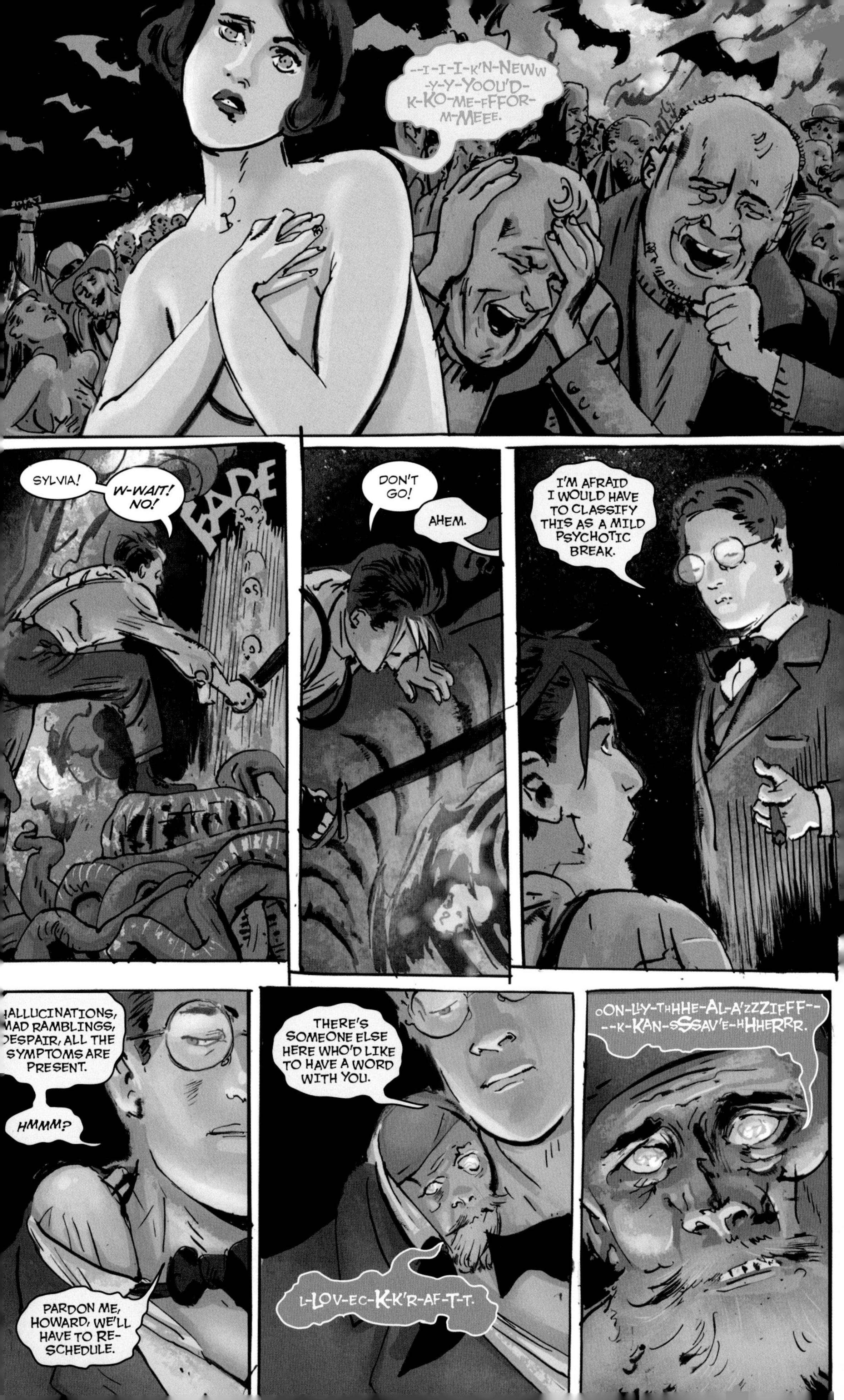
--I-I-I-K'N-NEWW -Y-Y-YOOU'D-K-KO-ME-FFOR-M-MEEE.
SYLVIA!
W-WAIT! NO!
FADE
DON'T GO!
AHEM.
I'M AFRAID I WOULD HAVE TO CLASSIFY THIS AS A MILD PSYCHOTIC BREAK.
HALLUCINATIONS, MAD RAMBLINGS, DESPAIR, ALL THE SYMPTOMS ARE PRESENT.
HMMM?
PARDON ME, HOWARD, WE'LL HAVE TO RE-SCHEDULE.
THERE'S SOMEONE ELSE HERE WHO'D LIKE TO HAVE A WORD WITH YOU.
L-LOV-EC-K-K'R-AF-T-T.
OON-LLY-THHHE-AL-A'ZZZIFFF--K-KAN-SSSAV'E-HHHERRR.

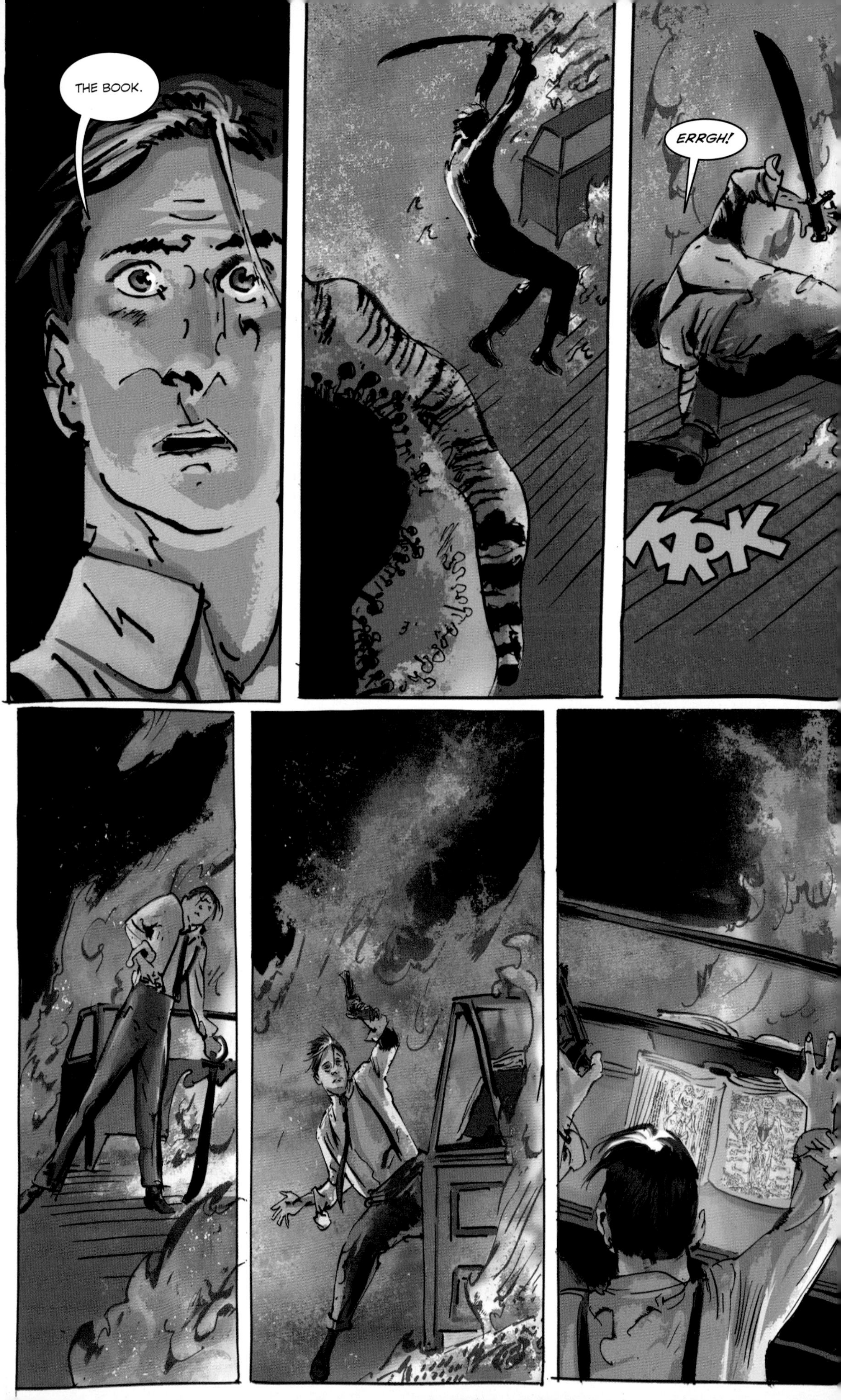
THE BOOK.
ERRGH!
KROK

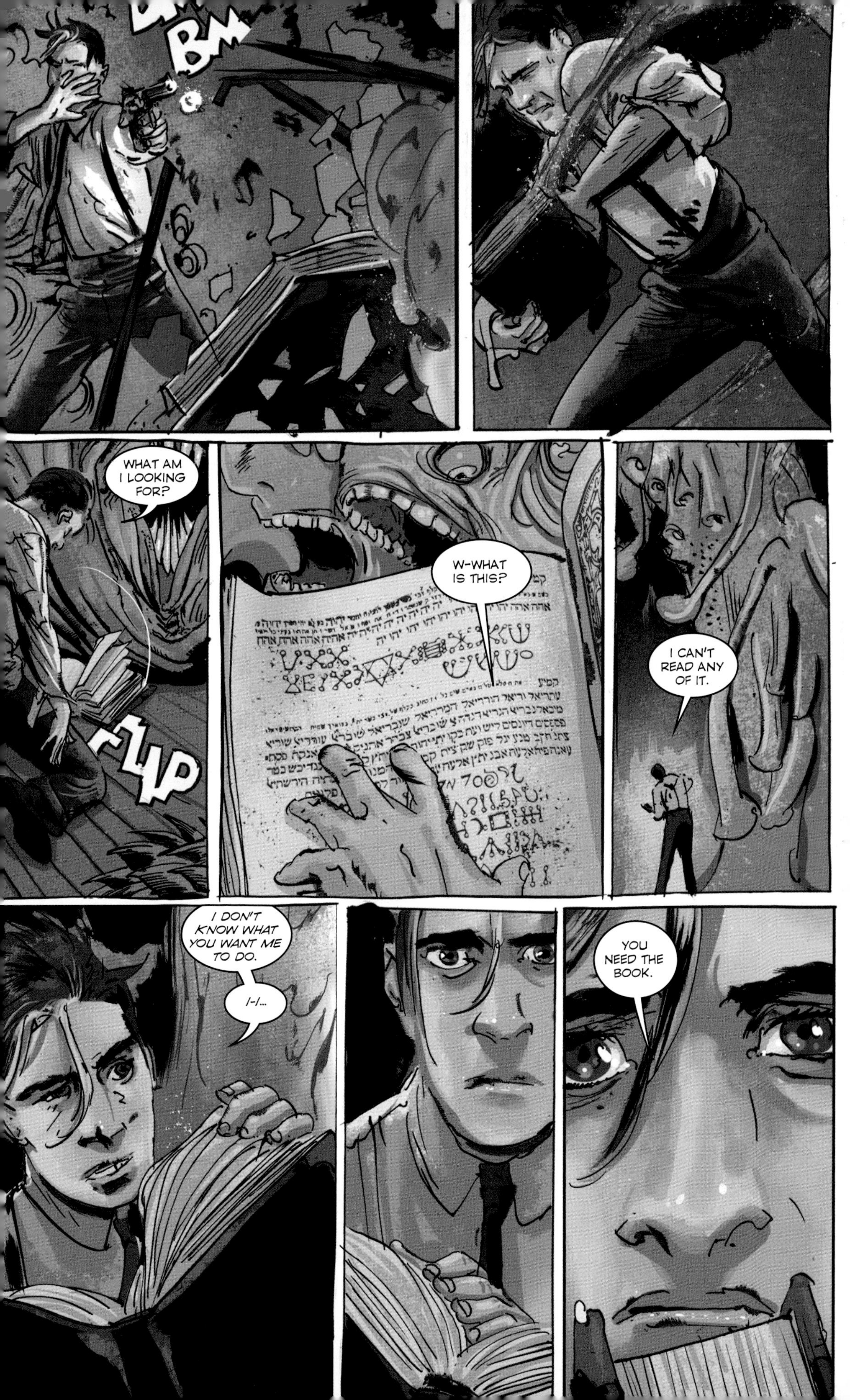
BM
WHAT AM I LOOKING FOR?
FLUP
W-WHAT IS THIS?
I CAN'T READ ANY OF IT.
I DON'T KNOW WHAT YOU WANT ME TO DO.
I-I...
YOU NEED THE BOOK.

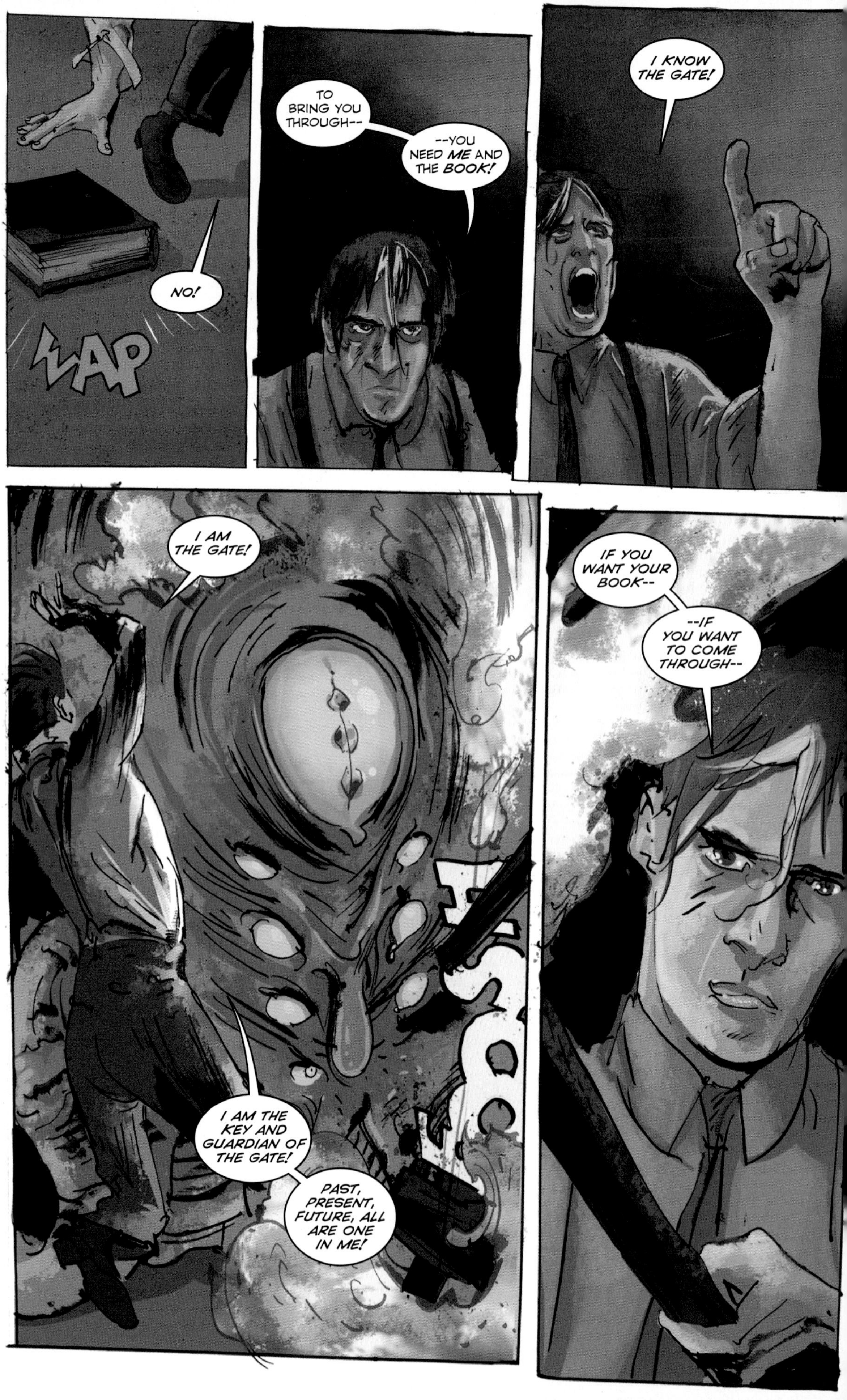
NO!
ZAP
TO BRING YOU THROUGH--
--YOU NEED ME AND THE BOOK!
I KNOW THE GATE!
I AM THE GATE!
I AM THE KEY AND GUARDIAN OF THE GATE!
PAST, PRESENT, FUTURE, ALL ARE ONE IN ME!
IF YOU WANT YOUR BOOK--
--IF YOU WANT TO COME THROUGH--

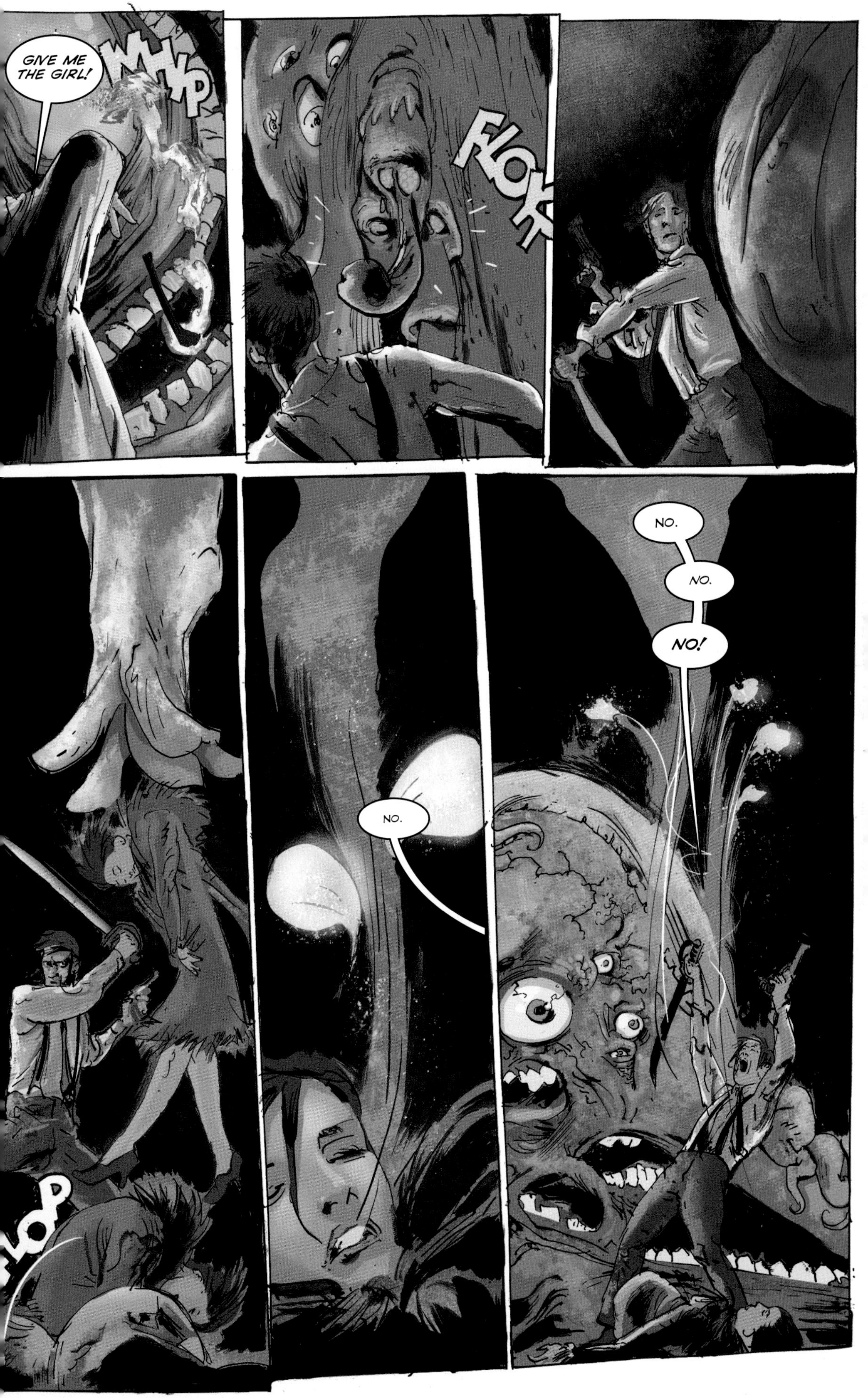

GIVE ME THE GIRL!
WHIP
FLOK
LOP
NO.
NO.
NO.
NO!

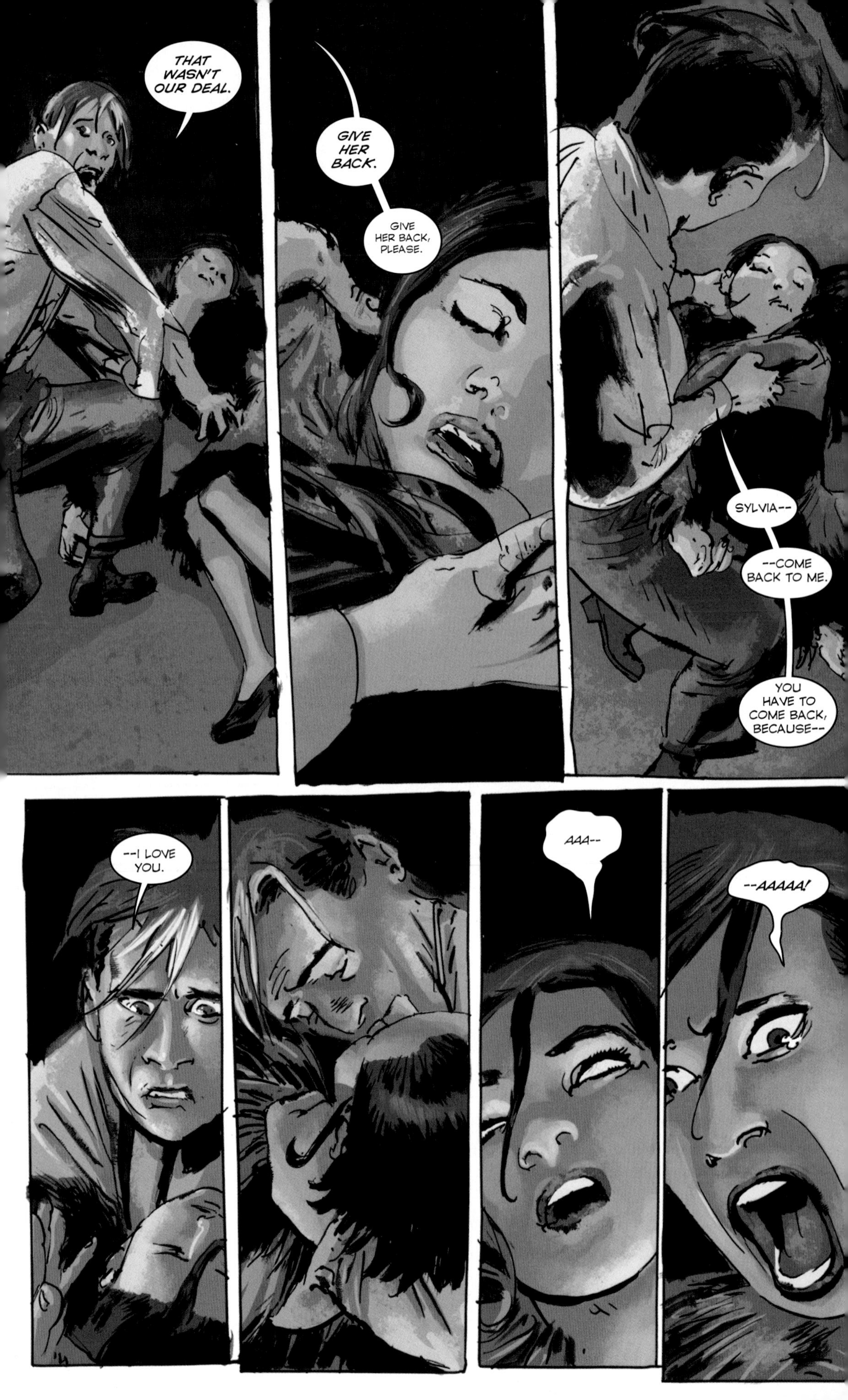
THAT WASN'T OUR DEAL.
GIVE HER BACK.
GIVE HER BACK, PLEASE.
SYLVIA--
--COME BACK TO ME.
YOU HAVE TO COME BACK, BECAUSE--
--I LOVE YOU.
AAA--
--AAAAA!

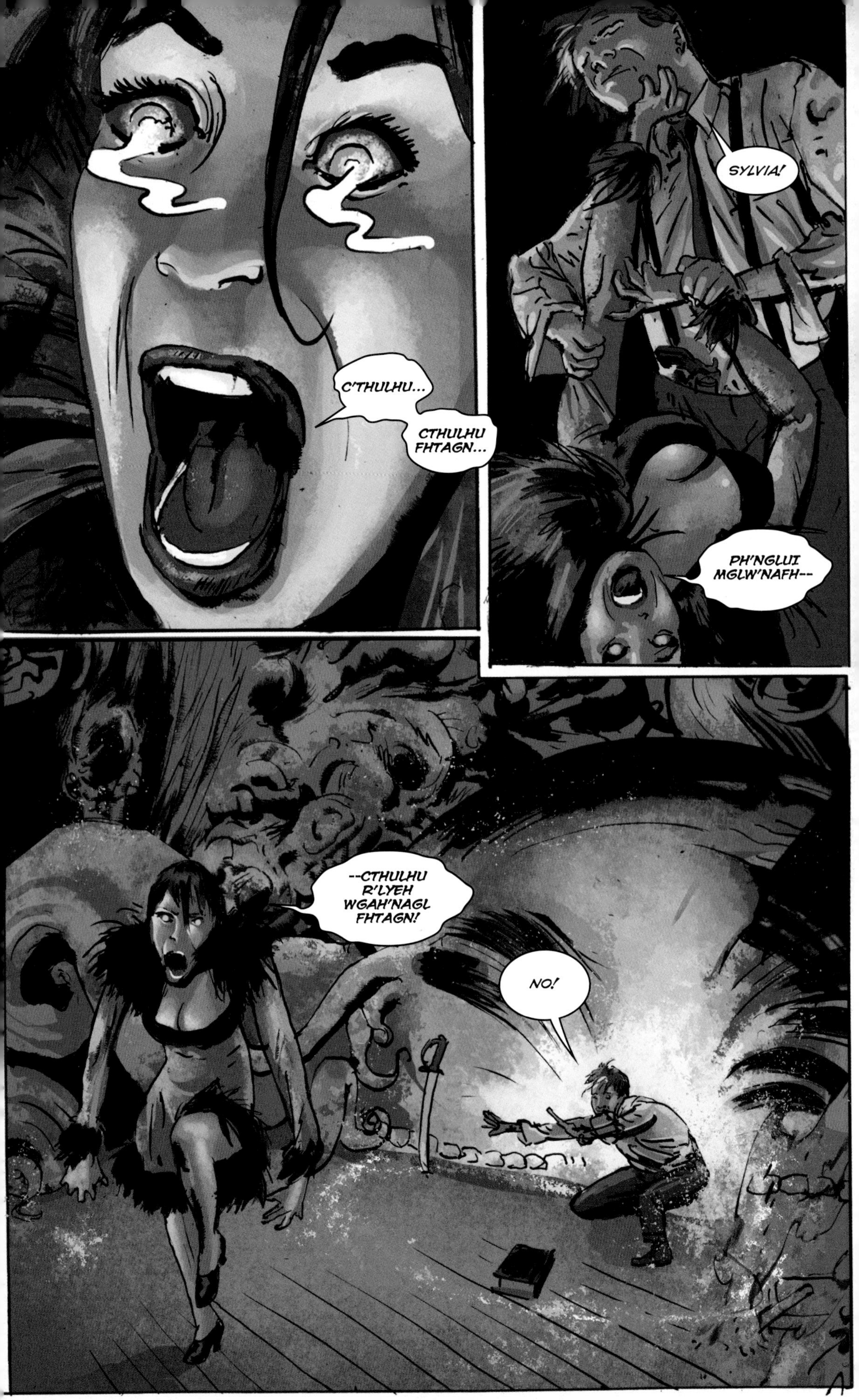
C'THULHU...
CTHULHU FHTAGN...
SYLVIA!
PH'NGLUI MGLW'NAFH--
--CTHULHU R'LYEH WGAH'NAGL FHTAGN!
NO!

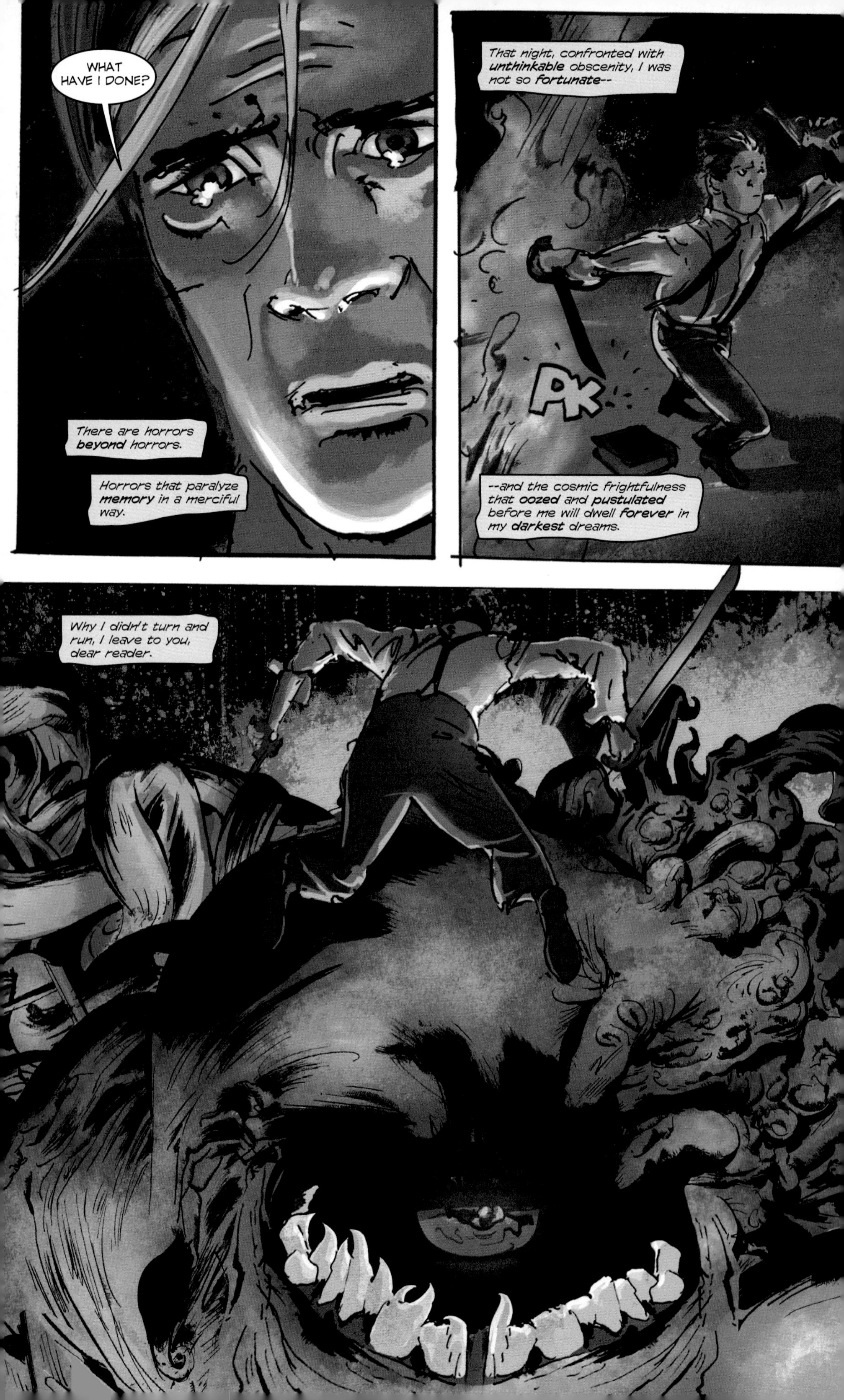
WHAT HAVE I DONE?
There are horrors beyond horrors.
Horrors that paralyze memory in a merciful way.
That night, confronted with unthinkable obscenity, I was not so fortunate--
PK
--and the cosmic frightfulness that oozed and pustulated before me will dwell forever in my darkest dreams.
Why I didn't turn and run, I leave to you, dear reader.

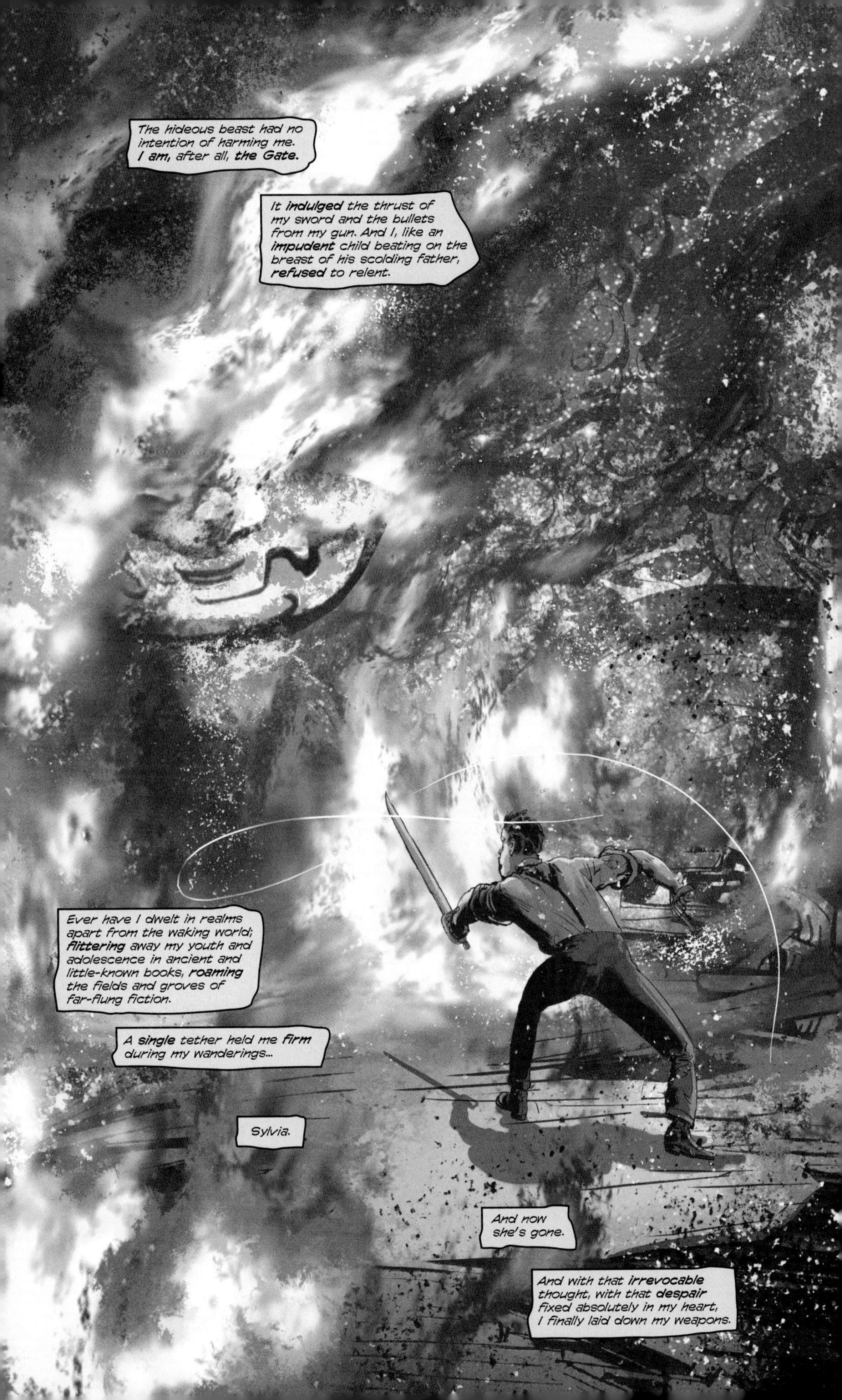
The hideous beast had no intention of harming me. I am, after all, the Gate.
It indulged the thrust of my sword and the bullets from my gun. And I, like an impudent child beating on the breast of his scolding father, refused to relent.
Ever have I dwelt in realms apart from the waking world; flittering away my youth and adolescence in ancient and little-known books, roaming the fields and groves of far-flung fiction.
A single tether held me firm during my wanderings...
Sylvia.
And now she's gone.
And with that irrevocable thought, with that despair fixed absolutely in my heart, I finally laid down my weapons.

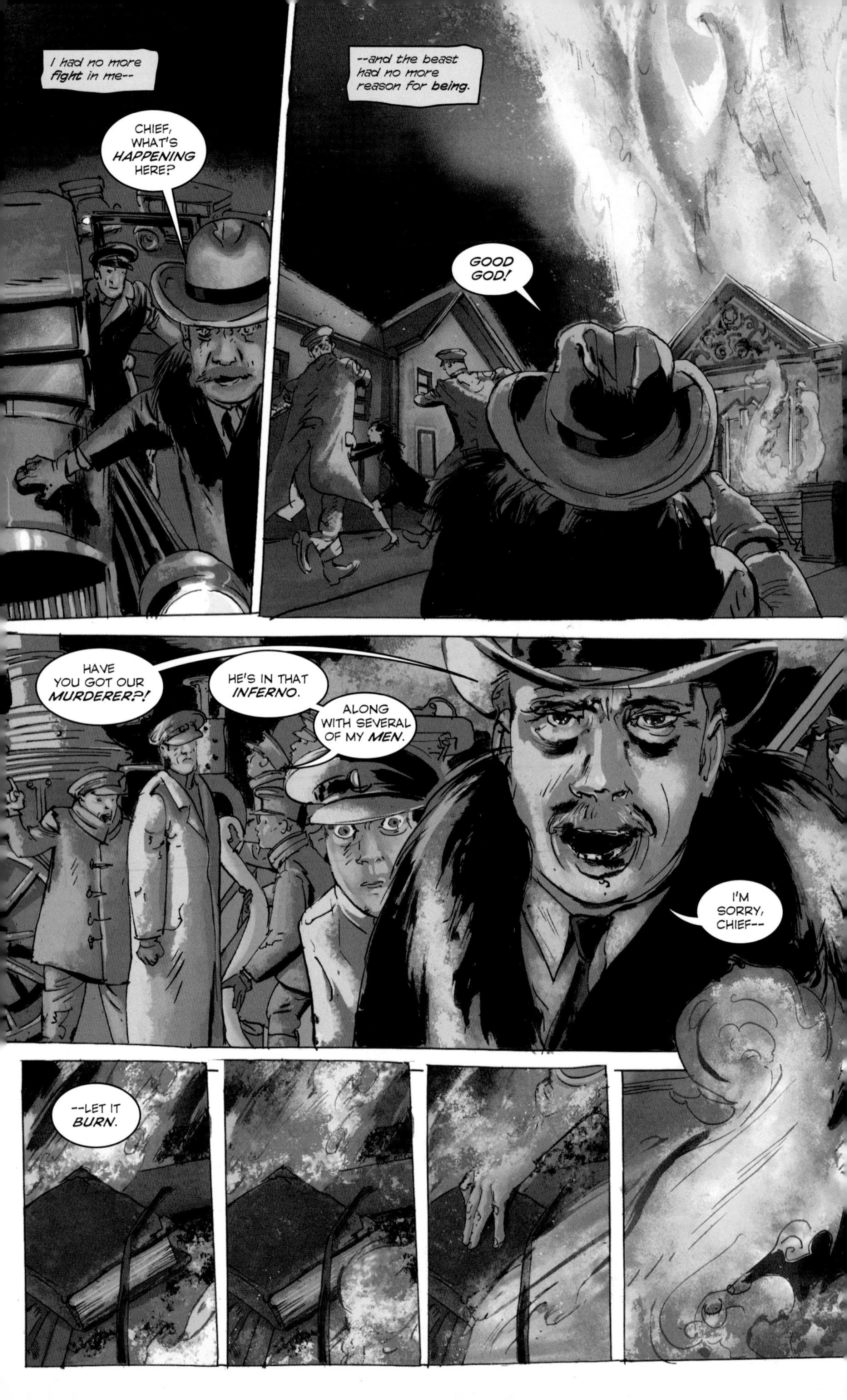
I had no more fight in me--
CHIEF, WHAT'S HAPPENING HERE?
--and the beast had no more reason for being.
GOOD GOD!
HAVE YOU GOT OUR MURDERER?!
HE'S IN THAT INFERNO.
ALONG WITH SEVERAL OF MY MEN.
I'M SORRY, CHIEF--
--LET IT BURN.

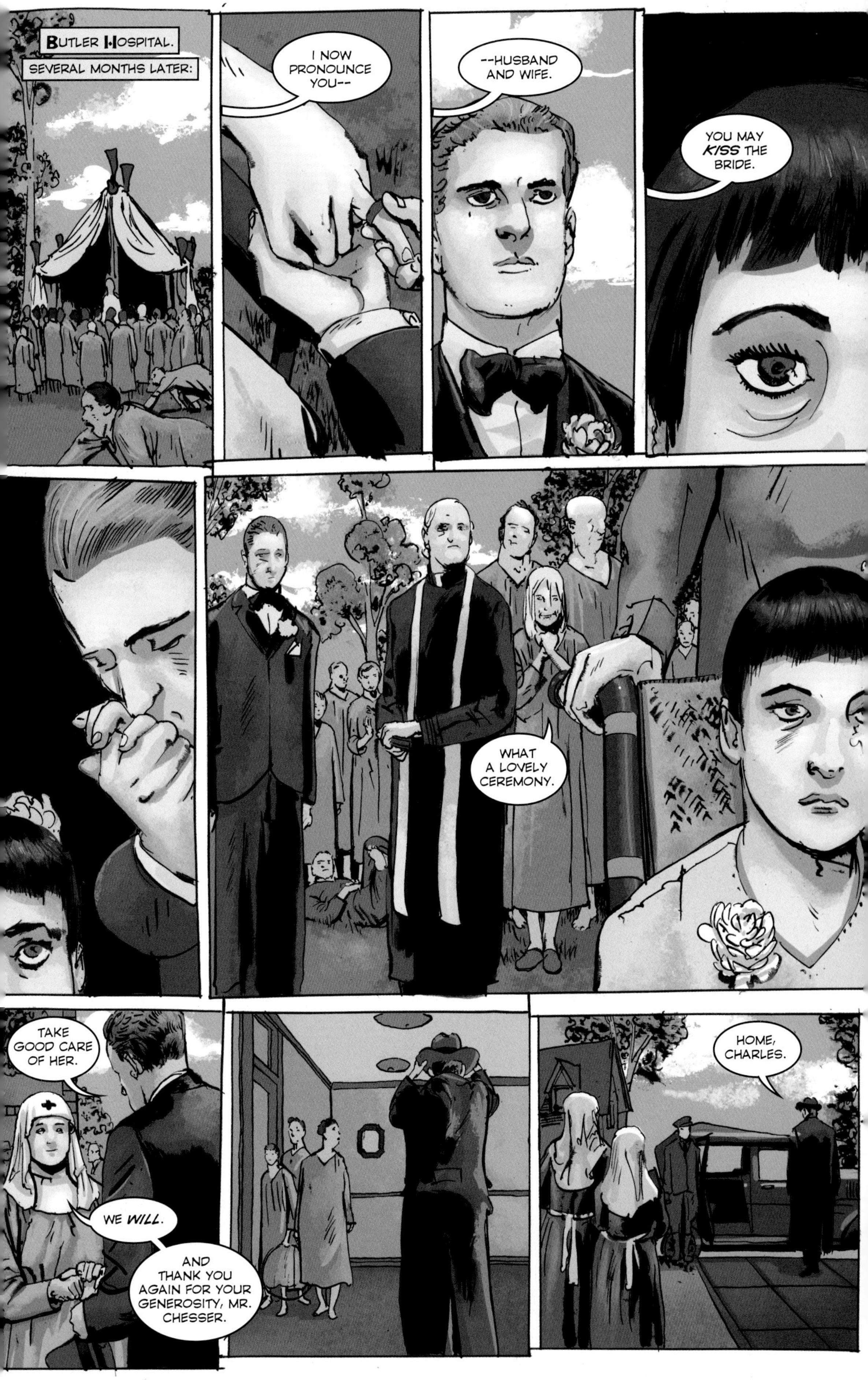
BUTLER HOSPITAL.
SEVERAL MONTHS LATER:
I NOW PRONOUNCE YOU--
--HUSBAND AND WIFE.
YOU MAY KISS THE BRIDE.
WHAT A LOVELY CEREMONY.
TAKE GOOD CARE OF HER.
WE WILL.
AND THANK YOU AGAIN FOR YOUR GENEROSITY, MR. CHESSER.
HOME, CHARLES.

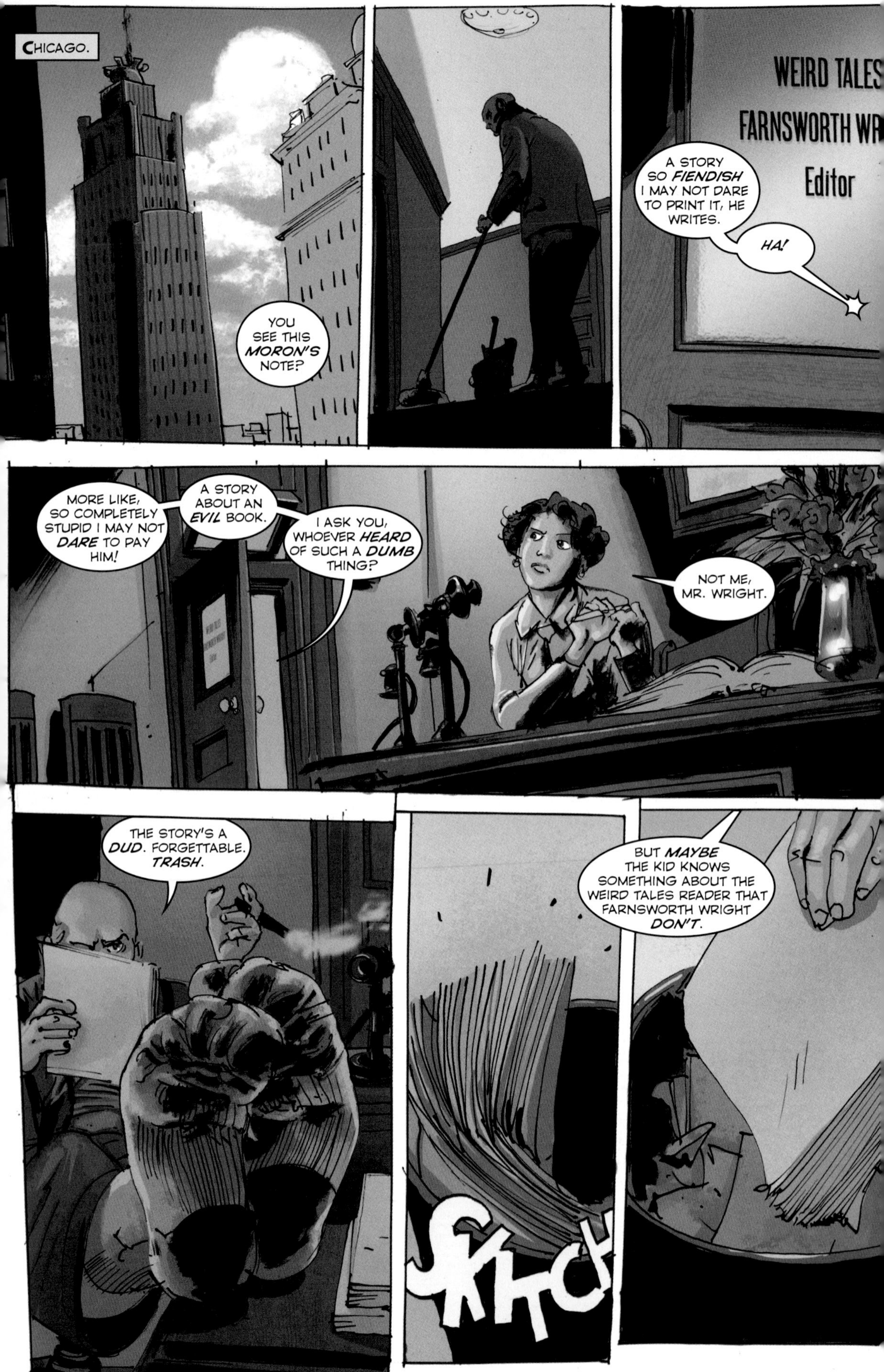
CHICAGO.
YOU SEE THIS *MORON'S* NOTE?
WEIRD TALES
FARNSWORTH WR
Editor
A STORY SO *FIENDISH* I MAY NOT DARE TO PRINT IT, HE WRITES.
HA!
MORE LIKE, SO COMPLETELY STUPID I MAY NOT *DARE* TO PAY HIM*!*
A STORY ABOUT AN *EVIL* BOOK.
I ASK YOU, WHOEVER *HEARD* OF SUCH A *DUMB* THING?
NOT ME, MR. WRIGHT.
THE STORY'S A *DUD*. FORGETTABLE. *TRASH*.
SKTCH
BUT *MAYBE* THE KID KNOWS SOMETHING ABOUT THE WEIRD TALES READER THAT FARNSWORTH WRIGHT *DON'T*.

CUT MR. LOVECRAFT A CHECK.
THE USUAL FEE?
MAKE IT FOR $240 BUCKS.
THAT'S A PENNY-AND-A-HALF A WORD, MR. WRIGHT! YOU AIN'T NEVER PAID THAT MUCH!
The Dunwich Horror
By
ard Phillips
DID I HIRE YOU TO BE A SECRETARY OR A MATHEMATICIAN?
CUT THE CHECK.
Mr. Wright,
Please find enclosed a copy of
latest novella. It is
Dunwich Horror. It takes place
amongst the wild domed hills of
upper Miskatonic Valley, far
of Arkham, and is based on
old New England legends---one of
which I heard only last month
my sojourn in Wilbraham.
HIS NOTE SAYS HE'S GONNA BE OUT OF TOWN AWHILE.
SEND IT TO HIS AUNTS IN PROVIDENCE.
ABROAD.
Only a cynic can create inspired horror.
PAK
SMK
For behind every masterpiece of the weird there must reside a driven daemonic force that despises humanity's petty illusions--
TIK
DAK DAK
TIK
SMAK
TAK
--and longs to pull them to pieces and mock them.

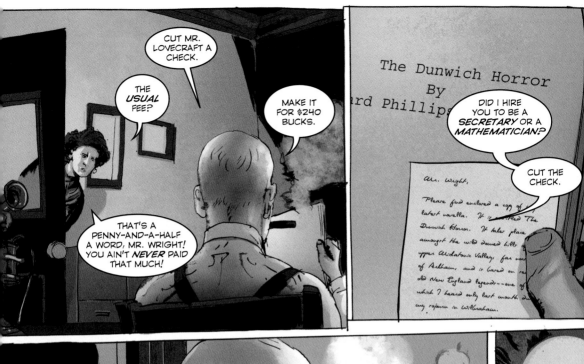

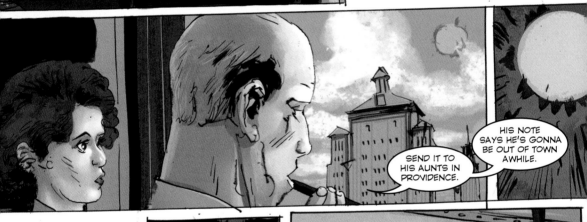

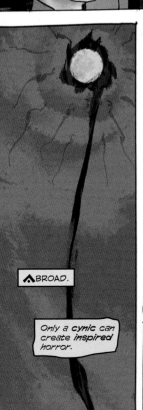

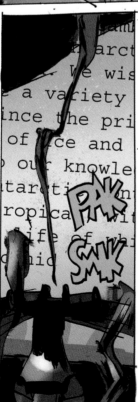

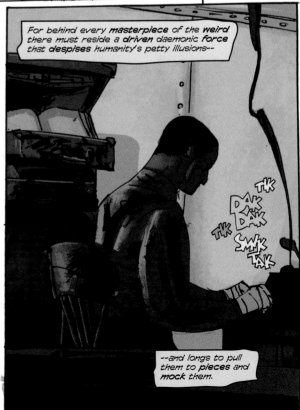

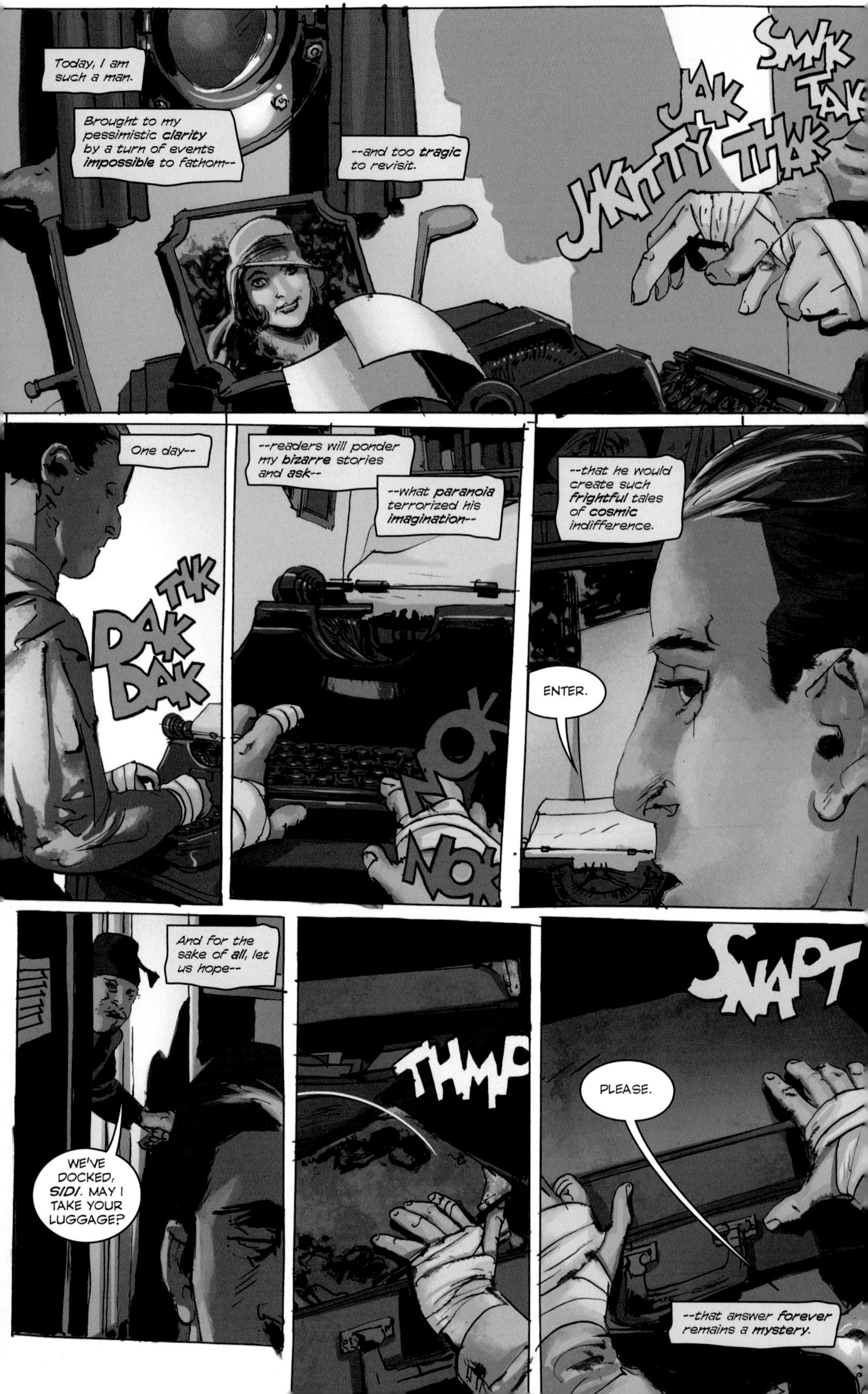

Today, I am such a man.
Brought to my pessimistic clarity by a turn of events impossible to fathom--
--and too tragic to revisit.
SWIK
JAK
TAK
J'KITTY THAK
One day--
DAK
TK
DAK
--readers will ponder my bizarre stories and ask--
--what paranoia terrorized his imagination--
NOK
NOK
--that he would create such frightful tales of cosmic indifference.
ENTER.
And for the sake of all, let us hope--
WE'VE DOCKED, SIDI. MAY I TAKE YOUR LUGGAGE?
THMC
SNAP
PLEASE.
--that answer forever remains a mystery.

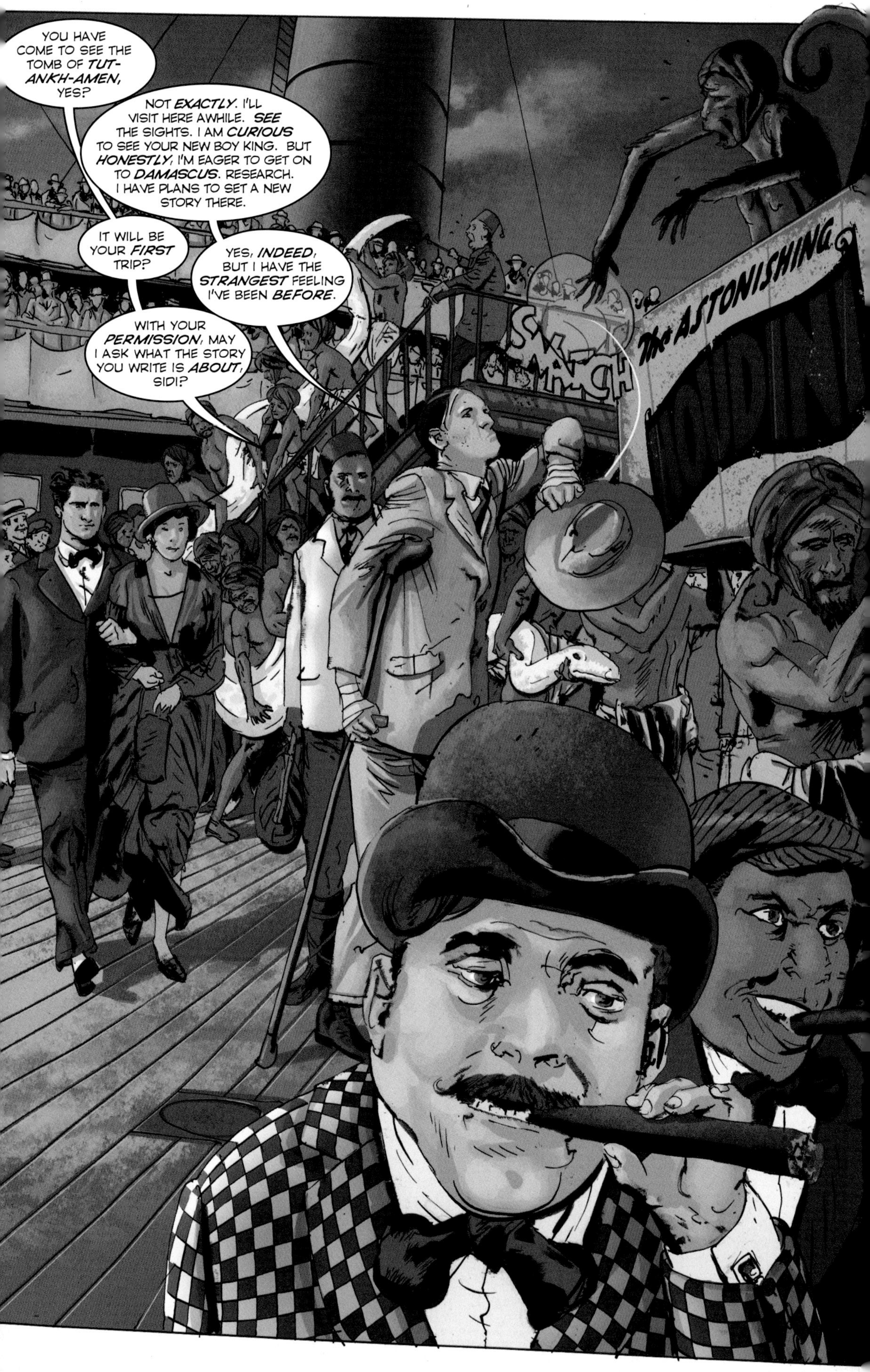
YOU HAVE COME TO SEE THE TOMB OF TUT-ANKH-AMEN, YES?
NOT EXACTLY. I'LL VISIT HERE AWHILE. SEE THE SIGHTS. I AM CURIOUS TO SEE YOUR NEW BOY KING. BUT HONESTLY, I'M EAGER TO GET ON TO DAMASCUS. RESEARCH. I HAVE PLANS TO SET A NEW STORY THERE.
IT WILL BE YOUR FIRST TRIP?
YES, INDEED, BUT I HAVE THE STRANGEST FEELING I'VE BEEN BEFORE.
WITH YOUR PERMISSION, MAY I ASK WHAT THE STORY YOU WRITE IS ABOUT, SIDI?
The ASTONISHING

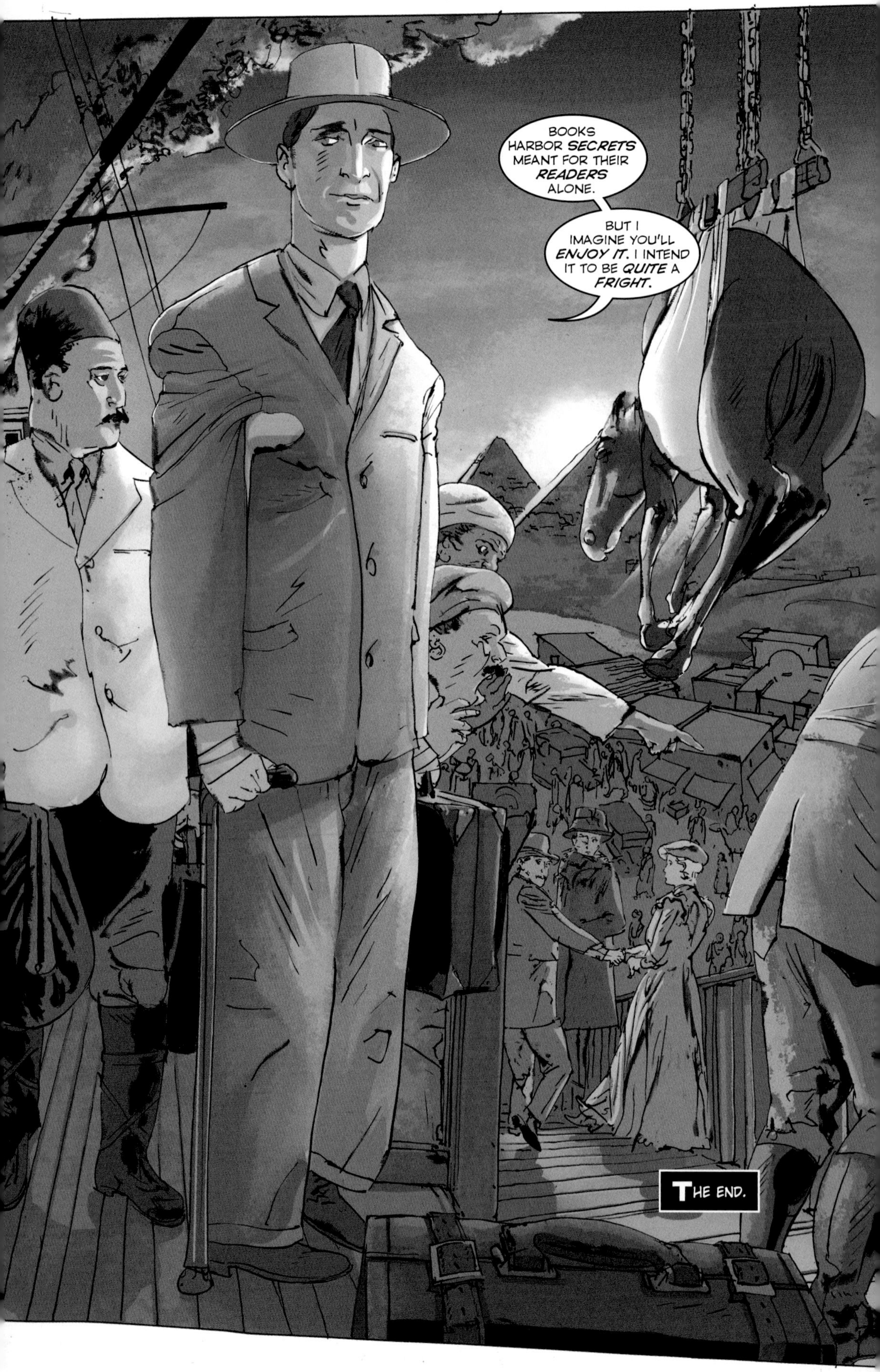
BOOKS HARBOR SECRETS MEANT FOR THEIR READERS ALONE.
BUT I IMAGINE YOU'LL ENJOY IT. I INTEND IT TO BE QUITE A FRIGHT.
THE END.

The hero's main feat is to overcome the monster of darkness: it is the long-hoped-for and expected triumph of consciousness over the unconscious.

-CARL jUNG

COVER GALLERY

A LIMITED EDITION PRINTING

July 2008

399¢

The *Strange Adventures of H.P.*

Lovecraft

Chapt. **1** ABOUT A WRITER AND HIS BOOK

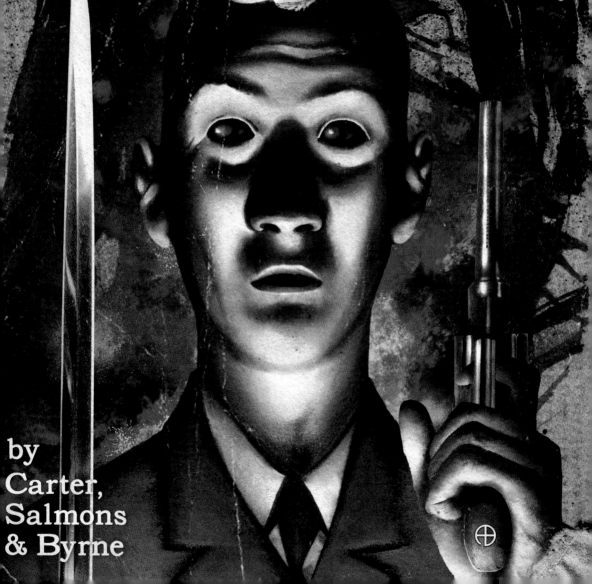

by
Carter,
Salmons
& Byrne

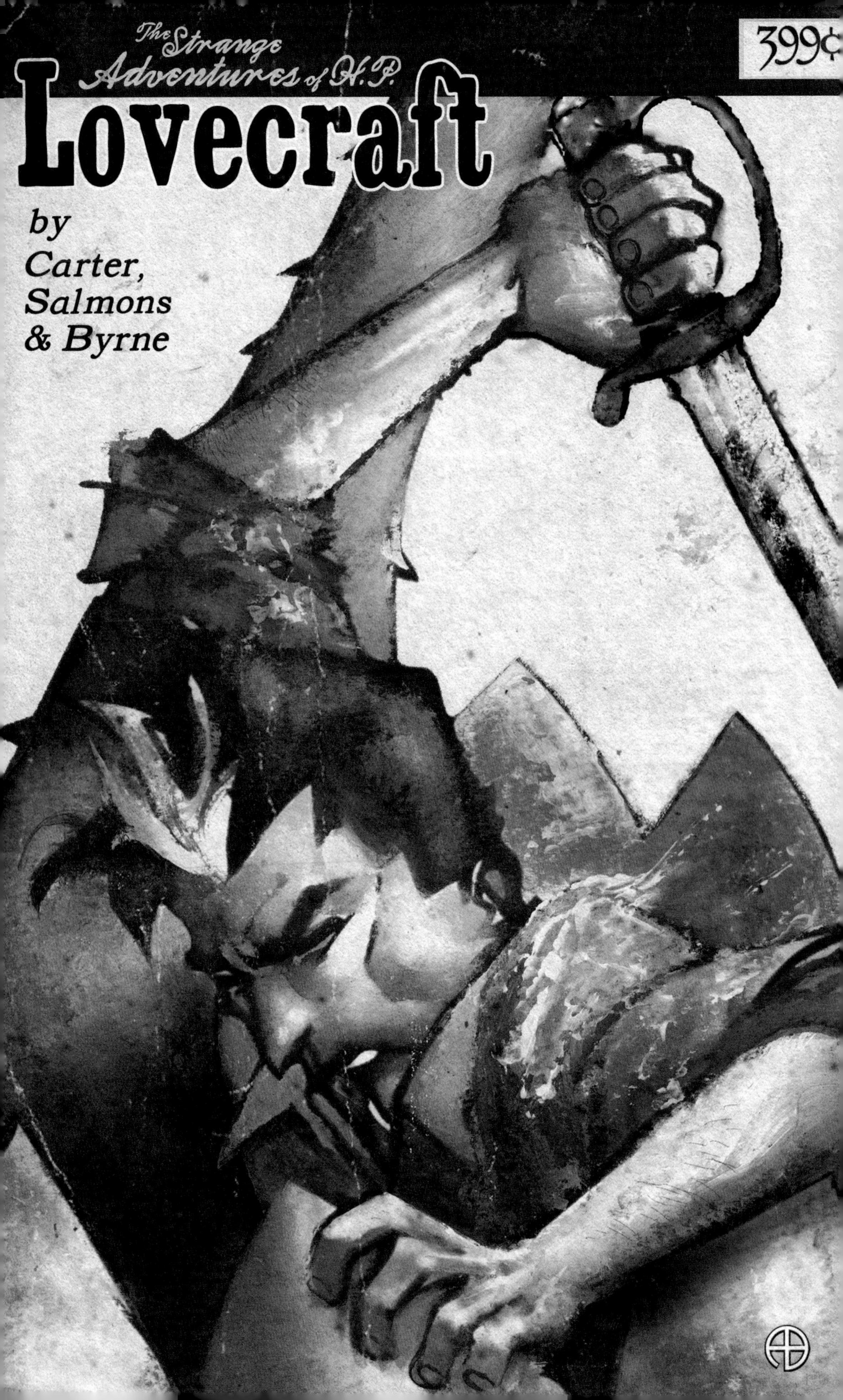
The Strange Adventures of H.P.
Lovecraft
399¢
by
Carter,
Salmons
& Byrne

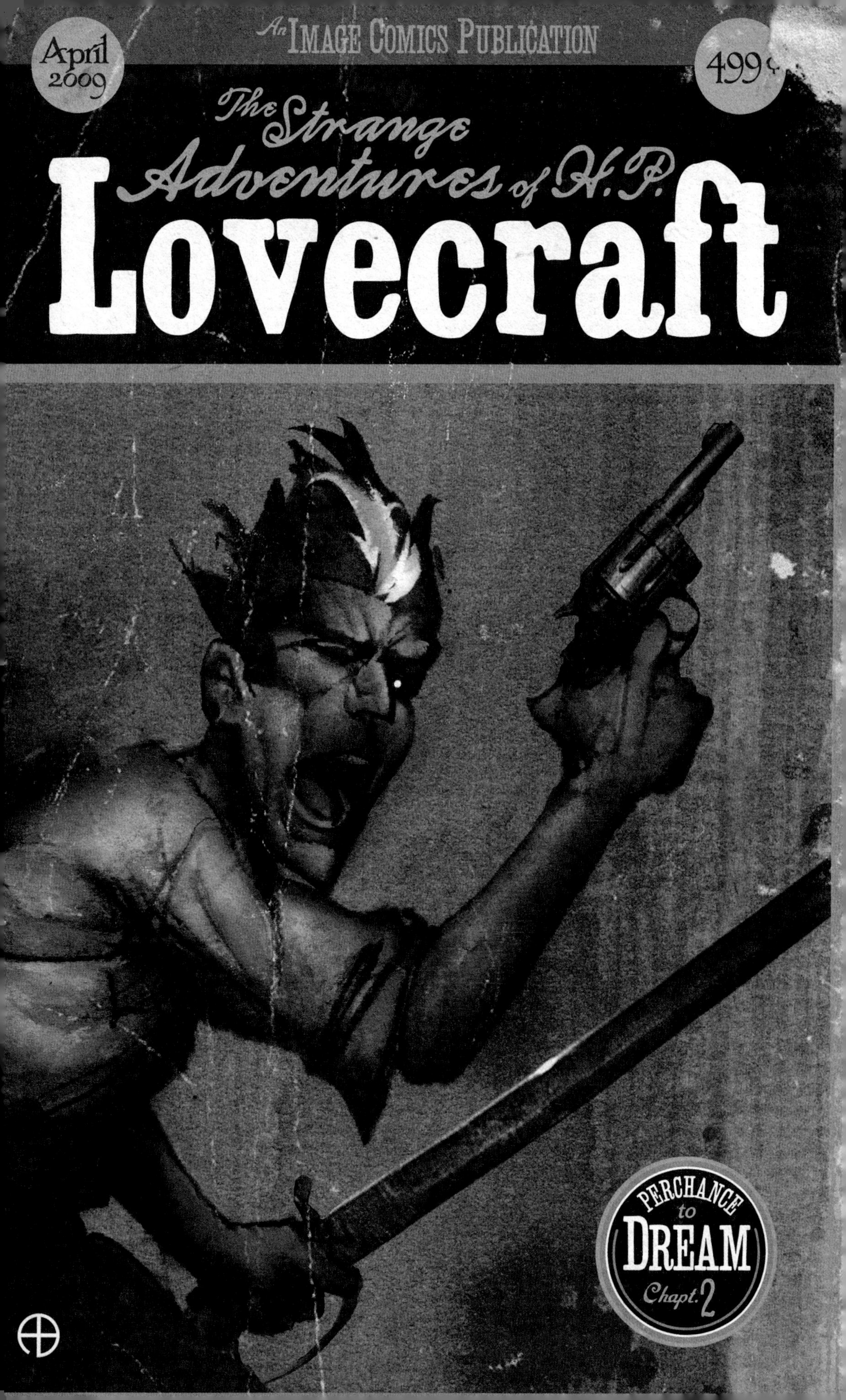

An Image Comics Publication
April 2009
499¢
The Strange Adventures of H.P.
Lovecraft
Perchance to Dream
Chapt. 2

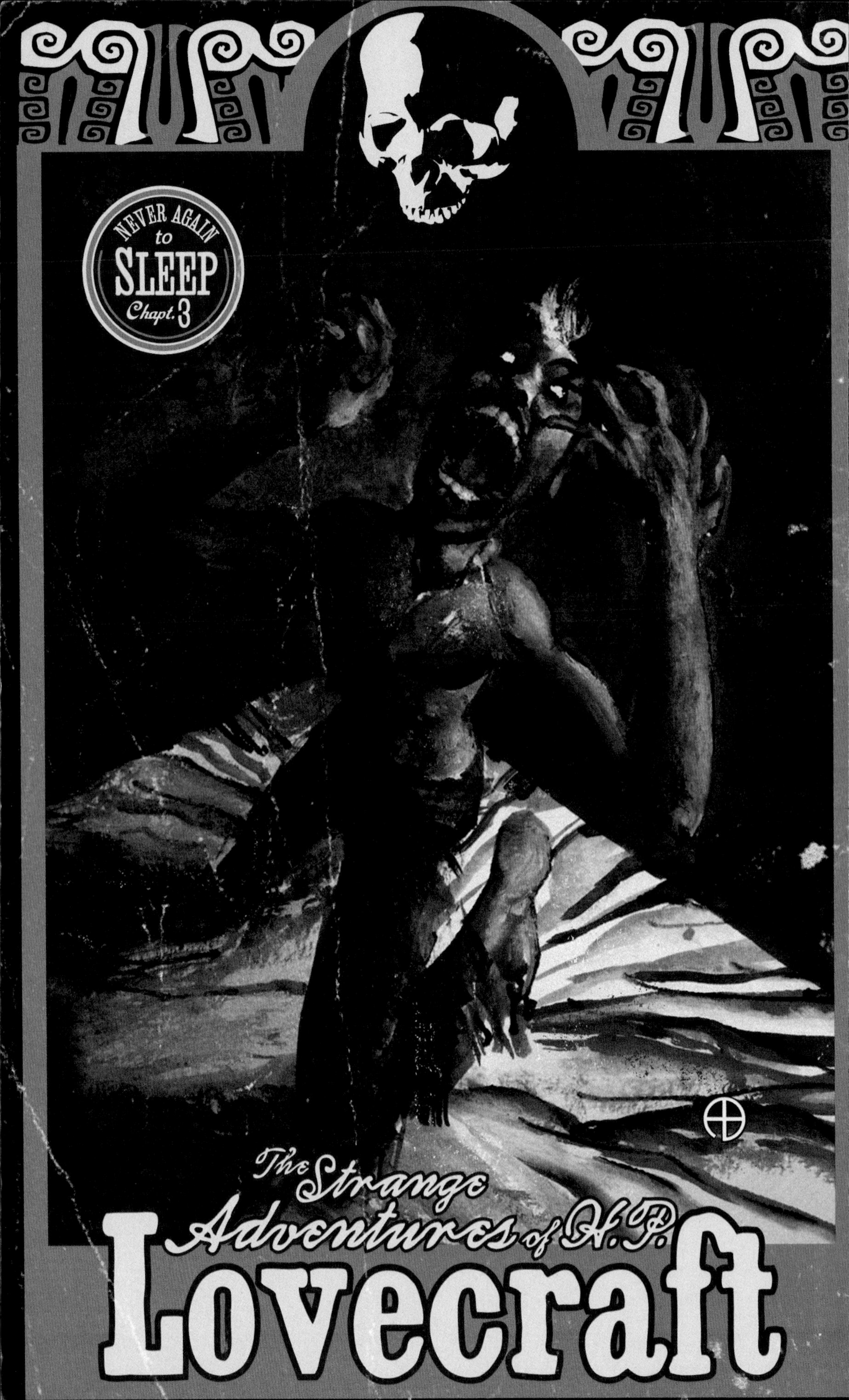
NEVER AGAIN to SLEEP
Chapt. 3
The Strange Adventures of H.P.
Lovecraft

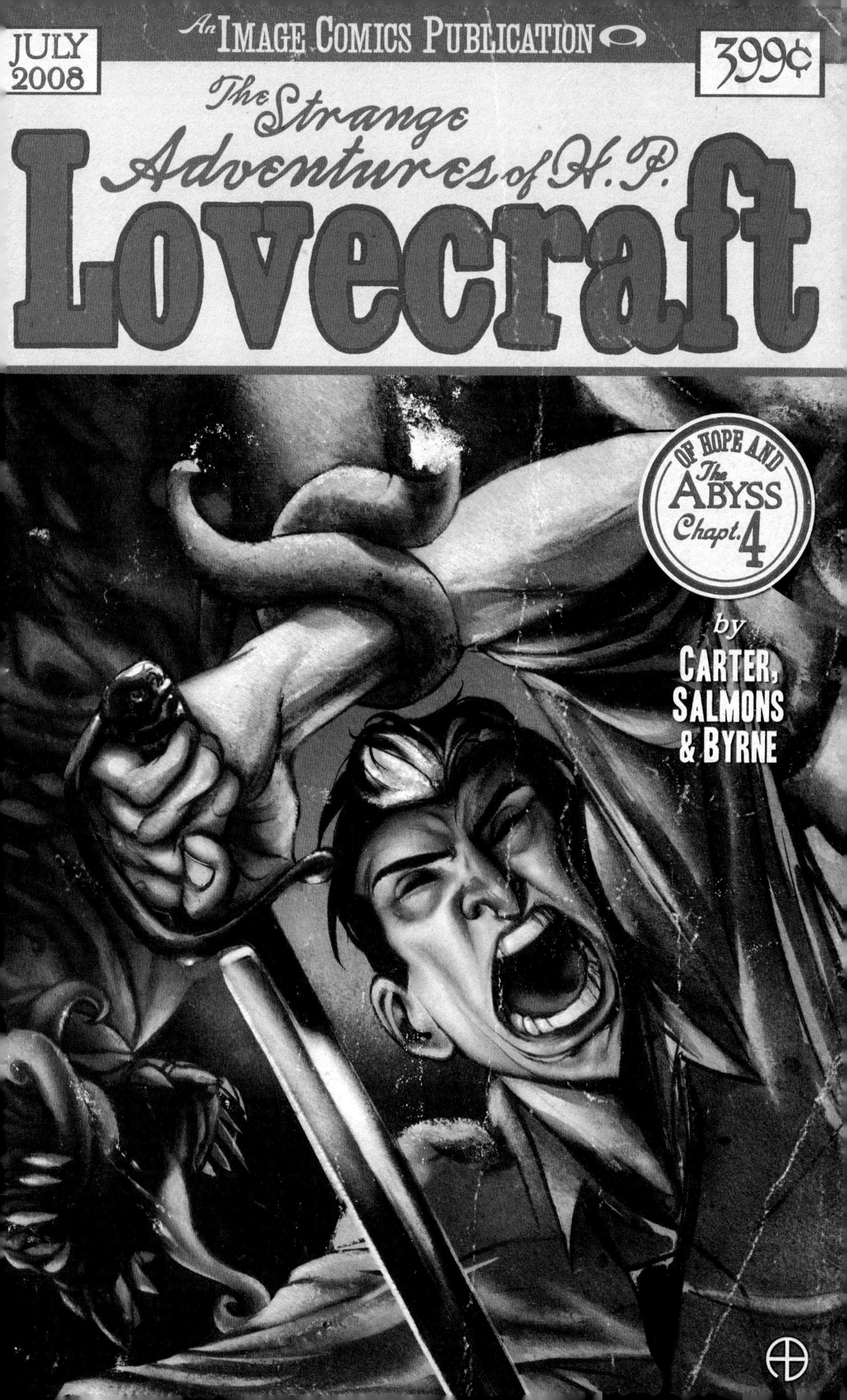
An Image Comics Publication
July 2008
399¢
The Strange Adventures of H. P. Lovecraft
Of Hope and The Abyss Chapt. 4
by
Carter, Salmons & Byrne

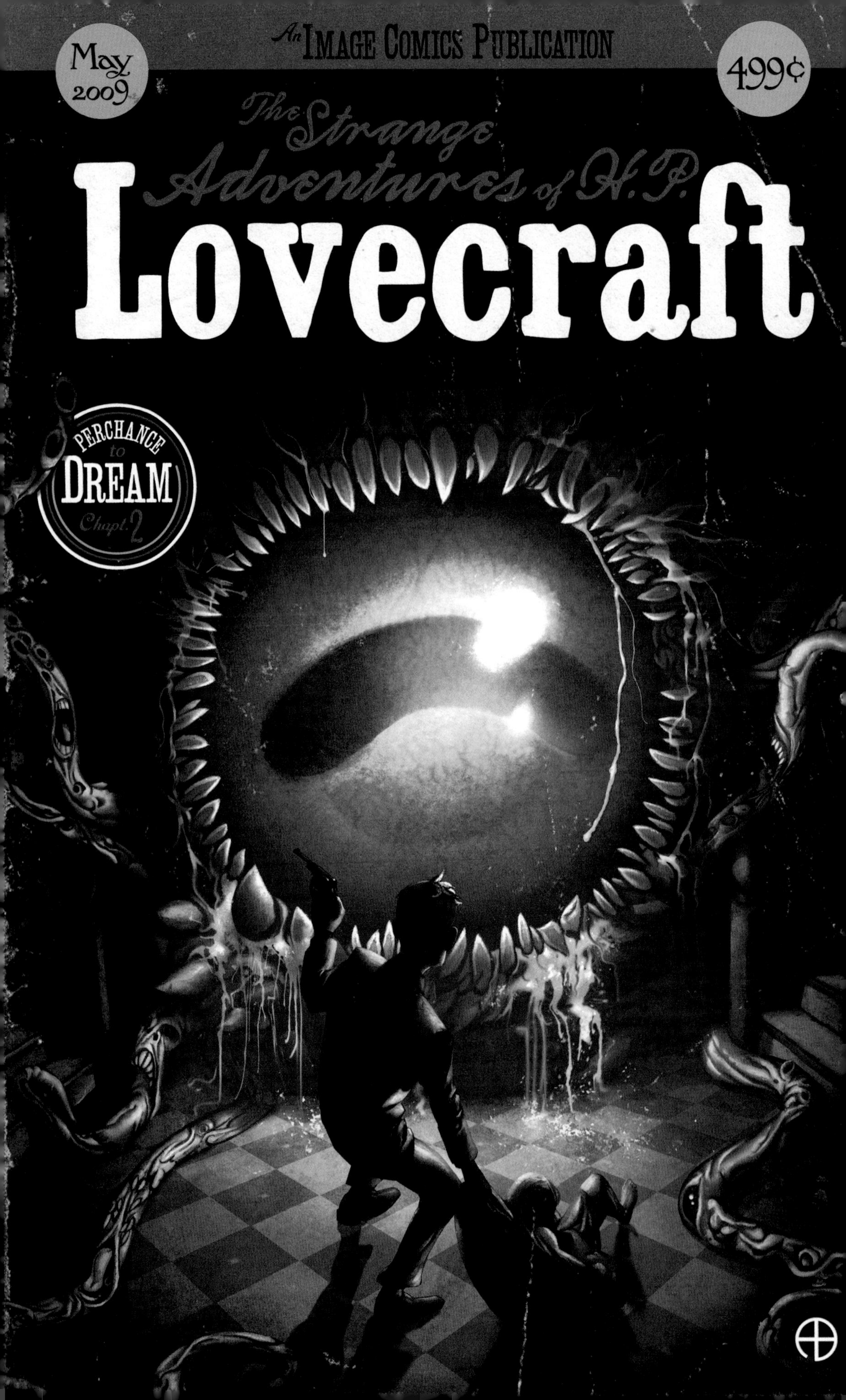
An Image Comics Publication
May 2009
499¢
The Strange Adventures of H.P.
Lovecraft
Perchance to Dream
Chapt. 2

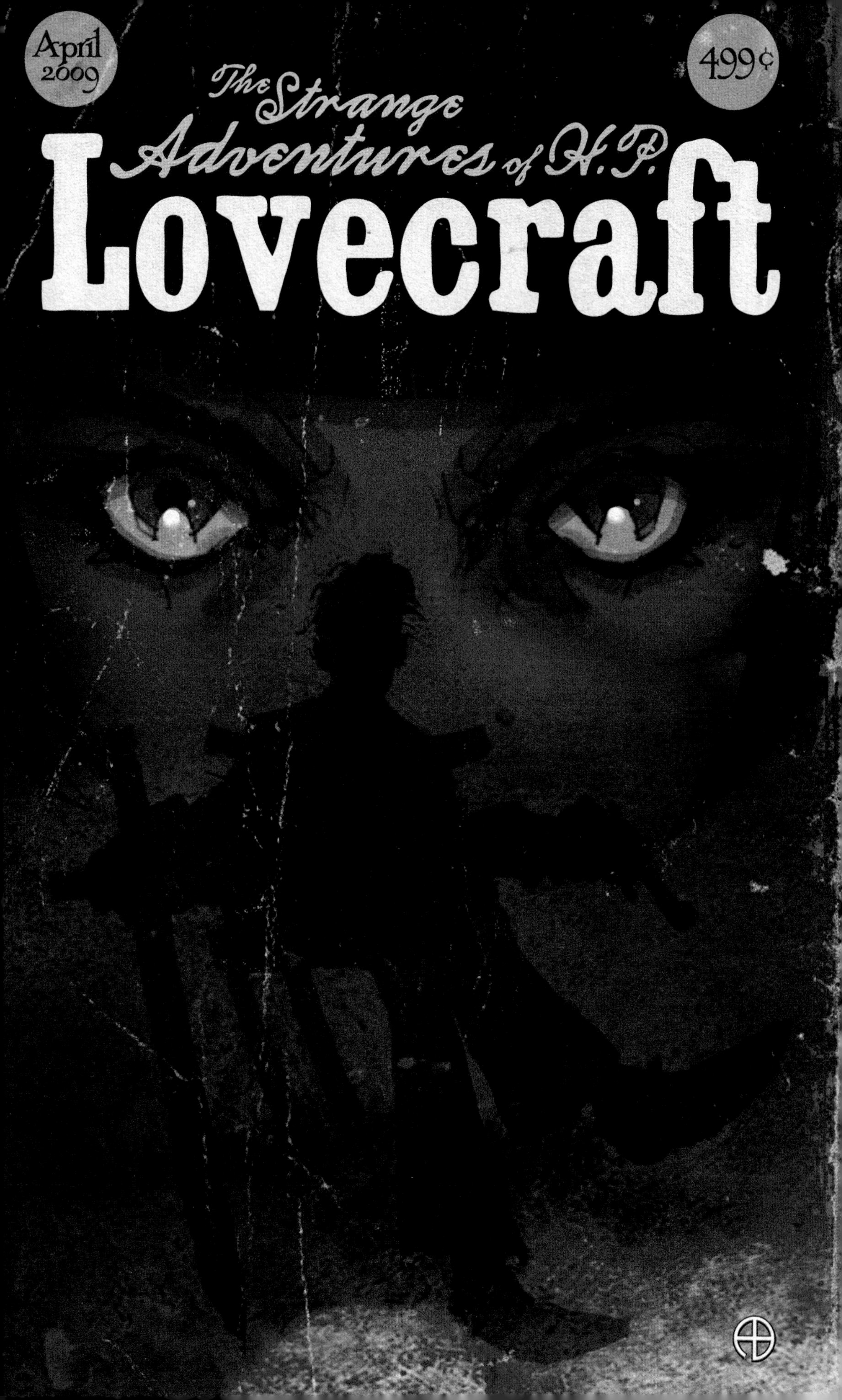
April
2009
The Strange
Adventures of H.P.
Lovecraft
499¢

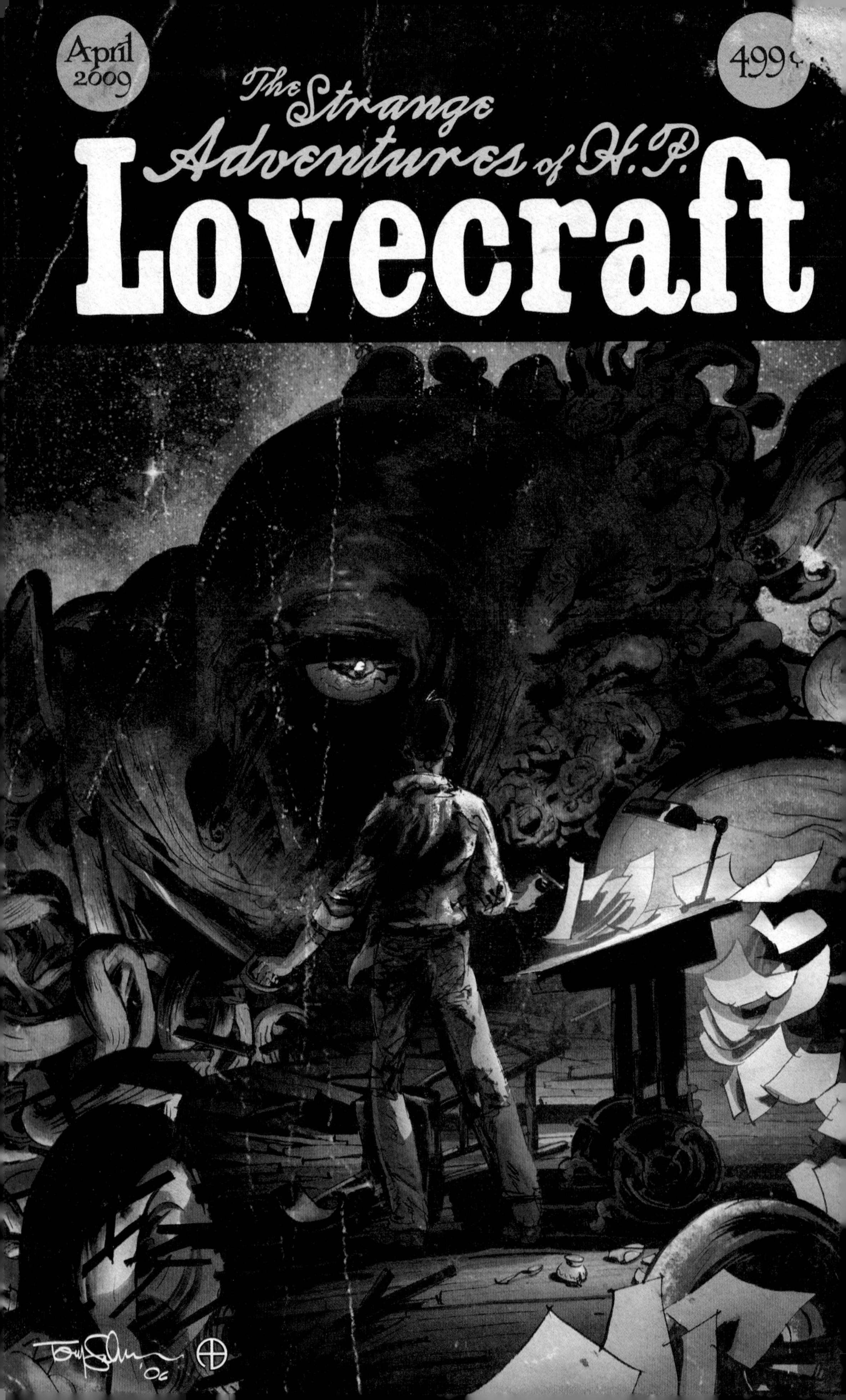
April 2009
499¢
The Strange Adventures of H.P.
Lovecraft